# HORIZONS

## Learning to Read

Fast Track A–B
Teacher Presentation Book 1

Siegfried Engelmann
Owen Engelmann
Karen Lou Seitz Davis

SRA/McGraw-Hill
Columbus, Ohio

SRA/McGraw-Hill

*A Division of The McGraw·Hill Companies*

Send all inquiries to:
SRA/McGraw-Hill
8787 Orion Place
Columbus, Ohio 43240-4027


ISBN 0-02-687501-2

2 3 4 5 6 7 8 9 AGK 00

# Table of Contents

**Materials:** Each child will need a pencil, crayons, a workbook and a textbook for every lesson.

═══════ EXERCISE 1 ═══════

## FOLLOWING DIRECTIONS

a. You're going to follow directions. You have to listen carefully and do what I tell you to do. Wait for my tap.

b. Listen: Touch your nose. Get ready. (Tap.) ✔
Hands down.
• Listen: Touch your head. Get ready. (Tap.) ✔
• Listen: Clap your hands one time. Get ready. (Tap.) ✔
• Listen: Hold up your pencil. Get ready. (Tap.) ✔
• Listen: Put your pencil down. Get ready. (Tap.) ✔

c. (Repeat step b until firm.)
• Good following directions.

**WORKBOOK**

d. Now you're going to follow directions about doing things in your workbook.

e. (Hold up a workbook.) This is your workbook. Hold up your workbook when I tap. Get ready. (Tap.) ✔
• Now you'll put your workbook down. Get ready. (Tap.) ✔

f. (Hold up and open a workbook to Lesson 1.) Now you'll open your workbook to the page that has a big number 1 on the top. That page is near the front of your workbook. Find the big 1 at the top of the page and touch it. Keep touching the 1. (Observe children and give feedback.)

g. Touch the picture of the star. Get ready. (Tap.) ✔
• Touch the picture of the tree. Get ready. (Tap.) ✔

• Touch the picture of the pig. Get ready. (Tap.) ✔
• Touch the number 1 at the top of the page. Get ready. (Tap.) ✔

h. Touch the space for your name just after the number 1. Get ready. (Tap.) ✔
• Everybody, print your name in that space. Then put your pencil down when you're finished.
(Observe children and give feedback.)

i. Everybody, touch the mouse. Keep touching it. ✔
• That mouse is trying to get to the cheese at the end of the trail. When I say "Go," start at the mouse and follow the trail to the cheese. Leave your finger on the cheese when you get to the end of the trail. Get ready. Go.
(Observe children and give feedback.)

j. Everybody, when I tap, touch the mouse again. Get ready. (Tap.) ✔
• We'll help the mouse get to the cheese by touching and saying the letters.
• The letter just after the mouse is **R.**
• (Teacher reference:)

| r | s | n | f | n | f | r | s |
|---|---|---|---|---|---|---|---|

• When I tap, touch just under the **R.** Do not cover up any part of the **R.** Get ready. (Tap.) ✔
(Observe children and give feedback.)
• The next letter is **S.** Touch under the **S.** Get ready. (Tap.) ✔
• The next letter is **N.** Touch under the **N.** Get ready. (Tap.) ✔
• The next letter is **F.** Touch under the **F.** Get ready. (Tap.) ✔

k. Keep touching under the **F** and get ready to tell me the next letter.
• What's the next letter? (Tap.) *N.*
Touch under the **N.** Get ready. (Tap.) ✔
• What's the next letter? (Tap.) *F.*
Touch under the **F.** Get ready. (Tap.) ✔
• What's the next letter? (Tap.) *R.*
Touch under the **R.** Get ready. (Tap.) ✔
• What's the last letter? (Tap.) *S.*
Touch under the **S.** Get ready. (Tap.) ✔

l. We helped the mouse get to the cheese. Good job of following directions.

- Here's a rule about one of these letters: Every **R** is supposed to have a circle around it.
- What's supposed to be around every **R**? (Signal.) *A circle.*
- (Write on the board:)

(r)

- Here's how to make a circle around an **R**.
m. Find each **R**. Make a circle around those **R**s. Put your pencil down when you're finished.
  (Observe children and give feedback.)
- (Write on the board:)

(r)  s  n  f  n  f  (r)  s

- Here's what you should have so far.
n. Here's a rule about another letter: Every **F** is supposed to have a line under it.
- What's supposed to be under every **F**? (Signal.) *A line.*
- (Write on the board:)

<u>f</u>

- Here's how to make a line under an **F**.
- Your turn: Make a line under each **F**. Put your pencil down when you're finished.
  (Observe children and give feedback.)
- (Write to show:)

(r)  s  n  <u>f</u>  n  <u>f</u>  (r)  s

- Here's what you should have so far.
o. Here's our last rule: Every **S** is supposed to have a line over it.
- What's supposed to be over every **S**? (Signal.) *A line.*
- (Write on the board:)

s̄

- Here's how to make a line over an **S**.
- Your turn: Make a line over each **S**. Put your pencil down when you're finished.
  (Observe children and give feedback.)
- (Write to show:)

(r)  s̄  n  <u>f</u>  n  <u>f</u>  (r)  s̄

- Here's what you should have. Raise your hand if you got everything right.

═══════ EXERCISE 2 ═══════

## SAY IT FAST

a. The next thing you're going to do is called **say it fast.** I'll show you how to do it.
- Here's a word a part at a time: **shoe** (pause) **lace.**
  I can say it fast: **shoelace.**
- Here's another word a part at a time: **snow** (pause) **ball.**
  I can say it fast: **snowball.**
b. Your turn: Listen: **ham** (pause) **burger.**
  Say it fast. (Signal.) *Hamburger.*
- New word: Listen: **stair** (pause) **way.**
  Say it fast. (Signal.) *Stairway.*
- New word: Listen: **milk** (pause) **shake.**
  Say it fast. (Signal.) *Milkshake.*
- New word: Listen: **pop** (pause) **corn.**
  Say it fast. (Signal.) *Popcorn.*
c. (Repeat step b until the group is firm.)

**Individual Turns**
- I'll call on different children to say it fast.
  (Call on individual children for one of the following tasks.)
- **Milk** (pause) **shake.** Say it fast. *Milkshake.*
- **Ham** (pause) **burger.** Say it fast. *Hamburger.*
- **Shoe** (pause) **lace.** Say it fast. *Shoelace.*
d. Here's a harder game. Some words have only two sounds. I can say those words fast.
- Listen: **mmm** (pause) **EEE.**
  I can say it fast: **me.**
- New word: Listen: **sss** (pause) **OOO.**
  I can say it fast: **so.**
e. Your turn: **mmm** (pause) **EEE.**
  Say it fast. (Signal.) *Me.*
- New word: **sss** (pause) **EEE.**
  Say it fast. (Signal.) *See.*
- New word: **nnn** (pause) **OOO.**
  Say it fast. (Signal.) *No.*
- Last word: **sss** (pause) **OOO.**
  Say it fast. (Signal.) *So.*

f. (Repeat step e until firm.)

**Individual Turns**

- I'll call on different children to say it fast. (Call on individual children for one of the following tasks.)
- nnn (pause) OOO. Say it fast. *No.*
- mmm (pause) EEE. Say it fast. *Me.*
- sss (pause) EEE. Say it fast. *See.*

## SOUNDS FROM LETTER NAMES

a. Now you're going to say letter names a part at a time. This is tough.
b. (Write on the board:)

**m s**

- (Point to **m.**)
- Everybody, what's the name of this letter? (Signal.) *M.*
- I can say the name **M** a part at a time. Listen: eee (pause) mmm. Listen again. eee (pause) mmm.
- Your turn: Say **M** a part at a time. Get ready. (Tap 2 times.) eee (pause) *mmm.*
c. (Point to **s.**)
- What's the name of this letter? (Signal.) *S.*
- I can say **S** a part at a time. Listen: eee (pause) sss.
- Your turn: Say **S** a part at a time. Get ready. (Tap 2 times.) eee (pause) *sss.*
d. Let's do that again. Listen: Say **M** a part at a time. Get ready. (Tap 2 times.) eee (pause) *mmm.*
- Say **S** a part at a time. Get ready. (Tap 2 times.) eee (pause) *sss.*

**Individual Turns**

- (Call on different children to say one of the letters a part at a time.)

**Note:** Do not erase letters.

## LETTER DICTATION

a. (Write on the board:)

_____

- - - - - - - - - - - - - - -

_____

- (Then write **f l s m** in the style children are to follow.)
- I'll touch these letters. You tell me their names.
- (Point to each letter.) What letter? (Children respond.)
b. Find the picture of the pencil and touch it. ✔
- You're going to write letters after the pencil.
- The first letter you'll write is **L**. What letter? (Signal.) *L.*
- Touch the space where you'll write **L**. ✔
- Write the letter **L**. (Observe children and give feedback. Accept approximations.)
c. Touch the space for the next letter. ✔
- You'll write the letter **F** in that space. What letter? (Signal.) *F.*
- Write the letter **F**. (Observe children and give feedback. Accept approximations.)
d. Touch the space for the last letter. ✔
- You'll write the letter **S** in that space. What letter? (Signal.) *S.*
- Write the letter **S** in the last space. (Observe children and give feedback. Accept approximations.)

## STORY TIME

a. I'm going to tell you a funny story. You have to listen very carefully.
- This story is about Mr. Mosely. He was very smart, but early in the morning he was always so sleepy that he would forget to say **all the parts of words.**
- What would he forget to say? (Signal.) *All the parts of words.*
- One morning, he wanted to ask his wife, "Where's my **toothbrush**?" But he didn't

say **toothbrush.** He said this: "Where's my **tooth**?"

- What did he say? (Signal.)
*Where's my tooth?*
- What did he want to say?
(Signal.) *Where's my toothbrush?*
- After he said, "Where's my tooth?" his wife said, "I hope your tooth is in your mouth."
- One morning, Mr. Mosely wanted to ask his wife, "Where is my **wallet**?" But he didn't say **wallet.** He said this: "Where is my **wall**?"
- What did he say? (Signal.)
*Where is my wall?*
- What did he want to say?
(Signal.) *Where is my wallet?*
- After he said, "Where is my wall?" his wife said, "I hope your **wall** is where it always is."
- One morning, Mr. Mosely's wife asked him what he wanted for breakfast. He tried to say, "I'd like a **pancake**." But he didn't say **pancake.** He said this: "I'd like a **pan**."
- What did he say? (Signal.) *I'd like a pan.*
- What did he want to say?
(Signal.) *I'd like a pancake.*

b. Let's do those one more time. I'll tell you what he said. You tell me what he was trying to say.

c. Here's what he said one morning: "Where's my **tooth**?"
- He said the word **tooth,** but what word was he trying to say? (Signal.) *Toothbrush.*
- He said **part** of the word **toothbrush.**
- What **part** did he say? (Signal.) *Tooth.*
- What part did he forget? (Signal.) *Brush.*

d. Here's what he said another morning: "Where is my **wall**?"
- He said **wall,** but what word was he trying to say? (Signal.) *Wallet.*
- He said part of the word **wallet.** What part did he say? (Signal.) *Wall.*
- What part did he forget? (Signal.) *Et.*

e. Here's what he said one morning: "I'd like a **pan**."
- What word was he trying to say?
(Signal.) *Pancake.*

- He said part of the word **pancake.** What part did he say? (Signal.) *Pan.*
- What part did he forget? (Signal.) *Cake.*

f. (Repeat steps c through e until firm.)

### TEXTBOOK

g. (Hold up a textbook.) Open your textbook to the page with the big number 1 on top. That's lesson 1.
(Observe children and give feedback.)
- These pictures show the story we just did.

h. Everybody, touch picture 1. ✔
- Mr. Mosely is in the bathroom, holding a tube of toothpaste. He's saying something to his wife. Everybody, what is he saying? (Signal.) *Where's my tooth?*

i. (Repeat step h until firm.)

j. Touch picture 2. ✔
- Mr. Mosely is in the bedroom looking for something and asking his wife where it is. What is he saying to his wife?
(Signal.) *Where's my wall?*

k. Turn to the next page and touch picture 3. ✔
- Mr. Mosely is in the kitchen telling his wife what he'd like for breakfast. What is he telling her? (Signal.) *I'd like a pan.*

l. (Repeat steps j and k until firm.)

### WORKBOOK

m. Close your textbook and go back to lesson 1 in your workbook. ✔
- Find the picture of Mr. Mosely. He's sitting at the table. Look at what his wife is putting on his plate. What is that?
(Signal.) *A pan.*
He's being served a great big pan for breakfast.
- If you look around in that picture, you'll see some of the other things he didn't say correctly. What do you see?

(Call on individual children. Idea: *Wallet, toothbrush.*)

n. Later you can color this picture.

===== EXERCISE 6 =====

## SOUNDS FROM LETTER NAMES

a. (Refer to the board:)

> **m    s**

b. Let's see who remembers how to say these letters a part at a time.

c. (Point to **m.**)
- First you'll tell me the **name** of this letter. Everybody, what's the **name?** (Signal.) *M.*
- Now say **M** a part at a time. Get ready. (Tap 2 times.) *eee* (pause) *mmm.*
- (Point to **s.**)
- What's the **name** of this letter? *S.*
- Say **S** a part at a time. Get ready. (Tap 2 times.) *eee* (pause) *sss.*

===== EXERCISE 7 =====

## HIDDEN PICTURE

> **Note:** Each child needs a blue, a green and a yellow crayon.

a. Find the picture on the next page of your workbook. ✔
- This picture has letters. The letters are in spaces.
- There are coloring rules for three of the spaces. After you color in the right spaces, you'll be able to see the hidden picture. Take out crayons that are blue, green and yellow.
(Observe children and give feedback.)
b. Touch the box for **M** above the picture. ✔
- Here's the coloring rule for **M:** All parts of the picture that have an **M** are blue. What color are all parts of the picture that have an **M**? (Signal.) *Blue.*
- Make a blue mark in the box for **M.** That will remind you of the rule. Raise your hand when you're finished.
(Observe children and give feedback.)
c. Touch the box for **S.** ✔

- Here's the coloring rule for **S:** All parts of the picture that have an **S** are yellow. What color? (Signal.) *Yellow.*
- Make a yellow mark in the box for **S.** That will remind you of the rule. Raise your hand when you're finished.
(Observe children and give feedback.)
d. All parts of the picture that are not blue or yellow are green. What color? (Signal.) *Green.*
- Make a green mark in the empty box. Raise your hand when you're finished.
(Observe children and give feedback.)
e. Now you can color the picture. Find each space that has the letter **M** in it and color that space blue. Be very careful. Remember, color just the spaces that have an **M.** If a space does not have the letter **M** do not color it.
(Observe children and give feedback.)
f. Now color the spaces that have an **S** in them. Those spaces are yellow. Be careful. If a space does not have the letter **S** do not color it.
(Observe children and give feedback.)
g. Now color the spaces that have no letter in them. They are green. Be careful.
(Observe children and give feedback.)
h. Name some of the things in the hidden picture. (Call on individual children. Idea: *Sun, sky, grass, trees, lake.*)

===== EXERCISE 8 =====

## LETTER PRINTING

a. (Write on the board:)

> ====================
> - - - - - - - - - - - - -
> ====================

b. Touch the picture of the dog. ✔
- You're going to write the letter **R** on the line after the dog. I'll write that letter on the board. I'll show you where to start the letter and how to make it. Watch carefully.
- (Write lowercase **r** in style children are to follow.)
c. Everybody, touch the first space after the dog. ✔

- You're going to write your first **R** in that space. Put your pencil on the place you're going to start writing. ✔
- Make your **R** in that space. Put your pencil down when you're finished.
(Observe children and give feedback.)
d. Touch the space for your next **R**. ✔
- Write an **R** in that space. Put your pencil down when you're finished.
(Observe children and give feedback.)
- Later, you'll finish the row by writing **R**s in the rest of the spaces.
e. Touch the picture of the skunk. ✔
- You're going to write the letter **N** after the skunk. I'll write that letter on the board. I'll show you where to start that letter and how to make it. Watch carefully.
- (Write **n** in the style children are to follow **below** the letter **r**.)
f. Everybody, touch the space after the skunk. ✔
- You're going to write your first **N** in that space. Put your pencil on the place you're going to start writing. ✔

- Make your **N**. Put your pencil down when you're finished.
(Observe children and give feedback.)
- Touch the space for your next **N**. ✔
- Write an **N** in that space. Put your pencil down when you're finished.
(Observe children and give feedback.)
g. Later, you'll finish the row by writing **N**s in the rest of the spaces.

═══════════ EXERCISE 9 ═══════════

## INDEPENDENT WORK

a. Find the ladybug. ✔
- After the ladybug there are some spaces where you can practice writing your name later. See how neatly you can print it.
b. Later, you can color the picture of Mr. Mosely on page 1 of your workbook.

**Independent Work Summary**
- Color story picture.
- Letter printing (finish lines of **r, n**).
- Write name three times.

**Materials:** Each child will need a red, a blue and a green crayon for exercise 9.

===== EXERCISE 1 =====

## SOUNDS FROM LETTER NAMES

a. (Write on the board:)

**s    m**

- Last time, you said the names of these letters a part at a time. Let's see who can remember how to do that.

b. (Point to **s.**)
- First you'll tell me the name of this letter. Everybody, what's the name? (Signal.) *S.*
- I can say **S** a part at a time. Listen: eee (pause) sss.
- Say **S** a part at a time. Get ready. (Tap 2 times.) *eee* (pause) *sss.*

c. (Point to **m.**)
- What's the name of this letter? (Signal.) *M.*
- Say **M** a part at a time. Get ready. (Tap 2 times.) *eee* (pause) *mmm.*

===== EXERCISE 2 =====

## SAY IT FAST

a. Last time, you said words fast.
- Listen: **tooth** (pause) **brush.** Say it fast. (Signal.) *Toothbrush.*
- Listen: **wash** (pause) **cloth.** Say it fast. (Signal.) *Washcloth.*

b. Here are harder words. I'll say them a part at a time.

c. Listen: **mmm** (pause) **III.** Say it fast. (Signal.) *My.*
- Listen: **sh sh sh** (pause) **EEE.** Say it fast. (Signal.) *She.*
- Listen: **mmm** (pause) **EEE.** Say it fast. (Signal.) *Me.*
- Listen: **nnn** (pause) **OOO.** Say it fast. (Signal.) *No.*

d. (Repeat step c until firm.)

### Individual Turns
- I'll call on different children to say it fast.

(Call on individual children for one of the following tasks.)
- **mmm** (pause) **III.** Say it fast. *My.*
- **sh sh sh** (pause) **EEE.** Say it fast. *She.*
- **mmm** (pause) **EEE.** Say it fast. *Me.*
- **nnn** (pause) **OOO.** Say it fast. *No.*

===== EXERCISE 3 =====

## WORD vs. LETTER NAME

a. I'll say some letter names. Listen: **D, J, M, S.**
- I'll say some words: **little, were, cars, girls.**

b. Your turn to tell me if I say a letter name or a word.

c. **M.** Is that a letter name or a word? (Signal.) *Letter name.*
- **Only.** Is that a letter name or a word? (Signal.) *Word.*
- **Running.** Is that a letter name or a word? (Signal.) *Word.*
- **F.** Is that a letter name or a word? (Signal.) *Letter name.*
- **The.** Is that a letter name or a word? (Signal.) *Word.*
- **S.** Is that a letter name or a word? (Signal.) *Letter name.*
- **Brown.** Is that a letter name or a word? (Signal.) *Word.*

d. (Repeat step c until firm.)

### Individual Turns
- Your turn to say a letter name. (Call on several children.)
- Your turn to say a word. (Call on several children. Praise words.)

===== EXERCISE 4 =====

## FOLLOWING DIRECTIONS

a. You're going to follow directions. You have to listen carefully and do what I tell you to do. Remember, wait for my tap.

b. Listen: Clap your hands one time. Get ready. (Tap.) ✔
- Listen: Touch your ears. Both ears. Get ready. (Tap.) ✔

- Listen: Hold up your pencil. Get ready. (Tap.) ✔
- Listen: Put your pencil down. Get ready. (Tap.) ✔
- Listen: Touch your nose. Get ready. (Tap.) ✔
- Hands down.
c. (Repeat step b until firm.)
- Good following directions.

**WORKBOOK**

d. Now you're going to follow directions about doing things in your workbook.
- Open your workbook to the page that has a big number 2 on the top. Touch the big 2 on the top of the page and keep touching it.
  (Observe children and give feedback.)
- Everybody, touch the space for your name just after the number 2. Get ready. (Tap.) ✔
- Everybody, print your name in that space. Then put your pencil down when you're finished.
  (Observe children and give feedback.)
e. Everybody, touch the picture of the mouse. Get ready. (Tap.) ✔
- Touch the picture of the hamburger. Get ready. (Tap.) ✔
f. (Repeat step e until firm.)
g. Everybody, when I tap, touch the picture of the mouse again. Get ready. (Tap.) ✔
- This time the mouse is trying to follow the trail to the hamburger.
- The letter just after the mouse is **N**.
- (Teacher reference:)

| n | s | l | e | a | l | f | o | s | n |

- When I tap, touch just under the **N**. Get ready. (Tap.) ✔
- The next letter is **S**. What letter? (Tap.) S. Touch under the **S**. Get ready. (Tap.) ✔
- Everybody, touch under the next letter. Get ready. (Tap.) ✔
  Tell me the name of that letter. (Tap.) L.

- Touch under the next letter. Get ready. (Tap.) ✔
  Tell me the name of that letter. (Tap.) E.
- Touch under the next letter. Get ready. (Tap.) ✔
  Tell me the name of that letter. (Tap.) A.
- Touch under the next letter. Get ready. (Tap.) ✔
  Tell me the name of that letter. (Tap.) L.
- Touch under the next letter. Get ready. (Tap.) ✔
  Tell me the name of the letter. (Tap.) F.
- Touch under the next letter. Get ready. (Tap.) ✔
  Tell me the name of the letter. (Tap.) O.
- Touch under the next letter. Get ready. (Tap.) ✔
  Tell me the name of the letter. (Tap.) S.
- Touch under the last letter. Get ready. (Tap.) ✔
  Tell me the name of the letter. (Tap.) N.
h. You helped the mouse get to the hamburger. Nice job.
i. Here's a rule about one of these letters: Every **L** is supposed to have a box around it.
- What's supposed to be around every **L**? (Signal.) A box.
- (Write on the board:)

| l |

- Find the **L**s on the path. Make a box around each of those **L**s. Put your pencil down when you're finished.
  (Observe children and give feedback.)
- (Write on the board:)

| n | s | l | e | a | l | f | o | s | n |

- Here's what you should have so far.
j. Here's a rule about another letter: Every **S** is supposed to have a line **over** it. What's supposed to be over every **S**? (Signal.) A line.
- Make a line over each **S**. Put your pencil down when you're finished.
  (Observe children and give feedback.)
- (Write to show:)

| n | s̄ | l | e | a | l | f | o | s̄ | n |

- Here's what you should have. Raise your hand if you got everything right.

═══ EXERCISE 5 ═══

## SAY IT SLOWLY

a. You've said letter names a part at a time. You can also say other words a part at a time. The first word is **me.** What word? (Signal.) *Me.*

b. My turn to say the parts of **me.** Listen: **mmm** (pause) **EEE.**

- Your turn. I'll tap for each part. You'll say the parts of (pause) **me.** Get ready. (Tap 2 times.) *mmm    EEE.*

- (Repeat until firm.)

c. My turn to say the parts of **see.** Listen: **sss** (pause) **EEE.**

- Your turn: Say the parts of **see.** Get ready. (Tap 2 times.) *sss    EEE.*

d. My turn to say the parts of **no.** Listen: **nnn** (pause) **OOO.**

- Your turn: Say the parts of **no.** Get ready. (Tap 2 times.) *nnn    OOO.*

e. My turn to say the parts of **eat.** Listen: **EEE** (pause) **t.**

- Your turn: Say the parts of **eat.** Get ready. (Tap 2 times.) *EEE    t.*

## Individual Turns

- I'll call on different children to say words a part at a time.
  (Call on individual children for one of the following tasks.)
- Say **no** a part at a time. *nnn    OOO.*
- Say **see** a part at a time. *sss    EEE.*
- Say **me** a part at a time. *mmm    EEE.*
- Say **eat** a part at a time. *EEE    t.*

═══ EXERCISE 6 ═══

## LETTER DICTATION

a. (Write on the board:)

- (Then write **n f l m s** in the style children are to follow.)

- I'll touch these letters. You tell me the names.
- (Point to each letter.) What letter? (Children respond.)

b. Touch the picture of a pencil. ✔

- You're going to write letters after the pencil. Remember to use your best printing. The first letter you'll write is **F.** What letter? (Signal.) *F.*

- Touch the space where you'll write **F.** ✔

- Write the letter **F.**
  (Observe children and give feedback. Accept approximations.)

c. Touch the space for the next letter. ✔

- You'll write the letter **S** in that space. What letter? (Signal.) *S.*

- Write the letter **S.**
  (Observe children and give feedback. Accept approximations.)

d. Touch the space for the next letter. ✔

- You'll write the letter **L** in that space. What letter? (Signal.) *L.*

- Write the letter **L.**
  (Observe children and give feedback. Accept approximations.)

e. Touch the space for the next letter. ✔

- You'll write the letter **N** in that space. What letter? (Signal.) *N.*

- Write the letter **N.**
  (Observe children and give feedback. Accept approximations.)

f. Touch the space for the last letter. ✔

- You'll write the letter **M** in that space. What letter? (Signal.) *M.*

- Write the letter **M.**
  (Observe children and give feedback. Accept approximations.)

═══ EXERCISE 7 ═══

## SOUNDS FROM LETTER NAMES

a. (Write on the board:)

**m    s**

b. (Point to **m.**)

- Everybody, what's the name of this letter? (Signal.) *M.*

- I can say **M** a part at a time. Listen: **eee** (pause) **mmm.**

- Your turn: Say **M** a part at a time. Get ready. (Tap 2 times.) *eee    mmm.*
c. Listen: When you read words, you don't say the names of the letters. You say the **sounds.**
- The sound for **M** is the last part of the letter name. It's **mmm.** Everybody, say the sound that **M** makes. Get ready. (Signal.) *mmm.*
d. (Point to **s.**)
- I can say **S** a part at a time. Listen: **eee** (pause) **sss.**
- Your turn: Say **S** a part at a time. Get ready. (Tap 2 times.) *eee    sss.*
- The sound for **S** is the last part of the letter name. It's **sss.** Everybody, say the sound that **S** makes. Get ready. (Signal.) *sss.*
e. This time I'll say each letter name a part at a time. You'll say the sound.
f. (Point to **m.**)
  The name is **eee** (pause) **mmm.** What's the sound? (Signal.) *mmm.*
- (Point to **s.**)
  The name is **eee** (pause) **sss.** What's the sound? (Signal.) *sss.*
g. (Repeat step f until firm.)

*DRILL name sound*

**Individual Turns**
- (Repeat step f, calling on individual children.)

═══════ EXERCISE 8 ═══════

**STORY TIME**

a. This is a story about the worst day that Mr. Mosely ever had. He was so sleepy on this day that he forgot to say a lot of word parts.
- He said his first silly thing just after he got out of bed. He couldn't find one of his slippers. He wanted to ask his wife, "Have you seen my **slipper**?" But he didn't say **slipper.**
  He said, "Have you seen my **slip**?"
- What did he say?
  (Signal.) *Have you seen my slip?*
- What did he want to say? (Signal.) *Have you seen my slipper?*

- After he said, "Have you seen my **slip**?" his wife looked at him and said, "No. What does your **slip** look like?"
b. Mr. Mosely said his next silly thing when he was tying his shoes. He wanted to tell his wife that he broke his **shoelace.** But he didn't say **shoelace.** He said this: "I broke my **shoe.**"
- What did he say?
  (Signal.) *I broke my shoe.*
- What did he want to say?
  (Signal.) *I broke my shoelace.*
- After he said, "I broke my **shoe**," Mrs. Mosely said, "I didn't know that somebody could really break a **shoe.**"
c. That same morning, Mr. Mosely wanted to ask his wife, "Do I have a yellow tie in my **dresser**?" But he didn't say **dresser.** He said: "Do I have a yellow tie in my **dress**?"
- What did he say? (Signal.)
  *Do I have a yellow tie in my dress?*
- What did he want to say? (Signal.)
  *Do I have a yellow tie in my dresser?*
- After he said, "Do I have a yellow tie in my **dress**," his wife said, "I didn't even know that you had a **dress.**"
d. Mr. Mosely said his last silly thing when he was walking downstairs. He wanted to say, "Please close the door to the **bedroom.**" But he didn't say **bedroom.**
- Here's what he said: "Please close the door to the **bed.**"
- What did he say? (Signal.)
  *Please close the door to the bed.*
- What did he want to say? (Signal.)
  *Please close the door to the bedroom.*
- After he said, "Please close the door to the **bed**," his wife looked at him and said, "Dear, our **bed** does not have a door."
- That was a very bad morning for Mr. Mosely. Let's help him out. I'll tell you what he said. You tell me what word he was trying to say.
e. Here's what he said first: "Have you seen my **slip**?"
- He said the word **slip.** What word was he trying to say? (Signal.) *Slipper.*
- The next thing he said was, "I broke my **shoe.**"

- He said the word **shoe.** What word was he trying to say? (Signal.) *Shoelace.*
- Here's the next thing he said: "Do I have a yellow tie in my **dress**?"
- What word was he trying to say? (Signal.) *Dresser.*
- Here's the last thing he said: "Close the door to the **bed.**"
- What word was he trying to say? (Signal.) *Bedroom.*

## TEXTBOOK

f. (Hold up a textbook.) Open your textbook to the page with the big number 2 on top. That's lesson 2.
   (Observe children and give feedback.)
- The top picture shows what Mr. Mosely's bedroom really looked like. The bottom picture is a silly picture that shows how it would look if the things Mr. Mosely said were true.
- In the silly picture, Mr. Mosely's wife is holding a slip. What did Mr. Mosely want her to find? (Signal.) *Slipper.*
- Mr. Mosely is holding something. What is that? (Signal.) *A dress.*
- And it has a yellow tie in it.
- Remember, in the story he wanted to know if his yellow tie was in the dresser. But what did he say instead of **dresser**? (Signal.) *Dress.*
- Look at that thing next to his sock. That's a broken shoe. In the story he didn't have a broken shoe. What was broken? (Signal.) *Shoelace.*
- But what did he tell his wife was broken? (Signal.) *Shoe.*
- In the silly picture, there's a door to his bed. He wanted his wife to close a door. Where did the door lead to? (Signal.) *The bedroom.*
- What did he say instead of the **door to the bedroom**? (Signal.) *Door to the bed.*

## WORKBOOK

g. Close your textbook and go back to lesson 2 in your workbook. ✔
- Find the picture of Mr. Mosely. Later, you'll color this picture. Remember what color his tie is.

=== EXERCISE 9 ===

### HIDDEN PICTURE

*Note:* Each child needs a red, a blue and a green crayon.

a. Find the picture on the next page of your workbook. ✔
- This picture has a lot of letters. The letters are in spaces.
- There are coloring rules for four of the spaces. Take out crayons that are red, blue and green.
  (Observe children and give feedback.)
b. Touch the box for **A** above the picture. ✔
- Here's the coloring rule for **A:** All parts of the picture that have an **A** are red. What color are all parts of the picture that have an **A**? (Signal.) *Red.*
- Make a red mark in the box for **A.** That will remind you of the rule. Raise your hand when you're finished.
  (Observe children and give feedback.)
c. Touch the box for **E.** ✔
- Here's the coloring rule for **E:** All parts of the picture that have an **E** are blue. What color? (Signal.) *Blue.*
- Make a blue mark in the box for **E.** That will remind you of the rule. Raise your hand when you're finished.
  (Observe children and give feedback.)
d. Touch the boxes for **O** and **M** at the top of the picture.
- Here's the rule for **O** and **M:** All parts of the picture that have **O** or **M** are green. What color? (Signal.) *Green.*
- Make a green mark in the boxes for **O** and **M.** Raise your hand when you're finished.

(Observe children and give feedback.)

e. Now you can color the green parts of the picture. Find each space that has the letter **O** or **M** in it and color that space green. Be very careful. Remember, color just the spaces that have an **O** or **M.** If a space does not have the letter **O** or **M** do not color it yet.
(Observe children and give feedback.)

f. Now color the spaces that have an **A** in them. Be careful. If a space does not have the letter **A** do not color it yet.
(Observe children and give feedback.)

g. Now color the spaces that have an **E** in them. Be careful. If a space does not have the letter **E** do not color it.

h. Name some of the things in the hidden picture. (Call on individual children. Idea: *Flower, leaves, stem, sky, grass, clouds.*)

====== EXERCISE 10 ======

## LETTER PRINTING

a. (Write on the board:)

b. Touch the picture of the mouse. ✔
• You're going to write the letter **N** on the line after the mouse. I'll write the letter on the board. I'll show you where to start the letter and how to make it. Watch carefully.
• (Write lowercase **n** in style children are to follow.)
• Everybody, touch the first space after the mouse. ✔
• You're going to write your first **N** in that space. Put your pencil on the place you're going to start writing. ✔

• Make your **N.** Put your pencil down when you're finished.
(Observe children and give feedback.)
• Touch the space for your next **N.** ✔
• Write an **N** in that space. Put your pencil down when you're finished.
(Observe children and give feedback.)
• Later, you'll finish the row by writing Ns in the rest of the spaces.

c. Touch the picture of the moon. ✔
• You're going to write the letter **M** on the line after the moon. I'll write the letter on the board. I'll show you where to start that letter and how to make it. Watch carefully.
• (Write lowercase **m** in the style children are to follow below the **n.**)
• Everybody, touch the space after the moon. ✔
• You're going to write your first **M** in that space. Put your pencil on the place you're going to start writing. ✔
• Make your **M.** Put your pencil down when you're finished.
(Observe children and give feedback.)
• Touch the space for your next **M.** ✔
• Write an **M** in that space. Put your pencil down when you're finished.
(Observe children and give feedback.)
• Later, you'll finish the row of Ms by writing an **M** in the rest of the spaces.

d. Remember to color the picture of Mr. Mosely.

## Independent Work Summary
• Color story picture (tie=yellow).
• Letter printing (finish lines of **n, m**).

**Materials:** Each child will need a red, a brown and a yellow crayon for exercise 9.

## EXERCISE 1

**SOUNDS FROM LETTER NAMES**

a. (Write on the board:)

**f    l**

b. (Point to **f.**)
- Tell me the name of this letter. Get ready. (Signal.) *F.*
- I can say **F** a part at a time: **eee** (pause) **fff.**
- Your turn. Say **F** a part at a time. Get ready. (Tap 2 times.) *eee    fff.*
- (Point to **l.**)
- What's the name of this letter? (Signal.) *L.*
- Say **L** a part at a time. Get ready. (Tap 2 times.) *eee    lll.*

c. (Repeat step b until firm.)

d. Listen: When you read words, you don't say the names of these letters. You say the **sounds.**
- The sound for **F** is the last part of the letter name. It's **fff.** Everybody, say the sound that **F** makes. Get ready. (Tap.) *fff.*
- The sound for **L** is the last part of the letter name. It's **lll.** Everybody, say the sound that **L** makes. Get ready. (Tap.) *lll.*

e. I'll say each letter name a part at a time. Then you tell me the **sound** the letter makes when you read.

f. (Point to **f.**)
- This letter is **F.** Listen: **eee** (pause) **fff.** What sound does **F** make? (Signal.) *fff.*
- (Point to **l.**)
- This letter is **L.** Listen: **eee** (pause) **lll.** What sound does **L** make? (Signal.) *lll.*

g. (Repeat step f until firm.)

**Note:** Do not erase letters.

## EXERCISE 2

**SAY IT FAST**

a. Last time, you said words fast.
- Listen: **to** (pause) **day.** Say it fast. (Signal.) *Today.*
- Listen: **be** (pause) **fore.** Say it fast. (Signal.) *Before.*

b. Here are harder words. I'll say them a part at a time.
- Listen: **mmm** (pause) **EEE.** Say it fast. (Signal.) *Me.*
- Listen: **sh   sh   sh** (pause) **III.** Say it fast. (Signal.) *Shy.*
- Listen: **mmm** (pause) **III.** Say it fast. (Signal.) *My.*
- Listen: **sss** (pause) **OOO.** Say it fast. (Signal.) *So.*

c. (Repeat step b until firm.)

**Individual Turns**
- I'll call on different children to say it fast. (Call on individual children for one of the following tasks.)
- **mmm** (pause) **III.** Say it fast. *My.*
- **sh sh sh** (pause) **III.** Say it fast. *Shy.*
- **mmm** (pause) **EEE.** Say it fast. *Me.*
- **sss** (pause) **OOO.** Say it fast. *So.*

## EXERCISE 3

**WORD vs. LETTER NAME**

a. I'll say some letter names. Listen: **S, N, K, L.**
- I'll say some words: **man, running, pretty, the.**

b. Your turn to tell me if I say a letter name or a word.
- **Face.** Is that a letter name or a word? (Signal.) *Word.*
- **F.** Is that a letter name or a word? (Signal.) *Letter name.*
- **M.** Is that a letter name or a word? (Signal.) *Letter name.*
- **Sad.** Is that a letter name or a word? (Signal.) *Word.*
- **Sister.** Is that a letter name or a word? (Signal.) *Word.*

**3**

- **D.** Is that a letter name or a word?
  (Signal.) *Letter name.*
- **Arm.** Is that a letter name or a word?
  (Signal.) *Word.*
c. (Repeat step b until firm.)

**Individual Turns**
- Your turn to say a letter name.
  (Call on several children.)
- Your turn to say a word.
  (Call on several children. Praise words.)

═══════ EXERCISE 4 ═══════
## FOLLOWING DIRECTIONS

a. You're going to follow directions. Listen carefully and do what I tell you to do. Remember, wait for my tap.
b. Listen: Touch your ear. One ear. Get ready. (Tap.) ✔
- Listen: Touch your head. Get ready. (Tap.) ✔
- Hands down.
c. (Repeat step b until firm.)
- Good following directions.

**WORKBOOK**

d. Now you're going to follow directions about doing things in your workbook. Open your workbook to the page that has a big number 3 on the top. Touch the big 3 on the top of the page and keep touching it.
  (Observe children and give feedback.)
- Everybody, touch the space for your name just after the number 3. Get ready. (Tap.) ✔
- Everybody, print your name in that space. Put your pencil down when you're finished.
  (Observe children and give feedback.)
e. Everybody, touch the picture of the monkey. Get ready. (Tap.) ✔
- Touch the picture of the banana. Get ready. (Tap.) ✔

f. (Repeat step e until firm.)
g. Everybody, when I tap, touch the picture of the monkey again. Get ready. (Tap.) ✔
- We're going to help the monkey get to the banana.
- The letter just after the monkey is **M.**
- (Teacher reference:)

| m a l o n m e n a m |

- When I tap, touch just under the **M.** Get ready. (Tap.) ✔
- The next letter is **A.** What letter? (Tap.) *A.* Touch under the **A.** Get ready. (Tap.) ✔
- Everybody, touch under the next letter. Get ready. (Tap.) ✔
  Tell me the name of that letter. (Tap.) *L.*
- Touch under the next letter. Get ready. (Tap.) ✔
  Tell me the name of that letter. (Tap.) *O.*
- Touch under the next letter. Get ready. (Tap.) ✔
  Tell me the name of that letter. (Tap.) *N.*
- Touch under the next letter. Get ready. (Tap.) ✔
  Tell me the name of that letter. (Tap.) *M.*
- Touch under the next letter. Get ready. (Tap.) ✔
  Tell me the name of that letter. (Tap.) *E.*
- Touch under the next letter. Get ready. (Tap.) ✔
  Tell me the name of that letter. (Tap.) *N.*
- Touch under the next letter. Get ready. (Tap.) ✔
  Tell me the name of that letter. (Tap.) *A.*
- Touch under the last letter. Get ready. (Tap.) ✔
  Tell me the name of that letter. (Tap.) *M.*
h. OOO! That monkey is going to like that banana.
i. Here's a rule about one of these letters: Every **A** is supposed to have a circle around it.
- What's supposed to be around every **A?** (Signal.) *A circle.*
- (Write on the board:)

- Find the **A**s on the trail to the banana. Make a circle around each of those **A**s. Put your pencil down when you're finished.
  (Observe children and give feedback.)
- (Write on the board:)

m (a) l o n m e n (a) m

- Here's what you should have so far.
 j. Here's a rule about another letter: Every **M** is supposed to have a line under it. What's supposed to be under every **M?** (Signal.) *A line.*
- Make a line under each **M.** Put your pencil down when you're finished.
  (Observe children and give feedback.)
- (Write to show:)

m (a) l o n m e n (a) m

- Here's what you should have so far.
 k. Here's a rule about another letter: Every **N** is supposed to have a line over it. What's supposed to be over every **N?** (Signal.) *A line.*
- Make a line over each **N.** Put your pencil down when you're finished.
  (Observe children and give feedback.)
- (Write to show:)

m (a) l o n̄ m e n̄ (a) m

- Here's what you should have. Raise your hand if you got everything right.

═══════════ EXERCISE 5 ═══════════
## SAY IT SLOWLY

a. You're going to say words a part at a time. The first word is **see.** What word? (Signal.) *See.*
b. My turn to say the parts of **see.** Listen: **sss** (pause) **EEE.**
- Your turn. I'll tap for each part. You'll say the parts of (pause) **see.** Get ready. (Tap 2 times.) *sss EEE.*
- (Repeat step b until firm.)
c. My turn to say the parts of **am.** Listen: **aaa** (pause) **mmm.**
- Your turn: Say the parts of **am.** Get ready.

(Tap 2 times.) *aaa mmm.*
d. My turn to say the parts of **so.** Listen: **sss** (pause) **OOO.**
- Your turn: Say the parts of **so.** Get ready. (Tap 2 times.) *sss OOO.*
e. My turn to say the parts of **at.** Listen: **aaa** (pause) **t.**
- Your turn: Say the parts of **at.** Get ready. (Tap 2 times.) *aaa t.*

**Individual Turns**
- I'll call on different children to say words a part at a time. (Call on individual children for one of the following tasks.)
- Say **so** a part at a time. *sss OOO.*
- Say **am** a part at a time. *aaa mmm.*
- Say **eat** a part at a time. *EEE t.*
- Say **at** a part at a time. *aaa t.*

═══════════ EXERCISE 6 ═══════════
## LETTER DICTATION

a. (Write on the board:)

- (Then write **f m n l s** in the style children are to follow.)
- I'll touch these letters. You tell me the names.
- (Point to each letter.) What letter? (Children respond.)
b. Touch the pencil. ✔
- You're going to write letters after the pencil. The first letter you'll write is **N.** What letter? (Signal.) *N.*
- Touch the space where you'll write **N.** ✔
- Write the letter **N.**
  (Observe children and give feedback. Accept approximations.)
c. Touch the space for the next letter. ✔
- You'll write the letter **F** in that space. What letter? (Signal.) *F.*
- Write the letter **F.**
  (Observe children and give feedback. Accept approximations.)
d. Touch the space for the next letter. ✔

- You'll write the letter **L** in that space. What letter? (Signal.) *L.*
- Write the letter **L.**
  (Observe children and give feedback. Accept approximations.)
e. Touch the space for the next letter. ✔
- You'll write the letter **M** in that space. What letter? (Signal.) *M.*
- Write the letter **M.**
  (Observe children and give feedback. Accept approximations.)
f. Touch the space for the last letter. ✔
- You'll write the letter **S** in that space. What letter? (Signal.) *S.*
- Write the letter **S.**
  (Observe children and give feedback. Accept approximations.)

=============== EXERCISE 7 ===============

## SOUNDS FROM LETTER NAMES

a. (Refer to the board:)

f  l

b. (Point to **f.**)
- Everybody, what's the name of this letter? (Signal.) *F.*
- I can say **F** a part at a time. Listen: **eee** (pause) **fff.**
- Your turn: Say **F** a part at a time. Get ready. (Tap 2 times.) *eee    fff.*
- The sound for **F** is the last part of the letter name. It's **fff.** Everybody, say the sound that **F** makes. Get ready. (Signal.) *fff.*
c. (Point to **l.**)
- I can say **L** a part at a time. Listen: **eee** (pause) **lll.**
- Your turn: Say **L** a part at a time. Get ready. (Tap 2 times.) *eee    lll.*
- The sound for **L** is the last part of the letter name. It's **lll.** Everybody, say the sound that **L** makes. Get ready. (Signal.) *lll.*
d. This time I'll say each letter name a part at a time. You'll say the sound.
- (Point to **f.**)
  The name is **eee** (pause) **fff.** What's the sound? (Signal.) *fff.*

- (Point to **l.**)
  The name is **eee** (pause) **lll.** What's the sound? (Signal.) *lll.*
e. (Repeat step d until firm.)

### Individual Turns
- (Repeat step d, calling on different children.)

=============== EXERCISE 8 ===============

## STORY TIME

a. Today we have another story about Mr. Mosely.
- One day, Mr. Mosely woke up very early. It was dark in the house. And he was very tired, so you know what he forgot. His wife said, "All the power is off, so we have no light or heat in the house." Mr. Mosely said, "Can you light a **can**?"
- What did he say? (Signal.) *Can you light a can?*
- Mr. Mosely didn't want to say **can.** He wanted to say **candle.** What word did he want to say? (Signal.) *Candle.*
- What word did he say? (Signal.) *Can.*
- His wife said, "I can't light a can, but I can light a candle." And that's what she did.
b. As Mr. Mosely got dressed, he dropped his keys and he couldn't see them. He asked his wife, "Do you see my keys on the **car**?"
- What did he say? (Signal.) *Do you see my keys on the car?*
- He didn't want to say the word **car.** What word do you think he wanted to say? (Signal.) *Carpet.*
- What word did he say? (Signal.) *Car.*
- His wife said, "I see your keys on the carpet, not on the car." She handed him the keys.
c. After he got dressed, he went downstairs to eat breakfast. His wife said, "We don't have power, so you'll have to eat a cold breakfast. What do you want?" He said, "Can I have some **corn**?"
- What did he say? (Signal.) *Can I have some corn?*

- He didn't want to say the word **corn.** What do you think he wanted to say? (Signal.) *Cornflakes.*
- His wife said, "You don't want corn. You want cornflakes, don't you?"

d. As Mr. Mosely ate, he said, "Too bad we don't have any power. I would like some **cough.**"
- What word did he say? (Signal.) *Cough.*
- What word do you think he wanted to say? (Signal.) *Coffee.*

e. After he ate his cornflakes, his wife asked him, "Where did you leave the letters you wanted to mail?"
He thought for a minute and said, "They are on the top shelf of the **book.**"
- Where did he say they were? (Signal.) *On the top shelf of the book.*
- He didn't want to say the word **book.** What word do you think he wanted to say instead of book? (Signal.) *Bookcase.*

f. Then the heat came on and Mr. Mosely said, "Now I am **hap.**"
- What did he say? (Signal.) *Now I am hap.*
- What did he want to say? (Signal.) *Now I am happy.*

g. Let's do those words again. Here's what Mr. Mosely said first, "Can you light a **can?**"
What word did he want to say instead of **can?** (Signal.) *Candle.*
- Here's the next thing he said, "Do you see my keys on the **car?**"
What word did he want to say instead of **car?** (Signal.) *Carpet.*
- Here's the next thing he said, "Can I have some **corn?**"
What word did he want to say instead of **corn?** (Signal.) *Cornflakes.*
- Here's the next thing he said, "I would like some **cough.**"
What word did he want to say instead of **cough?** (Signal.) *Coffee.*
- Then he said that the letters were on the top shelf of the **book.**
What word did he want to say instead of **book?** (Signal.) *Bookcase.*
- The last thing he said was, "Now I am **hap.**"

What word did he want to say instead of **hap?** (Signal.) *Happy.*

TEXTBOOK

h. Open your textbook to the page with the big number 3 on top. That's lesson 3. (Observe children and give feedback.)
- The top picture shows Mr. Mosely in his bedroom in the dark. He is holding a candle. He wanted to ask his wife if she could light a candle. What did he ask her to light instead? (Signal.) *Can.*
- Look at the bottom picture on that page. Mr. Mosely dropped his keys on the carpet. You can see his keys right by Mr. Mosely's hand. He wanted to ask her, "Do you see my keys on the carpet?" What did he ask her instead? (Signal.) *Do you see my keys on the car?*

i. Touch the top picture on the next page. ✔
- That picture shows Mr. Mosely telling his wife where the letters were. You can see the letters on the top shelf of the bookcase. Mr. Mosely did not tell his wife that they were on the top shelf of the bookcase. Instead, he told her that they were on the top shelf of what? (Signal.) *Book.*
- Have you ever heard of a book with shelves? (Signal.) *No.*
- Touch the bottom picture on that page. ✔
- Mr. Mosely has a big smile on his face. He is trying to tell his wife that he is happy. But he didn't say **happy.** What did he say? (Signal.) *Hap.*
- I think Mr. Mosely is very **sil.**

j. Close your textbook and go back to lesson 3 in your workbook. ✔

- Find the picture of Mr. Mosely. ✔
  This is a **silly** picture. It looks like Mr. Mosely is coughing. Look in his bowl. What is that? (Signal.) *Corn.*
- What's that thing that is burning on the table? (Signal.) *Can.*
- Look around the room and you'll see his keys somewhere. Touch them. ✔
- What are his keys on? (Call on a child.) *A toy car.*
- You can also see his letters somewhere. Touch them. ✔
- What are his letters on? (Call on a child.) *Shelf of a book.*

k. Later, you can color this picture.

━━━━━━━━ EXERCISE 9 ━━━━━━━━

## HIDDEN PICTURE

> ***Note:*** Each child needs a red, a brown and a yellow crayon.

a. Find the picture on the next page of your workbook. ✔
- This picture has a lot of letters. The letters are in spaces.
- There are coloring rules for four of the spaces. Take out crayons that are red, brown and yellow.
  (Observe children and give feedback.)
b. Touch the box for **N** above the picture. ✔
- Here's the coloring rule for **N:** All parts of the picture that have an **N** are red. What color are all parts of the picture that have an **N?** (Signal.) *Red.*
- Make a red mark in the box for **N.** That will remind you of the rule. Raise your hand when you're finished.
  (Observe children and give feedback.)
c. Touch the box for **F.** ✔
- Here's the coloring rule for **F:** All parts of the picture that have an **F** are brown. What color? (Signal.) *Brown.*
- Make a brown mark in the box for **F.** That will remind you of the rule. Raise your hand when you're finished.
  (Observe children and give feedback.)
d. Touch the boxes for **A** and **L** at the top of the picture.

- Here's the rule for **A** and **L:** All parts of the picture that have **A** or **L** are yellow. What color? (Signal.) *Yellow.*
- Make a yellow mark in the boxes for **A** and **L.** Raise your hand when you're finished.
  (Observe children and give feedback.)
e. Later, you can color the picture. Be careful. Remember, don't color parts that don't have a letter.

━━━━━━━━ EXERCISE 10 ━━━━━━━━

## LETTER PRINTING

a. (Write on the board:)

b. Touch the picture of the cat. ✔
- You're going to write the letter **L** on the line after the cat. I'll write the letter on the board. I'll show you where to start the letter and how to make it. Watch carefully.
- (Write lowercase **l** in style children are to follow.)
- Everybody, touch the first space after the cat. ✔
- You're going to write your first **L** in that space. Put your pencil on the place you're going to start writing. ✔
- Make your **L.** Put your pencil down when you're finished.
  (Observe children and give feedback.)
- Touch the space for your next **L.** ✔
- Write an **L** in that space. Put your pencil down when you're finished.
  (Observe children and give feedback.)
- Later, you'll finish the row by writing Ls in the rest of the spaces.
c. Touch the picture of the cup. ✔
- You're going to write the letter **F** on the line after the cup. I'll write the letter on the board. I'll show you where to start that letter and how to make it. Watch carefully.
- (Write lowercase **f** in the style children are to follow.)

- Everybody, touch the space after the cup. ✔
- You're going to write your first **F** in that space. Put your pencil on the place you're going to start writing. ✔
- Make your **F**. Put your pencil down when you're finished.
  (Observe children and give feedback.)
- Touch the space for your next **F**. ✔
- Write an **F** in that space. Put your pencil down when you're finished.
  (Observe children and give feedback.)

- Later, you'll finish the row of **F**s by writing an **F** in the rest of the spaces.

d. Remember to color the picture of Mr. Mosely and to color the hidden picture.

**Independent Work Summary**
- Color story picture.
- Color hidden picture (**f**=brown, **n**=red, **a**=yellow, **l**=yellow).
- Letter printing (finish lines of **l**, **f**).

## 4

---EXERCISE 1---

### SAY IT FAST

a. I'll say some words a time. You'll say them
- Li
  Sa
- Lis
  Say
b. I'll s ound at a **time**
- c. Listen: (pause) OOO.
  Say it fast. (Signal.) *No.*
- Listen: iii (pause) nnn.
  Say it fast. (Signal.) *In.*
  Yes, we are **in** this room.
- Listen: aaa (pause) nnn.
  Say it fast. (Signal.) *An.*
d. (Repeat step c until firm.)
- e. Now I'll say three-sound words a sound at a time.
- Listen: fff (pause) EEE (pause) t. Once more: fff (pause) EEE (pause) t.
  Say it fast. (Signal.) *Feet.*
- Listen: rrr (pause) aaa (pause) nnn. Once more: rrr (pause) aaa (pause) nnn.
  Say it fast. (Signal.) *Ran.*
- Here's another three-sound word. It's tough.
- Listen: rrr (pause) AAA (pause) nnn. Once more: rrr (pause) AAA (pause) nnn.
  Say it fast. (Signal.) *Rain.*
f. (Repeat step e until firm.)

### Individual Turns
- I'll call on different children to say it fast.
  (Call on individual children for one of the following tasks.)
- nnn (pause) OOO. Say it fast. *No.*
- aaa (pause) nnn. Say it fast. *An.*
- rrr (pause) aaa (pause) nnn. Say it fast. *Ran.*
- rrr (pause) AAA (pause) nnn. Say it fast. *Rain.*

---EXERCISE 2---

### LETTER vs. SOUND

a. I'll say some letter names. Listen: **S, M, F, L.**
- I'll say some letter sounds. Listen: **sss, mmm, fff, lll.**
- b. Your turn to tell me if I say a letter name or a sound.
- Listen: **mmm.** Is that a letter name or a sound? (Signal.) *Sound.*
- Listen: **S.** Is that a letter name or a sound? (Signal.) *Letter name.*
- Listen: **L.** Is that a letter name or a sound? (Signal.) *Letter name.*
- Listen: **fff.** Is that a letter name or a sound? (Signal.) *Sound.*
- Listen: **sss.** Is that a letter name or a sound? (Signal.) *Sound.*
- Listen: **M.** Is that a letter name or a sound? (Signal.) *Letter name.*
- Listen: **lll.** Is that a letter name or a sound? (Signal.) *Sound.*
- Listen: **F.** Is that a letter name or a sound? (Signal.) *Letter name.*
c. (Repeat step b until firm.)

### Individual Turns
- Your turn to say a letter name.
  (Call on several children.)
- Your turn to say a sound.
  (Call on several children. Praise words.)

---EXERCISE 3---

### SOUNDS FROM LETTER NAMES

a. (Write on the board:)

| s | m | f | l |
|---|---|---|---|

- First, you'll tell me the name of each letter.
- (Point to each letter.) What's the name of this letter? (Children respond.)
b. I'll say each letter name a part at a time. Then you tell me the **sound** the letter makes when you read.
- c. (Point to **s.**)
  This letter is **S.** Listen: **eee** (pause) **sss.**
  What sound does **S** make? (Signal.) *sss.*

- (Point to **m.**)
  This letter is **M**. Listen: **eee** (pause) **mmm.**
  What sound does **M** make?
  (Signal.) *mmm.*
- (Point to **f.**)
  This letter is **F**. Listen: **eee** (pause) **fff.**
  What sound does **F** make? (Signal.) *fff.*
- (Point to **l.**)
  This letter is **L**. Listen: **eee** (pause) **lll.**
  What sound does **L** make? (Signal.) *lll.*

d. (Repeat step c until firm.)

**Individual Turns**

- Let's do it again. I'll call on different children to tell me the sounds.
- (Repeat step c, calling on individual children.)

====== EXERCISE 4 ======

**FOLLOWING DIRECTIONS**

a. Open your workbook to the page that has a big number 4 on the top. Touch the big 4 at the top of the page and keep touching it.
   (Observe children and give feedback.)
- Touch the space for your name just after the number 4. Get ready. (Tap.) ✔
- Everybody, print your name in that space. Put your pencil down when you're finished.
   (Observe children and give feedback.)

b. You're going to follow directions. You have to listen carefully and do what I tell you to do. Remember to wait for my tap.

c. Everybody, when I tap, touch the picture of the dinosaur. Get ready. (Tap.) ✔
- (Teacher reference:)

| m  f  e  s  l |
|---|

- The first letter in the dinosaur is **M**. When I tap, touch under the **M**. Get ready. (Tap.) ✔

- Touch under the next letter. Get ready. (Tap.) ✔
  Tell me the name of that letter. (Tap.) *F.*
- Touch under the next letter. Get ready. (Tap.) ✔
  Tell me the name of that letter. (Tap.) *E.*
- Touch under the next letter. Get ready. (Tap.) ✔
  Tell me the name of that letter. (Tap.) *S.*
- Touch under the last letter. Get ready. (Tap.) ✔
  Tell me the name of that letter. (Tap.) *L.*

d. (Repeat step c until firm.)
e. Touch the elephant. Get ready. (Tap.) ✔
- (Teacher reference:)

| s  m  f  n  r |
|---|

- We're going to help the elephant get some peanuts.
- Touch under the first letter after the elephant. Get ready. (Tap.) ✔
  Tell me the name of that letter. (Tap.) *S.*
- Touch under the next letter. Get ready. (Tap.) ✔
  Tell me the name of that letter. (Tap.) *M.*
- Touch under the next letter. Get ready. (Tap.) ✔
  Tell me the name of that letter. (Tap.) *F.*
- Touch under the next letter. Get ready. (Tap.) ✔
  Tell me the name of that letter. (Tap.) *N.*
- Touch under the last letter. Get ready. (Tap.) ✔
  Tell me the name of that letter. (Tap.) *R.*

f. That elephant got all of those peanuts because you knew the letters.

g. Here's a rule about one of those letters: Every **L** is supposed to have a line under it. What's supposed to be under every **L**? (Signal.) *A line.*
- Find the **L**s. Make a line under each of those **L**s. Don't forget to look at the dinosaur and at the peanuts. Put your pencil down when you're finished.
   (Observe children and give feedback.)

h. Here's a rule about another letter: Every **M** is supposed to have a line over it. What's supposed to be over every **M**? (Signal.) *A line.*

- Your turn: Make a line over each **M.** Don't forget to look at the dinosaur and at the peanuts. Put your pencil down when you're finished.
  (Observe children and give feedback.)
i. Here's a rule about another letter: Every **F** is supposed to have a box around it. What's supposed to be around every **F**? (Signal.) *A box.*
- Your turn: Make a box around each **F.** Put your pencil down when you're finished.
  (Observe children and give feedback.)
j. (Write on the board:)

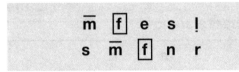

- Here's what you should have. Raise your hand if you got everything right.

========= EXERCISE 5 =========
## SAY IT SLOWLY

a. You're going to say words a sound at a time.
- Listen to this word: **me.**
  I can say it a sound at a time. Listen: **mmm** (pause) **EEE.**
- Your turn: Say **me** a sound at a time. Get ready. (Tap 2 times.) *mmm    EEE.*
b. Listen to this word: **no.**
  Say **no** a sound at a time. Get ready. (Tap 2 times.) *nnn    OOO.*
- Listen to this word: **eat.**
  I can say **eat** a sound at a time: **EEE** (pause) t.
- Your turn. Say **eat** a sound at a time. Get ready. (Tap 2 times.) *EEE    t.*
c. (Repeat step b until firm.)
d. Here's a word that has **three** parts: **feet.**
  Listen to the sounds in **feet:**
  **fff** (pause) **EEE** (pause) t.
- Once more: **fff** (pause) **EEE** (pause) t.
- Your turn: Say all three sounds for **feet.** Get ready. (Tap 3 times.) *fff    EEE    t.*
- Again: Say the three sounds in **feet.** Get ready. (Tap 3 times.) *fff    EEE    t.*

e. New word: **seat.**
  Say all three sounds for **seat.** Get ready. (Tap 3 times.) *sss    EEE    t.*
f. Last word: **meet.**
  Say all three sounds for **meet.** Get ready. (Tap 3 times.) *mmm    EEE    t.*
g. You're saying the sounds in three-sound words.

**Individual Turns**
- I'll call on different children to say words a part at a time.
  (Call on individual children for one of the following tasks.)
- Say **me** a part at a time. *mmm    EEE.*
- Say **eat** a part at a time. *EEE    t.*
- Say the three sounds in **meet.** *mmm    EEE    t.*
- Say the three sounds in **seat.** *sss    EEE    t.*

========= EXERCISE 6 =========
## STORY TIME

**Note:** Do not say words inside brackets, such as **[eat].** Those words are for teacher reference only.

a. Here's a story about an animal. I'll tell you the story, but you'll have to help me with the words I don't say fast.
  **[Sam]**
b. Listen: There once was a bunny named **sss** (pause) **aaa** (pause) **mmm.**
- Listen to his name again: **sss** (pause) **aaa** (pause) **mmm.**
- What's the bunny's name? (Signal.) *Sam.*
  **[eat]**
c. Sam loved to **EEE** (pause) t.
- Listen to the word again: **EEE** (pause) t.
- What word? (Signal.) *Eat.*
- What did Sam love to do? (Signal.) *Eat.*
  **[hop]**
d. Sam's mom said, "If you don't stop eating, you won't be able to **h** (pause) **ooo** (pause) p."
- Listen to the word again: **h** (pause) **ooo** (pause) p.

- What word? (Signal.) *Hop.*
- What wouldn't Sam be able to do? (Signal.) *Hop.*

**[ate]**

e. But Sam didn't listen.
   Sam **AAA** (pause) **t** and **AAA** (pause) **t.**
- Listen to the word again: **AAA** (pause) **t.**
- What word? (Signal.) *Ate.*
- What did Sam do? (Signal.) *Ate.*
- Yes, Sam ate and ate.

**[fun]**

f. One day, the other bunnies said, "Let's go hop over to the pond and have some **fff** (pause) **uuu** (pause) **nnn**."
- Once more: They were going to have **fff** (pause) **uuu** (pause) **nnn.**
- What were the other bunnies going to have? (Signal.) *Fun.*
- So the bunnies hopped off to the pond— all the bunnies except for Sam.

**[go]**

g. Sam said, "My legs do not want to **g** (pause) **OOO**."
- Listen to the word again: **g** (pause) **OOO.**
- What word? (Signal.) *Go.*
- What wouldn't his legs do? (Signal.) *Go.*

**[hop]**

h. At last he got to the pond. But it took him a long time because he could not **h** (pause) **ooo** (pause) **p.**
- Listen to that word again: **h** (pause) **ooo** (pause) **p.**
- What word? (Signal.) *Hop.*
- What couldn't Sam do? (Signal.) *Hop.*

**[home]**

i. When he finally got to the pond, the other bunnies were finished playing and they said, "Well, it's time for us to go back **h** (pause) **OOO** (pause) **mmm**."
- Listen again: They were going **h** (pause) **OOO** (pause) **mmm.**
- Where were they going? (Signal.) *Home.*

**[no]**

j. Sam had to turn around and go back home. When he got there, he was very tired, and he said to himself, "Is this a lot of fun? **nnn** (pause) **OOO**."
- Listen again: **nnn** (pause) **OOO.**
- What word? (Signal.) *No.*
- Was Sam having fun? (Signal.) *No.*

## TEXTBOOK

k. Open your textbook to the page with the big number 4 on top.
   (Observe children and give feedback.)
- Those are pictures of the story.

**[eat]**

l. Touch the first picture. ✔
- That picture shows that Sam loved to **EEE** (pause) **t.**
- What did he love to do? (Signal.) *Eat.*
- What do you think his mom is saying to him? (Call on a child. Ideas: *Don't eat so much; If you don't stop eating, you won't be able to hop.*)

**[go]**

m. Touch the second picture. ✔
- That picture shows the bunnies hopping to the pond. You can see Sam. His legs wouldn't **g** (pause) **OOO.**
- What wouldn't they do? (Signal.) *Go.*
- He is way behind the others.

**[home]**

n. Touch the picture on the next page. You have to turn your book sideways. ✔
- That shows the bunnies after they got **h** (pause) **OOO** (pause) **mmm.**
- Where were they? (Signal.) *Home.*
- One bunny looks very, very tired. Which bunny is that? (Signal.) *Sam.*
- And was he having fun? (Signal.) *No.*

## WORKBOOK

o. Close your textbook and go back to lesson 4 in your workbook. ✔
- This is like the picture that's in your textbook.
- Later, you can color this picture. All the bunnies are brown and white.

## LETTER DICTATION

a. (Write on the board:)

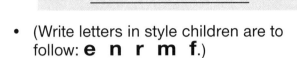

- (Write letters in style children are to follow: **e  n  r  m  f**.)
- You're going to tell me the **name** of each letter, not the sound. Don't get fooled.
- (Point to each letter.) What's the letter name? (Children respond.)

b. Turn to side 2 of your worksheet. ✔
- Touch the pencil at the top of the page. ✔

c. You're going to write letters after the pencil. The first letter you'll write is **R**. What letter? (Signal.) *R.*
- Touch the place where you'll write **R**. ✔
- Write the letter **R**. (Observe children and give feedback.) Accept approximations.)

d. Touch the space for the next letter. ✔
- You'll write the letter **F** in that space. What letter? (Signal.) *F.*
- Write the letter **F**. (Observe children and give feedback. Accept approximations.)

e. Touch the space for the next letter. ✔
- You'll write the letter **E** in that space. What letter? (Signal.) *E.*
- Write the letter **E**. (Observe children and give feedback. Accept approximations.)

f. Touch the space for the next letter. ✔
- You'll write the letter **N** in that space. What letter? (Signal.) *N.*
- Write the letter **N**. (Observe children and give feedback. Accept approximations.)

g. Touch the space for the last letter. ✔
- You'll write the letter **M** in that space. What letter? (Signal.) *M.*
- Write the letter **M**. (Observe children and give feedback. Accept approximations.)

## COLORING GAME

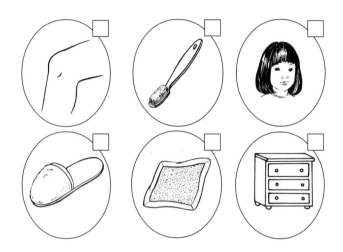

a. Find the star. ✔
   You're going to color some of these pictures.
- You won't color the others. I'll give you clues about the pictures.

b. Here's a clue about the first picture you'll color. Remember, don't say anything. The picture shows a **wash** (pause) **cloth.**
- You'll put a little mark in the box of the picture that shows a **wash** (pause) **cloth.**
- (Hold up a workbook. Point to the box in the first picture.) The mark doesn't go in this box.
- (Point to the box in the picture of the washcloth.) The mark goes in this box.
- Put a little mark in the box. ✔
   That mark will remind you which picture to color.

**[knee]**

c. Here's a clue about the next picture you'll color. The picture shows a **nnn** (pause) **EEE.**
- Put a little mark in the box of the picture that shows a **nnn** (pause) **EEE.** ✔

**[she]**

d. Here's a clue about the last picture you'll color. It's a picture of **sh sh sh** (pause) **EEE.**
- Put a mark in the box of the picture that shows **sh sh sh** (pause) **EEE.** ✔

e. Later you'll color the pictures that have a mark in the box. Remember, **don't** color any of the other pictures.

==== EXERCISE 9 ====

## LETTER PRINTING

a. (Write on the board:)

b. Touch the cat at the bottom of the page. ✔
- You're going to write the letter **S** on the line after the cat. I'll write the letter on the board. I'll show you where to start the letter and how to make it. Watch carefully.
- (Write lowercase **S** in style children are to follow.)
- Everybody, touch the first space after the cat. ✔
- You're going to write your first **S** in that space. Put your pencil on the place where you're going to start writing. ✔
- Make your **S.** Put your pencil down when you're finished.
  (Observe children and give feedback.)
- Touch the space for your next **S.** ✔
- Write an **S** in that space. Put your pencil down when you're finished.
  (Observe children and give feedback.)
- Later, you'll finish the row by writing **S**s in the rest of the spaces.
c. Touch the picture of the flower. ✔

- You're going to write the letter **R** on the line after the flower. I'll write the letter on the board. I'll show you where to start that letter and how to make it. Watch carefully.
- (Write lowercase **r** in the style children are to follow.)
- Everybody, touch the space after the flower. ✔
- You're going to write your first **R** in that space. Put your pencil on the place you're going to start writing. ✔
- Make your **R.** Put your pencil down when you're finished.
  (Observe children and give feedback.)
- Touch the space for your next **R.** ✔
- Write an **R** in that space. Put your pencil down when you're finished.
  (Observe children and give feedback.)
- Later, you'll finish the row by writing **R**s in the rest of the spaces.
d. Remember to color the picture of the bunnies. They are brown and white.
- Remember to color the pictures that have a mark in the box. Don't color the pictures without a mark.

**Independent Work Summary**
- Color story picture (bunnies are brown and white).
- Color pictures with marks (**washcloth, knee, she**).
- Letter printing (finish lines of **s, r**).

**5**

Materials: Each child will need scissors and paste to complete exercise 6.

=== EXERCISE 1 ===

**SOUNDS FROM LETTER NAMES**

a. (Write on the board:)

**l    s    f    m    n**

- First you'll say each letter name a part at a time. Then you'll tell me the sound the letter makes.

b. (Point to **l**.)
- This letter is **L**. Say **L** a part at a time. Get ready. (Tap 2 times.) *eee    lll.*
- What sound does **L** make? (Signal.) *lll.*

c. (Point to **s**.)
- This letter is **S**. Say **S** a part at a time. Get ready. (Tap 2 times.) *eee    sss.*
- What sound does **S** make? (Signal.) *sss.*

d. (Point to **f**.)
- This letter is **F**. Say **F** a part at a time. Get ready. (Tap 2 times.) *eee    fff.*
- What sound does **F** make? (Signal.) *fff.*

e. (Point to **m**.)
- This letter is **M**. Say **M** a part at a time. Get ready. (Tap 2 times.) *eee    mmm.*
- What sound does **M** make? (Signal.) *mmm.*

f. (Point to **n**.)
- This letter is **N**. Say **N** a part at a time. Get ready. (Tap 2 times.) *eee    nnn.*
- What sound does **N** make? (Signal.) *nnn.*

**Note:** Do not erase letters.

**WORKBOOK**

=== EXERCISE 2 ===

**SOUND-TO-LETTER DICTATION**

a. Open your workbook to lesson 5. There's a big 5 on top. Write your name in the blank after the 5. Put your pencil down when you're finished.
(Observe children and give feedback.)

b. You're going to write letters, but I'm not going to tell you the letter names. I'm going to tell you the sounds.

c. Let's practice.
- Listen: The sound is **mmm**. Everybody, what letter makes the sound **mmm?** (Signal.) *M.*
- New sound: **sss**. Everybody, what letter makes the sound **sss?** (Signal.) *S.*
- New sound: **fff**. What letter makes the sound **fff?** (Signal.) *F.*

d. (Repeat step c until firm.)

e. (Point to letters on the board:)

**l    s    f    m    n**

- You'll write some of the letters that are on the board.

f. Touch the pencil on your worksheet. ✔
- Everybody, touch number 1 after the picture of the pencil. ✔
- Here's the sound for number 1. Listen: **mmm.**
Say that sound. Get ready. (Signal.) *mmm.*
- Write the letter that makes the sound **mmm.** Put your pencil down when you're finished.
(Observe children and give feedback. Accept approximations.)
- (Write on the board:)

1. m    2.    3.    4.

---

26    *Lesson 5*

- Here's what you should have. Check your work.
Raise your hand if you wrote the letter **M.**
g. Everybody, touch number 2. ✔
Here's the sound letter 2 makes.
Listen: **fff.**
Say that sound. Get ready. (Signal.) *fff.*
- Write the letter that makes the sound **fff** in the space for 2. Put your pencil down when you're finished.
(Observe children and give feedback. Accept approximations.)
- (Write to show:)

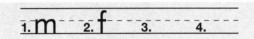

- Check your work. Here's what you should have. Raise your hand if you wrote the letter **F.**
h. Touch number 3. ✔
Here's the sound letter 3 makes.
Listen: **sss.**
Say that sound. Get ready. (Signal.) *sss.*
- Write the letter that makes the sound **sss** in the space for 3. Put your pencil down when you're finished.
(Observe children and give feedback. Accept approximations.)
- (Write in the third space: **S.**)
- Check your work. Here's what you should have. Raise your hand if you wrote the letter **S.**
i. Touch number 4. ✔
Here's the sound letter 4 makes.
Listen: **lll.**
What sound? (Signal.) *lll.*
- Write the letter that makes the sound **lll** in the space for 4. Put your pencil down when you're finished.
(Observe children and give feedback. Accept approximations.)
- (Write in the fourth space: **l.**)
- Check your work. Here's what you should have. Raise your hand if you wrote the letter **L.**
j. Raise your hand if you got all the letters right.

## SAY IT FAST

a. Get ready to say words fast.
- Listen: **aaa** (pause) **t.**
Say it fast. (Signal.) *At.*
- Listen: **aaa** (pause) **mmm.**
Say it fast. (Signal.) *Am.*
b. Listen to a three-sound word.
Listen: **mmm** (pause) **aaa** (pause) **nnn.**
Say it fast. (Signal.) *Man.*
- Listen to another three-sound word:
**rrr** (pause) **aaa** (pause) **t.**
Say it fast. (Signal.) *Rat.*
- Listen to another three-sound word:
**mmm** (pause) **EEE** (pause) **t.**
Say it fast. (Signal.) *Meet.*
- Listen: **sss** (pause) **EEE** (pause) **t.**
Say it fast. (Signal.) *Seat.*
- Last word: **rrr** (pause) **AAA** (pause) **nnn.**
Say it fast. (Signal.) *Rain.*

**Individual Turns**
- I'll call on different children to say it fast. (Call on individual children for one of the following tasks.)
- **aaa** (pause) **t.** Say it fast. *At.*
- **aaa** (pause) **mmm.** Say it fast. *Am.*
- **rrr** (pause) **aaa** (pause) **t.** Say it fast. *Rat.*
- **mmm** (pause) **EEE** (pause) **t.** Say it fast. *Meet.*
- **sss** (pause) **EEE** (pause) **t.** Say it fast. *Seat.*
- **rrr** (pause) **AAA** (pause) **nnn.** Say it fast. *Rain.*
- **mmm** (pause) **aaa** (pause) **nnn.** Say it fast. *Man.*

## STORY TIME

***Note:*** Do not say words inside brackets, such as **[sad]**. Those words are for teacher reference only.

**5**

a. Here's more of the story about Sam the bunny. I'll tell you the story, but you'll have to help me with the words I don't say fast. Listen:

**[sad]**

b. When we left Sam he was very **sss** (pause) **aaa** (pause) **d.**
• Listen to the word again: **sss** (pause) **aaa** (pause) **d.**
• What word? (Signal.) *Sad.*
• Yes, Sam felt sad.

**[hop]**

c. He was sad because he could not **h** (pause) **ooo** (pause) **p.**
• Listen to the word again: **h** (pause) **ooo** (pause) **p.**
• What word? (Signal.) *Hop.*
• What couldn't Sam do? (Signal.) *Hop.*

**[ate]**

d. He couldn't hop because he **AAA** (pause) **t** and **AAA** (pause) **t.**
• What did he do? (Signal.) *Ate and ate.*

**[fun]**

e. The other bunnies went places and had **fff** (pause) **uuu** (pause) **nnn.**
• Listen to the word again: **fff** (pause) **uuu** (pause) **nnn.**
• What did the other bunnies have? (Signal.) *Fun.*
• But Sam couldn't keep up with them so he didn't have fun. One day, Sam was watching his brothers and sisters play with the other bunnies. They were jumping and hopping and running.

**[sit]**

f. Sam said to himself, "They hop and jump, but all I do is **sss** (pause) **iii** (pause) **t.**"
• Listen to the word again: **sss** (pause) **iii** (pause) **t.**
• What word? (Signal.) *Sit.*
• What does Sam do? (Signal.) *Sit.*

**[eat]**

g. Then Sam said to himself, "While I sit here, I think I will **EEE** (pause) **t.**"
• What did he plan to do? (Signal.) *Eat.*

**[move]**

h. He looked at some tasty clover blossoms in front of him, but just as he was going to start eating them, he noticed that the clover started to **mmm** (pause) **oo oo oo** (pause) **vvv.**
• Listen to the word again: **mmm** (pause) **oo oo oo** (pause) **vvv.**
• What word? (Signal.) *Move.*
• What did the clover start to do? (Signal.) *Move.*
• Then Sam noticed that the clover was moving because a tiny gray mouse was carrying it. That mouse was working very hard.
• Sam said, "Where are you going with that clover?"

**[sick]**

i. The mouse said in a squeaky little voice, "I'm bringing it to a friend who is **sss** (pause) **iii** (pause) **k.**"
• Listen to the word again: **sss** (pause) **iii** (pause) **k.**
• What word? (Signal.) *Sick.*
• How did the mouse's friend feel? (Signal.) *Sick.*

**[fed]**

j. The mouse continued, "And my friend has a big family with a lot of little mice that need to be **fff** (pause) **eee** (pause) **d.**"
• Listen to the word again: **fff** (pause) **eee** (pause) **d.**
• What word? (Signal.) *Fed.*
• What needs to happen to the little mice? (Call on a child. Idea: *They need to be fed.*)

k. Sam thought for a moment and then said, "Maybe I can help." What do you think Sam will do to help? (Children respond.)
• Do you think it will be easy for Sam to help? (Children respond.)

## TEXTBOOK

l. Open your textbook to the page with the big number 5.
(Observe children and give feedback.)
• Touch the first picture. ✔
**[sit]**
• That picture shows Sam watching his brothers and sisters. They hop and jump, but all he does is **sss** (pause) **iii** (pause) **t.**
• What does he do? (Signal.) *Sit.*
• If you look carefully at that picture, you can see some clover that is moving.
m. Touch the picture on the next page. ✔
**[sick]**
• That picture shows the mouse bringing clover to feed a friend who is **sss** (pause) **iii** (pause) **k.**
• How does the friend feel? (Signal.) *Sick.*

## WORKBOOK

n. Close your textbook and go back to lesson 5 in your workbook. ✔
o. You can see another picture of Sam and the mouse. Later, you can color the picture. Remember what colors Sam and the mouse are.

=== EXERCISE 5 ===

**SOUNDS FROM LETTER NAMES**

a. (Write on the board:)

**r f l m s n**

• Tell me the name of each letter when I touch under it.
b. (Point to **r.**)
Everybody, what letter? (Signal.) *R.*
• (Repeat for remaining letters.)
c. Touch the picture of the skunk. ✔
• Right after the skunk are the same letters I have on the board. For all these letters the sound is the last part of the name.

d. The first letter is **R.** Touch under that letter. ✔
• I can say **R** a sound at a time:
**ah ah ah** (pause) **rrr.**
Your turn: Say **R** a part at a time. Get ready. (Tap 2 times.) *ah ah ah    rrr.*
• The sound for **R** is **rrr.**
Tell me the sound. (Signal.) *rrr.*
e. The next letter is **F.** Touch under that letter. ✔
Say **F** a part at a time. Get ready. (Tap 2 times.) *eee    fff.*
• Tell me the sound. (Signal.) *fff.*
f. The next letter is **L.** Touch under that letter. ✔
• Say **L** a part at a time. Get ready. (Tap 2 times.) *eee    lll.*
• Tell me the sound. (Signal.) *lll.*
g. The next letter is **M.** Touch under that letter. ✔
• Say **M** a part at a time. Get ready. (Tap 2 times.) *eee    mmm.*
• Tell me the sound. (Signal.) *mmm.*
h. The next letter is **S.** Touch under that letter. ✔
• Say **S** a part at a time. Get ready. (Tap 2 times.) *eee    sss.*
• Tell me the sound. (Signal.) *sss.*
i. The last letter is **N.** Touch under that letter. ✔
• Say **N** a part at a time. Get ready. (Tap 2 times.) *eee    nnn.*
• Tell me the sound. (Signal.) *nnn.*
j. Go back to the first letter—that's **R.** Touch under **R.** ✔
• Say **R** a part at a time. Get ready. (Tap 2 times.) *ah ah ah    rrr.*
• Tell me the sound. (Signal.) *rrr.*

**Individual Turns**
• (Call on different children to do one of the following tasks.)
• Say **M** a part at a time. *eee    mmm.*
Tell me the sound. *mmm.*
• Say **N** a part at a time. *eee    nnn.*
Tell me the sound. *nnn.*
• Say **F** a part at a time. *eee    fff.*
Tell me the sound. *fff.*
• Say **R** a part at a time. *ah ah ah    rrr.*
Tell me the sound. *rrr.*

- Say **L** a part at a time. *eee    lll.*
  Tell me the sound. *lll.*
- Say **S** a part at a time. *eee    sss.*
  Tell me the sound. *sss.*

━━━━━━━ EXERCISE 6 ━━━━━━━
## MATCHING PUZZLE

> **Note:** Each child needs a paid of scissors and paste.

a. Turn to side 2 of your worksheet. ✔
- This is a new kind of matching game.
b. Touch the letters in the boxes at the top of the page. ✔
- The first letter is **M.** Touch it. ✔
- I'll say the rest of the letters. You touch them: **S, L, R, F, N.**
c. Go down to the letters at the bottom of the page. ✔
- You're going to cut out those letters. Cut carefully along the dotted lines. When you're done, you should have six letters. Put them in a neat row. Raise your hand when you're finished.
  (Observe children and give feedback.)
d. Now, take each of the letters you cut out and put it right on top of the same letter up above. Find the **M** in your row and put it right over the **M** above. Then do the same thing for the other letters.
  (Observe children and give feedback.)
- Now, turn the letters over so the heavy line is at the bottom, and you will see a secret picture. Start with the letter **M.** Turn it over and put it right where it was. ✔
- Now do the same thing for the other letters.
  (Observe children and give feedback.)
e. What's in the hidden picture?
  (Signal.) *Mouse.*
- Now you can paste the parts of the picture in place.

━━━━━━━ EXERCISE 7 ━━━━━━━
## SAY IT SLOWLY

a. You're going to say words a part at a time.
- The first word is **an.** What word? (Signal.) *An.*
  It has two sounds. Listen: **aaa** (pause) **nnn.**
- Your turn: Say **an** a part at a time. Get ready. (Tap 2 times.) *aaa    nnn.*
b. New word: **ear.**
  What word? (Signal.) *Ear.*
  Listen: **EEE** (pause) **rrr.**
- Say **ear** a part at a time. Get ready. (Tap 2 times.) *EEE    rrr.*
- What word? (Signal.) *Ear.*
c. Here's a word that has **three** sounds: **fan.**
  What word? (Signal.) *Fan.*
  Listen: **fff** (pause) **aaa** (pause) **nnn.**
- Your turn: Say all three sounds in **fan.** Get ready. (Tap 3 times.) *fff    aaa    nnn.*
- What word? (Signal.) *Fan.*
d. New word: **meal.**
  What word? (Signal.) *Meal.*
  Listen: **mmm** (pause) **EEE** (pause) **lll.**
- Say all three sounds for **meal.** Get ready. (Tap 3 times.) *mmm    EEE    lll.*
- What word? (Signal.) *Meal.*
e. New word: **fear.**
  Listen: **fff** (pause) **EEE** (pause) **rrr.**
- Say all three sounds for **fear.** Get ready. (Tap 3 times.) *fff    EEE    rrr.*
- What word? (Signal.) *Fear.*

**Individual Turns**
- (Call on different children for one of the following tasks.)
- Say the sounds for **an.** *aaa    nnn.*
- Say the sounds for **fan.** *fff    aaa    nnn.*
- Say the sounds for **fear.** *fff    EEE    rrr.*
- Say the sounds for **meal.** *mmm    EEE    lll.*

=========== EXERCISE 8 ===========

## LETTER PRINTING

a. (Write on the board:)

b. Touch the picture of the flower. ✔
- You're going to write the letter **M** on the line after the flower. I'll write the letter on the board. I'll show you where to start the letter and how to make it. Watch carefully.
- (Write lowercase **m** in style children are to follow.)
- Everybody, touch the first space after the flower. ✔
- You're going to write your first **M** in that space. Put your pencil on the place you're going to start writing. ✔
- Make your **M**. Put your pencil down when you're finished.
  (Observe children and give feedback.)
- Touch the space for your next **M**. ✔
- Write an **M** in that space. Put your pencil down when you're finished.
  (Observe children and give feedback.)

- Later, you'll finish the row by writing Ms in the rest of the spaces.
c. Touch the picture of the cat. ✔
- You're going to write the letter **S** on the line after the cat. I'll write the letter on the board. I'll show you where to start that letter and how to make it. Watch carefully.
- (Write lowercase **S** in the style children are to follow.)
- Everybody, touch the space after the cat. ✔
- You're going to write your first **S** in that space. Put your pencil on the place you're going to start writing. ✔
- Make your **S**. Put your pencil down when you're finished.
  (Observe children and give feedback.)
- Touch the space for your next **S**. ✔
- Write an **S** in that space. Put your pencil down when you're finished.
  (Observe children and give feedback.)
- Later, you'll finish the row of Ss.

## Independent Work Summary
- Color story picture (Sam=brown and white, mouse=gray).
- Letter printing (finish lines of **m**, **s**).

**6**

## SOUNDS FROM LETTER NAMES

a. (Write on the board:)

```
l   r   s   n   f
```

• Tell me the name of each letter.

b. (Point to **l**.)
   Everybody, what letter? (Signal.) *L.*
• (Repeat for remaining letters.)

**WORKBOOK**

c. Everybody, open your workbook to the page with the big 6 at the top of it. Write your name in the blank after the 6. Pencils down when you're finished. ✔
• Touch the picture of the frog. ✔
   That frog is going to jump and land on the lily pads.
• (Teacher reference:)

```
l   r   s   n   f
```

d. Touch under the **L**. ✔
   What's the **sound** for the letter **L**? (Signal.) *lll.*
   What **letter**? (Signal.) *L.*
e. Touch under the **R**.
   What's the **sound** for the letter **R**? (Signal.) *rrr.*
   What **letter**? (Signal.) *R.*
f. (Repeat step e for remaining items.)

═══════════ EXERCISE 2 ═══════════

## SAY IT SLOWLY

a. You're going to say words a part at a time. You've said the sounds for some of these words before.
b. The first word is **an**.
   What word? (Signal.) *An.*
   Say **an** a part at a time. Get ready.
   (Tap 2 times.) *aaa   nnn.*

• Here's a word that has three sounds: **fan**.
   Say all three sounds of **fan**. Get ready.
   (Tap 3 times.) *fff   aaa   nnn.*
c. (Repeat step b until firm.)
d. New word: **ran**.
   Say all three sounds for **ran**. Get ready.
   (Tap 3 times.) *rrr   aaa   nnn.*
e. (Repeat step d until firm.)

### Individual Turns
• (Call on different children for one of the following tasks.)
• Say the sounds in **ran**. *rrr   aaa   nnn.*
• Say the sounds in **fan**. *fff   aaa   nnn.*
• Say the sounds in **an**. *aaa   nnn.*

═══════════ EXERCISE 3 ═══════════

## LETTER NAMES IN WORDS
### Long Vowels

a. (Write on board:)

```
e   o   a   i
```

b. These letters sometimes make a sound that is the same as the letter name.
• (Point to **e**.)
   What's the letter name? (Signal.) *E.*
   **E** sometimes makes the sound **EEE**.
• (Point to **o**.)
   What's the letter name? (Signal.) *O.*
   **O** sometimes makes the sound **OOO**.
• (Point to **a**.)
   What's the letter name? (Signal.) *A.*
• **A** sometimes makes the sound **AAA**.
• (Point to **i**.)
   What's the letter name? (Signal.) *I.*
• **I** sometimes makes the sound **III**.
c. Find the picture of the fish. ✔
• (Teacher reference:)

```
e   o   a   i
```

• I'll say words that have the letter names in them. You'll hear a letter name in each word. You'll touch the letter that you hear.
d. Listen: The first word is **eat**.
   What word? (Signal.) *Eat.*

- I'll say **eat** a sound at a time: **EEE   t.**
  Everybody, say the letter name you hear
  in **EEE   t.** (Signal.) *E.*
- Touch the letter you hear in **EEE   t. ✔**
- You should be touching letter **E.**
e. New word: **ice.**
  What word? (Signal.) *Ice.*
- I'll say the sounds in **ice. III   sss.** Say
  the letter name you hear in **ice.**
  (Signal.) *I.*
- Touch the letter your hear in **ice. ✔**
- Everybody, what letter are you touching?
  (Signal.) *I.*
f. New word: **mail.**
  What word? (Signal.) *Mail.*
- Listen: **mmm   AAA   lll.** Say the letter
  name you hear in **mmm   AAA   lll.**
  (Signal.) *A.*
- Touch the letter you hear in **mail. ✔**
- Everybody, what letter are you touching?
  (Signal.) *A.*
g. Last word: **soap.**
  What word? (Signal.) *Soap.*
- Listen: **sss   OOO   p.** Say the letter
  name you hear in **sss   OOO   p.**
  (Signal.) *O.*
- Touch the letter you hear in **soap. ✔**
- Everybody, what letter are you touching?
  (Signal.) *O.*
h. (Repeat steps d through g until firm.)

================ EXERCISE 4 ================
## LETTER NAMES

a. (Write on the board:)

> **d   t   p   v**

- I'll touch these letters and tell you the
  names.
  (Touch and identify each letter: **D, T,
  P, V.**)
b. Find the airplane. ✔
  These are the same letters.
- Touch under the first letter. ✔
  What's the name of that letter?
  (Signal.) *D.*
- Touch under the next letter. ✔
  What's the name of that letter?
  (Signal.) *T.*

- Touch under the next letter. ✔
  What's the name of that letter?
  (Signal.) *P.*
- Touch under the last letter. ✔
  What's the name of that letter?
  (Signal.) *V.*

================ EXERCISE 5 ================
## MATCHING LETTERS

a. Touch the picture of the dog. ✔
- Here's the rule for the letters: Draw lines
  to connect the letters that are the same.
b. The line is already drawn from the blue **N**
  to the black **N.**
- Touch that line. ✔
- You can see that the line goes from the
  blue dot to the black dot.
c. Touch the blue **D.** ✔
- There's a black **D** that should be
  connected to the blue **D.**
- Draw a line from the blue dot to the black
  dot. Connect the two **D**s. Pencils down
  when you're finished.
  (Observe children and give feedback.)
- You've drawn a line from the blue **D** to
  the black **D.**
d. The next blue letter is **T.**
- Draw a line to connect that **T** with the
  black **T.** Then draw a line for the last
  letters. Make sure you have lines that
  connect the letters that are the same.
  Pencils down when you're finished.
  (Observe children and give feedback.)

================ EXERCISE 6 ================
## STORY TIME

a. I'm going to tell you more about Sam the
  Bunny.
b. In the last story, Sam met a mouse
  who was helping a friend.
                                    **[sick]**
  That friend was **sss   iii   k.**
- How did the friend feel? (Signal.) *Sick.*
                                    **[fed]**
c. The friend had a lot of little mice that
  needed to be **fff   eee   d.**
- Listen to that word again: **fff   eee   d.**

- What word? (Signal.) *Fed.*
- Yes, the little mice needed to be fed.
- Sam said that he wanted to help.

**[nice]**

d. The mouse said, "That would be very **nnn   lll   sss**."
- Listen to that word again:
   **nnn   lll   sss.**
- What word? (Signal.) *Nice.*

**[back]**

e. Then the mouse said, "I will load some things on your **b   aaa   k**."
- Listen to that word again: **b   aaa   k.**
- What word? (Signal.) *Back.*

**[is]**

f. "When we get your back loaded, you can take it to the place where my friend **iii   zzz**."
- Listen to that word again: **iii   zzz.**
- What word? (Signal.) *Is.*
- So the mouse loaded piles of clover on Sam's back. Then the mouse loaded grass, some carrot greens and some tiny flowers for dessert.

**[go]**

g. Then the mouse said, "Let's **g   OOO**."
- Listen to that word again: **g   OOO.**
- What word? (Signal.) *Go.*
- Yes, the mouse said, "Let's go."

**[move]**

h. And Sam tried to go, but he could not **mmm   oo oo oo   vvv**.
- Listen to that word again:
   **mmm   oo oo oo   vvv.**
- What word? (Signal.) *Move.*
- What couldn't Sam do? (Signal.) *Move.*
- The mouse said, "Oh dear, you are not in very good shape, are you?" Sam got a big tear in his eye.

**[no]**

i. Then he said, "**nnn   OOO**."
- Listen to that word again: **nnn   OOO.**
- What word? (Signal.) *No.*
- What did Sam say? (Signal.) *No.*

**[back]**

j. The little mouse shook her head and said, "Well, I'd better start unloading the stuff from your **b   aaa   k**."
- Listen to that word again: **b   aaa   k.**

- What word? (Signal.) *Back.*

**[load]**

k. After the mouse had tossed off most of the stuff, Sam said, "I think I can carry a small **lll   OOO   d**."
- Listen to that word again: **lll   OOO   d.**
- What word? (Signal.) *Load.*
- What did Sam think he could carry? (Signal.) *A small load.*
- The mouse said, "Well, that will be some help."

**[big]**

l. Sam said, "I can take a lot of small loads instead of one load that is **b   iii   g**."
- Listen to that word again: **b   iii   g.**
- What word? (Signal.) *Big.*
- Yes, what kind of load can't Sam take? (Signal.) *A big one.*
- We'll see what happens next time.

**TEXTBOOK**

m. Open your textbook to the page with the big number 6. ✔
- The first picture shows Sam asking the mouse what she is doing. What do you think that mouse will say? (Call on different children. Accept reasonable responses.)
n. Touch the next picture. ✔
- What's happening in that picture? (Call on a child. Idea: *Mouse is loading things onto Sam's back.*)
- What kinds of things is the mouse loading onto Sam's back? (Call on different children. Idea: *Clover, grass, carrot greens and tiny flowers.*)
- Where are they going to take those things? (Call on a child. Idea: *To the mouse's sick friend.*)
o. Touch the last picture. ✔
- That picture shows Sam with a full load. What is that mouse trying to do? (Call on a child. Idea: *Move Sam.*)

- Why isn't Sam moving? (Call on different children. Ideas: *Eats too much; too fat; out of shape; load is too big.*)
p. Later, you'll find that same picture in your workbook. Remember to make things the right color when you color them later.

## WORKBOOK

- Now close your textbook and go back to lesson 6 in your workbook. ✔

=== EXERCISE 7 ===

## SOUND-TO-LETTER DICTATION

a. (Write on the board:)

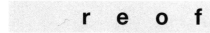

- You're going to write letters on your worksheet, but I'm not going to tell you the letter names. I'm going to tell you the sounds.
b. Let's practice.
- Listen: The sound is **fff.**
Everybody, what letter makes the sound **fff?** (Signal.) *F.*
- New sound: **EEE.**
Everybody, what letter makes the sound **EEE?** (Signal.) *E.*
- New sound: **OOO.**
What letter makes the sound **OOO?** (Signal.) *O.*
c. Find the picture of the tree at the bottom of your worksheet.
- Touch number 1 after the tree. ✔
- Here's the sound for number 1. Listen: **fff.**
What sound? (Signal.) *fff.*
- Write the letter that makes the sound **fff** in space number 1. Pencils down when you're finished.

(Observe children and give feedback. Accept approximations.)
- Check your work. You wrote the letter that makes the sound **fff.**
- What letter? (Signal.) *F.*
- (Write on the board:)

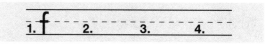

- Here's what you should have. Raise your hand if you wrote the letter **F.**
d. Touch number 2. ✔
Here's the sound letter 2 makes. Listen: **EEE.**
What sound? (Signal.) *EEE.*
- Write the letter that makes the sound **EEE** in the space for number 2. Pencils down when you're finished.
(Observe children and give feedback. Accept approximations.)
- You wrote the letter that makes the sound **EEE.**
- What letter? (Signal.) *E.*
- (Write in the second space: **e.**)
- Check your work. Raise your hand if you got it right.
e. Touch number 3. ✔
Here's the sound letter 3 makes. Listen: **OOO.**
What sound? (Signal.) *OOO.*
- Write the letter that makes the sound **OOO** in the space for number 3. Pencils down when you're finished.
(Observe children and give feedback. Accept approximations.)
- You wrote the letter that makes the sound **OOO.**
- What letter? (Signal.) *O.*
- (Write in the third space: **O.**)
- Check your work. Raise your hand if you got it right.
f. Touch number 4. ✔
Listen: **rrr.**
What sound? (Signal.) *rrr.*

- Write the letter that makes the sound **rrr** in the space for number 4. Pencils down when you're finished.
  (Observe children and give feedback. Accept approximations.)
- You wrote the letter that makes the sound **rrr.**
- What letter? (Signal.) *R.*
- (Write in the last space: **r.**)
- Check your work.
g. Raise your hand if you got everything right.

=========== EXERCISE 8 ===========

**COLORING GAME**

a. Turn to side 2 of your worksheet. ✔
- Find the pictures at the top of the page. You're going to color some of these pictures. You won't color the others.
- (Teacher reference:)

[s] [eat] [rain] [m]

- I'll give you clues about the pictures. Don't say anything. Just make a mark in the box.
b. Here's a clue about a picture: The picture shows the letter **eee    sss.**
- Put a mark in the box when you see: **eee    sss.** ✔
c. Here's a clue about the next picture: Somebody in this picture likes to **EEE    t.**
- Put a mark in the box where somebody likes to **EEE    t.** ✔
d. Here's a clue about the next picture: That picture shows **rrr    AAA    nnn.**
- Put a mark in the picture that shows **rrr    AAA    nnn.** ✔

e. Here's a clue about the last picture: The last picture shows **eee    mmm.**
- Put a mark in the box where you see: **eee    mmm.** ✔
f. Let's see who put marks on the right pictures.
- You should have a mark where you see **eee    sss.** What letter is that? (Signal.) *S.*
- You should have a mark in the box that shows an **S.**
g. You should have a mark where you see somebody who likes to **EEE    t.** What does he like to do? (Signal.) *Eat.*
- You should have a mark in the box that shows a rabbit eating.
h. You should have a mark in the picture that shows **rrr    AAA    nnn.** What word is that? (Signal.) *Rain.*
- You should have a mark in the box that shows **rain.**
i. You should have a mark where you see **eee    mmm.** What letter is that? (Signal.) *M.*
- You should have a mark in the box that shows an **M.**
j. Raise your hand if you got everything right.
k. Later you will color some of the pictures.
- Here's the rule: Color the pictures that have a mark in the box.
- Will you color all the pictures? (Signal.) *No.*
- Will you color pictures that don't have a mark in the box? (Signal.) *No.*
- Which pictures will you color? (Signal.) *Ones with a mark in the box.*
- Remember the rule. Don't get fooled.

======= EXERCISE 9 =======

## LETTER PRINTING

a. Find the ball. ✔
• You'll write letters on these lines.
b. (Write on the board:)

• (Write in style children are to follow:  **r
n**.)
**s**

• These are letters that you'll write.
• What letter goes on the first line?
(Signal.) *R.*

• What letter goes on the next line?
(Signal.) *N.*
• What letter goes on the last line?
(Signal.) *S.*
c. Write the first letter for each line. Write an
**R,** an **N** and an **S.** Pencils down when
you've done that much.
(Observe children and give feedback.)
d. When you write the rest of the letters,
make them carefully.

**Independent Work Summary**
• Color story picture.
• Color pictures with marks (**m, s,
rain, eat**).
• Letter printing (finish lines of **r, n, s**).

# 7

**Materials:** Each child will need scissors and paste to complete exercise 8.

## WORKBOOK

### EXERCISE 1

**LETTER NAMES IN WORDS**
**Long Vowels**

a. Everybody, open your workbook to lesson 7 and write your name. ✔

b. Find the apple. ✔

• (Teacher reference:)

| | |
|---|---|
| o | a |
| i | e |

• Touch under the first letter. ✔
• What letter? (Signal.) *O.*
• Touch under the letter next to O. ✔
• What letter? (Signal.) *A.*
• The next letter is just below the O. It's the letter I. Touch under that letter. Everybody, what letter? (Signal.) *I.*
• Touch under the last letter. What letter? *E.*

c. I'll say words that have letter names in them. You'll hear the names **O, A, I** and **E.**

d. Listen: The first word is **fold.** What word? (Signal.) *Fold.*
• I'll say the sounds. You touch the letter as soon as you hear a letter name:
**fff OOO III d.**
• Everybody, what letter are you touching? (Signal.) *O.*

e. Next word: **she.** What word? (Signal.) *She.*
• I'll say the sounds. You touch the letter you hear: **sh sh sh EEE.**
• Everybody, what letter are you touching? (Signal.) *E.*

f. Next word: **mile.** What word? (Signal.) *Mile.*
• Touch the letter you hear. Listen: **mmm III III.**

• Everybody, what letter are you touching? (Signal.) *I.*

g. Next word: **ate.** What word? (Signal.) *Ate.*
• Touch the letter you hear. Listen: **AAA t.**
• Everybody, what letter are you touching? (Signal.) *A.*

h. (Repeat steps d through g until firm.)

i. Raise your hand if you got all the letters right.

### EXERCISE 2

**SAY IT FAST**

a. You're going to figure out the mystery words. I'll tell you the **sounds** of the word. You'll say those sounds. Then you'll tell me the mystery word.

b. Here are clues for the first word: The first sound in that word is **sss.** The next sound is **EEE.**  *See*
• What's the **first** sound? (Signal.) *sss.*
• What's the **next** sound? (Signal.) *EEE.*
• I'll say both sounds: **sss EEE.**
• Your turn: Say both those sounds. Get ready. (Tap 2 times.) *sss EEE.*
• Say it fast. (Signal.) *See.*
• What's the first mystery word? (Signal.) *See.*

c. Here are clues for the next mystery word. The first sound is **nnn.** The next sound is **OOO.**
• What's the **first** sound? (Signal.) *nnn.*  *no*
• What's the **next** sound? (Signal.) *OOO.*
• I'll say both sounds: **nnn OOO.**
• Your turn: Say both those sounds. Get ready. (Tap 2 times.) *nnn OOO.*
• Say it fast. (Signal.) *No.*
• What's the mystery word? (Signal.) *No.*

d. Here are clues for the next mystery word. *am* The first sound is **aaa.** The next sound is **mmm.**
• What's the **first** sound? (Signal.) *aaa.*
• What's the **next** sound? (Signal.) *mmm.*
• I'll say both sounds: **aaa mmm.**
• Your turn: Say both those sounds. Get ready. (Tap 2 times.) *aaa mmm.*
• Say it fast. (Signal.) *Am.*

- What's the mystery word? (Signal.) *Am.*
e. Here are clues for the last mystery word. The first sound is **EEE.** The next sound is **rrr.**
- What's the **first** sound? (Signal.) *EEE.* *ear*
- What's the **next** sound? (Signal.) *rrr.*
- I'll say both sounds: **EEE   rrr.**
- Your turn: Say both those sounds. Get ready. (Tap 2 times.) *EEE   rrr.*
- What's the mystery word? (Signal.) *Ear.*

**Individual Turns**
- (Call on different children for one of the following tasks.)
- **aaa   mmm.** Say it fast. *Am.*
- **sss   EEE.** Say it fast. *See.*
- **nnn   OOO.** Say it fast. *No.*
- **EEE   rrr.** Say it fast. *Ear.*

========== EXERCISE 3 ==========

## LETTER vs. SOUND

a. I'll say some letter names. Listen: **R, L, N, F.**
- I'll say some letter sounds. Listen: **rrr, lll, nnn, fff.**
b. Your turn to tell me if I say a letter name or a sound.
- Listen: **F.** Is that a letter name or a sound? (Signal.) *Letter name.*
- Listen: **fff.** Is that a letter name or a sound? (Signal.) *Sound.*
- Listen: **lll.** Is that a letter name or a sound? (Signal.) *Sound.*
- Listen: **L.** Is that a letter name or a sound? (Signal.) *Letter name.*
- Listen: **R.** Is that a letter name or a sound? (Signal.) *Letter name.*
- Listen: **nnn.** Is that a letter name or a sound? (Signal.) *Sound.*
- Listen: **rrr.** Is that a letter name or a sound? (Signal.) *Sound.*
- Listen: **N.** Is that a letter name or a sound? (Signal.) *Letter name.*
c. (Repeat step b until firm.)

**Individual Turns**
- Your turn to say a letter name. (Call on several children.)

- Your turn to say a sound. (Call on several children.)

========== EXERCISE 4 ==========

## SOUNDS FROM LETTER NAMES

a. (Write on the board:)

**l   r   m   s   n**

- Each of these letters makes the sound that is at the end of the letter name. First you'll tell me the letter names.
b. (Point to **l.**)
- What's the name? (Signal.) *L.*
- (Repeat for remaining items.)
c. Now you'll tell me the sounds.
- (Point to **l.**) What sound does L make? (Signal.) *lll.*
- (Point to **r.**) What sound does R make? (Signal.) *rrr.*
- (Point to **m.**) What sound does M make? (Signal.) *mmm.*
- (Point to **s.**) What sound does S make? (Signal.) *sss.*
- (Point to **n.**) What sound does N make? (Signal.) *nnn.*
d. (Repeat step c until firm.)

**Individual Turns**
- (Repeat step c, calling on different children.)

========== EXERCISE 5 ==========

## READING WORDS

a. You're so good with your sounds that you're ready to read words.
- (Write on board:)

**me**

- This is a word. You can tell it's a word because the line goes under more than one letter. The line goes under **M** and **E.**
- Listen: You read words by saying the **sounds** for the letters. Then you say the word fast.

b. (Touch under **m.**) The first letter is **M.**
   What's the sound for that letter?
   (Signal.) *mmm.*
• (Touch under **e.**) The next letter is **E.**
   What's the sound for that letter?
   (Signal.) *EEE.*
c. I'll go back to the beginning of the word
   and touch under the letters again.
• (Touch under **m.**) Everybody, what's the
   sound? (Signal.) *mmm.*
• (Touch under **e.**) Everybody, what's the
   sound? (Signal.) *EEE.*
• Say both those sounds again. Get ready.
   (Tap 2 times.) *mmm   EEE.*
• Say it fast. (Signal.) *Me.*
• You just read the word **me.**
   Congratulations. You are reading.
d. Find the picture of the ladybug on your
   worksheet. ✔
   There's a word after the ladybug. You're
   going to read that word.
• The first letter is **N.** Touch the bar
   under **N.** ✔
   What's the sound for that letter?
   (Signal.) *nnn.*
• Touch the bar under the next letter. ✔
   What's the sound for that letter?
   (Signal.) *OOO.*
e. Go back to the ladybug.
• I'll say the sounds. You'll touch under the
   letters when I say the sounds.
• Listen: **nnn   OOO.**
• Again. Back to the ladybug. Get ready to
   touch.
• Listen: **nnn   OOO.**
f. (Repeat step e until firm.)
g. Listen to those sounds again:
   **nnn   OOO.**
   Everybody, say both those sounds. Get
   ready. (Tap 2 times.) *nnn   OOO.*
• Say it fast. (Signal.) *No.*
   You just read the word **no.** Good for you.
h. Touch the fish. ✔
• There's a word after the fish. You're
   going to read that word.
• Touch the bar under the first letter. ✔
   What's the sound for that letter?
   (Signal.) *mmm.*

• Touch the bar under the next letter. ✔
   What's the sound for that letter?
   (Signal.) *EEE.*
i. Go back to the fish.
• I'll say the sounds. You'll touch under the
   letters when I say the sounds.
• Listen: **mmm   EEE.**
• Again. Back to the fish. Get ready to
   touch.
• Listen: **mmm   EEE.**
j. (Repeat step i until firm.)
k. Listen to the sounds again: **mmm   EEE.**
• Everybody, say both those sounds. Get
   ready. (Tap 2 times.) *mmm   EEE.*
• Say it fast. (Signal.) *Me.*
   You just read the word **me.** Good for you.

**Individual Turns**
• (Call on individual children for one of the
   following tasks.)
• Touch the ladybug. Touch under the
   letters when I say the sounds:
   **nnn   OOO.** Say it fast. *No.*
• Touch the fish. Touch under the letters
   when I say the sounds: **mmm   EEE.**
   Say it fast. *Me.*

━━━━━━━━ EXERCISE 6 ━━━━━━━━
**STORY TIME**
a. This is more about Sam the bunny. I'll tell
   you this part of the story, but you'll have
   to help me with the words I don't say fast.
                                      **[mouse]**
b. When we left Sam, he was trying to help
   a little **mmm   ow   sss.**
• What word? (Signal.) *Mouse.*
                                      **[back]**
c. The mouse piled clover, carrot greens,
   tiny flowers and grass on Sam's
   **b   aaa   k.**
• Listen again: **b   aaa   k.**
• What word? (Signal.) *Back.*
                                      **[move]**
d. But when all that stuff was on Sam's
   back, he could not
   **mmm   oo oo oo   vvv.**
• Listen again: **mmm   oo oo oo   vvv.**

- What word? (Signal.) *Move.*
- Yes, with all that stuff on Sam's back he could not move.
- He said he would try to do smaller loads. So on his first trip, he carried a small bundle of clover.

**[big]**

e. The little mouse carried a bundle that was just as **b   iii   g.**
- Listen again: **b   iii   g.**
- What word? (Signal.) *Big.*
- Yes, the mouse's bundle was just as big as Sam's.
- The mouse led Sam to the sick friend's house. Sam was very tired when he finally got there. He was ready to quit, but all the little mice were so happy to have things to eat.

**[Sam]**

f. "Oh, thank you," they said to **sss   aaa   mmm.**
- Listen again: **sss   aaa   mmm.**
- What word? (Signal.) *Sam.*
- Who did the little mice thank? (Signal.) *Sam.*

**[down]**

g. So Sam said to himself, "I can't let those little mice **d   ow   nnn.**"
- Listen again: **d   ow   nnn.**
- What word? (Signal.) *Down.*
- Yes, Sam couldn't let the little mice down.
- So he went back with the mouse, and the mouse piled another load on Sam's back.

**[mouse]**

h. Then Sam and the mouse took the load to the sick **mmm   ow   sss.**
- Listen again: **mmm   ow   sss.**
- What word? (Signal.) *Mouse.*
- All day long Sam carried loads of things to the sick mouse.

**[eating]**

i. Sam didn't notice it at the time, but when he was carrying load after load he did not spend time **EEE   t   ing.**
- Listen again: **EEE   t   ing.**
- What word? (Signal.) *Eating.*
- What wasn't Sam doing? (Signal.) *Eating.*

**[hard]**

j. And he also didn't notice that by the end of the day, carrying a load was not as

**h   ar   d.**
- Listen again: **h   ar   d.**
- What word? (Signal.) *Hard.*
- Yes, it was getting easier for him to carry things. That's good.

**TEXTBOOK**

k. Open your textbook to lesson 7. ✔
- Touch the first picture. ✔
That shows Sam carrying a bundle and the mouse carrying a bundle. Where are Sam and the mouse taking the bundles? (Signal.) *To a sick friend's.*
- Who is carrying the bigger bundle? (Call on a child. Ideas: *Neither one; They are about the same size.*)
- Sam looks very tired. Does Sam want to quit, or is he ready to carry another load? (Signal.) *He wants to quit.*
l. Touch the next picture. ✔
Some little mice are talking to Sam after he brought them a bundle of food. What are the little mice saying to Sam? (Signal.) *Thank you.*
- Is Sam going to quit now, or is he going to carry another load? (Signal.) *Carry another load.*
m. Touch the picture on the next page. ✔
That shows Sam at the end of the day. What are Sam and the mouse doing? (Call on a child. Idea: *Carrying another load.*)
- Does Sam look tired? (Signal.) *No.*
- Does the mouse look tired? (Signal.) *Yes.*
- Sam was so busy carrying loads all day that he **wasn't** doing something else. What was that? (Signal.) *Eating.*
- If Sam keeps working out and watching what he eats, he will get in shape.

**WORKBOOK**

n. Close your textbook and go back to

lesson 7 in your workbook. ✔

- You can see a picture of Sam and the mouse. Somebody forgot to show the loads they are carrying. Later, you can draw a load for the mouse and a load for Sam.

========== EXERCISE 7 ==========

## WRITING WORDS

a. You're going to write words. I'll tell you the sounds for the words. You'll write the letters for those sounds.
- Touch the picture of the cat. ✔
- The word you'll write on that line is **me.** What word? (Signal.) *Me.*
- Say **me** a sound at a time. Get ready. (Tap 2 times.) *mmm    EEE.*

b. Let's do it again.
Say the first sound in **me.** (Signal.) *mmm.*
Say the next sound in **me.** (Signal.) *EEE.*
- The first sound is **mmm.** The next sound is **EEE.**
- Touch the bar for the first letter. ✔
That's where you'll write the letter for **mmm.**
- Touch the next bar. ✔
That's where you'll write the letter for **EEE.**

c. Your turn: Write the letters for the word **me.** Pencils down when you're finished. **(Observe children and give feedback. Accept approximations for e.)**
- (Write on the board:)

<u>me</u>

- Here's what you should have. This is the word **me.** Raise your hand if you got it right.
- You're not only reading words. You're also writing words.

d. Touch the picture of the pencil. ✔
- The word you'll write on that line is **so.** What word? (Signal.) *So.*
- Say the word **so** a sound at a time. Get ready. (Tap 2 times.) *sss    OOO.*

e. Let's do it again.
Say the first sound in **so.** (Signal.) *sss.*
Say the next sound in **so.** (Signal.) *OOO.*

f. (Repeat step e until firm.)

g. Everybody, put your finger on the pencil. ✔
I'll say the sounds in **so.** You'll touch the bars.
- The first sound is **sss.** Touch the bar for **sss.** ✔
- The next sound is **OOO.** Touch the bar for **OOO.** ✔

h. (Repeat step g until firm.)

i. Your turn: Write the letters for the word **so.** Pencils down when you're finished. (Observe children and give feedback.)
- (Write on the board:)

<u>so</u>

- Here's what you should have. This is the word **so.** Raise your hand if you got it right.
- You are **so** smart.

========== EXERCISE 8 ==========

## MATCHING PUZZLE

**Note:** Each child needs scissors and paste.

a. Turn to side 2 on your worksheet.
- Touch the top box of letters. The first letter is **V.** Touch it. ✔
- I'll say the rest of the letters. You touch them: **T, U, R, H, S.**

b. Go down to the letters at the bottom of the page.
- You're going to cut out those letters. Cut carefully along the dotted lines. When you're done, you should have six letters. Put them in a neat row. (Observe children and give feedback.)
- Now, take each of the letters you cut out and put it right on top of the same letter up above. Raise your hand when you've done that much. (Observe children and give feedback.)
- Now, turn the letters over so the heavy line is at the bottom, and you will see a secret picture. ✔

- What's the secret picture?
  (Signal.) *School bus.*
- You can paste the parts of the picture
  in place.

===================== EXERCISE 9 =====================

## CROSS-OUT GAME

a. Touch the **R** in the corner of the box. ✔
- This is a cross-out exercise. The **R** is
  crossed out. That tells you the rule for
  this game.
b. Listen to the rule: Cross out every **R** in
  the big box. What's the rule? (Signal.)
  *Cross out every R in the big box.*
- (Repeat until firm.)
c. Cross out all the **R**s, but not any of the
  other letters. Raise your hand when
  you're finished.
  (Observe children and give feedback.)
- You should have crossed out four **R**s.
  Count them. See if you found all of them.
  Raise your hand if you did.

===================== EXERCISE 10 =====================

## LETTER PRINTING

a. Find the pig. ✔
- You'll write letters on these lines.
b. (Write on the board:)

- (Write in style children are to follow: **r n. m**)
- These are letters that you'll write.
- What letter goes on the first line?
  (Signal.) *R.*
- What letter goes on the next line?
  (Signal.) *N.*
- What letter goes on the last line?
  (Signal.) *M.*
c. Write the first letter for each line. Write an
  **R,** an **N** and an **M.** Pencils down when
  you've done that much.
  (Observe children and give feedback.)
d. When you write the rest of the letters,
  make them carefully.

===================== EXERCISE 11 =====================

## INDEPENDENT WORK

- Remember to fix up the story picture by
  drawing a load for Sam and a load for the
  mouse. Remember, the loads have to be
  about the same size. See if you can make
  good loads. Remember what color the
  loads are.

**Independent Work Summary**
- Complete and color story picture (one
  same-size load each).
- Letter printing (finish lines of **r, n, m**).

**8**

**Materials:** Each child will need a brown, a green and a blue crayon for exercise 8.

---EXERCISE 1---

## SAY IT FAST

a. You're going to figure out the mystery words. I'll tell you the sounds of the word. You'll say those sounds. Then you'll tell me the mystery word.

b. Here are clues for the first word.
- The first sound is **aaa.**
  The next sound is **nnn.**
- What's the **first** sound? (Signal.) *aaa.*
  What's the **next** sound? (Signal.) *nnn.*
  Yes, **aaa  nnn.**
- Say both those sounds. Get ready. (Tap 2 times.) *aaa  nnn.*
- Say it fast. (Signal.) *An.*
- What's the first mystery word? (Signal.) *An.*

c. Here are clues for the next mystery word.
- The first sound is **sss.**
  The next sound is **OOO.**
- What's the **first** sound? (Signal.) *sss.*
  What's the **next** sound? (Signal.) *OOO.*
- Say both those sounds. Get ready. (Tap 2 times.) *sss  OOO.*
- Say it fast. (Signal.) *So.*
- You figured out the mystery word. What is it? (Signal.) *So.*

d. Here are clues for the next mystery word. It has three sounds.
- The first sound is **fff.**
  The next sound is **EEE.**
  The last sound is **lll.**
- Listen. The sounds are: **fff  EEE  lll.**
- What's the **first** sound? (Signal.) *fff.*
  What's the **next** sound? (Signal.) *EEE.*
  What's the **last** sound? (Signal.) *lll.*
- Say those three sounds. Get ready. (Tap 3 times.) *fff  EEE  lll.*
- Again. Get ready. (Tap 3 times.) *fff  EEE  lll.*
- Say it fast. (Signal.) *Feel.*

- You figured out the mystery word. What is it? (Signal.) *Feel.*

e. Here are clues for the last mystery word.
- The first sound is **mmm.**
  The next sound is **aaa.**
  The last sound is **nnn.**
- Listen. The sounds are: **mmm  aaa  nnn.**
- What's the **first** sound? (Signal.) *mmm.*
  What's the **next** sound? (Signal.) *aaa.*
  What's the **last** sound? (Signal.) *nnn.*
- Say those three sounds. Get ready. (Tap 3 times.) *mmm  aaa  nnn.*
- Again. Get ready. (Tap 3 times.) *mmm  aaa  nnn.*
- Say it fast. (Signal.) *Man.*
- You figured out the mystery word. What is it? (Signal.) *Man.*

### Individual Turns
- I'll call on different children to say it fast. (Call on individual children for one of the following tasks.)
- **fff  EEE  lll.** Say it fast. *Feel.*
- **aaa  nnn.** Say it fast. *An.*
- **mmm  aaa  nnn.** Say it fast. *Man.*
- **sss  OOO.** Say it fast. *So.*

---EXERCISE 2---

## SOUND REVIEW

a. Today we'll do the textbook first. Open your textbook to lesson 8. Touch the picture of the snake. ✔
- (Teacher reference:)

| r | s | m | e | o | n | i |
|---|---|---|---|---|---|---|

- There are letters on the snake. You're going to say the **sounds** for the letters. Get ready to move pretty quickly.

b. Touch under the first letter. ✔
  Everybody, tell me the sound. Get ready. (Signal.) *rrr.*

- Touch under the next letter. ✔
  What's the sound? (Signal.) *sss.*
  (To correct:)
  The letter name is **S.** Say **S** a part at a time. *eee   sss.*
  So what sound does that letter make? *sss.*
- c. Touch under the next letter. ✔
  What's the sound? (Signal.) *mmm.*
- d. (Repeat for remaining items.)

**Individual Turns**

- I can say all those sounds on the snake. Listen and follow along: **rrr, sss, mmm, EEE, OOO, nnn, III.**
  I'm a champ at saying sounds.
- Who wants to say all the sounds?
- (Call on several children to say all the sounds.)

════════ EXERCISE 3 ════════

**READING WORDS**

a. You're going to read words.
- Touch the pencil. ✔
- (Teacher reference:)

| <u>so</u> | <u>no</u> | <u>see</u> |
|---|---|---|

- There's a word after the pencil. The letters are **S** and **O.**
- Touch under the first letter. ✔
  Everybody, what's the **sound** for that letter? (Signal.) *sss.*
- Touch under the next letter. ✔
  What's the **sound** for that letter? (Signal.) *OOO.*
- Go back to the pencil.
  I'll say the sounds. You'll touch under the letters.
- Listen: **sss   OOO.**
- Go back to the pencil. Listen and touch again: **sss   OOO.**
- Everybody, touch and say both those sounds. Get ready.
  (Tap 2 times.) *sss   OOO.*

- Say it fast. (Signal.) *So.*
  You just read the word **so.** Good for you.
b. Touch the ladybug. ✔
  There's a word after the ladybug. The letters are **N** and **O.**
- Touch under the first letter. ✔
  Everybody, what's the sound for that letter? (Signal.) *nnn.*
- Touch under the next letter. ✔
  What's the sound for that letter? (Signal.) *OOO.*
- Go back to the ladybug.
  I'll say the sounds. You'll touch under the letters.
- Listen: **nnn   OOO.**
  Listen to the sounds again: **nnn   OOO.**
- Everybody, touch and say both those sounds. Get ready. (Tap 2 times.) *nnn   OOO.*
- Say it fast. (Signal.) *No.*
  You just read the word **no.**
c. Find the hamburger. ✔
- The word has two **Es.**
d. Here's the rule about two **Es.** You don't say **EEE** two times—you say **EEE** once.
- That word is **see.**
- I'll say the sounds in **see.** You'll touch. When I say the sound **EEE,** touch the bar for the **Es.**
- Get ready: **sss   EEE.**
- Your turn to touch and **say the sounds** with me. Get ready: *sss   EEE.*
- Say it fast. (Signal.) *See.*

**Individual Turns**

- (Call on different children to say the sounds for one of the words and say it fast.)
- Read the word after the pencil. *[So.]*
- Read the word after the ladybug. *[No.]*
- Read the word after the hamburger. *[See.]*

**8**

## STORY TIME

a. This is the last part of the story about Sam. I'll tell the story, but you'll have to help with the words I don't say fast.

b. When we left Sam, he was helping the mouse who was helping a sick mouse. Sam carried load after load.

**[sore]**

c. At the end of the day he was very **sss OOO rrr.**
- Listen again: **sss OOO rrr.**
- What word? (Signal.) *Sore.*
- How did Sam feel at the end of the day? (Signal.) *Sore.*
- The next morning Sam was **sss OOO rrr.**
- How did he feel the next morning? (Signal.) *Sore.*
- For a while, he thought he was too sore to do work for the sick mouse, but then he remembered all those little mice and how grateful they were. Sam decided to help out again.

**[loads]**

d. Sam carried many **lll OOO d zzz.**
- Listen again: **lll OOO d zzz.**
- What word? (Signal.) *Loads.*
- Sam carried many loads.

**[more]**

e. And each time he carried a load he was able to carry **mmm OOO rrr** and **mmm OOO rrr.**
- How much could Sam carry? (Signal.) *More and more.*
- At the beginning of the day, he was able to carry one bunch of grass, carrot greens, tiny flowers and clover.

**[four]**

f. By the end of the day, he could carry **fff OOO rrr.**
- Listen again: **fff OOO rrr.**
- What word? (Signal.) *Four.*
- How many bunches of grass, carrot greens and clover could Sam carry? (Signal.) *Four.*
- Wow, he was getting stronger and stronger.

**[more]**

g. And the next day, he carried even **mmm OOO rrr.**
- What word? (Signal.) *More.*

**[sore]**

h. And he wasn't even very **sss OOO rrr.**
- What word? (Signal.) *Sore.*

**[no]**

i. Did he spend a lot of time eating that day?—The answer is **nnn OOO.**
- What's the answer? (Signal.) *No.*
- The next day Sam helped out again.

**[hop]**

j. And Sam noticed that he could take a little **h ooo p.**
- Listen again: **h ooo p.**
- What word? (Signal.) *Hop.*
- What could Sam take? (Signal.) *A little hop.*

**[fine]**

k. By the end of that day, the sick mouse said that she was feeling **fff lll nnn.**
- Listen again: **fff lll nnn.**
- What word? (Signal.) *Fine.*
- How did she feel? (Signal.) *Fine.*

**[more]**

l. She said that she didn't need Sam to help any **mmm OOO rrr.**
- What word? (Signal.) *More.*

**[kiss]**

m. All the little mice came up and gave Sam a great big **k iii sss.**
- Listen again: **k iii sss.**
- What word? (Signal.) *Kiss.*
- What did the little mice give Sam? (Signal.) *A kiss.*

n. Find the picture of Sam and the mice.
- What's happening in that picture? (Call on a child. Idea: *All the little mice are kissing Sam.*)

**[fence]**

o. When Sam went back to the other bunnies, they were playing the game of hop over the **fff eee nnn sss.**
- Listen again: **fff eee nnn sss.**
- What word? (Signal.) *Fence.*
- What were the other bunnies hopping over? (Signal.) *The fence.*

**[that]**

p. One of them said to Sam, "Don't you wish you could do **ththth    aaa    t**?"

• Listen again: **ththth    aaa    t.**

• What word? (Signal.) *That.*

**[this]**

q. Sam smiled to himself and said, "Watch **ththth    iii    sss.**"

• Listen again: **ththth    iii    sss.**

• What word? (Signal.) *This.*

• What did Sam say? (Signal.) *Watch this.*

• Then he hopped over the fence. "Wow," the other bunnies said.

**[hop]**

r. "Sam can really **h    ooo    p**."

• Listen again: **h    ooo    p.**

• What word? (Signal.) *Hop.*

s. Find the pictures on the next page. ✔

• These are pictures that show Sam at different times in the story. You can tell when the picture takes place by the number of bunches Sam is carrying. Remember, at the end of the first day, he was carrying one bunch.

t. How much was he carrying at the end of the next day? (Signal.) *Four bunches.*

• And he was carrying even more than four on the last day that he helped out.

u. Touch the first picture. ✔

• Raise your hand when you know how many bunches he is carrying in that picture. Everybody, how many bunches is he carrying? (Signal.) *Six.*

• Six bunches is more than four bunches, so on which day does he carry more than four bunches—the second day, or the last day? (Signal.) *Last day.*

v. Touch the next picture. ✔

• Raise your hand when you know how many bunches he's carrying.

• Everybody, how many bunches is he carrying? (Signal.) *One.*

• So does that picture take place on the first day, the second day or the last day? (Signal.) *First day.*

w. Touch the next picture. ✔

• Raise your hand when you know how many bunches he's carrying.

• Everybody, how many bunches? (Signal.) *Four.*

• So the picture took place on the second day.

x. Listen: Touch the picture that shows Sam on the first day. ✔

• How many bunches is he carrying? (Signal.) *One.*

• Touch the picture that shows Sam on the second day. ✔

• How many bunches is he carrying? (Signal.) *Four.*

• Touch the picture that shows Sam on the third day. ✔

• How many bunches is he carrying? (Signal.) *Six.*

═══════ EXERCISE 5 ═══════

## LETTER NAMES IN WORDS
### Long Vowels

a. Close your textbook. Go to lesson 8 in your workbook and write your name. ✔

b. Find the cat. ✔

• (Teacher reference:)

| | | | |
|---|---|---|---|
| a | e | o | i |

• Tell me the letters.

• Touch under the first letter. What letter? (Signal.) *A.*

• Touch under the next letter. What letter? (Signal.) *E.*

• Touch under the next letter. What letter? (Signal.) *O.*

• Touch under the last letter. What letter? (Signal.) *I.*

c. I'll say words that have those letter names in them. You'll touch the letter you hear.

d. Listen: The first word is **for.** What word? (Signal.) *For.*

• I'll say the sounds. You'll hear one letter name. Touch the letter as soon as you hear the name: **fff    OOO    rrr.**

• Everybody, what letter are you touching? (Signal.) *O.*

**8**

e. Next word: **meet.** What word?
(Signal.) *Meet.*
- I'll say the sounds. You touch the letter
you hear: **mmm    EEE    t.**
- Everybody, what letter are you touching?
(Signal.) *E.*

f. Next word: **sore.** What word?
(Signal.) *Sore.*
- I'll say the sounds. You touch the letter
you hear: **sss    OOO    rrr.**
- Everybody, what letter are you touching?
(Signal.) *O.*

g. Next word: **eat.** What word? (Signal.) *Eat.*
- I'll say the sounds. You touch the letter
you hear: **EEE    t.**
- Everybody, what letter are you touching?
(Signal.) *E.*

h. Last word: **sail.** What word? (Signal.) *Sail.*
- I'll say the sounds. You touch the letter
you hear: **sss    AAA    lll.**
- Everybody, what letter are you touching?
(Signal.) *A.*

i. (Repeat steps d through h until firm.)

j. Raise your hand if you got all the letters
right.

═══════════ EXERCISE 6 ═══════════

**WRITING WORDS**

a. You're going to write words. You've done
some of them before.

b. Touch the star. ✔
- You'll write the word **no** on the line after
the star.
What word? (Signal.) *No.*
- Say **no** a sound at a time. Get ready.
(Tap 2 times.) *nnn    OOO.*
- Let's do that again.
Say the first sound in **no.** (Signal.) *nnn.*
Say the next sound in **no.** (Signal.) *OOO.*
- The first sound is **nnn.** Touch the bar for
that sound. ✔
The next sound is **OOO.** Touch the bar
for that sound. ✔
- Write the letters for the word **no.** Pencils
down when you're finished.
(Observe children and give feedback.)

- Check your work.
- (Write on the board:)

| |
|---|
| **<u>no</u>** |

- Here's what you should have. This is
the word **no.** Raise your hand if you
got it right.

c. Touch the line for the spider. ✔
You'll write the word **me** on that line.
What word? (Signal.) *Me.*
- Say **me** a sound at a time. Get ready.
(Tap 2 times.) *mmm    EEE.*
- Let's do that again.
Say the first sound in **me.** (Signal.) *mmm.*
Say the next sound in **me.** (Signal.) *EEE.*
- The first sound is **mmm.** Touch the bar
for that sound. ✔
The next sound is **EEE.** Touch the bar for
that sound. ✔
- Write the letters for the word **me.** Pencils
down when you're finished.
(Observe children and give feedback.)
- (Write on the board:)

| |
|---|
| **<u>me</u>** |

- Here's the word **me.** Raise your hand if
you got it right.

**Individual Turns**
- You're going to read the words you
made.
(Call on different children to say the
sounds for one of the words and say
it fast.)
- Read the word after the star. *[No.]*
- Read the word after the spider. *[Me.]*

====== EXERCISE 7 ======

## LETTER PRINTING

a. Find the fish. ✔
• You'll write letters on these lines.
b. (Write on the board:)

• (Write in style children are to follow: **s o r** .)

• These are letters that you'll write.
• What letter goes on the first line? (Signal.) *S.*
• What letter goes on the next line? (Signal.) *O.*
• What letter goes on the last line? (Signal.) *R.*
c. Write the first letter on each line. Pencils down when you've done that much. (Observe children and give feedback.)
d. When you write the rest of the letters, make them carefully.

====== EXERCISE 8 ======

## HIDDEN PICTURE

**Note:** Each child needs a brown, a green and a blue crayon.

a. Turn to side 2 of your worksheet. ✔
• This hidden picture has a lot of letters. The letters are in spaces.
• There are coloring rules for three of the letters. Take out crayons that are brown, green and blue. (Observe children and give feedback.)

b. Touch the box for **M** above the picture. ✔
• Here's the coloring rule for **M:** All parts of the picture that have an **M** are brown.
• What color are all parts of the picture that have an **M?** (Signal.) *Brown.*
• Make a brown mark in the box for **M.** That will remind you of the rule. Raise your hand when you're finished. (Observe children and give feedback.)
c. Touch the box for **N** above the picture. ✔
• Here's the coloring rule for **N:** All parts of the picture that have an **N** are blue. What color? (Signal.) *Blue.*
• Make a blue mark in the box for **N.** That will remind you of the rule. Raise your hand when you're finished. (Observe children and give feedback.)
d. Touch the box for **S** above the picture. ✔
• Here's the rule for **S:** All parts of the picture that have an **S** are green. What color? (Signal.) *Green.*
• Make a green mark in the box for **S.** Raise your hand when you're finished. (Observe children and give feedback.)
e. Later, you can color the parts of the picture.

====== EXERCISE 9 ======

## INDEPENDENT WORK
### Matching: Letters

• Find the skunk. ✔
• You'll draw lines to show letters that are the same.

**Independent Work Summary**
• Letter printing (finish lines of **s, o, r**).
• Color the hidden picture (**m**=brown, **n**=blue, **s**=green).
• Connect matching letters.

## 9

**Materials:** Each child will need a brown, a blue and a green crayon for exercise 9.

=====EXERCISE 1=====

## SAY IT FAST

a. You're going to figure out the mystery words. I'll tell you the sounds of the word. You'll say those sounds. Then you'll tell me the mystery word.

b. Here are clues for the first word.
- The first sound is **aaa.**
  The next sound is **mmm.**
- What's the **first** sound? (Signal.) *aaa.*
  What's the **next** sound? (Signal.) *mmm.*
  Yes, **aaa  mmm.**
- Say both those sounds. Get ready.
  (Tap 2 times.) *aaa  mmm.*
- Say it fast. (Signal.) *Am.*
- What's the first mystery word?
  (Signal.) *Am.*

c. Here are clues for the next mystery word.
- The first sound is **sss.**
  The next sound is **EEE.**
- What's the **first** sound? (Signal.) *sss.*
  What's the **next** sound? (Signal.) *EEE.*
- Say both those sounds. Get ready.
  (Tap 2 times.) *sss  EEE.*
- Say it fast. (Signal.) *See.*
- You figured out the mystery word. What is it? (Signal.) *See.*

d. Here are clues for the next mystery word. It has three sounds.
- The first sound is **sss.**
  The next sound is **EEE.**
  The last sound is **mmm.**
- What's the **first** sound? (Signal.) *sss.*
  What's the **next** sound? (Signal.) *EEE.*
  What's the **last** sound? (Signal.) *mmm.*
- Say those three sounds. Get ready.
  (Tap 3 times.) *sss  EEE  mmm.*
- Again. Get ready. (Tap 3 times.)
  *sss  EEE  mmm.*
- Say it fast. (Signal.) *Seem.*
- You figured out the mystery word. What is it? (Signal.) *Seem.*

e. Here are clues for the last mystery word.
- The first sound is **rrr.**

The next sound is **aaa.**
The last sound is **nnn.**
- What's the **first** sound? (Signal.) *rrr.*
  What's the **next** sound? (Signal.) *aaa.*
  What's the **last** sound? (Signal.) *nnn.*
- Say those three sounds. Get ready.
  (Tap 3 times.) *rrr  aaa  nnn.*
- Again. Get ready. (Tap 3 times.)
  *rrr  aaa  nnn.*
- Say it fast. (Signal.) *Ran.*
- You figured out the mystery word. What is it? (Signal.) *Ran.*

## Individual Turns
- I'll call on different children to say it fast. (Call on individual children for one of the following tasks.)
- **sss  EEE  mmm.** Say it fast. *Seem.*
- **aaa  mmm.** Say it fast. *Am.*
- **rrr  aaa  nnn.** Say it fast. *Ran.*
- **sss  EEE.** Say it fast. *See.*

=====EXERCISE 2=====

## SOUND REVIEW

a. Open your textbook to lesson 9. Touch the picture of the bunny. ✔
- After the bunny are carrots.
- (Teacher reference:)

| e | f | r | l | n | o |

- We're going to help the bunny get carrots by saying the **sounds** for the letters.
  Get ready to move pretty quickly.

b. Touch under the first letter. ✔
  Everybody, tell me the sound. Get ready. (Signal.) *EEE.*
- Touch under the next letter. ✔
  What's the sound? (Signal.) *fff.*
- Touch under the next letter. ✔
  What's the sound? (Signal.) *rrr.*
- Touch under the next letter. ✔
  What's the sound? (Signal.) *lll.*

- Touch under the next letter. ✔
  What's the sound? (Signal.) *nnn.*
- Touch under the last letter. ✔
  What's the sound? (Signal.) *OOO.*

**Individual Turns**

- I can say all those sounds after the bunny
  the fast way. Listen and follow along:
  **EEE, fff, rrr, lll, nnn, OOO.**
  I'm a champ at saying sounds.
- Who wants to say all the sounds?
- (Call on several children to say all the
  sounds.)

══════ EXERCISE 3 ══════

**READING WORDS**

a. You're going to read words.
- Touch the wagon. ✔
- (Teacher reference:)

| | |
|---|---|
| 1. <u>s</u><u>e</u><u>e</u> | 3. <u>m</u> <u>e</u> |
| 2. <u>s</u><u>e</u><u>e</u><u>m</u> | 4. <u>n</u> <u>o</u> |

b. The words have numbers in front of
   them.
- Touch number 1. ✔
- Touch number 2. ✔
- Words 1 and 2 have funny spellings.
  Each word has two **Es.** Remember the
  rule about two **Es:** You don't say **EEE**
  two times—you say **EEE** once.
c. Touch number 1 again. ✔
- The word after number 1 is **see.**
- What word? (Signal.) *See.*
- I'll say the sounds in **see.** You'll touch.
  When I say the sound **EEE,** touch the bar
  for the two **Es.**
- Get ready: **sss    EEE.**
d. Your turn to touch and **say the sounds**
   with me. Get ready. (Tap 2 times.)
   *sss    EEE.*
- Say it fast. (Signal.) *See.*
e. Touch number 2. ✔
- Word 2 has two **Es.**
- You'll just say the sound once.
- Touch under the first letter of word 2. ✔
  Everybody, what is the sound?
  (Signal.) *sss.*

- Touch the bar for the **Es.** ✔
  What's the sound? (Signal.) *EEE.*
- Touch under the last letter. ✔
  Everybody, what's the sound?
  (Signal.) *mmm.*
f. Your turn to touch and say the sounds
   with me. Get ready. (Tap 3 times.)
   *sss    EEE    mmm.*
- Again. Get ready. (Tap 3 times.)
  *sss    EEE    mmm.*
- Say it fast. (Signal.) *Seem.*
- Good reading.
g. Touch word 3. ✔
- The letters are **M** and **E.**
- Touch under the first letter. ✔
  Everybody, what's the **sound** for that
  letter? (Signal.) *mmm.*
- Touch under the next letter. ✔
  What's the **sound** for that letter?
  (Signal.) *EEE.*
- Go back to the first letter of word 3.
  I'll say the sounds. You'll touch under the
  letters.
- Listen: **mmm    EEE.**
- Back to the first letter. Listen and touch
  again: **mmm    EEE.**
- Everybody, touch and say both those
  sounds. Get ready. (Tap 2 times.)
  *mmmm    EEE.*
- Say it fast. (Signal.) *Me.*
  You just read the word **me.** Good for you.
h. Touch word 4. ✔
- The letters are **N** and **O.**
- Touch under the first letter. ✔
  Everybody, what's the sound for that
  letter? (Signal.) *nnn.*
- Touch under the next letter. ✔
  What's the sound for that letter?
  (Signal.) *OOO.*
- Go back to the first letter of word 4. ✔
  I'll say the sounds. You'll touch under the
  letters.
- Listen: **nnn    OOO.**
  Listen to the sounds again: **nnn    OOO.**
- Everybody, touch and say both those
  sounds. Get ready. (Tap 2 times.)
  *nnn    OOO.*
- Say it fast. (Signal.) *No.*
- You just read the word **no.**

**Individual Turns**

- (Call on different children to say the sounds for one of the words and say it fast.)
- Read word 1. *[See.]*
- Read word 2. *[Seem.]*
- Read word 3. *[Me.]*
- Read word 4. *[No.]*

═══════ EXERCISE 4 ═══════

**STORY TIME**

a. I'm going to tell you part of a story.

**[boy]**

- This is a story about a **b    oy.**
- Listen again: **b    oy.**
- What word? (Signal.) *Boy.*
- Yes, a **boy.** That boy's name was Bob.

**[late]**

b. Every time Bob went out with his pals he came home **lll    AAA    t.**
- Listen again: **lll    AAA    t.**
- What word? (Signal.) *Late.*
- Yes, he came home **late.**

**[hike]**

c. One day, his pals asked Bob if he could go on a **h    lll    k.**
- Listen again: **h    lll    k.**
- What word? (Signal.) *Hike.*
- Yes, they wanted Bob to go on a **hike** with them.

**[dad]**

d. So Bob asked his **d    aaa    d.**
- Listen again: **d    aaa    d.**
- Who did Bob ask? (Signal.) *Dad.*
- Yes, he asked his **dad.**

**[path]**

e. And his dad said Bob could go, but he told Bob to stay near the **p    aaa    ththth.**
- Listen again: **p    aaa    ththth.**
- What word? (Signal.) *Path.*

**[four]**

f. Yes, he had to stay near the **path** and he had to come home by **fff    OOO    rrr.**
- Listen again: **fff    OOO    rrr.**
- What word? (Signal.) *Four.*
- Bob and his pals said they would be back by **four.**

**[mile]**

g. They hiked for a **mmm    lll    lll.**
- Listen again: **mmm    lll    lll.**
- What word? (Signal.) *Mile.*

**[mud]**

h. Yes, they hiked for a **mile** and they came to a hill of **mmm    uuu    d.**
- Listen again: **mmm    uuu    d.**
- What word? (Signal.) *Mud.*
- His pals played in the **mud.** At first Bob stayed near the path.

**[pals]**

i. But then Bob joined his **p    aaa    lll    zzz.**
- Listen again: **p    aaa    lll    zzz.**
- What word? (Signal.) *Pals.*
- When Bob got home, he looked like a hill of mud.

**[time]**

j. He didn't get home on **t    lll    mmm.**
- Listen again: **t    lll    mmm.**
- What word? (Signal.) *Time.*
- Yes, he didn't get home on **time.**

**[mad]**

k. And his dad was **mmm    aaa    d.**
- Listen again: **mmm    aaa    d.**
- How did his dad feel? (Signal.) *Mad.*

l. Find the picture of Bob and his dad at the bottom of the page. Bob just asked his dad if he could go on a hike. His dad said yes, and he's telling Bob something else. What's that? (Call on a child. Idea: *Come home by four.*)

m. Find the pictures on the next page. ✔
- These are two pictures of Bob. One shows him before the hike, and the other shows him after the hike.
- Touch the picture of Bob before the hike. ✔
- Are you touching the first picture or the second picture? (Signal.) *Second.*
- How do you know that picture took place before the hike? (Call on a child. Idea: *No mud.*)
- Touch the picture of Bob after the hike. ✔
- How do you know that picture took place after the hike? (Call on a child. Idea: *All muddy.*)

## WORKBOOK

===== EXERCISE 5 =====

### LETTER NAMES IN WORDS
#### Long Vowels

a. Close your textbook. Go to lesson 9 in your workbook and write your name. ✔
- Find the teddy bear. ✔
- (Teacher reference:)

| | |
|---|---|
| o | e |
| i | a |

b. Tell me the letters.
- Touch under the first letter. What letter? (Signal.) *O.*
- Touch under the letter next to **O**. What letter? (Signal.) *E.*
- Touch under the letter below the **O**. What letter? (Signal.) *I.*
- Touch under the last letter. What letter? (Signal.) *A.*

c. I'll say words that have those letter names in them. You'll touch the letter you hear.

d. Listen: The first word is **or**. What word? (Signal.) *Or.*
- I'll say the sounds. You'll hear one letter name. Touch the letter as soon as you hear the name: **OOO    rrr.**
- Everybody, what letter are you touching? (Signal.) *O.*

e. Next word: **rain**. What word? (Signal.) *Rain.*
- I'll say the sounds. You touch the letter you hear: **rrr    AAA    nnn.**
- Everybody, what letter are you touching? (Signal.) *A.*

f. Next word: **ear**. What word? (Signal.) *Ear.*
- I'll say the sounds. You touch the letter you hear: **EEE    rrr.**
- Everybody, what letter are you touching? (Signal.) *E.*

g. Next word: **fine**. What word? (Signal.) *Fine.*
- I'll say the sounds. You touch the letter you hear: **fff    III    nnn.**

- Everybody, what letter are you touching? (Signal.) *I.*

h. Last word: **rope**. What word? (Signal.) *Rope.*
- I'll say the sounds. You touch the letter you hear: **rrr    OOO    p.**
- Everybody, what letter are you touching? (Signal.) *O.*

i. (Repeat steps d through h until firm.)

j. Raise your hand if you got all the letters right.

===== EXERCISE 6 =====

### WRITING WORDS

a. You're going to write words. You've done some of them before.

b. Touch the star. ✔
- You'll write the word **or** on the line after the star.
What word? (Signal.) *Or.*
- I'll say **or** a sound at a time: **OOO    rrr.**
- Your turn. Get ready. (Tap 2 times.) *OOO    rrr.*
- Let's do that again.
Say the first sound in **or**. (Signal.) *OOO.*
Say the next sound in **or**. (Signal.) *rrr.*
- The first sound is **OOO**. Touch the bar for that sound. ✔
The next sound is **rrr**. Touch the bar for that sound. ✔
- Write the letters for the word **or**. Pencils down when you're finished.
(Observe children and give feedback.)
- Check your work.
- (Write on the board:)

<u>**or**</u>

- Here's what you should have. This is the word **or**. Raise your hand if you got it right.

c. Touch the line after the spider. ✔
You'll write the word **so** on that line.
What word? (Signal.) *So.*
- Say **so** a sound at a time. Get ready. (Tap 2 times.) *sss    OOO.*
- Let's do that again.
Say the first sound in **so**. (Signal.) *sss.*
Say the next sound in **so**. (Signal.) *OOO.*

- The first sound is **sss.** Touch the bar for that sound. ✔
  The next sound is **OOO.** Touch the bar for that sound. ✔
- Write the letters for the word **so.** Pencils down when you're finished.
  (Observe children and give feedback.)
- (Write on the board:)

**SO**

- Here's the word **so.** Raise your hand if you got it right.

**Individual Turns**
- You're going to read the words you made.
  (Call on different children to say the sounds for one of the words and read it.)
- Read the word after the star. *[Or.]*
- Read the word after the spider. *[So.]*

=====EXERCISE 7=====

**LETTER PRINTING**

a. Find the dinosaur. ✔
- You'll write letters on these lines.
b. (Write on the board:)

- (Write in style children are to follow: **r e s**.)
- These are letters that you'll write.
- What letter goes on the first line? (Signal.) *R.*
- What letter goes on the next line? (Signal.) *E.*
- What letter goes on the last line? (Signal.) *S.*
c. Write the first letter on each line. Pencils down when you're finished.
  (Observe children and give feedback.)
d. When you write the rest of the letters, make them carefully.

=====EXERCISE 8=====

**CROSS-OUT AND CIRCLE GAME**

a. Turn to side 2 of your worksheet. ✔
- Find the boxes with the crossed-out **M** and circled **N.**
- This is a very tough exercise.
b. Touch the letter **M.** ✔
- That letter is crossed out. That tells you one rule for the game. Listen: Cross out every **M.** The 5 under the **M** tells you that there are 5 **M**s to cross out.
c. Touch the letter **N.** ✔
  There is a circle around the **N.** That tells you the other rule. Listen: Circle every **N.**
- Your turn: What is the rule for every **N?** (Signal.) *Circle every N.*
- The 6 under the **N** tells you how many **N**s there are. How many? (Signal.) *Six.*
d. Listen: What's the rule for every **M?** (Signal.) *Cross out every M.*
- Cross out the **M**s and circle the **N**s. Pencils down when you're finished.
  (Observe children and give feedback.)
e. Check your cross-outs and circles to make sure you crossed out **five M**s and circled **six N**s.

=====EXERCISE 9=====

**HIDDEN PICTURE**

*Note:* Each child needs a brown, a blue and a green crayon.

a. Find the picture at the bottom of your worksheet. ✔
- This picture has a lot of letters. The letters are in spaces.
- There are coloring rules for three of the letters. Take out crayons that are brown, green and blue.
  (Observe children and give feedback.)
b. Touch and say the names of the letters.
- First letter. What's the name? (Signal.) *T.*
- Next letter. What's the name? (Signal.) *R.*
- Last letter. What's the name? (Signal.) *P.*
c. Touch the box for **R** above the picture. ✔
- Here's the coloring rule for **R:** All parts of the picture that have an **R** are brown.

- What color are all parts of the picture that have an **R?** (Signal.) *Brown.*
- Make a brown mark in the box for **R.** That will remind you of the rule. Raise your hand when you're finished.
  (Observe children and give feedback.)

d. Touch the box for **P.** ✔
- Here's the coloring rule for **P:** All parts of the picture that have a **P** are blue. What color? (Signal.) *Blue.*
- Make a blue mark in the box for **P.** That will remind you of the rule. Raise your hand when you're finished.
  (Observe children and give feedback.)

e. Touch the box for **T** at the top of the picture. ✔
- Here's the rule for **T:** All parts of the picture that have a **T** are green. What color? (Signal.) *Green.*
- Make a green mark in the box for **T.** Raise your hand when you're finished.
  (Observe children and give feedback.)

f. Later, you can color the parts and find the hidden picture.

**Independent Work Summary**
- Letter printing (finish lines of **r, e, s**).
- Color the hidden picture (**t**=green, **r**=brown, **p**=blue).

---

**Materials:** Each child will need crayons and scissors.

**Note:** Administer WORD WRITING to the entire group. Individually administer the rest of the test.

---

**WORKBOOK**

===== EXERCISE 1 =====

## TEST—Group Administered

### Part 1: WORD WRITING

a. Open your workbook to lesson 10, test 1. ✔
   This is a test.
• Write your name at the top of the page.
b. Find the cat. ✔
• You're going to write some words.
c. Touch line 1. ✔
• The word for that line is **me.** What word? (Signal.) *Me.*
• Say the sounds in **me.** Get ready. (Tap 2 times.) *mmm    EEE.*
• Write the word **me** on line 1. Pencils down when you're finished.
   (Observe children but do not give feedback.)
d. Touch line 2. ✔
• The word for that line is **no.** What word? (Signal.) *No.*
• Say the sounds in **no.** Get ready. (Tap 2 times.) *nnn    OOO.*
• Write the word **no** on line 2. Pencils down when you're finished.
   (Observe children.)

===== EXERCISE 2 =====

## STORYBOOK
## Coloring

**Note:** Each child needs crayons.

• While I'm listening to each child read, you can color the pictures on side 1 and side 2. The pictures show the story of Sam the bunny.

===== EXERCISE 3 =====

## TEST—Individually Administered

**Note:** Individually administer the rest of the test: SOUNDS and WORD READING. Mark all errors. Record the test results on the Test Summary Sheet for test 1.

### Part 2: SOUNDS

a. Turn to side 2. ✔
• Find the dinosaur. ✔
• Touch and say the **sound** for each letter. [*lll, sss, mmm.*]
b. Find the skunk. ✔
• Touch and say the **sound** for each letter. [*rrr, nnn, fff.*]
c. Find the spider. ✔
• Touch and say the **sound** for each letter. [*OOO, lll, EEE.*]

### Part 3: WORD READING

d. Find the flower. ✔
• Touch and say each sound. [*sss    OOO.*]
• Say it fast. [*So.*]
e. Find the tree. ✔
• Touch and say the sound. [*mmm    EEE.*]
• Say it fast. [*Me.*]
f. Find the ball. ✔
• Touch and say the sound. [*sss    EEE    mmm.*]
• Say it fast. [*Seem.*]

## EXERCISE 4

### STORYBOOK
#### Take Home

**Note:** Each child needs scissors.

a. (Remove perforated test sheet from workbook.)
b. (Direct children to cut along the dotted line.)
c. (Collect test part of sheets.)
d. (Direct children to fold the booklet along the fold line so that the title is showing.)
e. Now you can take the storybook home and tell the story to your family.

## EXERCISE 5

### MARKING THE TEST

- (Record all test results on the lesson 10, Test 1 Summary Sheet. Reproducible Summary Sheets are at the back of the Teacher's Guide.)

## EXERCISE 6

### TEST REMEDIES

- (Provide any necessary remedies for Test 10 before presenting lesson 11. Test Remedies are discussed in the Teacher's Guide.)

## EXERCISE 7

### LITERATURE BOOK

- (See Teacher's Guide.)

**Materials:** Each child will need a red, a blue and a yellow crayon (exercise 7) and lined paper (exercise 9).

## TEXTBOOK

### EXERCISE 1
**DOUBLE LETTERS**

a. Open your textbook to lesson 11. Find the camel. ✔
• (Teacher reference:)

| ll    nn    ee |
|---|

b. There are letters on the camel. You see the same letters two times. These are called **double letters.**
• What are they called? (Signal.) *Double letters.*
• You've read words with double **E.** Remember, when you read words that have double letters, you say the sound just once.
c. Touch the bar for the first double letter. ✔
   This is double **L.** What sound does double **L** make? (Signal.) *lll.*
• Touch the bar for the next double letter. ✔
   This is double **N.** What sound does double **N** make? (Signal.) *nnn.*
• Touch the bar for the last double letter. ✔
   This is double **E.** What sound does double **E** make? (Signal.) *EEE.*
d. Let's do it again.
• You touch the bar and say the sounds.
• Touch the bar under double **L.** What sound? (Signal.) *lll.*
• Next bar. What sound? (Signal.) *nnn.*
• Last bar. What sound? (Signal.) *EEE.*
e. Remember how to say the sounds for double letters. You'll be reading words with those letters.

### EXERCISE 2
**LETTER NAMES IN WORDS**
**Long Vowels**

a. Find the snake. ✔
• (Teacher reference:)

| o    a    i    e |
|---|

b. Touch under the first letter. What letter? (Signal.) *O.*
• Next letter. What letter? (Signal.) *A.*
• Next letter. What letter? (Signal.) *I.*
• Last letter. What letter? *E.*
c. I'll say words that have those letter names in them. You'll touch the letter you hear.
d. Listen: The first word is **feel.** What word? (Signal.) *Feel.*
• I'll say the sounds. You'll hear one letter name. Touch the letter as soon as you hear the name: **fff    EEE    lll.**
• Everybody, what letter are you touching? (Signal.) *E.*
e. Next word: **for.** What word? (Signal.) *For.*
• I'll say the sounds. You touch the letter you hear: **fff    OOO    rrr.**
• Everybody, what letter are you touching? (Signal.) *O.*
f. Next word: **file.** What word? (Signal.) *File.*
• I'll say the sounds. You touch the letter you hear: **fff    III    lll.**
• Everybody, what letter are you touching? (Signal.) *I.*
g. Next word: **ice.** What word? (Signal.) *Ice.*
• I'll say the sounds. You touch the letter you hear: **III    sss.**
• Everybody, what letter are you touching? (Signal.) *I.*
h. (Repeat steps d through g until firm.)
i. Raise your hand if you got all the letters right.

### EXERCISE 3
**READING WORDS**

a. You're going to read some words.
• Touch the cactus. ✔

- (Teacher reference:)

> o r
>
> f o r

- The first word has the letters **O** and **R**.
- Touch under the first letter. ✔
  Everybody, what's the sound for that letter? (Signal.) *OOO.*
- Touch under the next letter. ✔
  Everybody, what's the sound for that letter? (Signal.) *rrr.*
- b. Go back to the first letter. ✔
- I'll say the sounds. You touch under the letters. Listen: **OOO   rrr.**
- c. Again. Back to the first letter. Get ready to touch. Listen: **OOO   rrr.**
- (Repeat until firm.)
- d. Everybody, touch and say those sounds. Get ready. (Tap 2 times.) *OOO   rrr.*
- Again. Touch and say those sounds. Get ready. (Tap 2 times.) *OOO   rrr.*
- Say it fast. (Signal.) *Or.*
- What word? (Signal.) *Or.*
  You just read the word **or.**
- e. Touch the next word. ✔
  That word has the letters **F, O** and **R.**
- Touch under the first letter. ✔
  Everybody, what's the sound?
  (Signal.) *fff.*
- Touch under the next letter. ✔
  What's the sound? (Signal.) *OOO.*
- Touch under the last letter. ✔
  What's the sound? (Signal.) *rrr.*
- f. Go back to the **F.** ✔
- I'll say the sounds. You'll touch under the letters. Listen: **fff   OOO   rrr.**
- g. Again. Back to the first letter. Get ready to touch. Listen: **fff   OOO   rrr.**
- (Repeat until firm.)
- h. Everybody, touch and say those sounds. Get ready. (Tap 3 times.)
  *fff   OOO   rrr.*
- Again. Get ready.
  (Tap 3 times.) *fff   OOO   rrr.*
- Say it fast. (Signal.) *For.*
- What word? (Signal.) *For.*
  You just read the word **for.**
- i. Touch the rock. ✔

- (Teacher reference:)

> m e
>
> s ee

- The first word has the letters **M** and **E.**
- Touch under the first letter. ✔
  Everybody, what's the sound for that letter? (Signal.) *mmm.*
- Touch under the next letter. ✔
  Everybody, what's the sound for that letter? (Signal.) *EEE.*
- j. Go back to the first letter. ✔
- I'll say the sounds. You touch under the letters. Listen: **mmm   EEE.**
- k. Again. Back to the first letter. Get ready to touch. Listen: **mmm   EEE.**
- (Repeat until firm.)
- l. Everybody, touch and say those sounds. Get ready. (Tap 2 times.) *mmm   EEE.*
- Again. Get ready. (Tap 2 times.)
  *mmm   EEE.*
- Say it fast. (Signal.) *Me.*
- What word? (Signal.) *Me.*
  You just read the word **me.**
- m. Touch the next word. ✔
  The word on that line has the letters **S** and **E.**
- Touch under the first bar. ✔
  Everybody, what's the sound?
  (Signal.) *sss.*
- Touch under the next bar. ✔
  What's the sound? (Signal.) *EEE.*
- n. Go back to the **S.** ✔
- I'll say the sounds. You'll touch under the letters. Listen: **sss   EEE.**
- o. Again. Back to the first letter. Get ready to touch. Listen: **sss   EEE.**
- (Repeat until firm.)
- p. Everybody, touch and say those sounds. Get ready. (Tap 2 times.) *sss   EEE.*
- Again. Get ready. (Tap 2 times.)
  *sss   EEE.*
- Say it fast. (Signal.) *See.*
- What word? (Signal.) *See.*
  You just read the word **see.** Good for you.

**Individual Turns**

(Call on different children to say the sounds for one of the words and say it fast.)

- Read the words in the cactus. *[Or, for.]*
- Read the words in the rock. *[Me, see.]*

═══════════ EXERCISE 4 ═══════════

**STORY TIME**

a. Here's a story about a new character, Clarabelle. I'll tell you the story, but you'll have to help me with the words I don't say fast.

b. Listen: Clarabelle was not a person. She was not a goat and not a dog.

**[cow]**

c. Clarabelle was a **c  ooo  www.**
- Listen to the word again:
  **c  ooo  www.**
- What word? (Signal.) *Cow.*
- Yes, Clarabelle was a cow.

**[pigs]**

d. She lived on a farm with a lot of cows and **p  iii  g  zzz.**
- Listen to the word again: **p  iii  g  zzz.**
- What word? (Signal.) *Pigs.*
- Yes, she lived on a farm with lots of cows and pigs.

**[ducks]**

e. There were also lots of **d  uuu  k  sss.**
- Listen to the word again: **d  uuu  k  sss.**
- What word? (Signal.) *Ducks.*

**[sheep]**

f. There were lots of ducks and there were horses and **sh sh sh  EEE  p.**
- Listen to the word again: **sh sh sh  EEE  p.**
- What word? (Signal.) *Sheep.*

**[goats]**

g. There were horses and sheep and there were **g  OOO  t  sss.**
- Listen again: **g  OOO  t  sss.**
- What word? (Signal.) *Goats.*
- On the farm, there were cows, pigs, ducks, horses, sheep and goats.
- Clarabelle loved to imitate others.

**[pond]**

h. If she saw a duck swim, she would jump in the **p  ooo  nnn  d.**
- Listen to the word again: **p  ooo  nnn  d.**
- What word? (Signal.) *Pond.*
- Yes, she'd jump in the pond and try to swim like a duck.

**[bus]**

i. If she saw a boy go to school, she'd try to do the same thing and get on the **b  uuu  sss.**
- Listen to the word again: **b  uuu  sss.**
- What word? (Signal.) *Bus.*
- Isn't that funny, she'd try to be like a child and get on a bus.
- And every time Clarabelle tried to be like someone else she got in trouble.

**[mud]**

j. Once, she saw pigs rolling in the **mmm  uuu  d.**
- Listen again: **mmm  uuu  d.**
- What word? (Signal.) *Mud.*
- Right, the pigs were rolling in the mud.

**[fun]**

k. Clarabelle said, "That looks like **fff  uuu  nnn.**"
- Listen again: **fff  uuu  nnn.**
- What word? (Signal.) *Fun.*
- What did rolling in the mud look like to Clarabelle? (Signal.) *Fun.*
- So she got in the mud and started to roll around.

**[mad]**

l. And the pigs got very **mmm  aaa  d.**
- How did they feel? (Signal.) *Mad.*
- Those pigs were really mad.

**[pen]**

m. One pig said, "This is not a cow pen. This is a pig **p  eee  nnn.**"
- What word? (Signal.) *Pen.*
- Yes, it was a pig pen.

**[room]**

n. Another pig said, "Yeah, and you're so big that when you roll around, we don't have any **rrr  oo oo oo  mmm.**"
- What didn't the pigs have? (Signal.) *Room.*

**[leave]**

o. So the pigs kept complaining until Clarabelle decided that she should **lll EEE vvv.**
• What was she going to do? (Signal.) *Leave.*
• So she stood up and walked out of the pig pen—plop, plop.

**[legs]**

p. She had mud on her **lll eee g zzz.**
• What part had mud? (Signal.) *Legs.*

**[nose]**

q. And she had mud on her **nnn OOO zzz.**
• What other part had mud? (Signal.) *Nose.*

**[back]**

r. She had mud on her front and mud on her **b aaa k.**
• There was mud on her front and her . . . (Signal.) *Back.*
• Name the parts of Clarabelle that had mud on them. (Call on a child. Ideas: *Legs, nose, front and back.*)
• She was so loaded with mud that she could hardly walk.

**[feels]**

s. She said, "I don't like the way all this mud **fff EEE lll zzz.**"
• What word? (Signal.) *Feels.*
• Yes, she didn't like the way mud feels.

**[me]**

t. She said, "I know how I can wash all this mud off **mmm EEE.**"
• What word? (Signal.) *Me.*
• And next time, you'll find out how she did that.

═══════ EXERCISE 5 ═══════

**STORY EXTENSION**
**Picture Comprehension**

a. Find the pictures of Clarabelle on the next page of your textbook. ✔
• Touch the first picture. ✔
• The first picture shows Clarabelle doing something. What is she doing? (Call on a child. Idea: *Getting on a school bus.*)

• Where does Clarabelle want to go? (Call on a child. Idea: *School.*)
• Yes, she wants to be like the children and go to school.
b. Touch the other picture. ✔
• This picture shows something that happened in the story.
• Who is that big muddy animal that is lying down? (Signal.) *Clarabelle.* She looks pretty happy.
• Do the pigs look happy? (Signal.) *No.*
• What do you think they're saying to Clarabelle? (Call on a child. Ideas: *Get out; This pen is not for cows.*)
• I wonder what the other animals are thinking.
c. This same picture is in your workbook. Later, you can color that picture. Clarabelle is brown. The mud is black.
d. Close your textbook. ✔

═══════ EXERCISE 6 ═══════

**WRITING WORDS**
**Introducing aaa**

a. You're going to say words a sound at a time.
• Listen: **an.** What word? (Signal.) *An.* Say **an** a sound at a time. Get ready. (Tap 2 times.) *aaa nnn.*
• Listen: **am.** What word? (Signal.) *Am.* Say **am** a sound at a time. Get ready. (Tap 2 times.) *aaa mmm.*
• Here's a three-sound word. Listen: **ran.** What word? (Signal.) *Ran.* Say **ran** a sound at a time. Get ready. (Tap 3 times.) *rrr aaa nnn.*
• Here's another three-sound word. Listen: **man.** What word? (Signal.) *Man.* Say **man** a sound at a time. Get ready. (Tap 3 times.) *mmm aaa nnn.*
b. In all the words you just said, one of the sounds is **aaa.**
• Listen: The sound **aaa** is spelled with the letter **A.** What **letter** do you write for the sound **aaa?** (Signal.) *A.*

c. (Write on the board in the style children are to follow:)

-n-r-a-

**WORKBOOK**

d. Open your workbook to lesson 11 and write your name. ✔
• Say the word **an** a sound at a time. Get ready. (Tap 2 times.) *aaa nnn.*
• Let's do that again.
  Say the first sound in **an**. (Signal.) *aaa.*
  Say the next sound in **an**. (Signal.) *nnn.*
• The first sound in **an** is **aaa**. What letter do you write for **aaa?** (Signal.) *A.*
e. Touch the moon. ✔
• Write the letters for **an**. Pencils down when you're finished.
  (Observe children and give feedback.)
• (Write on the board:)

-a-n-

• Here's the word **an**.
  The first letter is **A**.
  The next letter is **N**.
  Raise your hand if you got it right.
f. The next word is **ran**. What word? (Signal.) *Ran.*
• **Ran** has three sounds. Say **ran** a sound at a time. Get ready.
  (Tap 3 times.) *rrr aaa nnn.*
g. Let's do it again.
  Say the first sound in **ran**. (Signal.) *rrr.*
  Say the next sound in **ran**. (Signal.) *aaa.*
  Say the last sound in **ran**. (Signal.) *nnn.*
• (Repeat step g until firm.)
h. Touch the star. ✔
• Write the letters for **ran**. Remember what letter to write for **aaa**. Pencils down when you're finished.
  (Observe children and give feedback.)

• (Write on the board:)

r-a-n

• Here's the word **ran**.
• Your first letter should be **R**.
  Your next letter should be **A**.
  Your last letter should be **N**.

**Individual Turns**
• (Call on different children to say the sounds for one of the words and say it fast.)
• Read the word after the moon. *[An.]*
• Read the word after the star. *[Ran.]*

═══════ EXERCISE 7 ═══════
**HIDDEN PICTURE**

*Note:* Each child needs a red, a blue and a yellow crayon.

a. Find the cat. ✔
• This is a hidden picture. I'll tell you the coloring rules. You'll need a red crayon, a blue crayon and a yellow crayon.
b. Touch and say the names of the letters.
• First letter. What's the name? (Signal.) *F.*
• Next letter. What's the name? (Signal.) *D.*
• Last letter. What's the name? (Signal.) *V.*
c. Touch the box for the **V** at the top of the picture. ✔
• Here's the rule for **V**: All parts of the picture that have a **V** are blue. Make a blue mark in the box for **V**. Raise your hand when you're finished.
  (Observe children and give feedback.)
• Here's the rule for the **F**: All the parts of the picture that have an **F** are red. Make a red mark in the box for **F**. Raise your hand when you're finished.
  (Observe children and give feedback.)
• Here's the rule for **D**: All parts of the picture that have a **D** are yellow. Make a yellow mark in the box for **D**. Raise your hand when you're finished.
  (Observe children and give feedback.)
d. Later, you can color the parts to find the hidden picture.

================= **EXERCISE 8** =================

## INDEPENDENT WORK

### Matching: Letters

a. Turn to side 2 of your worksheet. Find the happy face. ✔

b. Later, you'll draw lines to match the letters.

### Cross-Out and Circle Game

c. Find the box with the crossed-out **P** and circled **T.** ✔

d. Touch the letter **T.** ✔
There is a circle around the **T.** That tells you one rule for the game. Listen: Circle every **T.**

• Your turn: What is the rule for every **T?** (Signal.) *Circle every T.*

• The 5 under the **T** tells you how many **T**s there are. How many? (Signal.) *Five.*

e. Touch the letter **P** in the box. ✔

• That letter is crossed out. That tells you the other rule for the game. Listen: Cross out every **P.**

• What's the rule for every **P?** (Signal.) *Cross out every P.*

• The 4 under the **P** tells you that there are four **P**s to cross out.

f. Later, you'll cross out the **P**s and circle the **T**s. Don't get fooled.

### LINED PAPER
================= **EXERCISE 9** =================

## LETTER PRINTING

> **Note:** Each child needs lined paper.

a. Print your name on the top line of your paper. Pencils down when you're finished.
(Observe children and give feedback.)

• You're going to write some new letters on your lined paper. I'll show you how to make them.

b. The first letter you'll write is **L.** What letter? (Signal.) *L.*

• Watch carefully.

• (Write in the style children are to follow.)

• Remember, the **L** is a tall letter that starts at the top line.

• Write two **L**s on the line below your name. Pencils down when you're finished. (Observe children and give feedback.)

c. The letter for the middle line is **I.** What letter? (Signal.) *I.*

• Watch carefully.

• (Write to show:)

• Remember, only the dot for the **I** goes above the dotted line.

• Make two **I**s on the line below your **L**s. Pencils down when you're finished. (Observe children and give feedback.)

d. (Write to show:)

• The letter for the bottom line is **O.** What letter? (Signal.) *O.*

• Make two **O**s on the line below your **I**s. Pencils down when you're finished. (Observe children and give feedback.)

e. Later, you'll complete each row. You can make ten letters on each row.

### Independent Work Summary

• Color story picture (Clarabelle=brown, mud=black).

• Hidden picture (**f**=red, **d**=yellow, **v**=blue).

• Matching game.

• Cross-out (**p**=4) and circle (**t**=5) game.

• Letter printing (10 each: **l**, **i**, **o**).

**12**

**Materials:** Each child will need a green, a blue and a brown crayon (exercise 9) and lined paper (exercise 10).

## EXERCISE 1

### SOUNDS

a. Last time you learned a new sound: **aaa.**
- Listen: **at.** What word? (Signal.) *At.*
- Say **at** a sound at a time. Get ready. (Tap 2 times.) *aaa t.*
- What's the first sound in **at?** (Signal.) *aaa.*
- What letter makes the sound **aaa?** (Signal.) *A.*
- Yes, the first sound in **at** is spelled **A.**

b. New word: **an.** What word? (Signal.) *An.*
- Say **an** a sound at a time. Get ready. (Tap 2 times.) *aaa nnn.*
- What's the first sound in **an?** (Signal.) *aaa.*
- What letter makes the sound **aaa?** (Signal.) *A.*

**TEXTBOOK**

c. Open your textbook to lesson 12. Find the kites. ✔
- (Teacher reference:)

| nn | ll | ee | a |
|----|----|----|---|

- There are letters in the kites. You'll tell me the sounds.

d. Touch the bar for the first double letter. ✔
- Everybody, tell me the sound. Get ready. (Signal.) *nnn.*

e. Touch the bar for the next double letter. ✔
- Everybody, tell me the sound. Get ready. (Signal.) *lll.*

f. Touch the next bar. ✔
- Everybody, tell me the sound. Get ready. (Signal.) *EEE.*

g. Touch the next bar. ✔
- You know two sounds for this letter. One sound for this letter is the **letter name.** Tell me that sound. Get ready. (Signal.) *AAA.*
- The letter sometimes makes a different sound. Tell me that sound. Get ready. (Signal.) *aaa.*
- Let's do those again. Tell me the sound that is the letter name. Get ready. (Signal.) *AAA.*
- Tell me the other sound. Get ready. (Signal.) *aaa.*

h. This time, you'll spell sounds. I'll say the sounds for the kites. You'll touch the letters and tell me the letter names.

i. Listen: The sound for one of the kites is **AAA.** Touch that kite. ✔
- Everybody, spell what's in the kite you are touching. Get ready. (Signal.) *A.*

j. Listen: The sound for one of the kites is **nnn.** Touch that kite. ✔
- Everybody, spell what's in the kite you are touching. Get ready. (Signal.) *N-N.*

k. Listen: The sound for one of the kites is **aaa.** Touch that kite. ✔
- Everybody, spell what's in the kite you are touching. Get ready. (Signal.) *A.*

l. Listen: The sound for one of the kites is **EEE.** Touch that kite. ✔
- Everybody, spell what's in the kite you are touching. Get ready. (Signal.) *E-E.*

m. (Repeat steps i through l until firm.)

**Individual Turns**
- (Call on different children to say the sounds for one or two of the kites.)

## EXERCISE 2

### READING WORDS

a. Find the birds. ✔
- (Teacher reference:)

| am | man | ran |
|----|-----|-----|

- These are words that have the letter **A.** In all these words, the letter **A** does not say its name. It makes the sound **aaa.** What sound? (Signal.) *aaa.*

b. Find the orange bird. Then touch under the first letter of the word. ✔
Everybody, what's the sound?
(Signal.) *aaa.*
- Touch under the next letter. ✔
What's the sound? (Signal.) *mmm.*
- Go back to the first letter. ✔
- I'll say the sounds. You touch under the letters. Listen: **aaa    mmm.** ✔
- Back to the first letter. ✔
- Listen and touch again: **aaa    mmm.** ✔
- Everybody, touch and say the sounds. Get ready. (Tap 2 times.) *aaa    mmm.*
- Say it fast. (Signal.) *Am.*
What word? (Signal.) *Am.*
You just read the word **am.** I **am** proud of you.

c. Touch the word on the blue bird. ✔
This word has three sounds. Remember the sound for the letter **A.**
- Touch under the first letter. ✔
Everybody, what's the sound?
(Signal.) *mmm.*
- Touch under the next letter. ✔
What's the sound? (Signal.) *aaa.*
- Touch under the last letter. ✔
What's the sound? (Signal.) *nnn.*
- Go back to the first letter. ✔
- I'll say the sounds. You touch under the letters. Listen: **mmm    aaa    nnn.** ✔
- Back to the first letter. ✔
- Listen and touch again:
**mmm    aaa    nnn.** ✔
- Everybody, touch and say the sounds: Get ready. (Tap 3 times.)
*mmm    aaa    nnn.*
- Say it fast. (Signal.) *Man.*
What word? (Signal.) *Man.*
You just read the word **man.**

d. Touch the word on the green bird. ✔
This word has three sounds.
- Touch under the first letter. ✔
Everybody, what's the sound?
(Signal.) *rrr.*
- Touch under the next letter. ✔
What's the sound? (Signal.) *aaa.*
- Touch under the last letter. ✔
What's the sound? (Signal.) *nnn.*
- Go back to the first letter. ✔

- I'll say the sounds. You touch under the letters. Listen: **rrr    aaa    nnn.** ✔
- Back to the first letter. ✔
- Listen and touch again:
**rrr    aaa    nnn.** ✔
- Everybody, touch and say the sounds. Get ready. (Tap 3 times.) *rrr    aaa    nnn.*
- Say it fast. (Signal.) *Ran.*
What word? (Signal.) *Ran.*
You just read the word **ran.**

**Individual Turns**
- (Call on different children to say the sounds for one of the words and say it fast.)
- Read the word on the blue bird. *[Man.]*
- Read the word on the green bird. *[Ran.]*
- Read the word on the orange bird. *[Am.]*

========= EXERCISE 3 =========
**SAYING THE SOUNDS**
**Long Vowels**

a. Find the hill. ✔
- (Teacher reference:)

| e    o    a |
|---|

- The letters on the hill sometimes say their names in words.
b. Touch under the first letter. ✔
What letter? (Signal.) *E.*
- Touch under the next letter. ✔
What letter? (Signal.) *O.*
- Touch the next letter. ✔
What letter? (Signal.) *A.*
c. Now you're going to touch the sounds you hear in words.
d. Listen: **safe.** What word? (Signal.) *Safe.*
- **Safe** has three sounds. Say **safe** a sound at a time. Get ready. (Tap 3 times.)
*sss    AAA    fff.*
- One of those sounds is a **letter name.** Touch the letter name you hear in **safe.** Get ready. (Signal.) ✔
- You should be touching the letter **A.** You can hear the name **A** in the word **safe.**
e. Next word: **aim.** What word?
(Signal.) *Aim.*

- Say the two sounds in **aim.** Get ready. (Tap 2 times.) *AAA   mmm.*
- Touch the letter name you hear in **aim.** Get ready. (Signal.) ✔
- You should be touching the letter **A.** You can hear the name **A** in the word **aim.**

f. Next word: **loaf.** What word? (Signal.) *Loaf.*
- **Loaf** has three sounds. Say **loaf** a sound at a time. Get ready. (Tap 3 times.) *lll   OOO   fff.*
- Touch the letter name you hear in **loaf.** Get ready. (Signal.) ✔
- You should be touching the letter **O.** You can hear the name **O** in the word **loaf.**

g. The last word is **seem.** What word? (Signal.) *Seem.*
- **Seem** has three sounds. Say the sounds in **seem.** Get ready. (Tap 3 times.) *sss   EEE   mmm.*
- Touch the letter name you hear in **seem.** Get ready. (Signal.) ✔
- You should be touching the letter **E.** You can hear the name **E** in the word **seem.**

========= EXERCISE 4 =========

## READING WORDS

a. Find the trucks. ✔
- (Teacher reference:)

| for    seem |
| --- |

- There are words that you've read before on the trucks.

b. Touch the yellow truck. Then touch under the first letter of the word. ✔
- Everybody, what's the first sound? (Signal.) *fff.*
- Touch under the next letter. ✔ What's the sound? (Signal.) *OOO.*
- Touch under the last letter. ✔ What's the sound? *rrr.*

c. Go back to the first letter. ✔
- Touch and say the sounds. Get ready. (Tap 3 times.) *fff   OOO   rrr.*

d. Again. Back to the first letter. Touch and say the sounds. Get ready. (Tap 3 times.) *fff   OOO   rrr.*
- (Repeat until firm.)

e. Everybody, say it fast. (Signal.) *For.*
- What word? (Signal.) *For.* You just read the word **for.**

f. Touch the green truck. Then touch under the first letter of the word. ✔
- Everybody, what's the first sound? (Signal.) *sss.*
- Touch under the next bar. ✔ What's the sound? (Signal.) *EEE.*
- Touch under the last letter. ✔ What's the sound? (Signal.) *mmm.*

g. Go back to the first letter. ✔ Touch and say the sounds. Get ready. (Tap 3 times.) *sss   EEE   mmm.*
- Again. Back to the first letter. Touch and say the sounds. Get ready. (Tap 3 times.) *sss   EEE   mmm.*
- Say it fast. (Signal.) *Seem.* What word? (Signal.) *Seem.* You just read the word **seem.**

## Individual Turns
- (Call on different children to say the sounds for one of the words and say it fast.)
- Read the word on the green truck. *[Seem.]*
- Read the word on the yellow truck. *[For.]*

========= EXERCISE 5 =========

## STORY TIME

**[cow]**

a. Last time I told a story about a **c   ooo   www.**
- Listen to the word again: **c   ooo   www.**
- What word? (Signal.) *Cow.*
- That cow was named Clarabelle, and she loved to do what others did.

**[mud]**

b. When we left Clarabelle, she was covered with **mmm   uuu   d.**
- What word? (Signal.) *Mud.*
- She had **mud** on her legs, on her nose, on her front and even on her back. She said she knew how to get rid of that mud.

**[pond]**

c. So she went to a **p   ooo   nnn   d.**
- Listen again: **p   ooo   nnn   d.**
- Where did she go? (Signal.) *Pond.*

**[ducks]**

d. When she got there, she saw some **d   uuu   k   sss.**
- What did she see? (Signal.) *Ducks.*
- Yes, some ducks were near the pond.

**[smell]**

e. When she got closer, one of the ducks said to the other ducks, "Do you see a big mound of mud that has a very bad **sss   mmm   eee   lll**?"
- Listen again: **sss   mmm   eee   lll.**
- What word? (Signal.) *Smell.*
- Yes, one duck said Clarabelle had a very bad smell.

**[pond]**

f. "Phew," the ducks said, and they jumped from the bank into the **p   ooo   nnn   d.**
- Listen again: **p   ooo   nnn   d.**
- What word? (Signal.) *Pond.*
- Yes, they jumped into the pond.

**[jump]**

g. Clarabelle said, "Those are nasty little ducks, but I like the way they **j   uuu   mmm   p.**"
- Listen again: **j   uuu   mmm   p.**
- What word? (Signal.) *Jump.*
- So Clarabelle got up on the bank. And all the ducks in the water kept laughing at her and saying things like, "What is that big heap of mud going to do?" And, "Get out of here, mud ball."

**[heap]**

h. But Clarabelle didn't pay any attention, even when they called her a big mud **h   EEE   p.**
- Listen again: **h   EEE   p.**
- What word? (Signal.) *Heap.*

**[jump]**

i. Clarabelle just took a great big **j   uuu   mmm   p.**
- What did she take? (Signal.) *Jump.*

**[mile]**

j. And when she hit the water, it made a splat that you could hear for a **mmm   lll   lll.**
- Listen again: **mmm   lll   lll.**

- How far away could you hear her hitting the water? (Signal.) *Mile.*
- And that water flew so high and so far that there was almost no water left in the pond.

**[field]**

k. Clarabelle's giant splat sent some of the ducks flying into the **fff   EEE   lll   d.**
- Listen again: **fff   EEE   lll   d.**
- What did these ducks go into? (Signal.) *Field.*

**[duck]**

l. And they were all flapping and squawking and yelling at Clarabelle. Clarabelle thought to herself, "I guess I cannot do things like a **d   uuu   k.**"
- What word? (Signal.) *Duck.*
- Poor Clarabelle. We'll find out more about her problem next time.

---

## EXERCISE 6

### STORY EXTENSION
### Picture Comprehension

a. Find the pictures of Clarabelle. ✔
- These pictures show things that happened in the story.
b. Touch the first picture. ✔
- Who is that big mud heap? (Signal.) *Clarabelle.*
- Where is she going? (Signal.) *To the pond.*
- What are the ducks saying? (Call on different children. Ideas: *Look at that mound of mud; That mud heap has a very bad smell; Get out of here, mud ball.*)
- What's that mud heap going to do? (Signal.) *Jump in the pond.*
c. Touch the next picture. ✔
- What is Clarabelle doing? (Call on a child. Idea: *Jumping into the pond.*)
- When she dives in, the other animals fly out.
- What kinds of animals do you see being splashed out of the pond? (Call on a child. Idea: *Frogs, fish, ducks.*)

- What do you think those ducks are saying to Clarabelle?
  (Call on a child. Ideas: *Get out of our pond; You shouldn't have done that.*)
- Only one animal in this picture looks very happy. Who is that? (Signal.) *Clarabelle.*
- After she finds out how mad she made the other animals, I don't think she'll be so happy.

## WORKBOOK

═══════ EXERCISE 7 ═══════

**WRITING WORDS**

a. Close your textbook. Go to lesson 12 in your workbook and write your name. ✔
- Find the cat. ✔
- You're going to write words on the lines.
- Touch line 1 after the cat. ✔
b. The word for line 1 is **fan**. What word? (Signal.) *Fan.*
- Say **fan** a sound at a time. Get ready. (Tap 3 times.) *fff    aaa    nnn.*
- Let's do that again.
  Say the first sound in **fan**. (Signal.) *fff.*
  Say the next sound in **fan**. (Signal.) *aaa.*
  Say the last sound in **fan**. (Signal.) *nnn.*
c. (Repeat step b until firm.)
d. Write **fan**. Remember what letter to write for **aaa**. Pencils down when you're finished. (Observe children and give feedback. Accept approximations for **f** and **a**.)
- (Write on the board in the style children are to follow:)

1. fan

- Here's the word **fan**. Check your word.
- The first letter is **F**.
- The next letter is **A**.
- The last letter is **N**.
- Raise your hand if you got it right. Good for you.

e. Touch line 2. ✔
- The word for 2 is **no**. What word? (Signal.) *No.*
- Say **no** a sound at a time. Get ready. (Tap 2 times.) *nnn    OOO.*
- Let's do that again.
  Say the first sound in **no**. (Signal.) *nnn.*
  Say the other sound in **no**. (Signal.) *OOO.*
f. (Repeat step e until firm.)
g. Write **no**. Pencils down when you're finished. (Observe children and give feedback. Accept approximations.)
- (Write on the board:)

2. no

- Here's the word **no**. Check your word.
- The first letter is **N**.
- The last letter is **O**.
- Raise your hand if you got it right.
h. Touch line 3. ✔
  The word for 3 is **for**. What word? (Signal.) *For.*
- **For** has three sounds. Say **for** a sound at a time. Get ready. (Tap 3 times.) *fff    OOO    rrr.*
- Let's do that again.
  Say the first sound in **for**. (Signal.) *fff.*
  Say the next sound in **for**. (Signal.) *OOO.*
  Say the last sound in **for**. (Signal.) *rrr.*
i. (Repeat step h until firm.)
j. Write **for**. Pencils down when you're finished. (Observe children and give feedback. Accept approximations for **f**.)
- (Write on the board:)

3. for

- Here's the word **for**. Check your word.
- The first letter is **F**.
- The second letter is **O**.
- The third letter is **R**.
- Raise your hand if you got it right.
k. Now you're going to read the words you wrote.
- Touch the word on line 1. ✔
- The sounds for that word are *fff    aaa    nnn.*

- Everybody, say those sounds. Get ready. (Tap 3 times.) *fff   aaa   nnn.*
- What word? (Signal.) *Fan.*
l. Touch the word on line 2. ✔
- The sounds for that word are **nnn   OOO.**
- Everybody, touch and say those sounds. Get ready. (Tap 2 times.) *nnn   OOO.*
- What word? (Signal.) *No.*
m. Touch the word on line 3. ✔
- The sounds for that word are: **fff   OOO   rrr.**
- Everybody, touch and say those sounds. Get ready. (Tap 3 times.) *fff   OOO   rrr.*
- What word? (Signal.) *For.*

**Individual Turns**
- I'll call on different children to read those words. (Call on different children to say the sounds for one of the words and say it fast.)
- We have some good readers.

═══════ EXERCISE 8 ═══════
**INDEPENDENT WORK**

**Matching: Letters**
a. Find the bunny. ✔
- Later, you'll draw lines to match the letters.

**Cross-Out Game**
b. Find the star. ✔
- Touch the little box with the letters crossed out. ✔
- That shows what you'll cross out. You'll cross out **double N.**
- What will you cross out? (Signal.) *Double N.*
- Yes, **double N.**
- How many **double N**s will you cross out? (Signal.) *Four.*
- Yes, four.
c. Later, you'll cross out the **double N**s. Don't get fooled and cross out an **N** by itself.

═══════ EXERCISE 9 ═══════
**HIDDEN PICTURE**

> *Note:* Each child needs a green, a blue and a brown crayon.

a. Turn to side 2 of your worksheet.
- This is a hidden picture. I'll tell you the coloring rules. You'll need a green crayon, a blue crayon and a brown crayon.
b. Touch the box for the capital **I** at the top of the picture. ✔
- Here's the rule for capital **I:** All parts of the picture that have a capital **I** are green. Make a green mark in the box for **I.** Raise your hand when you're finished. (Observe children and give feedback.)
- Here's the rule for capital **A:** All the parts of the picture that have a capital **A** are blue. Make a blue mark in the box for **A.** Raise your hand when you're finished. (Observe children and give feedback.)
- Here's the rule for regular **H:** All parts of the picture that have a regular **H** are brown. Make a brown mark in the box for **H.** Raise your hand when you're finished. (Observe children and give feedback.)
c. Later you can color the parts and find the hidden picture.

LINED PAPER
═══════ EXERCISE 10 ═══════
**LETTER PRINTING**

> *Note:* Each child needs lined paper.

a. Print your name on your lined paper. Pencils down when you're finished. (Observe children and give feedback.)
- You're going to write a new letter. That letter is **F.** I'll show you how to make it. Watch carefully.

- (Write in the style children are to follow:)

- Remember, **F** is a tall letter that starts near the top line. Make two **F**s on the line just below your name. Pencils down when you're finished.
  (Observe children and give feedback.)
b. The other letters you'll write are **L** and **I**.
- (Write to show:)

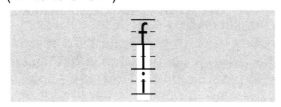

- Write two **L**s on the line below your **F**s. Write two **I**s on the line below your **L**s. Pencils down when you're finished.
  (Observe children and give feedback.)
c. Later, you'll complete each row. You can make ten letters on each row.

**Independent Work Summary**
- Matching game.
- Cross-out game (**nn**=4).
- Hidden picture (**I**=green, **A**=blue, **h**=brown).
- Letter printing (10 each: **f**, **l**, **i**).

**Material:** Each child will need lined paper (exercise 10).

━━━━━ EXERCISE 1 ━━━━━

## SOUNDS
### Introducing t

a. (Write on the board:)

| t |

- Everybody, what letter is this? (Signal.) *T.*
b. I'm going to tell you how to pronounce the sound for the letter **T.** I'll whisper the letter name. Listen carefully: (whisper **T**).
- Everybody, whisper the name. (Signal.) *T.*
- My turn to **whisper the first part** of the name, **T.** Listen: **t.**
- Your turn: Whisper the first part of the name. (Signal.) *t.*
- That's the sound the letter **T** makes. It's **always** a whisper sound.
c. You're going to say words a part at a time.
- Listen: **eat.** What word? (Signal.) *Eat.*
- Say **eat** a sound at a time. Get ready. (Tap 2 times.) *EEE    t.*
- What word? (Signal.) *Eat.*
d. New word: **at.** What word? (Signal.) *At.*
- Say **at** a sound at a time. Get ready. (Tap 2 times.) *aaa    t.*
- What word? (Signal.) *At.*
e. New word: **feet.** What word? (Signal.) *Feet.*
- Say **feet** a sound at a time. Get ready. (Tap 3 times.) *fff    EEE    t.*
- What word? (Signal.) *Feet.*
f. New word: **boat.** What word? (Signal.) *Boat.*
- Say **boat** a sound at a time. Get ready. (Tap 3 times.) *b    OOO    t.*
- What word? (Signal.) *Boat.*
g. New word: **ate.** What word? (Signal.) *Ate.*
- Say **ate** a sound at a time. Get ready. (Tap 2 times.) *AAA    t.*
- What word? (Signal.) *Ate.*

h. New word: **late.** What word? (Signal.) *Late.*
- Say **late** a sound at a time. Get ready. (Tap 3 times.) *lll    AAA    t.*
- What word? (Signal.) *Late.*
- (Point to **t.**)
- What sound does this letter make? (Signal.) *t.*
- Remember the sound **T** makes.

**Individual Turns**
- (Call on different children to sound out one of the following words: **at, feet, boat, ate, late.**)

━━━━━ EXERCISE 2 ━━━━━

## READING WORDS

a. Open your textbook to lesson 13. Find the bunny. ✔
- (Teacher reference:)

| 1. ram |
| 2. me |

- The first word has a letter that makes the sound **aaa.**
- Everybody, what letter makes the sound **aaa?** (Signal.) *A.*
- Yes, in some words **A** says its name. In other words, it says **aaa.**
b. Touch number 1. ✔
That word has three sounds. One of the sounds is **aaa.**
- Touch under the first letter of that word. ✔
Everybody, what's the first sound? (Signal.) *rrr.*
- Touch under the next letter. ✔
What's the sound? (Signal.) *aaa.*
Yes, **aaa.**
- Touch under the last letter. ✔
What's the sound? (Signal.) *mmm.*

c. Go back to the 1. ✔
   I'll say the sounds. You'll touch under the letters. Get ready: **rrr   aaa   mmm.** ✔
- (Repeat step c until firm.)
d. Go back to the 1. ✔
- This time, touch under the letters and say the sounds with me. Get ready.
   (Tap 3 times.) *rrr   aaa   mmm.*
- Once more. Touch under the letters and say the sounds. Get ready. (Tap 3 times.)
   *rrr   aaa   mmm.*
- Everybody, say it fast. (Signal.) *Ram.*
   What word did you just read?
   (Signal.) *Ram.*
- Yes, the car will **ram** into the truck.
e. Touch number 2. ✔
- That word has two sounds.
- Touch under the first letter. ✔
   Everybody, what's the sound?
   (Signal.) *mmm.*
- Touch under the last letter. ✔
   What's the sound? (Signal.) *EEE.*
f. Go back to the 2. ✔
- Touch and say the sounds. Get ready.
   (Tap 2 times.) *mmm   EEE.*
g. (Repeat step f until firm.)
h. Everybody, say it fast. (Signal.) *Me.*
   What word did you just read?
   (Signal.) *Me.*
- Good reading.

**Individual Turns**
- (Call on different children to say the sounds for one of the words and say it fast.)

════════ EXERCISE 3 ════════

**LETTER COMBINATIONS**
  **Introducing ai, oa, ea**

a. Find the heads of cabbage. ✔
- (Teacher reference:)

| ai   oa   ea |
|---|

- That rabbit is nibbling on those cabbages.
- These are letter combinations that you'll read in words. Each letter combination has a black letter and a blue letter.

- Here's the rule: The black letter says its name. The blue letter doesn't make any sound at all.
b. Touch the bar for the first combination. ✔
- That combination is spelled **A-I.** What's the name of the black letter in that combination? (Signal.) *A.*
- So the combination makes the sound **AAA.** What sound does the combination make? (Signal.) *AAA.*
- Yes, it says the name of the black letter. The **I** is blue so it doesn't make any sound at all.
c. Touch the bar for the next combination. ✔
- That combination is spelled **O-A.** What's the black letter? (Signal.) *O.*
- The black letter says its name. So what sound does the combination make? (Signal.) *OOO.*
- That's the sound the combination makes. Remember, the **A** is blue so it doesn't make any sound at all.
d. Touch the bar for the next combination. ✔
- That combination is spelled **E-A.** What's the black letter? (Signal.) *E.*
- The letter says its name. So what sound does the combination make? (Signal.) *EEE.*
- That's the sound the combination makes. Remember, the **A** is blue so it doesn't make any sound at all.
e. Let's do those combinations again.
- Touch the first combination. ✔
   What's the black letter? (Signal.) *A.*
   So what sound does the combination make? (Signal.) *AAA.*
- Touch the next combination. ✔
   What's the black letter? (Signal.) *O.*
   So what sound does the combination make? (Signal.) *OOO.*
- Touch the last combination. ✔
   What's the black letter? (Signal.) *E.*
   So what sound does the combination make? (Signal.) *EEE.*
f. (Repeat step e until firm.)

## EXERCISE 4

**READING WORDS**
**Words with Double Letters**

a. Find the hat. ✔
- (Teacher reference:)

> 1. s<u>ee</u>m
> 2. f<u>ee</u>l

- That looks like a farmer's hat. I hope that farmer is not nearby. He might not like the rabbit eating his cabbage.
- Word 1 has two **E**s. Remember, you just say the sound once.
- Touch and say the sounds.
  First sound. Get ready. (Signal.) *sss.*
  Next sound. Get ready. (Signal.) *EEE.*
  Last sound. Get ready. (Signal.) *mmm.*
- Touch and say those sounds again. Get ready. (Tap 3 times.) *sss    EEE    mmm.*
  Say it fast. (Signal.) *Seem.*
- Yes, they **seem** to be having fun.
b. Word 2 has two **E**s.
- Touch and say the sounds.
  First sound. Get ready. (Signal.) *fff.*
  Next sound. Get ready. (Signal.) *EEE.*
  Last sound. Get ready. (Signal.) *lll.*
- Touch and say those sounds again. Get ready. (Tap 3 times.) *fff    EEE    lll.*
  Say it fast. (Signal.) *Feel.*
- Yes, that would **feel** good.

**Individual Turns**
- (Call on different children to say the sounds for one or two of the words and say it fast.)

## EXERCISE 5

**STORY TIME**

a. I'm going to tell you more about Clarabelle, but I'm not going to say some of the words a part at a time. Instead, you will **read** those words.
b. Find the picture of the book. ✔

- (Teacher reference:)

> 1. am
> 2. me
> 3. no

- Touch word 1. ✔
- I'll say part of the story. Then you'll **read** word 1. Listen big and get ready to read the word when I tell you.
- When we left Clarabelle, she was in a pond. And she felt very sad. She said, "When those little ducks jumped in the pond, they made a tiny little ripple. But when I jumped in, I made a huge splat. I guess ducks don't make much splash because they are not as big as I . . ."
- Touch and say the sounds for word 1.
  First sound. (Signal.) *aaa.*
  Next sound. (Signal.) *mmm.*
- Go back to the first sound. Touch and say the sounds. Get ready.
  (Tap 2 times.) *aaa    mmm.*
  What word? (Signal.) *Am.*
- Yes, Clarabelle said, "They are not as big as I **am**."
c. Touch number 2. ✔
- I'll say the next part of the story. Then you'll read word 2.
- Clarabelle had jumped into the pond and had sent the water sailing. The pond was almost dry. The ducks had gone flying this way and that way. Some of them were in the field and some of them were in the trees. Clarabelle said to herself, "I don't blame those ducks for being mad at . . ."
- Say the sounds for word 2.
  First sound. (Signal.) *mmm.*
  Next sound. (Signal.) *EEE.*
- Go back to the first sound. Touch and say both sounds. Get ready.
  (Tap 2 times.) *mmm    EEE.*
- What word? (Signal.) *Me.*
- Yes, Clarabelle said, "I don't blame those ducks for being mad at **me**."
d. Touch word 3. ✔
- I'll say the last part of the story. Then you'll read word 3.

- Clarabelle started to climb out of the pond. The ducks were all around her. One was saying, "Look. That mud heap is really a cow. What's a **cow** doing in a **duck** pond?"
- "Yeah," the other ducks said. "Go find a cow pond, you big cow, you." Clarabelle tried to apologize. She said, "I'm really sorry about . . ."
- But the ducks would not listen. Clarabelle finally said, "Is there any way I can make up for what I did?"
- And all the ducks shouted in a very loud voice, ". . . ."
- Everybody, say the sounds for word 3. First sound. (Signal.) *nnn.* Next sound. (Signal.) *OOO.*
- Go back to the first sound. Touch and say both sounds again. Get ready. (Tap 2 times.) *nnn    OOO.*
- What word? (Signal.) *No.*
- That's what the ducks said when Clarabelle asked if there was anything she could do to make up for what she did. They said, "No!" Clarabelle was very sad.

## Second Reading

e. Let's read the story again.
- Touch word 1. ✔
- (Teacher reference:)

> 1. **am**
> 2. **me**
> 3. **no**

- I'll tell you part of the story, and then you'll read the words.
- Listen: Clarabelle was in a pond and she felt very sad. Here's what she said: "When those little ducks jumped in the pond, they made a tiny little ripple. But when I jumped in, I made a huge splat. I guess ducks don't make much splash because they are not as big as I . . ."
- Say the sounds for word 1. (Tap 2 times.) *aaa    mmm.*
- What word? (Signal.) *Am.*

- Clarabelle said, "Ducks are not as big as I am."
f. Touch word 2. ✔
- Clarabelle had jumped into the pond and had sent the water sailing. Ducks had gone flying into the trees and into the field. Clarabelle said, "I don't blame those ducks for being mad at . . ."
- Say the sounds for word 2. (Tap 2 times.) *mmm    EEE.*
- What word? (Signal.) *Me.*
- Yes, Clarabelle said, "I don't blame those ducks for being mad at me."
g. Touch word 3. ✔
- Clarabelle started to climb out of the pond. She asked the ducks, "Is there any way I can make up for what I did?"
- And all of the ducks shouted in a very loud voice, ". . . ."
- Say the sounds for word 3. (Tap 2 times.) *nnn    OOO.*
- What word? (Signal.) *No.*
- When Clarabelle asked if there was anything she could do to make up for what she did, the ducks said, "No."

## Individual Turns

- (Call on different children to say the sounds for one of the words and say it fast.)

══════════ EXERCISE 6 ══════════

## STORY EXTENSION
### Picture Comprehension

a. Find the picture of Clarabelle and the ducks. ✔
- Clarabelle is getting out of the pond. The water and the ducks are already out of the pond. Clarabelle has just asked the ducks if there is any way she can make up for what she did. Who can read what the ducks are saying to Clarabelle? (Call on a child. *No.*)
- Clarabelle doesn't look very happy, does she? *No.*

## WORKBOOK

b. Close your textbook. Go to lesson 13 in your workbook and write your name. ✔

c. Find the two pictures of the story. Touch the first picture. ✔

• Is this a picture of Clarabelle before or after she jumped in the pond? (Signal.) *Before.*

• She looks like a mud heap.

• Where are the ducks? (Call on a child. Idea: *In the pond.*)

d. Touch the next picture. ✔

• This is the same picture you just saw in your textbook, but you can't see what the ducks are saying.

• Is this a picture of Clarabelle before or after she jumped in the pond? (Signal.) *After.*

• Where are the ducks? (Call on individual children. Ideas: *Standing around the pond; in the trees.*)

• Later, you can color the pictures.

═══════ EXERCISE 7 ═══════

## READING SOUNDS

a. You learned a sound for the letter **T.** It's a whispered sound. Everybody, say the sound for the letter **T.** (Signal.) *t.*

b. Turn to side 2 of your worksheet and find the dog. ✔

• (Teacher reference:)

| s   t   f   t |
|---|

• I think that dog wants to eat those bones. Let's help her.

• You'll say the sound for each letter.

⌐c. Touch the first letter. ✔

│• Say the sound. Get ready. (Signal.) *sss.*

│• Next letter. Say the sound. Get ready. (Signal.) *t.*

│• Next letter. Say the sound. Get ready. (Signal.) *fff.*

└• Last letter. Say the sound. Get ready. (Signal.) *t.*

d. (Repeat step c until firm.)

e. This time, I'll say sounds for the blue bones. You'll touch the letters and tell me the names.

• (Teacher reference:)

| s   t   f |
|---|

⌐f. Listen: The sound for one of the blue bones is **t.** Touch that bone. ✔

│• Everybody, spell what's in the bone you are touching. Get ready. (Signal.) *T.*

│g. Listen: The sound for one of the blue bones is **sss.** Touch that bone. ✔

│• Everybody, spell what's in the bone you are touching. Get ready. (Signal.) *S.*

│h. Listen: The sound for one of the blue bones is **fff.** Touch that bone. ✔

└• Everybody, spell what's in the bone you are touching. Get ready. (Signal.) *F.*

i. (Repeat steps f through h until firm.)

**Individual Turns**

• (Call on different children to say the sounds.)

═══════ EXERCISE 8 ═══════

## INDEPENDENT WORK

**Cross-Out Game: Words**

a. Find the cross-out game on the doghouse. ✔

• This is a super hard cross-out game. You'll cross out a word.

b. Raise your hand when you can tell me the word that is crossed out in the small box.

• Everybody, what word? (Signal.) *Feel.*

c. Later you'll cross out **feel.**

• How many words will you cross out? (Signal.) *Four.*

• Be careful, and don't get fooled. Remember, the word **feel** has two **Es** in the middle. Make sure any word you cross out is spelled **F-E-E-L.**

**Matching: Letters**

d. Find the skunk. ✔

• Later, you'll draw lines to match the letters.

**13**

## WRITING WORDS

a. Find the star. ✔
- You're going to write some words.
b. Touch line 1. ✔
- The word for line 1 is **so.** What word? (Signal.) *So.*
- Say the sounds in **so.** Get ready. (Tap 2 times.) *sss    OOO.*
- Once more. Say the sounds in **so.** Get ready. (Tap 2 times.) *sss    OOO.*
c. Write the word **so** on line 1. Pencils down when you're finished. (Observe children and give feedback.)
d. Check your word.
- What letter did you write for **sss?** (Signal.) *S.*
- What letter did you write for **OOO?** (Signal.) *O.*
- Yes, the word **so** is spelled **S-O.**
e. Touch line 2. ✔
- The word for line 2 is **ran.** What word? (Signal.) *Ran.*
- Say the sounds in **ran.** Get ready. (Tap 3 times.) *rrr    aaa    nnn.*
- Once more. Say the sounds in **ran.** Get ready. (Tap 3 times.) *rrr    aaa    nnn.*
f. Tell me the letters you'll write for each sound.
- Listen: The first sound is **rrr.** What letter do you write? (Signal.) *R.*
- The next sound is **aaa.** What letter do you write? (Signal.) *A.*
- The last sound is **nnn.** What letter do you write? (Signal.) *N.*
g. Write the word **ran** on line 2. Pencils down when you're finished. (Observe children and give feedback.)
h. Check your word.
- What letter did you write for **rrr?** (Signal.) *R.*
- What letter did you write for **aaa?** (Signal.) *A.*
- What letter did you write for **nnn?** (Signal.) *N.*
- Yes, the word **ran** is spelled **R-A-N.**
i. Touch line 3. ✔
- The word for line 3 is **man.** What word? (Signal.) *Man.*

- Say the sounds in **man.** Get ready. (Tap 3 times.) *mmm    aaa    nnn.*
- Once more. Say the sounds in **man.** Get ready. (Tap 3 times.) *mmm    aaa    nnn.*
j. Write the word **man** on line 3. Pencils down when you're finished. (Observe children and give feedback.)
k. Check your word.
- What letter did you write for **mmm?** (Signal.) *M.*
- What letter did you write for **aaa?** (Signal.) *A.*
- What letter did you write for **nnn?** (Signal.) *N.*
- Yes, the word **man** is spelled **M-A-N.**

**Individual Turns**
- Now you're going to read the words you made. (Call on different children to say the sounds for one of the words and say it fast.)
- Read the word on line 1. *[So.]*
- Read the word on line 2. *[Ran.]*
- Read the word on line 3. *[Man.]*

## LETTER PRINTING

a. You'll write letters on lined paper.
b. (Write on the board in the style children are to follow:)

c. These are letters that you'll write.
- What letter goes on the first line? (Signal.) *F.*
- What letter goes on the next line? (Signal.) *I.*

- What letter goes on the last line? (Signal.) *M.*
- When you write the letters, make them carefully.

d. First, print your name on your paper. Then write two **F**s on the next line, two **I**s on the next line and two **M**s on the next line. Pencils down when you've done that much.

   **(Observe children and give feedback.)**

e. Later, you'll complete each line.

**Independent Work Summary**
- Color story pictures.
- Cross-out game (**feel**=4).
- Matching game.
- Letter printing (10 each: **f, i, m**).

**Materials:** Each child will need scissors and paste (exercise 6) and lined paper (exercise 10).

**TEXTBOOK**

=== EXERCISE 1 ===

## READING SOUNDS

a. You learned a sound for the letter **T.** It's a whispered sound. Everybody, say the sound for the letter **T.** (Signal.) *t.*

b. Open your textbook to lesson 14. Find the ruler. ✔

• (Teacher reference:)

| l | f | t | r | t |
|---|---|---|---|---|

• You'll say the sound for each letter.
• Touch the first letter. Say the sound. Get ready. (Signal.) *lll.*
• Next letter. Say the sound. Get ready. (Signal.) *fff.*
• Next letter. What sound? (Signal.) *t.*
• Next letter. What sound? (Signal.) *rrr.*
• Last letter. What sound? (Signal.) *t.*

**Individual Turns**
• (Call on different children to say the sounds.)

=== EXERCISE 2 ===

## WORD vs. SENTENCE

a. I'll say sentences. You'll tell me the first word and the second word in each sentence.

b. Listen: **I listen very well.**
• Say that sentence.
(Signal.) *I listen very well.*
The first word is **I.**
The second word is **listen.**
• **I listen very well.** What's the first word in that sentence? (Signal.) *I.*

What's the next word in that sentence? (Signal.) *Listen.*

c. New sentence: **My sister loves to read.**
• Say that sentence. (Signal.)
*My sister loves to read.*
The first word is **my.** What's the first word? (Signal.) *My.*
The second word is **sister.** What's the second word? (Signal.) *Sister.*
• **My sister loves to read.** What's the first word? (Signal.) *My.*
What's the second word? (Signal.) *Sister.*

d. New sentence: **Little bugs were in the air.**
• Say that sentence. (Signal.)
*Little bugs were in the air.*
The first word is **little.**
The next word is **bugs.**
• Listen: **Little bugs were in the air.** What's the first word? (Signal.) *Little.*
What's the next word? (Signal.) *Bugs.*

=== EXERCISE 3 ===

## READING WORDS

a. Find the backpack. ✔
• (Teacher reference:)

| 1. fan |
|---|
| 2. for |
| 3. ram |
| 4. or |

• A lot of children put their school supplies in backpacks.
• Two of these words have a letter that makes the sound **aaa.**
• Everybody, what letter makes the sound **aaa?** (Signal.) *A.*
• Yes, in some words **A** says its name. In other words, it says **aaa.**
• What sound does **A** make in some of these words? (Signal.) *aaa.*

b. Touch number 1. ✔
Word 1 has three sounds. One of the sounds is **aaa.**
• Touch under the first letter. ✔
Everybody, what's the sound? (Signal.) *fff.*

- Touch under the next letter. ✔
  What's the sound? (Signal.) *aaa.*
- Touch under the last letter. ✔
  What's the sound? (Signal.) *nnn.*

c. Go back to the 1. ✔
   I'll say the sounds. You'll touch under the letters. Get ready: **fff   aaa   nnn.** ✔

d. (Repeat step c until firm.)

e. This time, you'll touch and say the sounds. Get ready. (Tap 3 times.)
   *fff   aaa   nnn.*
- Once more. Touch and say the sounds. Get ready. (Tap 3 times.) *fff   aaa   nnn.*
- Say it fast. (Signal.) *Fan.*
- What word did you just read? (Signal.) *Fan.*

f. Touch under the first letter of word 2. ✔
- Everybody, what's the sound? (Signal.) *fff.*
- Touch under the next letter. ✔
- What's the sound? (Signal.) *OOO.*
- Touch under the last letter. ✔
- What's the sound? (Signal.) *rrr.*

g. I'll say the sounds. You'll touch under the letters. Get ready: **fff   OOO   rrr.** ✔

h. (Repeat step g until firm.)

i. This time, you'll touch and say the sounds. Get ready. (Tap 3 times.)
   *fff   OOO   rrr.*
- Everybody, say it fast. (Signal.) *For.*
- What word did you just read? (Signal.) *For.*
- Good reading.

j. Touch under the first letter of word 3. ✔
- Everybody, what's the sound? (Signal.) *rrr.*
- Next letter. What's the sound? (Signal.) *aaa.*
- Last letter. What's the sound? (Signal.) *mmm.*

k. I'll say the sounds. You'll touch under the letters. Get ready: **rrr   aaa   mmm.** ✔

l. (Repeat step k until firm.)

m. This time, you'll touch and say the sounds. Get ready. (Tap 3 times.)
   *rrr   aaa   mmm.*
- Everybody, say it fast. (Signal.) *Ram.*
  What word did you just read? (Signal.) *Ram.*

n. Touch under the first letter of word 4. ✔

- Everybody, what's the sound? (Signal.) *OOO.*
- Last letter. What's the sound? (Signal.) *rrr.*

o. I'll say the sounds. You'll touch under the letters. Get ready: **OOO   rrr.** ✔

p. (Repeat step o until firm.)

q. This time, you'll touch and say the sounds. Get ready. (Tap 2 times.)
   *OOO   rrr.*
- Everybody, say it fast. (Signal.) *Or.*
  What word did you just read? (Signal.) *Or.*

**Individual Turns**

- (Call on different children to say the sounds for one of the words and say it fast.)
- Read word 1. *[Fan.]*
- Read word 2. *[For.]*
- Read word 3. *[Ram.]*
- Read word 4. *[Or.]*

═══════ EXERCISE 4 ═══════

**LETTER COMBINATIONS**

a. Find the pair of scissors. ✔
- (Teacher reference:)

| o̲a̲   a̲i̲   e̲a̲ |
| --- |

- These are combinations that you'll read in words. Remember the rule: The black letter says its name. The blue letter doesn't make any sound at all.

b. Touch the bar for the first combination. ✔
   That combination is spelled **O-A.** What's the black letter? (Signal.) *O.*
- So what sound does the combination make? (Signal.) *OOO.*

c. Touch the bar for the next combination. ✔
   That combination is spelled **A-I.** What's the black letter? (Signal.) *A.*
- So what sound does the combination make? (Signal.) *AAA.*

d. Touch the bar for the last combination. ✔
   That combination is spelled **E-A.** What's the black letter? (Signal.) *E.*
- So what sound does the combination make? (Signal.) *EEE.*

e. (Repeat steps b through d until firm.)

**Individual Turns**
- (Call on different children.)
- Tell me the sound for each combination.

========= EXERCISE 5 =========

**STORY TIME**

a. Here's another story about Mr. Mosely.
- Listen: One morning, Mr. Mosely had to leave on a trip very, very early. So he was very, very tired. When he was packing things to go on the trip, he couldn't find his toothpaste or his hairbrush. So he asked his wife about these things.
b. He wanted to say, "Where is my toothpaste?" What did he want to say? (Signal.) *Where is my toothpaste?*
- But he said, "Where is my tooth?" What did he say? (Signal.) *Where is my tooth?*
- He wanted to say, "Where is my hairbrush?" What did he say instead? (Signal.) *Where is my hair?*
c. His wife drove him to the airport. On the way, he wanted to ask her about the airport. He wanted to say, "How long before we get to the airport?" What did he say instead? (Signal.) *How long before we get to the air?*
- His wife said, "Put your hand out the window and you can feel the air right now."
d. When Mr. Mosely and his wife got to the airport, he wanted to ask his wife what he should do with his suitcase. But he didn't ask about a suitcase. What did he ask about? (Signal.) *A suit.*
- He said, "What should I do with my suit?"
- She said, "Wear it."
e. At last, the plane was ready to leave. His wife said goodbye, but she didn't give him a kiss. Mr. Mosely wanted to ask her, "Aren't you going to kiss me goodbye?" But he didn't say goodbye. What did he say instead? (Signal.) *Good.*
- He said, "Aren't you going to kiss me good?"

- She said, "I always kiss you good." And she did.
f. That's the end of the story. I'll say some of the things that Mr. Mosely said in this story. You tell me what he was trying to say.
- He said, "Where is my tooth?" What was he trying to say? (Signal.) *Where is my toothpaste?*
- He said, "Where is my hair?" What was he trying to say? (Signal.) *Where is my hairbrush?*
- He said, "What should I do with my suit?" What was he trying to say? (Signal.) *What should I do with my suitcase?*
- He said, "Aren't you going to kiss me good?" What was he trying to say? (Signal.) *Aren't you going to kiss me goodbye?*

========= EXERCISE 6 =========

**STORY EXTENSION**
**Pictures: Comprehension and Cut-Out**

*Note:* Each child will need scissors and paste.

a. Find the picture of Mr. Mosely. ✔
- This is a picture of what Mr. Mosely would look like if he really didn't have the things he asked about.
b. He is bald. What did he ask about in the story? (Call on a child. Idea: *Where's my hair?*)
- He has something missing in his mouth. What did he ask about in the story? (Call on a child. Idea: *Where's my tooth?*)
- He has some clothing missing. What did he ask about in the story? (Call on a child. Idea: *Where's my suit?*)
c. (Repeat step b until firm.)

**WORKBOOK**

d. Close your textbook. Go to lesson 14 in your workbook and write your name. ✔
- Touch the picture of Mr. Mosely. ✔
- This is part of the picture you saw in your textbook, but you'll be able to fix Mr. Mosely up. At the bottom of the page is a tooth and some hair.

e. Later, you can cut out those things and paste them on Mr. Mosely.

━━━━━━━━ EXERCISE 7 ━━━━━━━━

## WRITING WORDS

a. You're going to write some words that have the letter **T**.
- (Write on the board in the style children are to follow:)

> tra

b. Find the spider. ✔
- Touch the space after 1. ✔
- Word 1 is **at**. What word? (Signal.) *At.* Yes, they looked **at** a pig.

c. Say **at** a sound at a time. Get ready. (Tap 2 times.) *aaa  t.*
- Say the first sound in **at**. (Signal.) *aaa.*
- Say the next sound in **at**. (Signal.) *t.*
- (Repeat step c until firm.)

d. What letter do you write for the sound **aaa**? (Signal.) *A.*
- What letter do you write for the sound **t**? (Signal.) *T.*
- Write the letters for **at**. Pencils down when you're finished.
(Observe children and give feedback.)
- Check your word.
- (Write on the board:)

> 1. at

- Here's what you should have.
- The first letter is **A**.
- The next letter is **T**.
- Raise your hand if you spelled **at, A-T**.

e. Touch the space for word 2. ✔

- Word 2 is **rat**. What word? (Signal.) *Rat.*
- **Rat** has three sounds.
- My turn to say **rat** a sound at a time: **rrr  aaa  t.**

f. Your turn: Say **rat** a sound at a time. Get ready. (Tap 3 times.) *rrr  aaa  t.*
- (Repeat step f until firm.)

g. Once more: Say the first sound in **rat**. (Signal.) *rrr.*
- Next sound. (Signal.) *aaa.*
- Last sound. (Signal.) *t.*
- (Repeat step g until firm.)

h. Write the word **rat**. Pencils down when you're finished.
(Observe children and give feedback.)
- Check your word.
- (Write on the board:)

> 1. rat

- Here's what you should have.
- The first letter is **R**.
- The next letter is **A**.
- The last letter is **T**.
- Raise your hand if you spelled **rat, R-A-T**.

i. Remember the whisper sound for the letter **T**.

**Individual Turns**
- (Call on different children to say the sounds for one or two of the words and say it fast.)

━━━━━━━━ EXERCISE 8 ━━━━━━━━

## WRITING WORDS FOR PICTURES

a. Turn to side 2 of your worksheet and find the cup. ✔
- The words in this part tell you about the pictures you'll fix up.

b. Touch number 1. ✔
- That's a name. It starts with capital **S**.
- Listen: You have heard some stories about an animal named . . . Touch and say the sounds for word 1. Get ready. (Tap 3 times.) *sss  aaa  mmm.*
- Say it fast. (Signal.) *Sam.*
- What name? (Signal.) *Sam.*

- Yes, you have heard some stories about an animal named **Sam.**
c. Touch number 2. ✔
- Listen: Sam was not a cow and not a . . . Word 2 tells which other animal Sam was not.
- Touch and say the sounds for word 2. Get ready. (Tap 3 times.) *rrr    aaa    mmm.*
- Say it fast. (Signal.) *Ram.*
- What word? (Signal.) *Ram.*
- Yes, Sam was not a cow and not a **ram.**
d. What was Sam? (Signal.) *A bunny.*
- And who did Sam help out? (Call on a child. Idea: *The mice.*)
- How did he help out the mice? (Call on a child. Idea: *Carried loads of grass, carrot greens, tiny flowers and clover to the mice.*)
e. Find the pictures below the words. ✔
- There's a picture of a cow, a bunny and a ram.
- One word you read is **Sam.**
- One word you read is **ram.**
f. You'll write the word **Sam** below the right picture and the word **ram** below the right picture. One picture won't have a word under it, so don't get fooled. Write your words. Pencils down when you're finished.
(Observe children and give feedback.)

═══════ EXERCISE 9 ═══════

**INDEPENDENT WORK**

**Matching: Letters**
a. Find the teddy bear. ✔
- (Teacher reference:)

|   |   |
|---|---|
| D | t |
| T | r |
| A | i |
| R | d |
| I | a |

- This is a new kind of matching game. Touch the letters in the first column. ✔
- All of those letters are capital letters.
b. What's the top letter? (Signal.) *D.*
- What's the next capital letter? (Signal.) *T.*
- What's the next capital letter? (Signal.) *A.*
- What's the next capital letter? (Signal.) *R.*
- What's the last capital letter? (Signal.) *I.*
c. (Repeat step b until firm.)
d. The letters in the other column are regular letters. You'll draw lines to the letters that are the same. Draw a line to match the **D** in the first column with the **d** in the other column.
(Observe children and give feedback.)
e. Later, you'll complete the matching game.

**Cross-Out Game: Words**
f. Find the cross-out game. ✔
- This is a super hard cross-out game. You'll cross out a word.
g. Raise your hand when you can tell me the word that is crossed out in the box.
- Everybody, what word? *Ran.*
h. Later, you'll cross out **ran.**
- How many words will you cross out? (Signal.) *Four.*
- Be careful, and don't get fooled. Make sure any word you cross out is spelled **R-A-N.**

LINED PAPER
EXERCISE 10

## LETTER PRINTING

**Note:** Each child needs lined paper.

a. You'll write letters on your lined paper.
b. (Write on the board in the style children are to follow:)

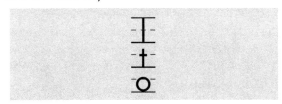

c. These are letters that you'll write.
• What letter goes on the first line?
(Signal.) *L.*

• What letter goes on the next line?
(Signal.) *T.*
• What letter goes on the last line?
(Signal.) *O.*
• When you write the letters, make them carefully.
d. First print your name on your paper. Then write two **L**s on the next line, two **T**s on the next line and two **O**s on the next line. Pencils down when you've done that much.
(Observe children and give feedback.)
e. Later, you'll complete each line.

## Independent Work Summary
• Cut and paste to complete story picture.
• Matching game.
• Cross-out game (**ran**=4).
• Letter printing (finish lines of **l**, **t**, **o**).

**15**

## TEXTBOOK

### EXERCISE 1

**READING SOUNDS**

a. Open your textbook to lesson 15. Find the school bus. ✔
- (Teacher reference:)

| a    f    o    t    r    ee |
| --- |

- There's a sound in each window.

b. Touch the first letter. ✔
- You know two sounds for that letter. One sound is the letter name. Say that sound. Get ready. (Signal.) *AAA.*
- Say the other sound. Get ready. (Signal.) *aaa.*
- Next letter. What sound? Get ready. (Signal.) *fff.*
- Next letter. What sound? Get ready. (Signal.) *OOO.*
- Next letter. What sound? Get ready. (Signal.) *t.*
- Next letter. What sound? Get ready. (Signal.) *rrr.*
- Last window. What sound? Get ready. (Signal.) *EEE.*

c. (Repeat step b until firm.)

**Individual Turns**
- (Repeat step b, calling on different children to respond.)

### EXERCISE 2

**LETTER COMBINATIONS**

a. The wheels on the bus have combinations that you'll read.

- (Teacher reference:)

| **ai**      **ea** |
| --- |

- Remember the rule: The black letter says its name. The blue letter doesn't make any sound at all.

b. Touch the bar for the combination in the first wheel. ✔
- That combination is spelled **A-I.** What's the black letter? (Signal.) *A.*
- So what sound does the combination make? (Signal.) *AAA.*
- Touch the bar for the combination in the other wheel. ✔
- That combination is spelled **E-A.** What's the black letter? (Signal.) *E.*
- So what sound does the combination make? (Signal.) *EEE.*

c. (Repeat step b until firm.)

**Individual Turns**
- (Call on different children.) Tell me the sound for each combination. *AAA, EEE.*

### EXERCISE 3

**READING WORDS**
**Words with Letter Combinations**

a. Find the school bell. ✔
- (Teacher reference:)

| 1. m**ea**n |
| --- |
| 2. r**ai**n |
| 3. m**ai**l |

- The words in the bell have letter combinations.

b. The letter combination in word 1 is **E-A.**
- Touch that combination. ✔
- What's the black letter in that combination? (Signal.) *E.*
- So when you say the sounds for the word, what sound will you say for the combination? (Signal.) *EEE.*
- Go back to number 1. ✔

- The word has three sounds. Those are the sounds for the **black** letters. Everybody, touch and say the sounds. Get ready. **(Tap 3 times.)** *mmm   EEE   nnn.*
- Again. Back to the 1. Touch and say the sounds for the black letters. Get ready. **(Tap 3 times.)** *mmm   EEE   nnn.*
- Say it fast. **(Signal.)** *Mean.* You read the word **mean.**

c. Touch the letter combination in word 2. ✔

- That combination is spelled **A-I.** What's the black letter in that combination? **(Signal.)** *A.*
- So when you say the sounds for the word, what sound will you say for that combination? **(Signal.)** *AAA.*
- The word has three sounds. Everybody, touch and say the sounds for the black letters. Get ready. **(Tap 3 times.)** *rrr   AAA   nnn.*
- Again. Back to the 2. Touch and say the sounds for the black letters. Get ready. **(Tap 3 times.)** *rrr   AAA   nnn.*
- Say it fast. **(Signal.)** *Rain.* You just read the word **rain.**

d. Touch the combination in word 3. ✔

- That combination is spelled **A-I.** What's
·  the black letter in that combination? **(Signal.)** *A.*
- So when you say the sounds, what sound will you say for the combination? **(Signal.)** *AAA.*
- The word has three sounds. Everybody, touch and say the sounds. Get ready. **(Tap 3 times.)** *mmm   AAA   lll.*
- Again. Back to the 3. Touch and say the sounds. Get ready. **(Tap 3 times.)** *mmm   AAA   lll.*
- Say it fast. **(Signal.)** *Mail.*
- You just read the word **mail.** How do you mail something? **(Call on a child. Ideas:** *Put a stamp on it; Take it to the post office or mailbox.***)**

e. Let's do those again.

- Touch number I. Touch and say the sounds for the black letters. Get ready. **(Tap 3 times.)** *mmm   EEE   nnn.*
- What word? **(Signal.)** *Mean.*

- Word 2. Touch and say the sounds for the black letters. Get ready. **(Tap 3 times.)** *rrr   AAA   nnn.*
- What word? **(Signal.)** *Rain.*
- Word 3. Touch and say the sounds for the black letters. Get ready. **(Tap 3 times.)** *mmm   AAA   lll.*
- What word? **(Signal.)** *Mail.*

f. Good reading words that have letter combinations.

**Individual Turns**

- **(Call on different children to read one of the words.)**

=== EXERCISE 4 ===

**STORY READING**

a. Find the words in the book. ✔

- (Teacher reference:)

| 1. see |
|--------|
| 2. no |
| 3. man |

- Those are words you'll read when we do the story.
- I'll say part of the story. Then you'll read.
- LIsten: There once was a goat named Gorman. Gorman lived on a farm. He was a lot like other goats, except there was something he did not do well.

b. Touch number 1. ✔

- That tells what he didn't do well. Everybody, touch and say the sounds. Get ready. **(Tap 2 times.)** *sss   EEE.*
- Say it fast. **(Signal.)** *See.*
- What didn't Gorman do well? **(Signal.)** *See.*
- Yes, Gorman did not see well.

c. Touch number 2. ✔

- One day Gorman bumped into something that moved. Did he bump into a cow?
- Everybody, touch and say the sounds for word 2. Get ready. **(Tap 2 times.)** *nnn   OOO.*
- Say it fast. **(Signal.)** *No.*

# 15

- Everybody, did Gorman bump into a cow? (Signal.) *No.*
- Gorman did not bump into a cow.
- Did Gorman bump into a horse? Touch number 2 again. Everybody, say it fast. (Signal.) *No.*
- Did Gorman bump into a horse? (Signal.) *No.*

d. Touch number 3. ✔
- Gorman didn't bump into a cow or a horse. Gorman bumped into a . . .
  Say the sounds for word 3. Get ready. (Tap 3 times.) *mmm    aaa    nnn.*
- Say it fast. (Signal.) *Man.*
- Yes, Gorman bumped into a what? (Signal.) *Man.*

e. Touch number 3 again. ✔
- Gorman did not know that it was a man. Gorman said, "You are a funny-looking goat."
- The man said, "I am not a goat."
- Gorman moved closer to the man and looked more carefully. Then Gorman said, "I can see you are not a goat. You are a funny-looking cow."
- The man said, "I am not a cow."
- Gorman took an even closer look at the man and said, "You are right. You are not a funny-looking cow. You are a funny-looking rooster."
- The man said, "I am a . . ."
  Say the sounds for number 3. Get ready. (Tap 3 times.) *mmm    aaa    nnn.*
- Say it fast. (Signal.) *Man.*
- Yes, the man said to Gorman, "I am a . . ." (Signal.) *Man.*

f. Let's do that story again, the fast way. Touch number 1 and get ready.
- There once was a goat named Gorman. Gorman lived on a farm. He was a lot like other goats, except there was something he did not do well.
- Number 1 tells what he didn't do well. Say the sounds for number 1. Get ready. (Tap 2 times.) *sss    EEE.*
- What word? (Signal.) *See.*

g. Touch number 2. ✔
- One day Gorman bumped into something that moved. Did he bump into a cow?

- Say the sounds for number 2. Get ready. (Tap 2 times.) *nnn    OOO.*
- What word? (Signal.) *No.*
- Did Gorman bump into a horse?
- Say the sounds for number 2. Get ready. (Tap 2 times.) *nnn    OOO.*
- What word? (Signal.) *No.*

h. Touch number 3. ✔
- Gorman didn't bump into a cow or a horse. Gorman bumped into a . . .
- Say the sounds for number 3. Get ready. (Tap 3 times.) *mmm    aaa    nnn.*
- What word? (Signal.) *Man.*
- Touch number 3 again. ✔
- Gorman did not know that it was a man. Gorman said, "You are a funny-looking goat."
- The man said, "I am not a goat."
- Gorman moved closer to the man and looked more carefully. Then Gorman said, "I can see you are not a goat. You are a funny-looking cow."
- The man said, "I am not a cow."
- Gorman took an even closer look at the man and said, "You are right. You are not a funny-looking cow. You are a funny-looking rooster."
- The man said, "I am a . . ."
- Say the sounds for number 3. Get ready. (Tap 3 times.) *mmm    aaa    nnn.*
- What word? (Signal.) *Man.*

i. You are reading parts of stories. Good for you.

===== EXERCISE 5 =====
## STORY EXTENSION
### Picture Comprehension

a. Find the pictures of Gorman. ✔
- These pictures show who Gorman thought he was talking to.
b. Touch the first picture. ✔
  Who is Gorman talking to in that picture? (Signal.) *A goat.*
  Yes, at first he thought the man was a goat.
- Touch the next picture. ✔
  Who is Gorman talking to in that picture? (Signal.) *A cow.*

Yes, then Gorman thought the man was a cow.
- Touch the last picture. ✔
  Who is Gorman talking to in that picture? (Signal.) *A rooster.*
  He must have thought that the man was a huge rooster.

**WORKBOOK**

c. Close your textbook. Go to lesson 15 in your workbook and write your name. ✔
  Find the pictures of Gorman. ✔
- These are the same pictures you just saw in your textbook.
d. Later, you'll color the pictures.

═══════ EXERCISE 6 ═══════

## WRITING WORDS

a. Find the spider. ✔
  You're going to write some words in the spider's web that have the letter **T.**
- Touch number 1. ✔
- Word 1 is **sat.** What word? (Signal.) *Sat.*
  Yes, they **sat** down.
b. Say **sat** a sound at a time. Get ready. (Tap 3 times.) *sss    aaa    t.*
- Say the first sound in **sat.** (Signal.) *sss.*
- Say the next sound in **sat.** (Signal.) *aaa.*
- Say the last sound in **sat.** (Signal.) *t.*
- (Repeat step b until firm.)
c. What letter do you write for the sound **sss?** (Signal.) *S.*
- What letter do you write for the sound **aaa?** (Signal.) *A.*
- What letter do you write for the sound **t?** (Signal.) *T.*
- Write the letters for **sat.** Pencils down when you're finished.
  (Observe children and give feedback.)
- Check your word.
- (Write on the board in the style children are to follow:)

1. ‾sat

d. Here's what you should have.
- The first letter is **S.**
- The next letter is **A.**
- The last letter is **T.**
- Raise your hand if you got it right.
e. Touch line 2. ✔
- Word 2 is **fat.** What word? (Signal.) *Fat.*
- **Fat** has three sounds.
f. Say **fat** a sound at a time. Get ready. (Tap 3 times.) *fff    aaa    t.*
- (Repeat step f until firm.)
g. Once more: Say the first sound in **fat.** (Signal.) *fff.*
- Next sound. (Signal.) *aaa.*
- Last sound. (Signal.) *t.*
- (Repeat step g until firm.)
h. Write the word **fat.** Pencils down when you're finished.
  (Observe children and give feedback.)
- Check your word.
- (Write on the board:)

2. ‾fat

i. Here's what you should have.
- The first letter is **F.**
- The next letter is **A.**
- The last letter is **T.**
- Raise your hand if you got it right.
j. Remember that whisper sound for the letter **T.**

### Individual Turns
- (Call on different children to read one or two of the words.)

═══════ EXERCISE 7 ═══════

## SAYING THE SOUNDS
### Long Vowels

a. Find the rabbit. ✔
- (Teacher reference:)

| a | i |
|---|---|
| o | e |

- These are letters that sometimes say their names in words. The letters are: **A, I, O,** and **E.**

- You're going to touch the sounds you hear in words.
b. Listen: **sail.** What word? (Signal.) *Sail.*
- **Sail** has three sounds. Say **sail** a sound at a time. Get ready. (Tap 3 times.) *sss   AAA   lll.*
- One of those sounds is a **letter name.** Touch the letter name you hear for **sail.** Get ready. (Signal.) ✔
- You should be touching the letter **A.** You can hear the name **A** in the word **sail.**
c. Next word: **life.** What word? (Signal.) *Life.*
- Say the three sounds in **life.** Get ready. (Tap 3 times.) *lll   III   fff.*
- Touch the letter name you hear in **life.** Get ready. (Signal.) ✔
- You should be touching the letter **I.** You can hear the name **I** in the word **life.**
d. Next word: **leap.** What word? (Signal.) *Leap.*
- **Leap** has three sounds. Say **leap** a sound at a time. Get ready. (Tap 3 times.) *lll   EEE   p.*
- Touch the letter name you hear for **leap.** Get ready. (Signal.) ✔
- You should be touching the letter **E.** You can hear the name **E** in the word **leap.**

=========== EXERCISE 8 ===========

## INDEPENDENT WORK

### Matching: Letters
a. Turn to side 2 of your worksheet, and find the matching game. ✔
b. Later, you'll draw lines to match the capital letters with the regular letters.

### Cross-Out Game
c. Find the cross-out game. ✔
d. Raise your hand when you can tell me the word you'll cross out.
- Everybody, what word? (Signal.) *Me.*
e. Later, you'll cross out **me.**
- How many words will you cross out? (Signal.) *Three.*

=========== EXERCISE 9 ===========

## HIDDEN PICTURE

> *Note:* Each child needs a green, a blue and a brown crayon.

a. Find the hidden picture at the bottom of your worksheet. ✔
- I'll tell you the coloring rules. You'll need a green crayon, a blue crayon and a brown crayon.
b. Touch the box for the **double L** at the top of the picture. ✔
- Here's the rule for **double L:** All parts of the picture that have a **double L** are blue. Make a blue mark in the box for **double L.** Raise your hand when you're finished.
  (Observe children and give feedback.)
- Here's the rule for **Y:** All parts of the picture that have a **Y** are green. Make a green mark in the box for **Y.** Raise your hand when you're finished.
  (Observe children and give feedback.)
- Here's the rule for the combination **E-A:** All parts of the picture that have **E-A** are brown. Make a brown mark in the box for **E-A.** Raise your hand when you're finished.
  (Observe children and give feedback.)
c. Later, you'll color all the parts of the picture.

## LINED PAPER
## ═══════ EXERCISE 10 ═══════
## LETTER PRINTING

**Note:** Each child needs lined paper.

a. (Write on the board in the style children are to follow:)

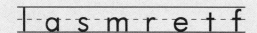

- You're going to write three rows of letters on your lined paper. I'll tell you the sounds for the letters you'll write.
b. Touch the top line you'll write a letter on. ✔
- The letter you'll write on that line makes the sound **rrr** in words. What sound? (Signal.) *rrr.*
- Write the letter for **rrr.** Pencils down when you're finished.
  (Observe children and give feedback.)
- (Write on the board:)

- Here's the letter you should have.
c. Touch the next line on your paper. ✔
- The letter you'll write on that line makes the sound **sss** in words. What sound? (Signal.) *sss.*

- Write the letter for **sss.** Pencils down when you're finished.
  (Observe children and give feedback.)
- (Write to show:)

- Here's the letter you should have.
d. Touch the next line on your paper. ✔
- The letter you'll write on that line makes the sound **t** in words. What sound? (Signal.) *t.*
- Write the letter for **t.** Pencils down when you're finished.
  (Observe children and give feedback.)
- (Write to show:)

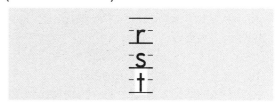

- Here's the letter you should have.
e. Later, you'll complete each line.

**Independent Work Summary**
- Color story pictures.
- Matching game.
- Cross-out game (**me**= 3).
- Color hidden picture (**ll**=blue, **ea**=brown, **y**=green).
- Letter printing (finish lines of **r, s, t**).

# 16

**Materials:** Children will need scissors, paste and lined paper.

## TEXTBOOK

### EXERCISE 1

**READING SOUNDS**

a. Open your textbook to lesson 16. Find the elephant. ✔
- (Teacher reference:)

| ea  f  o  t  oa |

- These are letters and letter combinations. Remember the rule for letter combinations. You say the sound for the black letter.

b. Touch the first combination. Say the sound. Get ready. (Signal.) *EEE.*
- Next letter. What sound? (Signal.) *fff.*
- Next letter. What sound? (Signal.) *OOO.*
- Next letter. What sound? (Signal.) *t.*
- Last combination. What sound? (Signal.) *OOO.*

c. (Repeat step b until firm.)

**Individual Turns**
- (Repeat step b, calling on different children.)

### EXERCISE 2

**READING WORDS**
**Words with Letter Combinations**

a. Find the lion. ✔
- (Teacher reference:)

| 1. f**oa**m |
| 2. s**ea**l |
| 3. r**ea**l |

- The words on the lion have letter combinations.

b. The letter combination in word 1 is **O-A.**
- Touch that combination. ✔
- What's the black letter in that combination? (Signal.) *O.*
- So when you say the sounds for the word, what sound will you say for the combination? (Signal.) *OOO.*
- The word has three sounds. Everybody, touch and say the sounds for the black letters. Get ready. (Tap 3 times.) *fff   OOO   mmm.*
- Again. Touch and say the sounds. Get ready. (Tap 3 times.) *fff   OOO   mmm.*
- Say it fast. (Signal.) *Foam.*
- What word? (Signal.) *Foam.*
- What is **foam?** (Call on a child. Ideas: *Suds, bubbles.*)

c. Touch the letter combination in word 2. ✔
- That combination is spelled **E-A.** What's the black letter in that combination? (Signal.) *E.*
- The word has three sounds. Everybody, touch and say the sounds for the black letters. Get ready. (Tap 3 times.) *sss   EEE   lll.*
- Again. Touch and say the sounds. Get ready. (Tap 3 times.) *sss   EEE   lll.*
- Say it fast. (Signal.) *Seal.*
- You just read the word **seal.** Who has seen pictures of seals swimming in the ocean?

d. Touch the combination in word 3. ✔
- That combination is spelled **E-A.** What's the black letter in that combination? (Signal.) *E.*
- The word has three sounds. Everybody, touch and say the sounds for the black letters. Get ready. (Tap 3 times.) *rrr   EEE   lll.*
- Again. Touch and say the sounds. Get ready. (Tap 3 times.) *rrr   EEE   lll.*
- Say it fast. (Signal.) *Real.*
- You just read the word **real.** That's a **real** achievement.

e. Let's do those again.
- Word 1. Say the sounds. Get ready. (Tap 3 times.) *fff   OOO   mmm.* What word? (Signal.) *Foam.*

- Word 2. Say the sounds. Get ready. (Tap 3 times.) *sss    EEE    lll.*
  What word? (Signal.) *Seal.*
- Word 3. Say the sounds. Get ready. (Tap 3 times.) *rrr    EEE    lll.*
  What word? (Signal.) *Real.*
- f. Good reading words that have letter combinations.

**Individual Turns**

- (Call on different children to say the sounds for each word and say the word fast.)

═══════ EXERCISE 3 ═══════

## STORY READING

a. Find the words in the book. ✔
- (Teacher reference:)

| 1. see |
| 2. me<u>a</u>n |
| 3. ram |
| 4. Sam |
| 5. am |

- Those are words you'll read. I'll say part of the story. Then you'll read part of that story.
- Listen: This story is about Clarabelle and Gorman.
- Touch word 1. ✔
- One day the farm animals were mad at Gorman because he was always bumping into them.
- Gorman said, "You would bump into other animals too, if you could not . . ." Everybody, touch and say the sounds for word 1. Get ready. (Tap 2 times.) *sss    EEE.*
- What word? (Signal.) *See.*
- Yes, Gorman said, "You would bump into other animals too, if you could not **see**."
b. Touch word 2. ✔
- Clarabelle said, "I think he is right. I will find out." She went into the barn, found an old gunny sack and stuck her head in it. Then she walked back outside with the bag over her head. She could see a little

bit through the sack, but not much. She was saying, "It is definitely hard to see with a sack over . . ." Bam. She bumped into a fence.
- Then she turned around and bumped into Horace, the horse. Horace said, "You did that on purpose. Stop that, you mean cow, you."
- Clarabelle said, "I am not . . ." Everybody, touch and say the sounds for the black letters in word 2. Get ready. (Tap 3 times.) *mmm    EEE    nnn.*
- Everybody, what word? (Signal.) *Mean.*
- Yes, Clarabelle said, "I am not **mean**."
c. Touch word 3. ✔
- Then Clarabelle said to Horace, "And you are a funny-looking . . ." Everybody, touch and say the sounds for word 3. Get ready. (Tap for each letter.) *rrr    aaa    mmm.*
- Everybody, what word? (Signal.) *Ram.*
- Yes, Clarabelle said, "You are a funny-looking **ram**."
d. Touch word 4. ✔
- Horace said, "I am not a ram."
- Clarabelle said, "If you are not a ram, you must be . . ." Everybody, touch and say the sounds for word 4. Get ready. (Tap 3 times.) *sss    aaa    mmm.*
- Everybody, what word? (Signal.) *Sam.*
- Horace said, "I am not a ram, and I am not **Sam**."
e. Touch word 5. ✔
- Clarabelle turned away and said, "This is no fun. I'm going back into the barn. Just then, she bumped into Gorman. Gorman said, "Who is bumping into me?"
- Clarabelle said, "I . . ." Everybody, touch and say the sounds for word 5. Get ready. (Tap 2 times.) *aaa    mmm.*
- What word? (Signal.) *Am.*
- Yes, when Gorman asked, "Who is bumping into me?" Clarabelle said, "I **am**."
- Did Gorman know who was talking? (Signal.) *No.*
f. Let's do the story one more time.
- Touch word 1. ✔

- One day the farm animals were mad at Gorman because he was always bumping into them.
- Gorman said, "You would bump into other animals too, if you could not . . ." Everybody, touch and say the sounds for word 1. Get ready. (Tap 2 times.) *sss    EEE.*
- What word? (Signal.) *See.*
g. Touch word 2. ✔
- Clarabelle went into the barn and came back out with an old gunny sack over her head. She could see a little bit through the sack, but not much. She bumped into Horace, the horse. Horace said, "Stop that, you mean cow, you."
- Clarabelle said, "I am not . . ." Everybody, touch and say the sounds for the black letters in word 2. Get ready. (Tap 3 times.) *mmm    EEE    nnn.*
- Everybody, what word? (Signal.) *Mean.*
- Yes, Clarabelle said, "I am not **mean**."
h. Touch word 3. ✔
- Then Clarabelle said to Horace, "And you are a funny-looking . . ." Everybody, touch and say the sounds for word 3. Get ready. (Tap 3 times.) *rrr    aaa    mmm.*
- Everybody, what word? (Signal.) *Ram.*
- Yes, Clarabelle said, "You are a funny-looking **ram**."
i. Touch word 4. ✔
- Horace said, "I am not a ram."
- Clarabelle said, "If you are not a ram, you must be . . ." Everybody, touch and say the sounds for word 4. Get ready. (Tap 3 times.) *sss    aaa    mmm.*
- Everybody, what word? (Signal.) *Sam.*
- Horace said, "I am not a ram, and I am not **Sam**."
j. Touch word 5. ✔
- Clarabelle turned away and bumped into Gorman. Gorman said, "Who is bumping into me?"
- Clarabelle said, "I . . ." Everybody, touch and say the sounds for word 5. Get ready. (Tap 2 times.) *aaa    mmm.*
- What word? (Signal.) *Am.*
- Yes, when Gorman asked, "Who is bumping into me?" Clarabelle said, "I **am**."

**Individual Turns**
- (Call on different children to read one of the words.)

═══════ EXERCISE 4 ═══════

**STORY EXTENSION**
**Picture Comprehension**

a. Find the pictures of Clarabelle. ✔
- These are pictures of the story, but they are not in the right order.
- Touch the first picture. ✔
  That shows Clarabelle bumping into Gorman.
- Touch the next picture. ✔
  What is Clarabelle bumping into? (Signal.) *The fence.*
- Touch the last picture. ✔
  Who is Clarabelle bumping into? (Signal.) *Horace the horse.*
b. Listen: In the story, what did Clarabelle bump into first: Gorman, the fence or Horace? (Signal.) *The fence.*
- In the story, who did she bump into next? (Signal.) *Horace.*
- In the story, who did she bump into last? (Signal.) *Gorman.*
c. (Repeat step b until firm.)

## EXERCISE 5

### STORY EXTENSION
**Cut-Out: Numbers**

**Note:** Each child will need scissors and paste.

a. Close your textbook. Go to lesson 16 in your workbook and write your name. ✔ Find the pictures at the top of your worksheet. ✔

b. These are the same pictures as the ones in your textbook. Next to the last picture are three numbers: 1, 2, 3. You'll cut the numbers out and paste them at the bottom of the right pictures. You'll paste 1 on the thing that happened first in the story. You'll paste 2 on the thing that happened next. You'll paste 3 on the thing that happened last.

c. Touch the picture that will have the number 1 on it. ✔

• You should be touching the picture of Clarabelle bumping into the fence.

## EXERCISE 6

### WRITING WORDS

a. Find the spider. ✔
You're going to write some words.

b. Touch number 1. ✔

• The word for line 1 is **tan**. What word? (Signal.) *Tan.*

• Say the three sounds in **tan**. Get ready. (Tap 3 times.) *t aaa nnn.*

• I'll say the three sounds in **tan**. You tell me the letter you write for each sound. First sound: **t**. What letter? (Signal.) *T.* Next sound: **aaa**. What letter? (Signal.) *A.* Last sound: **nnn**. What letter? (Signal.) *N.*

c. Write the word **tan** on line 1. Pencils down when you're finished. (Observe children and give feedback.)

• (Write on the board in the style children are to follow:)

1. $\overline{\text{tan}}$

• Here's what you should have. The word **tan** is spelled **T-A-N.**

d. Touch number 2. ✔

• The word for line 2 is **fan**. What word? (Signal.) *Fan.*

• Say the three sounds in **fan**. Get ready. (Tap 3 times.) *fff aaa nnn.*

• I'll say the three sounds in **fan**. You tell me the letter you write for each sound. First sound: **fff**. What letter? (Signal.) *F.* Next sound: **aaa**. What letter? (Signal.) *A.* Last sound: **nnn**. What letter? (Signal.) *N.*

e. Write the word **fan** on line 2. Pencils down when you're finished. (Observe children and give feedback.)

• (Write on the board:)

2. $\overline{\text{fan}}$

• Here's what you should have. The word **fan** is spelled **F-A-N.**

### Individual Turns
• (Call on different children to read one or two of the words.)

## 16

EXERCISE 7

## SAYING THE SOUNDS
### Long Vowels

a. Find the picture of the giraffe. ✔
- (Teacher reference:)

| a e i o |
|---|

- These are letters that sometimes say their names in words. The letters are: **A, E, I, O.**
- You're going to touch the sounds you hear in words.

b. Listen: **loan.** What word? (Signal.) *Loan.*
- Say the three sounds in **loan.** Get ready. (Tap 3 times.) *lll   OOO   nnn.*
- One of those sounds is a **letter name.** Touch the letter name you hear in **loan.** Get ready. (Signal.) ✔
- Everybody, what letter are you touching? (Signal.) *O.*
You can hear the name **O** in the word **loan.**

c. Next word: **nail.** What word? (Signal.) *Nail.*
- **Nail** has three sounds. Say **nail** a sound at a time. Get ready. (Tap 3 times.) *nnn   AAA   lll.*
- Touch the letter name you hear in **nail.** Get ready. (Signal.) ✔
- Everybody, what letter are you touching? (Signal.) *A.*
You can hear the name **A** in the word **nail.**

d. Next word: **fine.** What word? (Signal.) *Fine.*
- **Fine** has three sounds. Say **fine** a sound at a time. Get ready. (Tap 3 times.) *fff   III   nnn.*
- Touch the letter name you hear in **fine.** Get ready. (Signal.) ✔
- Everybody, what letter are you touching? (Signal.) *I.*
You can hear the name **I** in the word **fine.**

EXERCISE 8

## STORY EXTENSION
### Matching: Pictures

a. Turn to side 2 of your worksheet. ✔
Find the pictures at the top of the page.
b. This part shows pictures that are for a Mr. Mosely story. In that story Mr. Mosely asked for a **tooth,** but he really wanted **toothpaste.**
- He asked about his **hair,** but what did he really want to know about? (Signal.) *Hairbrush.*
- He asked about his **suit,** but what did he really want to know about? (Signal.) *Suitcase.*
- He asked about the **air,** but what did he really want to know about? (Signal.) *Airport.*
c. Touch the picture of the tooth. ✔
- All the things in that column are things he asked about—the tooth, the suit, the hair and the bottom picture that shows nothing. That's supposed to be air.
- The other column shows the things he wanted.
d. Draw a line from the tooth to the thing he really wanted to know about. Pencils down when you're finished. ✔
- You should have drawn a line to the toothpaste tube.
e. Later, you'll draw lines for the other objects.

EXERCISE 9

## INDEPENDENT WORK
### Matching: Letters

- Find the picture of a pencil. ✔
Later, you'll draw lines to match the capital letters with the regular letters.

## LETTER PRINTING

a. (Write on the board in the style children are to follow:)

- Get ready to write some letters on lined paper. ✔
- You're going to write three rows of letters. I'll tell you the sounds for the letters you'll write.

b. Touch the top line you'll write a letter on. ✔
- The letter you'll write on that line makes the sound **t** in words. What sound? (Signal.) *t.*
- Write the letter for **t.** Pencils down when you're finished.
(Observe children and give feedback.)
- (Write on the board:)

- Here's the letter you should have.
c. Touch the next line. ✔
- The letter you'll write on that line makes the sound **sss** in words. What sound? (Signal.) *sss.*
- Write the letter for **sss.** Pencils down when you're finished.
(Observe children and give feedback.)

- (Write to show:)

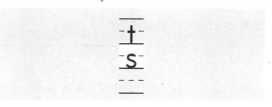

- Here's the letter you should have.
d. Touch the next line. ✔
- The letter you'll write on that line makes the sound **fff** in words. What sound? (Signal.) *fff.*
- Write the letter for **fff.** Pencils down when you're finished.
(Observe children and give feedback.)
- (Write to show:)

- Here's the letter you should have.
e. Later, you can complete the lines of letters.

### Independent Work Summary
- Cut and paste the numbers below story pictures (1=fence, 2=horse, 3=goat).
- Connect related pictures (**tooth**paste, **suit**case, **hair**brush, **air**port).
- Matching game.
- Letter printing (finish lines of **t, s, f**).

## 17

**Materials:** Each child will need scissors, paste and lined paper.

### ══════ EXERCISE 1 ══════

#### WORD vs. SENTENCE

a. I'll say sentences. You'll tell me the first word and the second word in each sentence.

b. Listen: **The girl was pretty.**
Say that sentence.
(Signal.) *The girl was pretty.*

• The first word is **the.**
The second word is **girl.**

• **The girl was pretty.**
What's the first word in that sentence?
(Signal.) *The.*
What's the next word in that sentence?
(Signal.) *Girl.*

c. New sentence: **A girl was pretty.**
Say that sentence.
(Signal.) *A girl was pretty.*

• What's the first word? (Signal.) *A.*
What's the second word? (Signal.) *Girl.*

d. (Repeat step c until firm.)

e. New sentence: **I see a bunny.**
Say that sentence. (Signal.) *I see a bunny.*

• The first word is **I.**
The next word is **see.**

• **I see a bunny.**
What's the first word? (Signal.) *I.*
What's the next word? (Signal.) *See.*

f. (Repeat step e until firm.)

### TEXTBOOK

### ══════ EXERCISE 2 ══════

#### ONE-LETTER WORDS

a. Open your textbook to lesson 17. Find the rock. ✔

• (Teacher reference:)

| I | a |
|---|---|

• These are letters that are used as words in the sentences you just said.

b. Touch the first letter. ✔

• It's capital **I.** That's the word for **I. I** am a teacher.

c. Touch the next letter. ✔
What letter is that? (Signal.) *A.*

• That's the word for **A. A** hat or **A** girl.

d. Later, you're going to read parts of a story that have the words **I** and **A.**

### ══════ EXERCISE 3 ══════

#### SOUNDS
#### Introducing Y as III

a. The letter name **Y** has two sounds.
Listen: **www III.**

b. Everybody, say the letter name **Y** a sound at a time. Get ready. (Tap 2 times.)
*www    III.*

• What's the first part of the name?
(Signal.) *www.*

• What's the last part of the name?
(Signal.) *III.*

• Yes, **III.** That's the sound **Y** makes in some words. What sound? (Signal.) *III.*

c. (Repeat step b until firm.)

d. Find the snake. ✔

• (Teacher reference:)

| r | m | l | y |
|---|---|---|---|

• All the letters on the snake make a sound that is the **last part of the letter name.** You'll touch and say the sound for each letter.

e. First letter. Everybody, what sound?
(Signal.) *rrr.*

• Next letter. Everybody, what sound?
(Signal.) *mmm.*

• Next letter. Everybody, what sound?
(Signal.) *lll.*

• Last letter. Everybody, what sound?
(Signal.) *III.*
Yes, **III.**

f. Say the sounds for the letters again.
- First letter. What sound? (Signal.) *rrr.*
- Next letter. What sound? (Signal.) *mmm.*
- Next letter. What sound? (Signal.) *lll.*
- Last letter. What sound? (Signal.) *lll.*

g. Remember the sound that **Y** makes in some words.

==========EXERCISE 4==========

**READING WORDS**
**Words with Letter Combinations**

a. Find the turtle. ✔
- (Teacher reference:)

> 1. l<u>oa</u>f
> 2. s<u>ea</u>l
> 3. r<u>ai</u>n
> 4. m<u>ea</u>n

- These words have letter combinations. You're going to read those words.

b. The letter combination in word 1 is **O-A.**
- Touch that combination. ✔
- What's the black letter in that combination? (Signal.) *O.*
- So when you say the sounds for the word, what sound will you say for the combination? (Signal.) *OOO.*
- Count the number of black letters in the word. ✔
  Everybody, how many black letters? (Signal.) *Three.*
- So how many sounds does the word have? (Signal.) *Three.*
- Everybody, touch and say the sounds. Get ready. (Tap 3 times.) *lll   OOO   fff.*
- Again. Touch and say the sounds. Get ready. (Tap 3 times.) *lll   OOO   fff.*
- Say it fast. (Signal.) *Loaf.*
- You just read the word **loaf.** A **loaf** of bread.

c. Touch the combination in word 2. ✔
- That combination is spelled **E-A.** What's the black letter in that combination? (Signal.) *E.*

- So when you say the sounds for the word, what sound will you say for that combination? (Signal.) *EEE.*
- Raise your hand when you know how many black letters are in the word. ✔
  How many black letters? (Signal.) *Three.*
- So how many sounds? (Signal.) *Three.*
- Everybody, touch and say the sounds. Get ready. (Tap 3 times.) *sss   EEE   lll.*
- Again. Touch and say the sounds. Get ready. (Tap 3 times.) *sss   EEE   lll.*
- Say it fast. (Signal.) *Seal.*
- You just read the word **seal.** A **seal** is an animal that spends a lot of time in the water.

d. Touch the combination in word 3. ✔
- That combination is spelled **A-I.** What's the black letter in that combination? (Signal.) *A.*
- So when you say the sounds, what sound will you say for that combination? (Signal.) *AAA.*
- Everybody, touch and say the sounds. Get ready. (Tap 3 times.) *rrr   AAA   nnn.*
- Again. Touch and say the sounds. Get ready. (Tap 3 times.) *rrr   AAA   nnn.*
- Say it fast. (Signal.) *Rain.*
- You just read the word **rain.**

e. Touch the combination in word 4. ✔
- That combination is spelled **E-A.** What's the black letter in that combination? (Signal.) *E.*
- So when you say the sounds, what sound will you say for the combination? (Signal.) *EEE.*
- Everybody, touch and say the sounds. Get ready. (Tap 3 times.)
  *mmm   EEE   nnn.*
- Again. Touch and say the sounds. Get ready. (Tap 3 times.) *mmm   EEE   nnn.*
- Say it fast. (Signal.) *Mean.*
- You just read the word **mean.**

f. Let's do those again.
- Touch word 1. Say the sounds. Get ready. (Tap 3 times.) *lll   OOO   fff.*
  What word? (Signal.) *Loaf.*
- Touch word 2. Say the sounds. Get ready. (Tap 3 times.) *sss   EEE   lll.*
  What word? (Signal.) *Seal.*

- Touch word 3. Say the sounds. Get ready. (Tap 3 times.) *rrr   AAA   nnn.* What word? (Signal.) *Rain.*
- Touch word 4. Say the sounds. Get ready. (Tap 3 times.) *mmm   EEE   nnn.*
- What word? (Signal.) *Mean.*

g. Good reading words that have combinations.

**Individual Turns**

- (Call on different children to read one of the words.)

═══════ **EXERCISE 5** ═══════

## SPACES BETWEEN WORDS

a. (Write on the board:)

> **a ram**

- You're going to read lines that have more than one word.
- I've written a line with two words on the board. These words are part of a story. Each word is underlined.

b. (Touch **a**.) The first word is **A**.
- (Touch space.) There's a space between that word and the next word.
- (Touch **ram**.) Then there's the second word.

c. This time, I'll touch and you'll tell me if I'm touching the first word, the space or the second word.
- (Touch first word.) What am I touching? (Signal.) *First word.*
- (Touch space.) What am I touching? (Signal.) *Space.*
- (Touch the second word.) What am I touching? (Signal.) *Second word.*

d. (Repeat step c until firm.)

e. Remember: When words are part of a story, each word is underlined, and there's a space between the words.

═══════ **EXERCISE 6** ═══════

## STORY READING

a. Find the book at the bottom of the page. ✔
- (Teacher reference:)

> 1. I am
> 2. a ram
> 3. I am mean.

- First you'll read these words. Then you'll read part of a story.

b. Touch number 1. ✔
- There are two words on line 1. The first word on that line is **I**. Touch the word **I**. ✔
- Touch the next word. ✔
  That word is **am**.
- Let's do line 1 again. Touch the first word. ✔
  You should be touching the word **I**.
- Touch the next word. ✔
  You should be touching the word **am**.

c. Touch number 2. ✔
  There are two words on line 2. The first word is **A**. Touch that word. ✔
  You should be touching the word **A**.
- The next word is **ram**. Touch that word. ✔
- Let's do line 2 again. Touch the first word. ✔
  You should be touching the word **A**.
- Touch the next word. ✔
  You should be touching the word **ram**.

d. Touch number 3. ✔
  Raise your hand when you know how many words are on that line.
- Everybody, how many? (Signal.) *Three.*
- The first word is **I**. Touch that word. ✔
  The next word is **am**. Touch that word. ✔
  The last word is **mean**. Touch that word. ✔
- Let's do line 3 again. Touch the first word. ✔
  You should be touching the word **I**.
- Touch the next word. ✔
  You should be touching the word **am**.
- Touch the last word. ✔
  You should be touching the word **mean**.

e. Your turn to read the words on each line.
- There are two words on line 1. Touch the first word. ✔
  Everybody, what word? (Signal.) *I.*
- Next word. Touch and say the sounds. Get ready. **(Tap 2 times.)** *aaa   mmm.* What word? (Signal.) *Am.*
- I'll read both words on line 1. You touch the words. Get ready. **I** (pause) **am.**

f. There are two words on line 2. Touch the first word. ✔
  Everybody, what word? (Signal.) *A.*
- Next word. Touch and say the sounds. Get ready. **(Tap 3 times.)** *rrr   aaa   mmm.* Everybody, what word? (Signal.) *Ram.*
- I'll read both words on line 2. You touch the words. Get ready. **A** (pause) **ram.**

g. There are three words on line 3. Touch the first word. ✔
  Everybody, what word? (Signal.) *I.*
- Next word. Touch and say the sounds. Get ready. **(Tap 2 times.)** *aaa   mmm.* Everybody, what word? (Signal.) *Am.*
- Next word. Touch and say the sounds. Get ready. **(Tap 3 times.)** *mmm   EEE   nnn.* Everybody, what word? (Signal.) *Mean.*
- I'll read the words on line 3. You touch the words. Get ready. **I** (pause) **am** (pause) **mean.**

h. Now I'll tell part of the story and you'll read part of it. This is a story about how Gorman became pals with another animal.
- One day Gorman was walking near the barn. He did not see where he was going, and he bumped into something that moved. That something said, "Hey, watch where you are going."
- Gorman asked, "Who is talking to me?"
- The animal that Gorman bumped into said . . .
- Touch number 1. ✔
- Everybody, tell me the first word. Get ready. (Signal.) *I.*
- Next word. Touch and say the sounds. Get ready. **(Tap 2 times.)** *aaa   mmm.*
- What word? (Signal.) *Am.*
- So Gorman asked, "Who is talking to

me?" and the animal that Gorman bumped into said, **"I am."**

i. Touch number 2. ✔
- Gorman said, "I can hear your voice, but I want to know what kind of animal you are. Are you a horse, or are you a cow?"
- The animal said, "I am . . ."
- Everybody, tell me the first word on line 2. Get ready. (Signal.) *A.*
- Next word. Touch and say the sounds. Get ready. **(Tap 3 times.)** *rrr   aaa   mmm.*
- What word? (Signal.) *Ram.*

j. So the animal told Gorman, "I am . . . (Signal.) *a ram."*
- (Repeat step j until firm.)

k. Touch number 3. ✔
- Gorman said, "Well, I'll see you later," and started to walk away. But after he went only a few steps the ram bumped into him.
- Gorman said, "Why did you bump into me?"
- And the ram said . . . Everybody, tell me the first word on line 3. Get ready. (Signal.) *I.*
- Next word. Touch and say the sounds. Get ready. **(Tap 2 times.)** *aaa   mmm.*
- What word? (Signal.) *Am.*
- Yes, **I am.**
- Touch the last word. Say the sounds. Get ready. **(Tap 3 times.)** *mmm   EEE   nnn.*
- What word? (Signal.) *Mean.*
- So Gorman asked the ram, "Why did you bump into me?"
- And what did the ram say? (Signal.) *I am mean.*
- He sounds like he's pretty mean.

l. Then the ram laughed and said, "I was just playing a joke, and we could be pals if you want."
- Gorman said, "Okay, I can always use another pal."
- And that's how Gorman and the ram became friends.

=== EXERCISE 7 ===
## COMPREHENSION

a. Go to the next page of your textbook. ✔
- This is a picture that shows part of the story. The ram had just bumped into Gorman. Those stars on Gorman's rear end mean that he is sore. That was where the ram bumped Gorman.
b. Touch the balloon that shows what the ram is saying. ✔
- There are words in the balloon. I'll read them. You touch them: **I** (pause) **am** (pause) **mean.**
- What did the ram say? (Signal.) *I am mean.*
c. Later, he'll say that he was just kidding, but I think he may be a pretty mean ram all right.

## WORKBOOK

=== EXERCISE 8 ===
## STORY EXTENSION
### Cut-Out: Words

*Note:* Each child will need scissors and paste.

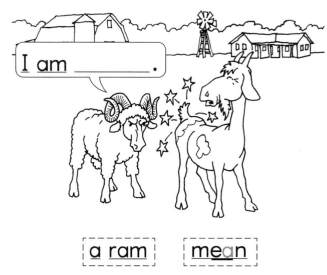

a ram    mean

a. Close your textbook. Go to lesson 17 in your workbook and write your name. ✔
- Find the picture of Gorman and the ram. The ram is saying, "I am . . .", but the rest of what he is saying is missing.
- Maybe he is saying, "I am mean."
- Maybe he is saying, "I am a ram."
- You can decide what the ram is saying.
b. Touch the words at the bottom of the page. ✔
- Later, you'll cut out what you want the ram to say and paste it.

=== EXERCISE 9 ===
## SOUNDS

a. Find the fence. ✔
- (Teacher reference:)

| y | e | t | y | s |
|---|---|---|---|---|

- You're going to say the sounds for the letters on the fence.

b. The first letter is **Y.** Say the name a part at a time. Get ready. (Tap 2 times.) *www III.*
• What sound does **Y** make? (Signal.) *III.*
c. Get ready to say the sounds for all the letters.
• First letter. What sound? (Signal.) *III.*
• Next letter. What sound? (Signal.) *EEE.*
• Next letter. What sound? (Signal.) *t.*
• Next letter. What sound? (Signal.) *III.*
• Last letter. What sound? (Signal.) *sss.*
d. (Repeat step c until firm.)

=======EXERCISE 10=======
## WRITING WORDS

a. Find the pencil. ✔
• You're going to write some words.
b. Touch number 1. ✔
• The word for line 1 is **ram.** What word? (Signal.) *Ram.*
• Say the three sounds in **ram.** Get ready. (Tap 3 times.) *rrr aaa mmm.*
• I'll say the three sounds in **ram.** You tell me the letter you write for each sound.
• First sound: **rrr.** What letter? (Signal.) *R.*
• Next sound: **aaa.** What letter? (Signal.) *A.*
• Next sound: **mmm.** What letter? (Signal.) *M.*
c. Write the word **ram** on line 1. Pencils down when you're finished.
(Observe children and give feedback.)
• (Write on the board in the style children are to follow:)

1. <u>ram</u>

• Here's what you should have. The word **ram** is spelled **R-A-M.**
d. Touch number 2. ✔
• The word for line 2 is **me.** What word? (Signal.) *Me.*
• Say the two sounds in **me.** Get ready. (Tap 2 times.) *mmm EEE.*
• I'll say the two sounds in **me.** You tell me the letter you write for each sound.
• First sound: **mmm.** What letter? (Signal.) *M.*

• Next sound: **EEE.** What letter? (Signal.) *E.*
e. Write the word **me** on line 2. Pencils down when you're finished.
(Observe children and give feedback.)
• (Write on the board:)

2. <u>me</u>

• Here's what you should have. The word **me** is spelled **M-E.**

## Individual Turns
• (Call on different children to read one or two of the words.)

=======EXERCISE 11=======
## INDEPENDENT WORK

### Cross-Out Game
a. Turn to side 2 of your worksheet. Find the cross-out game. ✔
b. The little box shows what you'll cross out.
• Raise your hand when you know what you'll cross out.
• Everybody, what word? (Signal.) *For.*
c. How many times will you cross it out? (Signal.) *Five.*

### Matching: Words with Pictures
d. Find the matching game at the bottom of the page. ✔
• You're going to draw lines to connect words with pictures of those words.
e. Raise your hand when you can tell me the first word.
• Everybody, what's the first word? (Signal.) *Ram.*
f. Find the right picture in the second column and draw a line to connect the word and the picture. Pencils down when you're finished.
(Observe children and give feedback.)
g. Later, you'll do the other words on your own.

## EXERCISE 12

### SPELLING SOUNDS

a. When you spell sounds, you say the letter names that make the sounds.
- My turn to spell **rrr** (pause) **R.**

b. Your turn: Spell **rrr.** (Signal.) *R.*
- Spell **mmm.** (Signal.) *M.*
- Spell **sss.** (Signal.) *S.*
- Spell **aaa.** (Signal.) *A.*
- Spell **t.** (Signal.) *T.*

### Individual Turns

- (Repeat step b, calling on different children to spell one of the sounds.)

### LINED PAPER
## EXERCISE 13

### LETTER PRINTING

a. (Write on the board in the style children are to follow:)

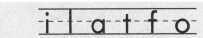

- Get ready to write some letters on lined paper. ✔
- You're going to write three rows of letters. I'll tell you the sounds for the letters you'll write.

b. Touch the top line you'll write a letter on. ✔
- The letter you'll write on that line makes the sound **t** in some words. What sound? (Signal.) *t.*
- Write the letter for **t.** Pencils down when you're finished.
  (Observe children and give feedback.)
- (Write on the board:)

- Here's the letter you should have.
c. Touch the next line. ✔
- The letter you'll write on that line makes the sound **III** in some words. What sound? (Signal.) *III.*
- Write the letter from the board that makes the sound **III.** Pencils down when you're finished.
  (Observe children and give feedback.)
- (Write to show:)

- Here's the letter you should have.
d. Touch the next line. ✔
- The letter you'll write on that line makes the sound **OOO** in words. What sound? (Signal.) *OOO.*
- Write the letter for **OOO.** Pencils down when you're finished.
  (Observe children and give feedback.)
- (Write to show:)

- Here's the letter you should have.
e. Later, you'll complete the lines of letters.

### Independent Work Summary

- Cut-out game (paste into the story picture **a ram** or **mean**).
- Cross-out game (**for**=5).
- Matching game (connect words to pictures).
- Letter printing (finish lines of **t, i, o**).

**Materials:** Each child will need scissors, paste and lined paper.

## TEXTBOOK

### EXERCISE 1

**SOUNDS**

a. Open your textbook to lesson 18. Find the baseball bat. ✔
- (Teacher reference:)

| y  s  i  f  y  e |
|---|

- First letter. What sound? (Signal.) *III.*
b. Next letter. What sound? (Signal.) *sss.*
c. (Repeat step b for remaining items.)
d. I'm going to say some words that have the letter **Y.**
- Listen: **my.** What word? (Signal.) *My.*
- Say the sounds in **my.** Get ready. (Tap 2 times.) *mmm   III.*
- What's the first sound in **my?** (Signal.) *mmm.*
- What's the other sound in **my?** (Signal.) *III.*
e. New word: **fly.** What word? (Signal.) *Fly.*
- **Fly** has three sounds. I'll say the sounds. **fff   lll   III.**
- Your turn: Say the sounds in **fly.** Get ready. (Tap 3 times.) *fff   lll   III.*
- What's the first sound? (Signal.) *fff.*
- What's the next sound? (Signal.) *lll.*
- What's the last sound? (Signal.) *III.* That sound is spelled with the letter **Y.**

### EXERCISE 2

**READING WORDS**

a. Find the baseball. ✔

- (Teacher reference:)

| 1. my |
|---|
| 2. try |
| 3. fly |

- These are words that have the letter **Y.**
b. Touch number 1. ✔
- Touch and say the sounds. Get ready. (Tap 2 times.) *mmm   III.*
- Again. Touch and say the sounds. Get ready. (Tap 2 times.) *mmm   III.*
- What word? (Signal.) *My.*
c. Touch number 2. ✔
- Touch and say the sounds. Get ready. (Tap 3 times.) *t   rrr   III.*
- Again. Touch and say the sounds. Get ready. (Tap 3 times.) *t   rrr   III.*
- What word? (Signal.) *Try.*
- Yes, we like it when you **try.**
d. Touch number 3. ✔
- Touch and say the sounds. Get ready. (Tap 3 times.) *fff   lll   III.*
- Again. Touch and say the sounds. Get ready. (Tap 3 times.) *fff   lll   III.*
- What word? (Signal.) *Fly.*

**Individual Turns**
- (Call on different children to read one of the words.)

### EXERCISE 3

**READING WORDS**
**Words with Letter Combinations**

a. Touch the baseball mitt. ✔
- (Teacher reference:)

| 1. e̲a̲t    2. ne̲a̲t    3. sa̲i̲l |
|---|

- These words have letter combinations. The letter combination in word 1 is **E-A.**
b. Touch that combination. ✔
- What's the black letter in that combination? (Signal.) *E.*
- So when you say the sounds for the word, what sound will you say for the combination? (Signal.) *EEE.*

- Raise your hand when you know how many black letters are in the word.
- Everybody, how many black letters? (Signal.) *Two.*
- So how many sounds? (Signal.) *Two.*
- Touch word 1. ✔
- Everybody, touch and say the sounds for the black letters. Get ready. (Tap 2 times.) *EEE    t.*
- Say it fast. (Signal.) *Eat.*
- You just read the word **eat.** ————
c. Touch the combination in word 2. ✔
- That combination is spelled **E-A.** What sound will you say for that combination? (Signal.) *EEE.*
- Touch word 2. ✔
- Everybody, touch and say the sounds for the black letters. Get ready. (Tap 3 times.) *nnn    EEE    t.*
- Again. Touch and say the sounds. Get ready. (Tap 3 times.) *nnn    EEE    t.*
- Say it fast. (Signal.) *Neat.*
- You just read the word **neat.** Please keep your desk **neat.** ————
d. Touch the combination in word 3. ✔
- That combination is spelled **A-I.** What sound will you say for the combination? (Signal.) *AAA.*
- Touch word 3. ✔
- Everybody, touch and say the sounds for the black letters. Get ready. (Tap 3 times.) *sss    AAA    lll.*
- Again. Touch and say the sounds. Get ready. (Tap 3 times.) *sss    AAA    lll.*
- Say it fast. (Signal.) *Sail.*
- You just read the word **sail.** The boat has a big **sail.** ————
e. Let's do those again.
- Touch word 1. ✔
  Say the sounds. Get ready. (Tap 2 times.) *EEE    t.*
  What word? (Signal.) *Eat.*
- Touch word 2. ✔
  Say the sounds. Get ready. (Tap 3 times.) *nnn    EEE    t.*
  What word? (Signal.) *Neat.*
- Touch word 3. ✔
  Say the sounds. Get ready. (Tap 3 times.) *sss    AAA    lll.*
  What word? (Signal.) *Sail.*

f. Good reading words that have letter combinations.

**Individual Turns**
- (Call on different children to read one of the words.)

═══════════ EXERCISE 4 ═══════════

## STORY READING

a. Touch the book. ✔
- (Teacher reference:)

> 1. **I am Sam.**
> 2. **at me**
> 3. **I see a man.**

- You're going to read part of a Clarabelle story.
b. One day Clarabelle was walking near the garden. She saw an animal she did not know. She looked at the animal and said, "Hello there. My name is Clarabelle."
- The other animal said . . .
c. Touch number 1. ✔
- There are three words on line 1. Touch the first word. ✔
- Everybody, what word? (Signal.) *I.*
- Touch the next word. Say the sounds. Get ready. (Tap 2 times.) *aaa    mmm.*
- Everybody, what word? (Signal.) *Am.*
- Touch the last word. Say the sounds. Get ready. (Tap 3 times.) *sss    aaa    mmm.*
- Everybody, what word? (Signal.) *Sam.*
d. Say all three words on line 1. Get ready. (Signal.) *I am Sam.*
- (Repeat step d until firm.)
e. That's what the animal said. Clarabelle introduced herself, and the other animal said, "I am Sam."
f. Sam was eating a great big carrot that he had pulled from the garden.
- Clarabelle said, "The farmer will not be happy if you eat things from the garden."
- Sam said, "Oh, I didn't know this was a garden. I don't want the farmer to be mad . . ."
- Touch number 2. ✔

- First word. Say the sounds. Get ready. (Tap 2 times.) *aaa   t.*
- Everybody, what word? (Signal.) *At.*
- Next word. Say the sounds. Get ready. (Tap 2 times.) *mmm   EEE.*
- Everybody, what word? (Signal.) *Me.*
- Say both words on line 2. Get ready. (Signal.) *At me.*
- Yes, Sam said, "I don't want the farmer to be mad . . ." (Signal.) *At me.*

g. Just then Clarabelle said, "Oh, oh. I have to leave." And she started to walk away from the garden very fast.
- Sam looked at her and said, "Why are you leaving?"
- She pointed over at the farmer's house and said . . .

h. Touch number 3. ✔
- First word. What word? (Signal.) *I.*
- Next word. Say the sounds. Get ready. (Tap 2 times.) *sss   EEE.*
- Everybody, what word? (Signal.) *See.*
- Yes, **I see . . .**
- Next word. Everybody, what word? (Signal.) *A.*
- Yes, **I see a** something.
- Last word. Say the sounds. Get ready. (Tap 3 times.) *mmm   aaa   nnn.*
- Everybody, what word? (Signal.) *Man.*

i. Say all the words on line 3. Get ready. (Signal.) *I see a man.*
- (Repeat step i until firm.)

j. That's what Clarabelle said.
- Why was she leaving the garden? (Signal.) *She saw a man.*
- And who do you think that man was? (Signal.) *The farmer.*
- And how do you think that man will feel about Sam eating carrots from the garden? (Call on a child. Idea: *He will be mad.*)

═══ EXERCISE 5 ═══

## COMPREHENSION

a. Go to the next page of your textbook. Touch the picture at the top of the page. ✔
- Clarabelle has just introduced herself, and the bunny is saying something.
- What is the bunny saying? (Call on a child to read: *I am Sam.*)

b. Touch the picture at the bottom of the page. ✔
- That picture shows Clarabelle leaving, and she is saying something.
- What is she saying? (Call on a child to read: *I see a man.*)
- What is Sam doing? (Call on a child. Idea: *Eating a carrot.*)

## WORKBOOK

=========== EXERCISE 6 ===========

**STORY EXTENSION**
   **Cut-Out: Words**

*Note:* Each child will need scissors and paste.

| I am Sam. | I am a man. |

c. Close your textbook. Go to lesson 18 in your workbook and write your name. ✔
d. Find the pictures that show the farmer and Sam. ✔
• There are two sentences under the pictures. (Call on a child to read them: *I am Sam. I am a man.*)
e. You'll cut out those sentences and paste them below the right pictures. Then you can color the pictures.

=========== EXERCISE 7 ===========

**MATCHING**
   **Missing Letters**

a. Turn to side 2 of your worksheet. Find the matching game. ✔
• This is a new kind of matching game. The lines are already drawn for each letter, but all the matching letters are missing.
b. Touch the letter **E.** ✔

• Follow the line to where the other **E** should be and write the **E** in that space. Pencils down when you're finished. (Observe children and give feedback.)
c. Touch the letter **F.** ✔
• Follow the line to where the other **F** should be and write the **F** in that space. Pencils down when you're finished. (Observe children and give feedback.)
d. Complete all the other letters. Write the missing **M,** the missing **O,** and the missing **I.** Pencils down when you're finished. (Observe children and give feedback.)

=========== EXERCISE 8 ===========

**WRITING WORDS**

a. Find the skunk. ✔
• You're going to write some words.
b. Touch line 1. ✔
• The word for that line is **so.** What word? (Signal.) *So.*
• Say **so** a sound at a time. Get ready. (Tap 2 times.) *sss    OOO.*
• Once more. Say the first sound in **so.** (Signal.) *sss.*
• Next sound. (Signal.) *OOO.*
c. (Repeat step b until firm.)
d. What letter do you write for the sound **sss?** (Signal.) *S.*
• What letter do you write for the sound **OOO?** (Signal.) *O.*
• Write the word **so.** Pencils down when you're finished. (Observe children and give feedback.)
• (Write on the board in the style children are to follow:)

1. <u>SO</u>

• Here's what you should have. **So** is spelled **S-O.**
e. Touch line 2. ✔
• The word for that line is **me.** What word? (Signal.) *Me.*
• Say **me** a sound at a time. Get ready. (Tap 2 times.) *mmm    EEE.*

- Once more. Say the first sound in **me.** (Signal.) *mmm.*
- Next sound. (Signal.) *EEE.*
f. (Repeat step e until firm.)
g. What letter do you write for the sound **mmm?** (Signal.) *M.*
- What letter do you write for the sound **EEE?** (Signal.) *E.*
- Write the word **me.** Pencils down when you're finished.
  (Observe children and give feedback.)
- (Write on the board:)

### 2. me

- Here's what you should have. **Me** is spelled **M-E.**
h. Touch line 3. ✔
- The word for that line is **man.** What word? (Signal.) *Man.*
- **Man** has three sounds. Say **man** a sound at a time. Get ready. (Tap 3 times.) *mmm   aaa   nnn.*
- Once more. Say the first sound in **man.** (Signal.) *mmm.*
- Next sound. (Signal.) *aaa.*
- Last sound. (Signal.) *nnn.*
i. (Repeat step h until firm.)
j. What letter do you write for the sound **mmm?** (Signal.) *M.*
- What letter do you write for the sound **aaa?** (Signal.) *A.*
- What letter do you write for the sound **nnn?** (Signal.) *N.*
- Write the word **man.** Pencils down when you're finished.
  (Observe children and give feedback.)
- (Write on the board:)

### 3. man

- Here's what you should have. **Man** is spelled **M-A-N.**
k. Let's read the words you just wrote.
- Word 1. Say the sounds. (Tap 2 times.) *sss   OOO.*
  What word? (Signal.) *So.*
- Word 2. Say the sounds. (Tap 2 times.) *mmm   EEE.*

---

- What word? (Signal.) *Me.*
- Word 3. Say the sounds. (Tap 3 times.) *mmm   aaa   nnn.*
  What word? (Signal.) *Man.*

==== EXERCISE 9 ====

## INDEPENDENT WORK
### Cross-Out Game

a. Find the cross-out game. ✔
- The little box shows what you'll cross out.
b. Raise your hand when you know what you'll cross out.
- Everybody, what word? (Signal.) *Mean.*
c. How many times will you cross it out? (Signal.) *Four.*

==== EXERCISE 10 ====

## SPELLING SOUNDS

a. When you spell sounds you say the letters that make the sounds.
b. Your turn: Spell the sound **t.** (Signal.) *T.*
- Spell the sound **aaa.** (Signal.) *A.*
- Spell the sound **sss.** (Signal.) *S.*
- Spell the sound **nnn.** (Signal.) *N.*
- Spell the sound **lll.** (Signal.) *L.*

### Individual Turns
- (Repeat step b, calling on different children to spell one of the sounds.)

## LINED PAPER
==== EXERCISE 11 ====

## LETTER PRINTING

a. Get ready to write letters on lined paper.
- Touch the top line you'll write on. ✔
- The letter you'll write on that line makes the sound **aaa** in some words. What sound? (Signal.) *aaa.*

- It also makes the sound **AAA** in some words. What letter makes those sounds? (Signal.) *A.*
- I'll show you how to write **A.**
- (Write **a** in the style children are to follow.)
- Write **A.** Pencils down when you're finished.
  (Observe children and give feedback.)
b. Touch the next line. ✔
- The letter you'll write on that line makes the sound **EEE** in some words. What sound? (Signal.) *EEE.*
- What letter makes that sound? (Signal.) *E.*
- I'll show you how to write **E.**
- (Write **e** below **a.**)
- Write the letter for **EEE.** Pencils down when you're finished.
  (Observe children and give feedback.)

c. Touch the next line. ✔
- The letter you'll write on that line makes the sound **t** in words. What sound? (Signal.) *t.*
- I'll show you how to write **T.**
- (Write **t** below **e.**)
- Write the letter for **t.** Pencils down when you're finished.
  (Observe children and give feedback.)
d. Later, you'll complete the lines of letters.

**Independent Work Summary**
- Cut and paste story sentences and color story pictures.
- Cross-out game (**mean**=4).
- Letter printing (finish lines of **a, e, t**).

**Materials:** Each child will need scissors, paste and lined paper.

## TEXTBOOK

========= EXERCISE 1 =========

### READING WORDS

a. Open your textbook to lesson 19. Find the dinosaur. ✔
- (Teacher reference:)

> 1. **A** <u>ram</u>
> 2. **A** <u>sail</u>
> 3. **A** <u>rat</u>
> 4. **A** <u>fan</u>

- There are two words on each line. The first word is **A.** The next word has a letter **A.** In some of those words, the **A** says **aaa.** In other words, the **A** says **AAA.** If there's no blue letter, the sound is **aaa.**
b. Number 1. What's the first word? (Signal.) *A.*
- Is there a blue letter in the next word? (Signal.) *No.*
- Touch and say the sounds for that word. Get ready. (Tap 3 times.) *rrr aaa mmm.*
- Say it fast. (Signal.) *Ram.*
c. Number 2. What's the first word? (Signal.) *A.*
- Is there a blue letter in the next word? (Signal.) *Yes.*
- Touch and say the sounds for that word. Get ready. (Tap 3 times.) *sss AAA lll.*
- Say it fast. (Signal.) *Sail.*
d. Number 3. What's the first word? (Signal.) *A.*
- Is there a blue letter in the next word? (Signal.) *No.*
- Touch and say the sounds for that word. Get ready. (Tap 3 times.) *rrr aaa t.*
- Say it fast. (Signal.) *Rat.*
e. Number 4. What's the first word? (Signal.) *A.*

- Is there a blue letter in the next word? (Signal.) *No.*
- Touch and say the sounds for that word. Get ready. (Tap 3 times.) *fff aaa nnn.*
- Say it fast. (Signal.) *Fan.*

**Individual Turns**
- (Call on different children to read one of the lines.)

========= EXERCISE 2 =========

### READING SOUNDS

a. Find the bunny. ✔
- (Teacher reference:)

> y oa y ai f ea

- Let's help the bunny get to the bunch of carrots.
b. Touch and say the sounds.
- First sound. Get ready. (Signal.) *lll.*
c. Next sound. Get ready. (Signal.) *OOO.*
d. (Repeat step c for remaining items.)

========= EXERCISE 3 =========

### READING WORDS
### Words with Y

a. Find the turtle. ✔
- (Teacher reference:)

> 1. **fly**
> 2. **try**
> 3. **my**

- These are words that have the letter **Y.**
- Touch number 1. ✔
- Touch and say the sounds. Get ready. (Tap 3 times.) *fff lll III.*
- Again. Touch and say the sounds. Get ready. (Tap 3 times.) *fff lll III.*
- What word? (Signal.) *Fly.*
- Yes, we would love to **fly.**
b. Touch number 2. ✔
- Touch and say the sounds. Get ready. (Tap 3 times.) *t rrr III.*
- Again. Touch and say the sounds. Get ready. (Tap 3 times.) *t rrr III.*
- What word? (Signal.) *Try.*

- Yes, we like it when you **try.**
c. Touch number 3. ✔
- Touch and say the sounds. Get ready.
  (Tap 2 times.) *mmm   lll.*
- Again. Touch and say the sounds. Get
  ready. (Tap 2 times.) *mmm   lll.*
- What word? (Signal.) *My.*
- Yes, **my** children are the smartest.

**Individual Turns**
- (Call on different children to read one of
  the words.)

═══════════════ EXERCISE 4 ═══════════════

**READING WORDS**
**Words with Letter Combinations**

a. Find the frog. ✔
- (Teacher reference:)

┌─────────────────────────────────────┐
│  1. m**ai**l    2. l**oa**f    3. **ea**t  │
│  4. n**ai**l    5. s**ea**l              │
└─────────────────────────────────────┘

- These words have letter combinations.
  You've read these words before.
b. Word 1. Touch and say the sounds for the
  black letters. Get ready.
  (Tap 3 times.) *mmm   AAA   lll.*
- Say it fast. (Signal.) *Mail.*
- What do you do when you **mail**
  something? (**Call on a child. Idea:** *Take it
  to the post office or put it in a mailbox.*)
c. Word 2. Touch and say the sounds for
  the black letters. Get ready.
  (Tap 3 times.) *lll   OOO   fff.*
- Say it fast. (Signal.) *Loaf.*
- You just read the word **loaf.**
d. Word 3. Touch and say the sounds for
  the black letters. Get ready.
  (Tap 2 times.) *EEE t.*
- Say it fast. (Signal.) *Eat.*
- Who likes to eat? (**Children respond.**)
e. Word 4. Touch and say the sounds for
  the black letters. Get ready.
  (Tap 3 times.) *nnn   AAA   lll.*
- Say it fast. (Signal.) *Nail.*

f. Word 5. Touch and say the sounds for
  the black letters. Get ready.
  (Tap 3 times.) *sss   EEE   lll.*
- Say it fast. (Signal.) *Seal.*
- You can **seal** an envelope. How do you
  do that? (**Call on a child. Idea:** *Lick the
  flap and close the envelope.*)

**Individual Turns**
- (Call on different children to read a word.)

═══════════════ EXERCISE 5 ═══════════════

**JOKE COMPREHENSION**
a. You're going to read some stories that
  make jokes.
- Go to the next page in your textbook.
  Touch the picture. ✔
- That picture shows a joke.
b. I'll tell you the joke. The refrigerator did
  not make things cold. It just didn't work.
- So two men carried the refrigerator to the
  dump.
- Clarabelle saw the refrigerator. She didn't
  know that men were carrying it. She saw
  just a refrigerator with legs going along
  the path. She said to the horse, "What a
  strange refrigerator."
- The horse said, "That refrigerator **does
  not run.**"
- Clarabelle said, "It must run. It has
  four legs."
- Listen: Did the refrigerator really work?
  (Signal.) *No.*
- That's why the horse said it didn't run.
  That means it didn't work. Clarabelle was
  not thinking about whether the
  refrigerator worked.
- Why did Clarabelle think that it could
  run? (**Call on a child. Idea:** *Because it
  had four legs.*)
c. Listen to the joke again. The refrigerator
  did not make things cold. It just didn't
  work.
- So two men carried the refrigerator to the
  dump.

- Clarabelle saw the refrigerator. She didn't know that men were carrying it. She saw just a refrigerator with legs going along the path. She said to the horse, "What a strange refrigerator." The horse said, "That refrigerator **does not run**."
- Clarabelle said, "It must run. It has four legs." Silly Clarabelle!

═══════════ EXERCISE 6 ═══════════

**STORY READING**

a. Go to the next page in your textbook. Find the book. ✔
- (Teacher reference:)

> 1. I e<u>a</u>t.
> 2. I e<u>a</u>t a lo<u>a</u>f.
> 3. I <u>sat</u>.

- We are going to read a story together. I'll read parts and you'll read parts.
b. Listen: A group of farm animals were talking. One of them said, "I love to swim in the pond. I swim every day." The animal who said that was a duck.
- Another animal said, "I run every day." That animal was a horse.
- Another animal said . . .
- Touch line 1. ✔
- First word. Everybody, what word? (Signal.) *I.*
- Next word. Say the sounds for the black letters. Get ready. (Tap 2 times.) *EEE   t.*
- What word? (Signal.) *Eat.*
- Say the words on line 1. Get ready. (Signal.) *I eat.*
- Sam was the animal who said, **"I eat."**
c. A bluebird said, "Well, everybody eats. I eat bread. I eat two **crumbs** of bread every morning."
- A raccoon said, "I eat two **slices** of bread every morning."
- Sam said, "I eat more than two slices of bread every morning."
- Then he said . . .
- Touch line 2. ✔
- First word? What word? (Signal.) *I.*

- Next word. Say the sounds. Get ready. (Tap 2 times.) *EEE   t.*
- What word? (Signal.) *Eat.*
- Next word. What word? (Signal.) *A.*
- Yes, Sam said, "I eat a something."
- Last word. Say the sounds for the black letters. Get ready. (Tap 3 times.) *lll   OOO   fff.*
- What word? (Signal.) *Loaf.*
- Say all four words on line 2. Get ready. (Signal.) *I eat a loaf.*
- How much bread does Sam eat? (Signal.) *A loaf.*
d. The horse said to Sam, "Today you must have done something more than just eat. What else did you do?"
- Sam said . . .
- Touch line 3. ✔
- First word. What word? (Signal.) *I.*
- Next word. Say the sounds. Get ready. (Tap 3 times.) *sss   aaa   t.*
- What word? (Signal.) *Sat.*
- Say both the words on line 3. Get ready. (Signal.) *I sat.*
- So Sam said he did something more than eat. What did he do? (Signal.) *Sat.*
- That's not very much.

═══════════ EXERCISE 7 ═══════════

**COMPREHENSION**

a. This time, you'll read parts of the story that are in pictures. Find picture 1. ✔

- Listen to that part of the story.

- One animal said, "I swim every day."
Who said that? (Signal.) *Duck.*
- Another animal said, "I run every day."
Which animal said that? (Signal.) *Horse.*
- Another animal said what you see in the picture. Everybody touch the words in the picture. ✔
What's that animal saying? (Call on a child to read: *I eat.*)
Which animal said that? (Signal.) *Sam.*
b. Go to the next page and touch picture 2. ✔

- Listen to that part of the story.
- An animal said, "I eat two crumbs of bread every morning."
Which animal said that?
(Signal.) *Bluebird.*
Touch the bluebird in the picture. ✔
- Another animal said, "I eat two slices of bread every morning."
Which animal said that?
(Signal.) *Raccoon.*
Touch the raccoon in the picture. ✔
- Sam said the words in the picture. What's Sam saying? (Call on a child to read: *I eat a loaf.*)
c. Touch picture 3. ✔

- Listen to that part.
- The horse asked Sam what else he did. Sam said the words in the picture.

- What's Sam saying? (Call on a child to read: *I sat.*)

━━━━━ **EXERCISE 8** ━━━━━
**STORY EXTENSION**
**Matching: Words with Pictures**

a. Close your textbook. Go to lesson 19 in your workbook and write your name.
- Find the pictures of Sam the bunny. ✔
b. There are two pictures. You're going to draw a line from each picture to the words that tell about the picture.
c. Touch the top picture. ✔
- What's Sam doing in that picture? (Signal.) *Sitting.*
d. Touch the bottom picture. ✔
- What's Sam doing in that picture? (Signal.) *Eating.*
e. Read the words. Then draw a line from each picture to the words that tell about it. Pencils down when you're finished. (Observe children and give feedback.)
f. Later, you'll color the pictures.

## EXERCISE 9

### MATCHING
#### Missing Letters

a. Find the matching game. ✔
* The lines show where the letters belong, but the letters are missing.
b. Touch the **R.** ✔
* Follow the line to where the other **R** should be and write it. Pencils down when you're finished.
(Observe children and give feedback.)
c. Later, you'll write the other missing letters.

## EXERCISE 10

### SPELLING WORDS

#### Oral

a. Your turn to spell some sounds.
* Spell **fff.** (Signal.) *F.*
* Spell **aaa.** (Signal.) *A.*
* Spell **sss.** (Signal.) *S.*
b. You can spell sounds. You can also spell words. When you spell words, you say the letters that make the sounds in the words.
c. Listen to this word: **me.** What word? (Signal.) *Me.*
* The sounds are **mmm    EEE.**
* How do you spell the sound **mmm?** (Signal.) *M.*
* How do you spell the sound **EEE?** (Signal.) *E.*
* Spell **me** again, and I'll write it on the board. Get ready. (Signal.) *M-E.*
* (Write on the board:)

| me |
|----|

d. New word. Listen: **so.** What word? (Signal.) *So.*
* The sounds are **sss    OOO.**
* Listen: How do you spell the sound **sss?** (Signal.) *S.*
* I low do you spell the sound **OOO?** (Signal.) *O.*
* Spell **so** again, and I'll write it on the board. Get ready. (Signal.) *S-O.*

* (Write on the board:)

| so |
|----|

e. New word. Listen: **no.** What word? (Signal.) *No.*
* The sounds are **nnn    OOO.**
* Listen: How do you spell the sound **nnn?** (Signal.) *N.*
* How do you spell the sound **OOO?** (Signal.) *O.*
* Spell **no** again, and I'll write it on the board. Get ready. (Signal.) *N-O.*
* (Write on the board:)

| no |
|----|

f. New word. Listen: **an.** What word? (Signal.) *An.*
* The sounds are **aaa    nnn.**
* Listen: How do you spell the sound **aaa?** (Signal.) *A.*
* How do you spell the sound **nnn?** (Signal.) *N.*
* Spell **an** again, and I'll write it on the board. Get ready. (Signal.) *A-N.*
* (Write on the board:)

| an |
|----|

#### Individual Turns

* (Call on different children to spell one of the words on the board.)
* You're spelling words. Good for you.

#### Written

g. (Erase the board.)
* Your turn to write three of the words we just spelled.
* Turn to side 2 of your worksheet. ✔ Find the tree and touch line 1. ✔
h. Write the word **no** on line 1. What word? (Signal.) *No.*
* Write it. Pencils down when you're finished.
(Observe children and give feedback.)

- (Write on the board in the style children are to follow:)

**1. no**

- Here's what you should have. **No** is spelled **N-O.**
i. Touch line 2. ✔
- Write the word **me** on line 2. What word? (Signal.) *Me.*
- Write it. Pencils down when you're finished.
(Observe children and give feedback.)
- (Write on the board:)

**2. me**

- Here's what you should have. **Me** is spelled **M-E.**
j. Touch line 3. ✔
- Write the word **an** on line 3. What word? (Signal.) *An.*
- Write it. Pencils down when you're finished.
(Observe children and give feedback.)
- (Write on the board:)

**3. an**

- Here's what you should have. **An** is spelled **A-N.**
k. Raise your hand if you got everything right.
- You're spelling and writing some hard words.

================= EXERCISE 11 =================

**INDEPENDENT WORK**

**Circle Game**
a. Find the circle game. ✔
- The little box shows what you'll circle.
b. Raise your hand when you know what you circle.
- Everybody, what word? (Signal.) *My.*
c. How many times will you circle it? (Signal.) *Four.*

**Cut-Out: Words**

> *Note:* Each child will need scissors and paste.

d. Find the pictures at the bottom of the page.
- Touch the first picture. ✔
What's in that picture? (Signal.) *A seal.*
- In the picture next to the seal is a **loaf.**
- Next to the loaf is some **mail.**
e. The words at the bottom of the page tell about the pictures. You'll read those words to yourself, cut them out, and paste them on the right pictures.

LINED PAPER
================ EXERCISE 12 ================
**LETTER PRINTING**

a. (Write the letters in the style children are to follow.)

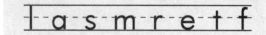

- Get ready to write letters on lined paper. ✔
- You're going to write three rows of letters. I'll tell you the sounds for the letters you'll write.
b. Touch the top line you'll write on. ✔
- The letter you'll write on that line makes the sound **EEE** in some words. What sound? (Signal.) *EEE.*
- Write the letter for **EEE.** Pencils down when you're finished.
(Observe children and give feedback.)
- (Write in the style children are to follow:)

- Here's the letter you should have.
c. Touch the next line. ✔
- The letter you'll write on that line makes the sound **fff** in words. What sound? (Signal.) *fff.*
- Write the letter for **fff.** Pencils down when you're finished.
  (Observe children and give feedback.)
- (Write to show:)

- Here's the letter you should have.
d. Touch the next line. ✔
- The letter you'll write on that line makes the sound **aaa** in some words and **AAA** in other words. What sound does it make in words with blue letters? (Signal.) *AAA.*
- What's the other sound it makes? (Signal.) *aaa.*

- Write the letter for those sounds. Pencils down when you're finished.
  (Observe children and give feedback.)
- (Write to show:)

- Here's the letter you should have.
e. Later, you can complete the lines of letters.

**Independent Work Summary**
- Color story pictures.
- Matching game.
- Circle game (**my**=4).
- Cut-out game.
- Letter printing (finish lines of **e, f, a**).

---

**Materials:** Each child will need scissors, paste and crayons.

**Note:** Administer WORD WRITING to the entire group. Individually administer the rest of the test.

---

## WORKBOOK

=========**EXERCISE 1**=========

### TEST–Group Administered

### Part 1: WORD WRITING

a. Open your workbook to lesson 20, test 2. ✔
   This is a test.
• Write your name at the top of the page. ✔
b. Find the dog. ✔
• You're going to write some words.
c. Touch line 1. ✔
• The word for that line is **me.** What word? (Signal.) *Me.*
• Say the sounds in **me.** Get ready. (Tap 2 times.) *mmm    EEE.*
• Write the word **me** on line 1. Pencils down when you're finished.
   (Observe children but do not give feedback.)
d. Touch line 2. ✔
• The word for that line is **for.** What word? (Signal.) *For.*
• Say the sounds in **for.** Get ready. (Tap 3 times.) *fff    OOO    rrr.*
• Write the word **for** on line 2. Pencils down when you're finished.
   (Observe children.)
e. Touch line 3. ✔
• The word for that line is **an.** What word? (Signal.) *An.*
• Say the sounds in **an.** Get ready. (Tap 2 times.) *aaa    nnn.*
• Write the word **an** on line 3. Pencils down when you're finished.
   (Observe children.)
f. Touch line 4. ✔

• The word for that line is **so.** What word? (Signal.) *So.*
• Say the sounds in **so.** Get ready. (Tap 2 times.) *sss    OOO.*
• Write the word **so** on line 4. Pencils down when you're finished.
   (Observe children.)

=========**EXERCISE 2**=========

### INDEPENDENT WORK
### Cut-Out: Pictures

**Note:** Each child needs scissors, paste and crayons.

a. Turn to side 2. ✔
• Find the little pair of scissors. ✔
b. There's a column of pictures. While I'm listening to each child read, you'll cut out the pictures. The pair of scissors shows you where to start cutting. Cut all the way down the dotted line. Then cut on the other dotted lines.
c. Next, you'll read each word on the page. Find the picture to go with each word and paste that picture above the word.
d. When you're all finished, you can color the pictures.

=========**EXERCISE 3**=========

### TEST–Individually Administered

**Note:** Individually administer the rest of the test: SOUNDS and WORD READING. Mark all errors. Record the test results on the Test Summary Sheet for test 2.

### Part 2: SOUNDS

a. Find the dinosaur. ✔
• Touch and say the **sound** for each letter. [*t, p, III.*]
b. Find the skunk. ✔
• Touch and say the **sound** for each combination. [*EEE, OOO, AAA.*]
c. Find the spider. ✔

- Touch and say the **sound** for each letter. [*fff, rrr, lll.*]

**Part 3: WORD READING**

d. Find the mouse. ✔
e. Touch number 1. ✔
- Touch and say the sound for each black letter. [*rrr   AAA   nnn.*]
- Say it fast. [*Rain.*]
f. Touch number 2. ✔
- Touch and say the sound for each black letter. [*sss   EEE   lll.*]
- Say it fast. [*Seal.*]
g. Touch number 3. ✔
- Touch and say the sound for each black letter. [*lll   OOO   fff.*]
- Say it fast. [*Loaf.*]
h. Touch number 4. ✔
- Touch and say the sound for each black letter. [*EEE   t.*]
- Say it fast. [*Eat.*]
i. Touch number 5. ✔
- Touch and say the sound for each black letter. [*t   rrr   lll.*]
- Say it fast. [*Try.*]

═══════ EXERCISE 4 ═══════

**MARKING THE TEST**

- (Record all test results on the lesson 20, Test 2 Summary Sheet. Reproducible Summary Sheets are at the back of the Teacher's Guide.)

═══════ EXERCISE 5 ═══════

**TEST REMEDIES**

- (Provide any necessary remedies for Test 2 before presenting lesson 21. Test Remedies are discussed in the Teacher's Guide.)

═══════ EXERCISE 6 ═══════

**LITERATURE BOOK**

- (See Teacher's Guide.)

**21**

**Materials:** Each child will need scissors, paste and lined paper.

=====EXERCISE 1=====

**READING SOUNDS**
**Introducing p**

a. (Write on the board:)

| t    p |
| --- |

- First, you'll tell me the letter names for these letters. Then you'll tell me the sounds.

b. What's the name of the first letter? (Signal.) *T.*
- Say **T** a part at a time. Get ready. (Tap 2 times.) *t   EEE.*
- What sound does **T** make? (Signal.) *t.*

c. The second letter name is **P.** The sound that letter makes is a whispered sound, **p.**
- Everybody, what sound does **P** make? (Signal.) *p.*

**TEXTBOOK**

d. Open your textbook to lesson 21. Find the mouse. ✔
- This mouse is going to follow the trail of cookies. Let's help the mouse by saying the sounds. They are all whispered sounds.
- (Teacher reference:)

| t   s   p   f   t   p |
| --- |

e. Touch and say the sounds.
- First sound. Get ready. (Signal.) *t.*

f. Next sound. Get ready. (Signal.) *sss.*

g. (Repeat step f for remaining sounds.)
h. This time, I'll say sounds for one of the **yellow** cookies.
- (Teacher reference:)

| t   s   p   f |
| --- |

- You'll touch the letter and then tell me the letter name.

i. Listen: The sound of a yellow cookie is **sss.**
- Touch the letter that makes the sound **sss.** ✔
- Everybody, what letter are you touching? (Signal.) *S.*

j. Listen: The sound of a yellow cookie is **t.**
- Touch the letter that makes the sound **t.** ✔
- Everybody, what letter are you touching? (Signal.) *T.*

k. Listen: The sound of a yellow cookie is **p.**
- Touch the letter that makes the sound **p.** ✔
- Everybody, what letter are you touching? (Signal.) *P.*

l. Listen: The sound of a yellow cookie is **fff.**
- Touch the letter that makes the sound **fff.** ✔
- Everybody, what letter are you touching? (Signal.) *F.*

m. (Repeat steps i through l until firm.)

=====EXERCISE 2=====

**READING WORDS**

a. Find the fish. ✔
- (Teacher reference:)

| 1. for | 4. na̲i̲l | 7. ant |
| --- | --- | --- |
| 2. e̲a̲t | 5. lo̲a̲n | 8. my |
| 3. see | 6. so | |

- These are words you've read before. Some of them have letter combinations.

b. Word 1. Touch and say the sounds. Get ready. (Tap 3 times.) *fff   OOO   rrr.*
- Say it fast. (Signal.) *For.*

c. Word 2. Touch and say the sounds for the black letters. Get ready. (Tap 2 times.) *EEE   t.*
- Say it fast. (Signal.) *Eat.*

d. Word 3. Touch and say the sounds. Get ready. (Tap 2 times.) *sss   EEE.*
- Say it fast. (Signal.) *See.*

e. Word 4. Touch and say the sounds for the black letters. Get ready. (Tap 3 times.) *nnn   AAA   lll.*

- Say it fast. (Signal.) *Nail.*
f. Word 5. Touch and say the sounds for the black letters. Get ready.
  (Tap 3 times.) *lll   OOO   nnn.*
- Say it fast. (Signal.) *Loan.*
g. Word 6. Touch and say the sounds. Get ready. (Tap 2 times.) *sss   OOO.*
- Say it fast. (Signal.) *So.*
h. Word 7. Touch and say the sounds. Get ready. (Tap 3 times.) *aaa   nnn   t.*
- Say it fast. (Signal.) *Ant.*
i. Word 8. Touch and say the sounds. Get ready. (Tap 2 times.) *mmm   III.*
- Say it fast. (Signal.) *My.*

**Individual Turns**
- (Call on different children to read one of the words.)

================ EXERCISE 3 ================

**STORY READING**

a. Find the book. ✔
- (Teacher reference:)

> 1. **I see no man.**
> 2. **My fan ran.**

- These are the parts of the story that you will read.
- Touch number 1. ✔
b. Listen to the first part of the story: A farmer had a fan that did not work. He took it to his barn so he could fix it. The farmer put the fan right on top of a bunch of ants who were on the floor. They yelled at the farmer, "Get this fan off us."
- But the farmer didn't hear them or see them. Just then, the farmer's wife called him. She said, "Come here right now."
- After the farmer left the barn, one of the ants peeked out from under the fan and said . . .
- Touch the first word on line 1. ✔
  What word? (Signal.) *I.*
- Next word. Touch and say the sounds. Get ready. (Tap 2 times.) *sss   EEE.*
  What word? (Signal.) *See.*
- Next word. Touch and say the sounds. Get ready. (Tap 2 times.) *nnn   OOO.*

- What word? (Signal.) *No.*
- So far, the ant said, "**I see no . . .**"
- Last word. Touch and say the sounds. Get ready. (Tap 3 times.)
  *mmm   aaa   nnn.*
  What word? (Signal.) *Man.*
- Everybody, what did the ant say? (Signal.) *I see no man.*
- Did the ant see a man? (Signal.) *No.*
- Why not? (Call on a child. Idea: *He'd left the barn.*)
c. The ants said, "Let's leave this barn."
- So all the ants started running as fast as they could run. They ran so hard that they moved the fan along the floor as they ran.
- The farmer came back into the barn just as the fan was running out the door. The farmer did not know that the ants were moving the fan. He said, "I must have fixed my fan because . . ."
- Read the words on line 2.
- First word. Touch and say the sounds. Get ready. (Tap 2 times.) *mmm   III.*
  What word? (Signal.) *My.*
- Next word. Touch and say the sounds. Get ready. (Tap 3 times.) *fff   aaa   nnn.*
  What word? (Signal.) *Fan.*
- Next word. Touch and say the sounds. Get ready. (Tap 3 times.) *rrr   aaa   nnn.*
  What word? (Signal.) *Ran.*
- Say all the words on line 2. Get ready. (Signal.) *My fan ran.*
- That's a joke. He thought he fixed the fan because . . . (Call on a child. Idea: *His fan ran.*)

================ EXERCISE 4 ================

**COMPREHENSION**

a. Find the story pictures. ✔
b. Touch picture 1. ✔
- The farmer had a fan that didn't work so he took it to his barn and put it on the floor. He didn't know that he put it on the ants.
c. Touch picture 2. ✔

I see no man.

- The farmer's wife called him and he left the barn. One of the ants peeked out from under the fan and said the words that are in the picture. Everybody, touch the words in the picture. ✔
- What's the ant saying? (Call on a child to read. *I see no man.*)
d. Next page. Touch picture 3. ✔

My fan ran.

- The ants decided to leave the barn so they started running as fast as they could. They moved the fan. When the farmer came into the barn, he saw the fan running out the door. He said, "I must have fixed my fan because . . ." Everybody, touch the words in the picture. ✔
- What's the man saying in the picture? (Call on a child to read. *My fan ran.*)

- His fan didn't really work, but it did run. Ho ho.

## WORKBOOK

### EXERCISE 5
### RHYMING WORDS

a. Close your textbook. Go to lesson 21 in your workbook and write your name. ✔
- Find the apple. ✔
- (Teacher reference:)

| 1. e<u>a</u>r |
|---|
| 2. ne<u>a</u>r |
| 3. te<u>a</u>r |

- These are difficult words.
b. Word 1. Touch and say the sounds for the black letters. Get ready. (Tap 2 times.) *EEE    rrr.*
- The word is **ear.** What word? (Signal.) *Ear.*
- Touch and say the sounds again. Get ready. (Tap 2 times.) *EEE    rrr.*
- Everybody, what word? (Signal.) *Ear.*
c. Word 2. Touch and say the sounds for the black letters. Get ready. (Tap 3 times.) *nnn    EEE    rrr.*
- Everybody, what word? (Signal.) *Near.*
d. Word 3. Touch and say the sounds for the black letters. Get ready. (Tap 3 times.) *t    EEE    rrr.*
- What word? (Signal.) *Tear.*
- Yes, Clarabelle had a big **tear** in her eye.
e. (Repeat steps b through d until firm.)

### Individual Turns
- (Call on different children to read one of the words.)

### EXERCISE 6
### MATCHING
#### Letters

a. Touch the worm. ✔
- I wonder if that worm took the bite out of

the apple.
- This is a matching game. Some of the letters are missing. Some of the matching lines are missing.
b. Later, you'll draw a line to connect the letters that are the same. Write any letters that are missing.

=== EXERCISE 7 ===

## CUT-OUT: WORDS

> **Note:** Each child needs scissors and paste.

a. Find the leaf. ✔
- This is a new kind of cut-out game.
b. Touch the top box. ✔
   There are words in the box. The first word is **I**. Touch it. ✔
c. Raise your hand when you know the word that is next to **I**.
- Everybody, what word is that? (Signal.) *See.*
d. Touch the word below **I**. ✔
   Raise your hand when you know the word.
- Everybody, what word? (Signal.) *No.*
e. Touch the last word. Raise your hand when you know that word.
- Everybody, what word? (Signal.) *Man.*
f. The same words are in the dotted boxes below. Cut out the words and put them over the words in the leaf box. Then turn them over and you'll see the secret picture. Raise your hand when you've made your secret picture. After you show it to me, I'll let you paste it in place. (Observe children and give feedback.)

=== EXERCISE 8 ===

## STORY EXTENSION
### Writing Words in Picture

a. Turn to side 2 of your worksheet. ✔
- Find the story picture. ✔
b. This is like the picture that's in your textbook, except the words are not in the picture. They are written below the

picture. You'll copy them in the picture so the farmer is saying, "My fan ran." Then you'll color the picture.

=== EXERCISE 9 ===

## SPELLING WORDS

### Oral

a. You're going to spell words. Remember, when you spell words, you say the letters that make the sounds in the words.
b. Listen: **so.** What word? (Signal.) *So.*
- The sounds are **sss OOO.**
- How do you spell the sound **sss**? (Signal.) *S.*
- How do you spell the sound **OOO**? (Signal.) *O.*
- So, how do you spell the word **so**? (Signal.) *S-O.*
- Spell it again, and I'll write it on the board. Get ready. (Signal.) *S-O.*
- (Write on the board:)

> **so**

c. New word. Listen: **me.** What word? (Signal.) *Me.*
- The sounds are **mmm   EEE.**
- Listen: How do you spell the sound **mmm**? (Signal.) *M.*
- How do you spell the sound **EEE**? (Signal.) *E.*
- So, how do you spell the word **me**? (Signal.) *M-E.*
- Spell it again, and I'll write it on the board. Everybody, spell **me**. Get ready. (Signal.) *M-E.*
- (Write on the board:)

> **me**

d. New word. Listen: **no.** What word? (Signal.) *No.*
- The sounds are **nnn   OOO.**
- Listen: How do you spell the sound **nnn**? (Signal.) *N.*
- How do you spell the sound **OOO**? (Signal.) *O.*
- So, how do you spell the word **no**? (Signal.) *N-O.*

- Spell it again, and I'll write it on the board. Get ready. (Signal.) *N-O.*
- (Write on the board:)

> **no**

e. New word. Listen: **am.** What word? (Signal.) *Am.*
- The sounds are **aaa   mmm.**
- Listen: How do you spell the sound **aaa?** (Signal.) *A.*
- How do you spell the sound **mmm?** (Signal.) *M.*
- So, how do you spell the word **am?** (Signal.) *A-M.*
- Spell it again, and I'll write it on the board. Get ready. (Signal.) *A-M.*
- (Write on the board:)

> **am**

- You're spelling words. Good for you.

**Individual Turns**
- (Call on different children to spell one of the words on the board.)

**Written**
f. (Erase the board.)
- Find the bunny. ✔
- Your turn to write some of the words we just spelled.
g. Touch line 1. ✔
- Write the word **so** on line 1. **So** on line 1. Pencils down when you're finished. (Observe children and give feedback.)
- (Write on the board:)

> **1. so**

- Here's what you should have. **So** is spelled **S-O.**
h. Touch line 2. ✔
- Write the word **no** on line 2. **No** on line 2. Pencils down when you're finished. (Observe children and give feedback.)
- (Write on the board:)

> **2. no**

- Here's what you should have. **No** is spelled **N-O.**

i. Touch line 3. ✔
- Write the word **am** on line 3. **Am** on line 3. Pencils down when you're finished. (Observe children and give feedback.)
- (Write on the board:)

> **3. am**

- Here's what you should have. **Am** is spelled **A-M.**
j. Raise your hand if you got everything right.

## LINED PAPER
## ═══════ EXERCISE 10 ═══════
### LETTER PRINTING

a. Get ready to write on lined paper. ✔
- Touch the top line you'll write on. ✔
- The letter you'll write on that line makes the sound **fff** in words. What sound? (Signal.) *fff.*
- Write the letter for **fff.** Pencils down when you're finished. (Observe children and give feedback.)
b. Touch the next line. ✔
- The letter you'll write on that line makes the sound **aaa** in some words. What sound? (Signal.) *aaa.*
- It also makes the sound **AAA** in some words. What letter makes those sounds? (Signal.) *A.*
- Write **A.** Pencils down when you're finished. (Observe children and give feedback.)
c. Touch the next line. ✔
- The letter you'll write on that line makes the sound **EEE** in some words. What sound? (Signal.) *EEE.*
- What letter makes that sound? (Signal.) *E.*
- Write the letter for **EEE.** Pencils down when you're finished. (Observe children and give feedback.)
d. Later, you'll complete the lines of letters.

**Independent Work Summary**
- Matching game.
- Story extension (copy sentence into story picture).
- Letter printing (finish lines of **f, a, e**).

**Materials:** Each child will need scissors, paste and lined paper.

## TEXTBOOK

### EXERCISE 1

**READING SOUNDS**

a. Open your textbook to lesson 22. Find the toy airplane. ✔
- (Teacher reference:)

| p | a | y | p | i | f | y | e |
|---|---|---|---|---|---|---|---|

- You'll say the sounds for these letters.
b. Touch the first letter. We learned that whispered sound last time. What sound? (Signal.) *p.*
c. Next letter. You know two sounds for that letter.
- One sound is the letter name. What sound is that? (Signal.) *AAA.*
- What's the other sound? (Signal.) *aaa.*
d. Next letter. What sound? (Signal.) *III.*
e. (Repeat step d for remaining letters.)

### EXERCISE 2

**READING WORDS**
**Words with P**

a. I'm going to say some words that have the letter **P.** Listen: **pat.** What word? (Signal.) *Pat.*
- Say the three sounds in **pat.** Get ready. (Tap 3 times.) *p   aaa   t.*
- What's the first sound in **pat?** (Signal.) *p.*
- That sound is spelled with the letter **P.**
b. New word: **map.** What word? (Signal.) *Map.*
- Say the three sounds in **map. Get ready.** (Tap 3 times.) *mmm   aaa   p.*
- What's the first sound in **map?** (Signal.) *mmm.*
- What's the next sound in **map?** (Signal.) *aaa.*

- What's the last sound in **map?** (Signal.) *p.*
- That sound is spelled with the letter **P.**
c. New word: **spy.** What word? (Signal.) *Spy.*
- I'll say the three sounds in spy: sss   p   III.
- Your turn. Say the three sounds in **spy.** Get ready. (Tap 3 times.) *sss   p   III.*
- What's the first sound in **spy?** (Signal.) *sss.*
- What's the next sound is **spy?** (Signal.) *p.*
- That sound is spelled with the letter **P.**
- What's the last sound in **spy?** (Signal.) *III.*
- That sound is spelled with the letter **Y.**
d. Find the toy truck. ✔
- (Teacher reference:)

> 1. **pal**
> 2. **le̲a̲p**
> 3. **so̲a̲p**
> 4. **spy**

- These are words that have the letter **P.**
e. Touch number 1. ✔
- The letter **A** makes the sound **aaa** in this word.
- Touch and say the sounds. Get ready. (Tap 3 times.) *p   aaa   III.*
- Again. Touch and say the sounds. Get ready. (Tap 3 times.) *p   aaa   III.*
- What word? (Signal.) *Pal.*
- Yes, a **pal** is a friend.
f. Touch number 2. ✔
- Touch and say the sounds for the black letters. Get ready. (Tap 3 times.) *III   EEE   p.*
- Again. Touch and say the sounds. Get ready. (Tap 3 times.) *III   EEE   p.*
- Yes, when you jump, you **leap.**
g. Touch number 3. ✔
- Touch and say the sounds for the black letters. Get ready. (Tap 3 times.) *sss   OOO   p.*
- Again. Touch and say the sounds. Get ready. (Tap 3 times.) *sss   OOO   p.*
- What word? (Signal.) *Soap.*

- When do you use **soap?** (Call on a child. Idea: *When I wash myself.*)

h. Touch number 4. ✔

- Say the sounds. Get ready. (Tap 3 times.) *sss   p   lll.*
- Again. Touch and say the sounds. Get ready. (Tap 3 times.) *sss   p   lll.*
- That word is **spy.** That's a tough word. What word? (Signal.) *Spy.*
- Yes, when you **spy** on somebody, you watch them when they don't know that you're watching.
- Your turn. Touch and say the sounds for word 4. Get ready. (Tap 3 times.) *sss   p   lll.*
- Everybody, what word? (Signal.) *Spy.*

i. You are reading some tough words.

**Individual Turns**
- (Call on different children to read one of the words.)

━━━━━━ EXERCISE 3 ━━━━━━

**READING WORDS**
**Words with Blue E**

a. (Write on the board:)

| a    i    o |
| --- |

- You're going to work with some new words that have a letter name. The letters on the board are the names you'll hear in these words.

b. Listen: **face.** What word? (Signal.) *Face.* You hear a letter name in the word **face.** What letter name? (Signal.) *A.*
- New word: **late.** What word? (Signal.) *Late.*
  You hear a letter name in the word **late.** What letter name? (Signal.) *A.*
- New word: **line.** What word? (Signal.) *Line.*
  You hear a letter name in the word **line.** What letter name? (Signal.) *I.*
- New word: **note.** What word? (Signal.) *Note.*
  You hear a letter name in the word **note.** What letter name? (Signal.) *O.*

c. (Repeat step b until firm.)

d. You're going to read words that have letter names in them.
- Find the toy sailboat. ✔
- (Teacher reference:)

| 1. **lin**e |
| --- |
| 2. **not**e |
| 3. **lat**e |

e. You've read letter combinations. One of the letters in the combination is blue. The other letter says its name. Sometimes, the letters are split up, and the blue letter is at the end of the word.

f. Touch word 1. ✔
- The blue **E** is at the end of the word. Touch it. ✔
- The blue **E** tells you that another letter in the word says its name. That letter is one of the letters on the board.
- Touch the letter that says its name in word 1. ✔
- You should be touching **I.**

g. Touch word 2. ✔
- The blue **E** at the end of the word tells you that another letter in the word says its name. It's one of the letters on the board. Touch the letter that says its name. ✔
- Everybody, what letter are you touching? (Signal.) *O.*

h. Touch word 3. ✔
- The blue **E** tells you that another letter says its name. Touch the letter that says its name. ✔
- Everybody, what letter are you touching? (Signal.) *A.*

i. (Repeat steps f through h until firm.)

j. Go back to word 1. ✔
- One of the letters says its name. What letter is that? (Signal.) *I.*
- You're going to touch and say the sounds for the black letters. Remember, don't say anything for the blue **E.** Touch and say the sounds. Get ready. (Tap 3 times.) *lll   lll   nnn.*
- What word? (Signal.) *Line.* You just read the word **line.**

k. Touch word 2. ✔

- Touch and say the sounds for the black letters. Get ready. **(Tap 3 times.)** *nnn   OOO   t.*
- What word? (Signal.) *Note.*
- You just read the word **note.**
l. Touch word 3. ✔
- Touch and say the sounds for the black letters. Remember to say the letter name for **A.** Get ready. **(Tap 3 times.)** *lll   AAA   t.*
- What word? (Signal.) *Late.*
  You just read the word **late.** We hate to be **late.**

**Individual Turns**
- (Call on different children to read one of the words.)

━━━━━━ **EXERCISE 4** ━━━━━━
**READING WORDS**
**Words with Letter Combinations**

a. Find the toy train. ✔
- (Teacher reference:)

| 1. mail | 2. seal | 3. neat |
|---|---|---|

- These words have blue letters. You'll say the sounds for each black letter and then say the word fast.
b. Word 1. Touch and say the sounds for the black letters. Get ready.
  **(Tap 3 times.)** *mmm   AAA   lll.*
- What word? (Signal.) *Mail.*
c. Word 2. Touch and say the sounds for the black letters. Get ready.
  **(Tap 3 times.)** *sss   EEE   lll.*
- What word? (Signal.) *Seal.*
d. Word 3. Touch and say the sounds for the black letters. Get ready.
  **(Tap 3 times.)** *nnn   EEE   t.*
- What word? (Signal.) *Neat.*

**Individual Turns**
- (Call on different children to read one or two of the words.)
- Remember, don't say sounds for blue letters.

━━━━━━ **EXERCISE 5** ━━━━━━
**STORY READING**

a. Find the book. ✔
- (Teacher reference:)

| 1. See me sail. |
|---|
| 2. I am a seal. |

- These are parts of the story you'll read.
- Touch line 1. ✔
b. One day, a skunk named Sinbad and his two daughters were out in a boat. They stopped at an island to have a picnic lunch. Sinbad and one of his daughters got out of the boat, but the other daughter stayed in the boat.
- Soon, Sinbad heard his daughter calling to him from the boat. He looked out over the lake, and there she was. She called out to her father . . .
- Read the words on line 1.
- First word. Say the sounds. Get ready. **(Tap 2 times.)** *sss   EEE.* What word? (Signal.) *See.*
- Next word. Say the sounds. Get ready. **(Tap 2 times.)** *mmm   EEE.* What word? (Signal.) *Me.*
- Last word. Say the sounds. Get ready. **(Tap 3 times.)** *sss   AAA   lll.* What word? (Signal.) *Sail.*
- Say the whole thing Sinbad's daughter said. (Signal.) *See me sail.*
- What was Sinbad's daughter doing? (Signal.) *Sailing.*
c. Touch line 2. ✔
- Sinbad called out, "I see you sailing, but you shouldn't be out there alone. Now get back to this island right away."
- She said, "I'm on my way, but I found a pal. I will bring my pal back with me."
- When the sailboat got closer, Sinbad could see something in the boat. He said, "Is your pal a dog?"
- She said, "No."
- Sinbad said, "Is your pal a fish?"
- She said, "No."
- Sinbad said, "Well, what is your pal?"
- The pal dove into the water. Then the pal came up and said . . .

- Read the words on line 2.
- First word. What word? (Signal.) *I.*
- Next word. Say the sounds. Get ready.
  (Tap 2 times.) *aaa   mmm.*
  What word? (Signal.) *Am.*
- Next word. What word? (Signal.) *A.*
- Yes, **I am a** something. Say the sounds
  for the last word. Get ready.
  (Tap 3 times.) *sss   EEE   lll.*
  What word? (Signal.) *Seal.*
- Say the whole thing the pal said.
  (Signal.) *I am a seal.*
- What kind of animal was the pal?
  (Signal.) *Seal.*

═══════════ EXERCISE 6 ═══════════

### COMPREHENSION

a. Next page. Find the story pictures. ✔
- This time you'll read parts of the story
  that are in the pictures.
b. Find picture 1. ✔

- Who is on the shore? (Signal.) *Sinbad
  and a daughter.*
- His other daughter is in the boat with
  somebody else. We can't see that animal
  well. Sinbad's daughter is saying
  something. Everybody, touch the words
  in the picture. What's she saying? (Call
  on a child to read. *See me sail.*)
c. Touch picture 2. ✔
- The boat is closer and Sinbad asks, "Is
  your pal a fish?" What did the daughter
  say? (Signal.) *No.*

d. Touch picture 3. ✔

- Then the pal dove into the water and
  came up. The pal said the words that are
  in the picture. What's the pal saying?
  (Call on a child to read. *I am a seal.*)

**WORKBOOK**

═══════════ EXERCISE 7 ═══════════

### STORY EXTENSION
### Cut-Out: Pictures

***Note:*** Each child will need scissors and
paste.

a. Close your textbook. Go to lesson 22 in
  your workbook and write your name. ✔
- Find the picture of the skunks and the
  seal. ✔
  It looks like Sinbad and the others are
  getting ready to have a picnic lunch.

- You can see two boxes that have words. You're going to cut out those boxes and paste them where they belong in the picture.
b. Touch the first box. ✔
- The first word is **A**. Touch and say the black letters for the next word. Get ready. (Tap 3 times.) *mmm   EEE   lll.*
- Everybody, what word? (Signal.) *Meal.*
- Yes, the words in the box say **a meal.**
- Those words go on the table where the picnic basket and the plates of food are. That's a meal.
c. Touch the second word box. ✔
- Raise your hand when you can say the words that are in that box.
- Everybody, what does the second box say? (Signal.) *A seal.*
- Those words go right near the seal.
d. Later, you'll cut those boxes out and paste them where they go in the picture.
- You can color the pictures.

================ EXERCISE 8 ================

## INDEPENDENT WORK

### Matching: Letters
a. Turn to side 2 of your worksheet. ✔
- Find the matching game at the top of the page. ✔
b. Some of the letters are missing. Some of the matching lines are missing.
- Later, you'll draw lines for the letters that are shown and write any letters that are missing.

### Circle Game
c. Find the circle game. ✔
- This is a super hard circle game. You'll circle a word.
d. Raise your hand when you can tell me the word that is circled in the small box. ✔
- Everybody, what word? (Signal.) *Ear.*
- How many words will you circle? (Signal.) *Five.*
e. Later, you'll circle **ear**. Be careful, and don't get fooled. Make sure any word you circle is spelled **E-A-R.**

================ EXERCISE 9 ================

## SPELLING WORDS

### Oral
a. I'll say words. You'll spell the words.
- Listen: **am.** What word? (Signal.) *Am.*
- How do you spell the word **am?** (Signal.) *A-M.*
- Spell **am** again, and I'll write it on the board. Get ready. (Signal.) *A-M.*
- (Write on the board:)

| am |
|----|

b. New word. Listen: **no.** What word? (Signal.) *No.*
- How do you spell the word **no?** (Signal.) *N-O.*
- Spell **no** again, and I'll write it on the board. Get ready. (Signal.) *N-O.*
- (Write on the board:)

| no |
|----|

c. New word. Listen: **or.** What word? (Signal.) *Or.*
- The sounds are **OOO   rrr.**
- Listen: What letter spells the sound **OOO?** (Signal.) *O.*
- How do you spell the sound **rrr?** (Signal.) *R.*
- So how do you spell the word **or?** (Signal.) *O-R.*
- Spell **or** again, and I'll write it on the board. Get ready. (Signal.) *O-R.*
- (Write on the board:)

| or |
|----|

d. New word. Listen: **for.** What word? (Signal.) *For.*
- The sounds are **fff   OOO   rrr.**
- Listen: How do you spell the sound **fff?** (Signal.) *F.*
- How do you spell the sound **OOO?** (Signal.) *O.*
- How do you spell the sound **rrr?** (Signal.) *R.*
- So how do you spell the word **for?** (Signal.) *F-O-R.*

- Spell **for** again, and I'll write it on the board. Get ready. (Signal.) *F-O-R.*
- (Write on the board:)

  for

**Individual Turns**
- (Call on different children to spell one of the words on the board.)

**Written**
e. (Erase board.)
- Your turn to write the words we just spelled.
f. Find the bunny. ✔
- Touch line 1. ✔
- Write the word **or** on line 1. **Or** on line 1. Pencils down when you're finished. (Observe children and give feedback.)
- (Write on the board:)

  1. or

- Here's what you should have. **Or** is spelled **O-R.**
g. Touch line 2. ✔
- Write the word **for** on line 2. **For** on line 2. Pencils down when you're finished. (Observe children and give feedback.)
- (Write on the board:)

  2. for

- Here's what you should have. **For** is spelled **F-O-R.**
h. Touch line 3. ✔
- Write the word **am** on line 3. **Am** on line 3. Pencils down when you're finished. (Observe children and give feedback.)
- (Write on the board:)

  3. am

- Here's what you should have. **Am** is spelled **A-M.**
i. Touch line 4. ✔
- Write the word **no** on line 4. **No** on line 4. Pencils down when you're finished. (Observe children and give feedback.)

- (Write on the board:)

  4. no

- Here's what you should have. **No** is spelled **N-O.**

LINED PAPER
**EXERCISE 10**

**LETTER PRINTING**

a. (Write on the board:)

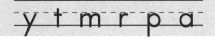

b. Get ready to write on lined paper. ✔
- Touch the top line. ✔
- The letter you'll write on that line makes the sound **aaa** in some words. What sound? (Signal.) *aaa.*
- It also makes the sound **AAA** in some words. What letter makes those sounds? (Signal.) *A.*
- Write **A.** Pencils down when you're finished. (Observe children and give feedback.)
c. Touch the next line. ✔
- The letter you'll write on that line makes the sound **III** in some words. What sound? (Signal.) *III.*
- There are two letters that sometimes make the sound **III.** One of those letters is **I.** You know another letter that sometimes makes the sound **III** in words. What letter? (Signal.) *Y.*
- I'll show you how to write **Y.**
- (Write **y** in the style children are to follow.)
- Write the letter **Y.** Pencils down when you're finished. (Observe children and give feedback.)
d. Touch the next line. ✔

- The letter you'll write on that line makes the sound **mmm** in words. What sound? (Signal.) *mmm.*
- Write the letter for **mmm.** Pencils down when you're finished.
  (Observe children and give feedback.)
- e. Later, you'll complete the lines of letters.

**Independent Work Summary**
- Story extension (cut and paste words in story picture. Color picture).
- Matching game.
- Circle game (**ear**=5).
- Letter printing (finish lines of **a**, **y**, **m**).

**23**

Materials: Each child will need scissors, paste and lined paper.

## TEXTBOOK

### EXERCISE 1
### READING SOUNDS

a. Open your textbook to lesson 23. Find the squirrel. ✔
- (Teacher reference:)

| p | ai | y | ea | i | oa | f | t | y | p |
|---|---|---|---|---|---|---|---|---|---|

- That squirrel is thinking about going down that tree.
b. Touch and say the sounds for the letters and combinations on the tree.
- First sound. Get ready. (Signal.) *p.*
c. Next sound. Get ready. (Signal.) *AAA.*
d. (Repeat step c for remaining items.)

### EXERCISE 2
### READING WORDS
#### Words with Y

a. Find the owl. ✔
- (Teacher reference:)

| 1. fry | 2. spy | 3. try |
|---|---|---|

- These are words that have the letter **Y.**
b. Touch number 1. ✔
- Touch and say the sounds. Get ready. (Tap 3 times.) *fff  rrr  III.*
- Again. Touch and say the sounds. Get ready. (Tap 3 times.) *fff  rrr  III.*
- What word? (Signal.) *Fry.*
- Yes, you **fry** things in a frying pan.
c. Touch number 2. ✔
- Touch and say the sounds. Get ready. (Tap 3 times.) *sss  p  III.*
- Again. Get ready. (Tap 3 times.) *sss  p  III.*
- What word? (Signal.) *Spy.*
- That's a tough word.

d. Touch number 3. ✔
- Touch and say the sounds. Get ready. (Tap 3 times.) *t  rrr  III.*
- Again. Get ready. (Tap 3 times.) *t  rrr  III.*
- What word? (Signal.) *Try.*
e. You are reading tough words.

**Individual Turns**
- (Call on different children to read one of the words.)

### EXERCISE 3
### READING WORDS
#### Words with Blue E

a. Find the bunny rabbit. ✔
- (Teacher reference:)

| 1. mole | 2. ate | 3. fine | 4. safe |
|---|---|---|---|

- These words have letter combinations that are split. The blue letter is at the end of the word. Another letter in the word says its name. That letter is **A, I** or **O.**
b. Touch the letter that says its name in word 1. Get ready. (Signal.) ✔
- Everybody, what letter are you touching? (Signal.) *O.*
c. Touch the letter that says its name in word 2. Get ready. (Signal.) ✔
- Everybody, what letter are you touching? (Signal.) *A.*
- Remember, the blue letter tells you that you'll say **AAA** for that letter, not **aaa.** What sound will you say? (Signal.) *AAA.*
d. Touch the letter that says its name in word 3. Get ready. (Signal.) ✔
- Everybody, what letter are you touching? (Signal.) *I.*
e. Touch the letter that says its name in word 4. Get ready. (Signal.) ✔
- Everybody, what letter are you touching? (Signal.) *A.*
f. Go back to word 1. ✔
- Touch and say the sounds for the black letters. Get ready. (Tap 3 times.) *mmm  OOO  III.*
- What word? (Signal.) *Mole.*

g. Word 2. Touch and say the sounds for the black letters. Get ready.
(Tap 2 times.) *AAA    t.*
• What word? (Signal.) *Ate.*
h. Word 3. Touch and say the sounds for the black letters. Get ready.
(Tap 3 times.) *fff    lll    nnn.*
• What word? (Signal.) *Fine.*
 i. Word 4. Touch and say the sounds for the black letters. Get ready.
(Tap 3 times.) *sss    AAA    fff.*
• What word? (Signal.) *Safe.*

**Individual Turns**
• (Call on different children to read one of the words.)

═══════════ EXERCISE 4 ═══════════
**READING WORDS**
**AAA vs. aaa Discrimination**

a. Find the snake. ✔
• (Teacher reference:)

> **1. pail    2. pal    3. ate    4. at**

b. These words have the letter **A.** In some words, the **A** says **aaa.** In other words, it says **AAA.** Remember the rule: If there's a blue letter, the sound is **AAA.** If there's no blue letter, the sound is **aaa.**
c. Word 1. Is there a blue letter in the word? (Signal.) *Yes.*
• Touch and say the sounds for the black letters. Get ready. (Tap 3 times.)
*p    AAA    lll.*
• Say it fast. (Signal.) *Pail.*
• Yes, a **pail** is a bucket.
d. Word 2. Is there a blue letter in the word? (Signal.) *No.*
• Touch and say the sounds. Get ready.
(Tap 3 times.) *p    aaa    lll.*
• Say it fast. (Signal.) *Pal.*
e. Word 3. Is there a blue letter in the word? (Signal.) *Yes.*
• Touch and say the sounds. Get ready.
(Tap 2 times.) *AAA    t.*
• Say it fast. (Signal.) *Ate.*
 f. Word 4. Is there a blue letter in the word? (Signal.) *No.*

• Touch and say the sounds. Get ready.
(Tap 2 times.) *aaa    t.*
• Say it fast. (Signal.) *At.*

**Individual Turns**
• (Call on different children to read one of the words.)

═══════════ EXERCISE 5 ═══════════
**STORY READING**

a. Find the book on the next page. ✔
• (Teacher reference:)

> **1. I feel rain.**
> **2. I am near my pal.**

• First, you're going to read sentences. Then you'll see the pictures.
b. Touch sentence 1. ✔
• First word. Everybody, what word? (Signal.) *I.*
• Next word. Touch and say the sounds. Get ready. (Tap 3 times.) *fff    EEE    lll.*
Again. Get ready. (Tap 3 times.)
*fff    EEE    lll.*
What word? (Signal.) *Feel.*
• Last word. Touch and say the sounds. Get ready. (Tap 3 times.) *rrr    AAA    nnn.*
• Say all the words in sentence 1.
(Signal.) *I    feel    rain.*
c. Sentence 2. There are a lot of words in that sentence.
• First word. What word? (Signal.) *I.*
• Next word. Touch and say the sounds. Get ready. (Tap 2 times.) *aaa    mmm.*
What word? (Signal.) *Am.*
• Next word. Touch and say the sounds. Get ready. (Tap 3 times.) *nnn    EEE    rrr.*
Again. Get ready. (Tap 3 times.)
*nnn    EEE    rrr.*
What word? (Signal.) *Near.*
• Yes, so far somebody is saying, **I am near** something.

- Next word. Touch and say the sounds. Get ready. **(Tap 2 times.)** *mmm III.* What word? **(Signal.)** *My.*
- Last word. Touch and say the sounds. Get ready. **(Tap 3 times.)** *p aaa III.* Again. Get ready. **(Tap 3 times.)** *p aaa III.* What word? **(Signal.)** *Pal.*
- Say all the words in sentence 2. **(Signal.)** *I am near my pal.*

### Second Reading

- Let's read the sentences again. **(Call on different children to read sentence 1 or sentence 2.)**

========== EXERCISE 6 ==========

### STORY EXTENSION
### Picture Comprehension

a. Find the story pictures. ✔
- Each picture shows what you just read.
b. Get ready to touch the picture that shows **"I feel rain."**
- Touch it. ✔
  (Observe children and give feedback.)
c. Get ready to touch the picture that shows **"I am near my pal."**
- Touch it. ✔
- Name the things that are in that picture. **(Call on a child. Idea:** *Boy, cow, girl.***)**
- I think you know who that cow is.

========== EXERCISE 7 ==========

### STORY EXTENSION
### Cut-Out: Words

**Note:** Each child will need scissors and paste.

a. Close your textbook. Go to lesson 23 in your workbook and write your name. ✔

b. Each picture has a space under it. You'll cut out the sentence that goes with the picture and paste the sentence under the picture. The sentences are at the bottom of the page.
c. Touch sentence 1. ✔
- You've read this sentence before. Raise your hand when you know what the sentence says. **(Call on a child.** *I feel rain.***)**
- One of the pictures shows somebody who could say, "I feel rain."
- Touch that picture. ✔
  That's where you'll paste sentence 1 when we're done, right below the bottom picture.
d. Touch sentence 2 at the bottom of the page. ✔
- Raise your hand when you know what the sentence says. **(Call on a child.** *I am near my pal.***)**
e. Later, you'll paste those words below the picture of the boy and the girl with their pal. Who is their pal? **(Signal.)** *Clarabelle.*
- Then, you can color the pictures.

========== EXERCISE 8 ==========

### INDEPENDENT WORK

### Writing Words for Pictures
a. Turn to side 2 of your worksheet. ✔
- Find the four words at the top of the page. ✔
b. Touch the first picture below the box of words. ✔
  What's that? **(Signal.)** *Fan.*
- Touch the picture next to the fan. What's that? **(Signal.)** *Sail.*
- What's that animal below the fan? **(Signal.)** *Mole.*
- What's in the last picture? **(Signal.)** *Soap.*
c. The words in the box above the pictures tell about the pictures. Later, you'll read the words and write them below the pictures they tell about.

**Matching: Letters and Combinations**

d. Find the apples. ✔
- This is a matching game. You'll draw lines to show letters that are the same and letter combinations that are the same. The combinations are not shown with blue letters.

━━━━━━ EXERCISE 9 ━━━━━━

## SPELLING WORDS

### Oral

a. I'll say words that have three sounds. You'll spell the words.
b. Listen: **fan.** What word? (Signal.) *Fan.*
- Say the three sounds in **fan.** Get ready. (Tap 3 times.) *fff aaa nnn.*
- How do you spell the sound **fff?** (Signal.) *F.*
- How do you spell the sound **aaa?** (Signal.) *A.*
- How do you spell the sound **nnn?** (Signal.) *N.*
- How do you spell the word **fan?** (Signal.) *F-A-N.*
c. (Repeat step b until firm.)
d. Spell **fan** again, and I'll write it on the board. (Signal.) *F-A-N.*
- (Write on the board:)

> **fan**

e. Listen: **for.**
- Say the three sounds in **for.** Get ready. (Tap 3 times.) *fff OOO rrr.*
- How do you spell the sound **fff?** (Signal.) *F.*
- How do you spell the sound **OOO?** (Signal.) *O.*
- How do you spell the sound **rrr?** (Signal.) *R.*
- How do you spell the word **for?** (Signal.) *F-O-R.*
f. (Repeat step e until firm.)
g. Spell **for** again, and I'll write it on the board. (Signal.) *F-O-R.*
- (Write on the board:)

> **for**

h. Listen: **ran.**
- Say the sounds in **ran.** Get ready. (Tap 3 times.) *rrr aaa nnn.*
- How do you spell the word **ran?** (Signal.) *R-A-N.*
i. (Repeat step h until firm.)
j. Spell **ran** again, and I'll write it on the board. (Signal.) *R-A-N.*
- (Write on the board:)

> **ran**

### Individual Turns

- (Call on different children to spell one of the words on the board.)

### Written

k. (Erase the board.)
l. Find the moon. ✔
- Your turn to write the words we just spelled.
m. Touch line 1. ✔
- Write the word **fan** on line 1. **Fan** on line 1. Pencils down when you're finished. (Observe children and give feedback.)
- (Write on the board:)

> **1. fan**

- Here's what you should have. **Fan** is spelled **F-A-N.**
n. Touch line 2. ✔
- Write the word **for** on line 2. **For** on line 2. Pencils down when you're finished. (Observe children and give feedback.)
- (Write on the board:)

> **2. for**

- Here's what you should have. **For** is spelled **F-O-R.**
o. Touch line 3. ✔
- Write the word **ran** on line 3. **Ran** on line 3. Pencils down when you're finished. (Observe children and give feedback.)
- (Write on the board:)

> **3. ran**

- Here's what you should have. **Ran** is spelled **R-A-N.**

p. Raise your hand if you got everything right.
• You're spelling and writing some hard words.

## LINED PAPER
## ══════ EXERCISE 10 ══════
## LETTER PRINTING

a. (Write on the board:)

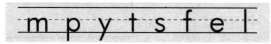

b. Get ready to write on lined paper. ✔
• Touch the top line. ✔
• The letter you'll write on that line makes the sound III in some words. What sound? (Signal.) *III.*
• Get ready to tell me which letter on the board makes that sound. Everybody, which letter? (Signal.) *Y.*
• Write **Y.** Pencils down when you're finished.
(Observe children and give feedback.)
c. Touch the next line. ✔
• The letter you'll write on that line makes the sound **p** in some words. What sound? (Signal.) *p.*

• What letter makes that sound? (Signal.) *P.*
• I'll show you how to write **P.**
• (Write **p** in the style children are to follow.)
• Write the letter for **p** under the **Y.** Pencils down when you're finished.
(Observe children and give feedback.)
d. Touch the next line. ✔
• The letter you'll write on that line makes the sound III in words. What sound? (Signal.) *III.*
• What letter makes that sound? (Signal.) *L.*
• Write the letter for III. Pencils down when you're finished.
(Observe children and give feedback.)
e. Later, you'll complete the lines of letters.

## Independent Work Summary
• Story extension (cut and paste sentences under appropriate pictures. Color pictures).
• Write appropriate words under pictures.
• Matching game.
• Letter printing (finish lines of **y**, **p**, **l**).

**Materials:** Each child will need a red and a blue crayon and lined paper.

═══════════ EXERCISE 1 ═══════════

## SAYING THE SOUNDS
### Blue-Letter Discrimination

a. You're going to say words a part at a time. Some of the words you'll say are spelled with a blue letter.

- Here's the rule: If you say a letter name, the word has a blue letter.

b. Listen: **same.** What word? (Signal.) *Same.*

- Say **same** a sound at a time. Get ready. (Tap 3 times.) *sss   AAA   mmm.*
- Again. Get ready. (Tap 3 times.) *sss   AAA   mmm.*
- Did you say a letter name? (Signal.) *Yes.* What letter name? (Signal.) *A.*
- You said a letter name. So does the word **same** have a blue letter? (Signal.) *Yes.*

c. New word: **Sam.** What word? (Signal.) *Sam.*

- Say **Sam** a sound at a time. **Get ready.** (Tap 3 times.) *sss   aaa   mmm.*
- Did you say a letter name? (Signal.) *No.*
- So does the word **Sam** have a blue letter? (Signal.) *No.*

d. Listen: **fine.** What word? (Signal.) *Fine.*

- Say the sounds in **fine.** Get ready. (Tap 3 times.) *fff   III   nnn.*
- Did you say a letter name? (Signal.) *Yes.*
- What letter name? (Signal.) *I.*
- You said a letter name. So does the word **fine** have a blue letter? (Signal.) *Yes.*

e. New word: **fin.** What word? (Signal.) *Fin.*

- Listen to the sounds in **fin: fff   iii   nnn.**
- Say the sounds in **fin.** Get ready. (Tap 3 times.) *fff   iii   nnn.*
- Did you say a letter name? (Signal.) *No.*
- So does the word **fin** have a blue letter? (Signal.) *No.*

f. New word: **fill.** What word? (Signal.) *Fill.*

- Say the sounds in **fill.** Get ready. (Tap 3 times.) *fff   iii   III.*

- Did you say a letter name? (Signal.) *No.*
- So does the word **fill** have a blue letter? (Signal.) *No.*

g. New word: **file.** What word? (Signal.) *File.*

- Say the sounds in **file.** Get ready. (Tap 3 times.) *fff   III   III.*
- Did you say a letter name? (Signal.) *Yes.*
- What letter name? (Signal.) *I.*
- You said a letter name. So does the word **file** have a blue letter? (Signal.) *Yes.*

h. I'll say the sounds for the words you just did. You tell me if the word has a blue letter.

- Listen: **fff   iii   III.** What word? (Signal.) *Fill.*
  Does **fill** have a blue letter? (Signal.) *No.*
- Listen: **fff   III   III.** What word? (Signal.) *File.*
  Does **file** have a blue letter? (Signal.) *Yes.*
- Listen: **sss   AAA   mmm.** What word? (Signal.) *Same.*
  Does **same** have a blue letter? (Signal.) *Yes.*
- Listen: **sss   aaa   mmm.** What word? (Signal.) *Sam.*
  Does **Sam** have a blue letter? (Signal.) *No.*
- Listen: **fff   iii   nnn.** What word? (Signal.) *Fin.*
  Does **fin** have a blue letter? (Signal.) *No.*
- Listen: **fff   III   nnn.** What word? (Signal.) *Fine.*
  Does **fine** have a blue letter? (Signal.) *Yes.*

═══ TEXTBOOK ═══

═══════════ EXERCISE 2 ═══════════

## READING SOUNDS

a. Open your textbook to lesson 24. Find the long dog at the top of the page. ✔

- That's a dachshund.
- (Teacher reference:)

| ai  p  oa  t  ea  y |
|---|

b. Touch and say the sounds for these letters and combinations.
• First sound. Get ready. (Signal.) *AAA.*
c. Next sound. Get ready. (Signal.) *p.*
d. (Repeat step c for remaining items.)

========= EXERCISE 3 =========

**RHYMING WORDS**

a. Find the squirrel. ✔
• (Teacher reference:)

> **1. at   2. sat   3. rat**

• There are no blue letters in these words, so do you say the name for the letter **A?** (Signal.) *No.*
b. Touch number 1. ✔
• Touch and say the sounds. Get ready. (Tap 2 times.) *aaa   t.*
• What word? (Signal.) *At.*
c. Touch number 2. ✔
• Touch and say the sounds. Get ready. (Tap 3 times.) *sss   aaa   t.*
• Again. Get ready. (Tap 3 times.) *sss   aaa   t.*
• What word? (Signal.) *Sat.*
d. Touch number 3. ✔
• Touch and say the sounds. Get ready. (Tap 3 times.) *rrr   aaa   t.*
• Again. Get ready. (Tap 3 times.) *rrr   aaa   t.*
• What word? (Signal.) *Rat.*
e. All those words rhyme. Listen: **at, sat, rat.**

**Individual Turns**
• (Call on different children to read one of the words.)

========= EXERCISE 4 =========

**READING WORDS**
**Blue-Letter Discrimination**

a. Find the cat. ✔
• (Teacher reference:)

> **1. pan   2. tan   3. ne̲a̲r   4. m̲a̲il**

• Some of these words have a blue letter so you say a letter name. Other words don't have a blue letter, so you don't say a letter name.
b. Word 1. Do you say a letter name? (Signal.) *No.*
• Touch and say the sounds. Get ready. (Tap 3 times.) *p   aaa   nnn.*
• Again. Get ready. (Tap 3 times.) *p   aaa   nnn.*
• What word? (Signal.) *Pan.*
c. Word 2. Do you say a letter name? (Signal.) *No.*
• Touch and say the sounds. Get ready. (Tap 3 times.) *t   aaa   nnn.*
• Again. Get ready. (Tap 3 times.) *t   aaa   nnn.*
• What word? (Signal.) *Tan.*
d. Word 3. Do you say a letter name? (Signal.) *Yes.*
• Touch and say the sounds. Get ready. (Tap 3 times.) *nnn   EEE   rrr.*
• Again. Get ready. (Tap 3 times.) *nnn   EEE   rrr.*
• What word? (Signal.) *Near.*
e. Word 4. Do you say a letter name? (Signal.) *Yes.*
• Touch and say the sounds. Get ready. (Tap 3 times.) *mmm   AAA   lll.*
• Again. Get ready. (Tap 3 times.) *mmm   AAA   lll.*
• What word? (Signal.) *Mail.*
f. (Repeat steps b through e until firm.)

**Individual Turns**
• (Call on different children to read one of the words.)

========= EXERCISE 5 =========

**READING WORDS**
**Words with Blue E**

a. (Write on the board:)

> **a   i   o**

b. Find the fish. ✔

- (Teacher reference:)

> 1. ate  2. sore  3. name  4. fine

- These words have letter combinations that are split. The blue letter is at the end of the word. Another letter in the word says its name. That's one of the letters on the board.
c. Touch the letter that says its name in word 1. Get ready. ✔
- Everybody, what letter are you touching? (Signal.) *A.*
- Remember, the blue letter tells you that you'll say **AAA** for that letter.
d. Touch the letter that says its name in word 2. Get ready. ✔
- Everybody, what letter are you touching? (Signal.) *O.*
e. Touch the letter that says its name in word 3. Get ready. ✔
- Everybody, what letter are you touching? (Signal.) *A.*
f. Touch the letter that says its name in word 4. Get ready. ✔
- Everybody, what letter are you touching? (Signal.) *I.*
g. Go back to word 1. ✔
- Touch and say the sounds for the black letters. Get ready. (Tap 2 times.) *AAA    t.*
- What word? (Signal.) *Ate.*
h. Word 2. Touch and say the sounds for the black letters. Get ready. (Tap 3 times.) *sss    OOO    rrr.*
- What word? (Signal.) *Sore.*
i. Word 3. Touch and say the sounds for the black letters. Get ready. (Tap 3 times.) *nnn    AAA    mmm.*
- What word? (Signal.) *Name.*
j. Word 4. Touch and say the sounds for the black letters. Get ready. (Tap 3 times.) *fff    III    nnn.*
- What word? (Signal.) *Fine.*

**Individual Turns**

- (Call on different children to read one of the words.)

═══════ **EXERCISE 6** ═══════

## SOUNDING OUT vs. SPELLING

a. Find the caterpillar. ✔
- (Teacher reference:)

> 1. ran    2. no

- For some of the work you'll do, you'll spell words. Remember, you say the letter names when you spell. For other words, you will say the sounds. That's not spelling. That's part of reading.
b. Touch word 1. Follow along and tell me if I say the sounds or spell.
- My turn: **rrr    aaa    nnn.** Did I say the sounds or spell? (Signal.) *Say the sounds.*
- My turn again: **R-A-N.** Did I say the sounds or spell? (Signal.) *Spell.*
- Your turn to **spell** word 1. Remember, say the letter names. Get ready. (Tap 3 times.) *R-A-N.*
- Did you say the sounds or spell? (Signal.) *Spell.*
- Now, touch and **say the sounds.** Get ready. (Tap 3 times.) *rrr    aaa    nnn.*
- Did you say the sounds or spell? (Signal.) *Say the sounds.*
- Raise your hand when you know word 1. Everybody, what word? (Signal.) *Ran.*
- Good reading.
c. Word 2. Tell me if I say the sounds or spell: **N-O.** Did I say the sounds or spell? (Signal.) *Spell.*
- Yes, **spell.**
- My turn again: **nnn    OOO.** Did I say the sounds or spell? (Signal.) *Say the sounds.*
- Your turn to spell the word. Remember, say the letter names. Get ready. (Tap 2 times.) *N-O.*
- Did you say the sounds or spell? (Signal.) *Spell.*
- Now, touch and say the sounds. Get ready. (Tap 2 times.) *nnn    OOO.*
- What did you do that time? (Signal.) *Say the sounds.*
- What word did you sound out? (Signal.) *No.*
- Good reading.

## EXERCISE 7

### STORY READING

A ram ran at me.

a. Find the story pictures. ✔
- The sentence you'll read tells about one of the pictures.
b. Touch the sentence under the pictures. ✔
- First word. What word? (Signal.) *A.*
c. Next word. Touch and say the sounds. Get ready. (Tap 3 times.)
  *rrr   aaa   mmm.*
- Again. Get ready. (Tap 3 times.)
  *rrr   aaa   mmm.*
- What word? (Signal.) *Ram.*
d. Next word. Touch and say the sounds. Get ready. (Tap 3 times.) *rrr   aaa   nnn.*
- Again. Get ready. (Tap 3 times.)
  *rrr   aaa   nnn.*
- What word? (Signal.) *Ran.*
- Yes, **a ram ran** somewhere.
e. Next word. Touch and say the sounds. Get ready. (Tap 2 times.) *aaa   t.*
- What word? (Signal.) *At.*
f. Next word. Touch and say the sounds. Get ready. (Tap 2 times.) *mmm   EEE.*
- What word? (Signal.) *Me.*
g. Touch the picture that shows somebody who is saying, "A ram ran at me." ✔
h. Touch a boy or girl in the other picture. ✔
- That person could say something else. Start with the word **I,** and say what that person could say. (Call on a child. *I ran at a ram.*)

---

**WORKBOOK**

## EXERCISE 8

### COMPREHENSION
### Independent Sentence Writing

I ran at a ram.

 _____
_____ .

a. Close your textbook. Go to lesson 24 in your workbook and write your name. ✔
- Find the story pictures. ✔
- These are like the pictures that are in your textbook, but the words under the picture are different.
b. Read the words that are under the picture.
- Touch the first word. ✔
  What word? (Signal.) *I.*
- Next word. Touch and say the sounds. Get ready. (Tap 3 times.) *rrr   aaa   nnn.*
  What word? (Signal.) *Ran.*
  Yes, **I ran.**
- Next word. Touch and say the sounds. Get ready. (Tap 2 times.) *aaa   t.*
  What word? (Signal.) *At.*
- Next word. What word? (Signal.) *A.*
- Last word. Touch and say the sounds. Get ready. (Tap 3 times.)
  *rrr   aaa   mmm.*
  What word? (Signal.) *Ram.*
- Say the whole sentence. (Signal.) *I ran at a ram.*

c. (Repeat step b until firm.)
d. Touch the picture that sentence tells about. ✔
- There is no sentence for the other picture.
e. Touch the star below the picture. ✔
- Later, you can write a sentence on that line. The sentence will say: **A ram ran at me.** What will the sentence say? (Signal.) *A ram ran at me.*
f. Remember to start with a capital letter.

===== EXERCISE 9 =====

## STORY EXTENSION
### Sentence Writing

a. Find the pencil. ✔
- You're going to write part of the story on these lines.
- (Write on the board:)

$$\underline{A \quad ram \quad ran.}$$

- Here's a part of the story you just read. It says: **A ram ran.** You'll write that sentence two times.
b. Touch line 1. ✔
- Find the space for the first word. You'll write the word **A** in that space. It will be a capital **A.** Write capital **A** in the space for the first word. Pencils down when you're finished.
  (Observe children and give feedback.)
c. Touch the space for the next word. ✔
- Write the word **ram** in the space for the second word. Pencils down when you're finished.
  (Observe children and give feedback.)
d. Touch the space for the last word. ✔
- Write the word **ran** in the space for that word. Pencils down when you're finished.
  (Observe children and give feedback.)
e. Later, you can write the same thing on the line below. You'll write: **A ram ran.**
- Then you can color the pictures.

===== EXERCISE 10 =====

## SPELLING WORDS

### Oral

a. I'll say words. You'll say the sounds and spell them.
b. Listen: **an.** What word? (Signal.) *An.*
- Say the sounds in **an.** Get ready. (Tap 2 times.) *aaa    nnn.*
- Spell the word **an.** Get ready. (Signal.) *A-N.*
- Spell it again, and I'll write it on the board. Get ready. (Signal.) *A-N.*
- (Write on the board:)

| an |
|----|

c. New word. Listen: **for.** What word? (Signal.) *For.*
- Say the sounds in **for.** Get ready. (Tap 3 times.) *fff    OOO    rrr.*
- Spell the word **for.** Get ready. (Signal.) *F-O-R.*
- Spell it again, and I'll write it on the board. Get ready. (Signal.) *F-O-R.*
- (Write on the board:)

| for |
|-----|

d. New word. Listen: **fan.** What word? (Signal.) *Fan.*
- Say the sounds in **fan.** Get ready. (Tap 3 times.) *fff    aaa    nnn.*
- Spell the word **fan.** Get ready. (Signal.) *F-A-N.*
- Spell it again, and I'll write it on the board. Get ready. (Signal.) *F-A-N.*
- (Write on the board:)

| fan |
|-----|

e. New word. Listen: **at.** What word? (Signal.) *At.*
- Say the sounds in **at.** Get ready. (Tap 2 times.) *aaa    t.*
- Spell the word **at.** Get ready. (Signal.) *A-T.*
- Spell it again, and I'll write it on the board. Get ready. (Signal.) *A-T.*

- (Write on the board:)

| at |
|:---:|

**Written**
f. (Erase the board.)
g. Find the bunny. ✔
- Your turn to write the words we just spelled.
h. Touch line 1. ✔
- Write the word **an** on line 1. Pencils down when you're finished.
(Observe children and give feedback.)
- (Write on the board:)

| 1. an |
|:---:|

- Here's what you should have. **An** is spelled **A-N.**
i. Touch line 2. ✔
- Write the word **at** on line 2. Pencils down when you're finished.
(Observe children and give feedback.)
- (Write on the board:)

| 2. at |
|:---:|

- Here's what you should have. **At** is spelled **A-T.**
j. Touch line 3. ✔
- Write the word **fan** on line 3. Pencils down when you're finished.
(Observe children and give feedback.)
- (Write on the board:)

| 3. fan |
|:---:|

- Here's what you should have. **Fan** is spelled **F-A-N.**
k. Touch line 4. ✔
- Write the word **for** on line 4. Pencils down when you're finished.
(Observe children and give feedback.)

- (Write on the board:)

| 4. for |
|:---:|

- Here's what you should have. **For** is spelled **F-O-R.**
l. Raise your hand if you got everything right.
- You're spelling and writing some hard words.

================= EXERCISE 11 =================
**INDEPENDENT WORK**

**Matching: Letters and Combinations**
a. Find the matching game. ✔
- You'll draw lines to show letters that are the same and letter combinations that are the same. The combinations are not shown with blue letters.

**Hidden Picture**

> **Note:** Each child needs a red and a blue crayon.

b. Find the hidden picture. ✔
- I'll tell you the coloring rules. You'll need a blue crayon and a red crayon.
c. Touch the box for the combination **O-A** at the top of the picture.
- Here's the rule for combination **O-A:** All the parts of the picture that have **O-A** are red. Make a red mark in the box for **O-A.** Raise your hand when you're finished.
(Observe children and give feedback.)
d. Here's the rule for combination **A-I:** All parts of the picture that have **A-I** are blue. Make a blue mark in the box for **A-I.** Raise your hand when you're finished.
e. Later, you can color the whole picture.

## LINED PAPER
### ━━━━ EXERCISE 12 ━━━━
## LETTER PRINTING

a. (Write on the board:)

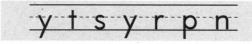

b. Get ready to write on lined paper. ✔
- Touch the top line. ✔
- The letter you'll write on that line makes the sound **p**. What sound? (Signal.) *p.*
- Which letter makes that sound? (Signal.) *P.*
- Write **P**. Pencils down when you're finished.
  (Observe children and give feedback.)
c. Touch the next line. ✔
- The letter you'll write on that line makes the sound **sss** in some words. What sound? (Signal.) *sss.*
- What letter makes that sound? (Signal.) *S.*

- Write the letter for **sss**. Pencils down when you're finished.
  (Observe children and give feedback.)
d. Touch the next line. ✔
- The letter you'll write on that line makes the sound **t** in words. What sound? (Signal.) *t.*
- Write the letter for **t**. Pencils down when you're finished.
  (Observe children and give feedback.)
e. Later, you'll complete the lines of letters.

**Independent Work Summary**
- Write appropriate sentence (**A ram ran at me**) under story picture.
- Story extension (copy once more: **A ram ran**).
- Color story pictures.
- Matching game.
- Hidden picture (**oa**=red, **ai**=blue).
- Letter printing (finish lines of **p, s, t**).

**25**

**Materials:** Each child will need scissors, paste and lined paper.

━━━━━━ EXERCISE 1 ━━━━━━

## SAYING THE SOUNDS
### Blue-Letter Discrimination

a. You're going to say words a part at a time. Some of the words you'll say are spelled with a blue letter.
- If you say a letter name, the word has a blue letter.

b. Listen: **ran.** What word? (Signal.) *Ran.*
- Say **ran** a sound at a time. Get ready. (Tap 3 times.) *rrr   aaa   nnn.* Again. Get ready. (Tap 3 times.) *rrr   aaa   nnn.*
- Did you say a letter name? (Signal.) *No.*
- So does the word **ran** have a blue letter? (Signal.) *No.*

c. New word: **rain.** What word? (Signal.) *Rain.*
- Say **rain** a sound at a time. Get ready. (Tap 3 times.) *rrr   AAA   nnn.*
- Did you say a letter name? (Signal.) *Yes.* What letter name? (Signal.) *A.*
- You said a letter name. So does the word **rain** have a blue letter? (Signal.) *Yes.*

d. Listen: **tape.** What word? (Signal.) *Tape.*
- Say the sounds in **tape.** Get ready. (Tap 3 times.) *t   AAA   p.*
- Did you say a letter name? (Signal.) *Yes.* What letter name? (Signal.) *A.*
- You said a letter name. So does the word **tape** have a blue letter? (Signal.) *Yes.*

e. New word: **tap.** What word? (Signal.) *Tap.*
- Say the sounds in **tap.** Get ready. (Tap 3 times.) *t   aaa   p.*
- Did you say a letter name? (Signal.) *No.*
- So does the word **tap** have a blue letter? (Signal.) *No.*

f. New word: **pin.** What word? (Signal.) *Pin.*
- Say the sounds in **pin.** Get ready. (Tap 3 times.) *p   iii   nnn.*
- Did you say a letter name? (Signal.) *No.*

- So does the word **pin** have a blue letter? (Signal.) *No.*

g. Last word: **pine.** What word? (Signal.) *Pine.*
- Say the sounds in **pine.** Get ready. (Tap 3 times.) *p   III   nnn.*
- Did you say a letter name? (Signal.) *Yes.*
- What letter name? (Signal.) *I.*
- You said a letter name. So does the word **pine** have a blue letter? (Signal.) *Yes.*

h. I'll say the sounds for the words you just did. You tell me if the word has a blue letter.
- Listen: t   aaa   p. What word? (Signal.) *Tap.* Does **tap** have a blue letter? (Signal.) *No.*
- Listen: rrr   AAA   nnn. What word? (Signal.) *Rain.* Does **rain** have a blue letter? (Signal.) *Yes.*
- Listen: p   III   nnn. What word? (Signal.) *Pine.* Does **pine** have a blue letter? (Signal.) *Yes.*
- Listen: p   iii   nnn. What word? (Signal.) *Pin.* Does **pin** have a blue letter? (Signal.) *No.*
- Listen: rrr   aaa   nnn. What word? (Signal.) *Ran.* Does **ran** have a blue letter? (Signal.) *No.*
- Listen: t   AAA   p. What word? (Signal.) *Tape.* Does **tape** have a blue letter? (Signal.) *Yes.*

━━━━━━ EXERCISE 2 ━━━━━━

## READING SOUNDS
### Introducing T-H

a. I'll say words that have a new letter combination. Sometimes the combination is whispered. Sometimes it isn't.

b. Listen: **math.**
- I'll say the last sound in **math: ththth.** That's a whispered sound.
- Your turn: Say the last sound in **math.** Get ready. (Signal.) *ththth.*

c. New word: **them.** Here's the **first** sound in **them: ththth.** That's an out-loud sound.

d. Your turn: Say the first sound in **them.** Get ready. (Signal.) *ththth.*
- Say the last sound in **math.** Get ready. (Signal.) *ththth.*

e. (Repeat step d until firm.)

f. (Write on the board:)

**th**

- Here's the new combination. The letters **T-H** make the sounds in the words **math** and **them.**
- What do you write for the sound **ththth?** (Signal.) *T-H.*

**TEXTBOOK**

g. Open your textbook to lesson 25. Find the bumblebee. ✔
- (Teacher reference:)

**th  y  p  oa  t  th  ai**

- There is a letter or a combination on each flower. Let's help the bumblebee go from flower to flower.

h. Touch and say the sounds.
- First flower. Say the out-loud sound. Get ready. (Signal.) *ththth.*
- Next flower. Say the sound. Get ready. (Signal.) *III.*

i. Next sound. Get ready. (Signal.) *p.*
- (Repeat for remaining items.)

**Individual Turns**
- (Call on different children to identify one or two sounds.)
- Remember the new combination. You'll read it in a lot of words.

---

**EXERCISE 3**

**READING WORDS**

a. Find the mushroom. ✔
- (Teacher reference:)

**1. ear   2. an   3. oar   4. feet**

b. Word 1. Touch and say the sounds. Get ready. (Tap 2 times.) *EEE   rrr.*
- What word? (Signal.) *Ear.*

c. Word 2. Touch and say the sounds. Get ready. (Tap 2 times.) *aaa nnn.*
- What word? (Signal.) *An.*

d. Word 3. Touch and say the sounds. Get ready. (Tap 2 times.) *OOO   rrr.*
- What word? (Signal.) *Or.*

e. Word 4. Touch and say the sounds. Get ready. (Tap 3 times.) *fff   EEE   t.*
- What word? (Signal.) *Feet.*

f. (Repeat steps b through e until firm.)

**Individual Turns**
- (Call on different children to read one of the words.)

---

**EXERCISE 4**

**READING WORDS**
**AAA vs. aaa Discrimination**

a. Find the ladybug. ✔
- (Teacher reference:)

| 1. pan | 2. pane |
|--------|---------|
| 3. ate | 4. at |

- These words have the letter **A.** Some of these words have a blue letter at the end. Remember: If a word has a blue letter, the letter **A** says its name.

b. Touch word 1. ✔
  Does it have a blue letter? (Signal.) *No.*
  So does **A** say its name? (Signal.) *No.*
- Touch word 2. ✔
  Does it have a blue letter? (Signal.) *Yes.*
  So does **A** say its name? (Signal.) *Yes.*
- Touch word 3. ✔
  Does it have a blue letter? (Signal.) *Yes.*
  So does **A** say its name? (Signal.) *Yes.*
- Touch word 4. ✔

**25**

Does it have a blue letter? (Signal.) *No.*
So does **A** say its name? (Signal.) *No.*

c. Go back to word 1. ✔

• It doesn't have a blue letter. So what **sound** do you say for the letter **A?** (Signal.) *aaa.*

• Touch and say the sounds.
First sound. (Signal.) *p.*
Next sound. (Signal.) *aaa.*
Last sound. (Signal.) *nnn.*

• Say those sounds again. Get ready. (Tap 3 times.) *p   aaa   nnn.*

• What word? (Signal.) *Pan.*

d. Touch word 2. ✔

• Does it have a blue letter? (Signal.) *Yes.*
So what sound do you say for the letter **A?** (Signal.) *AAA.*

• Touch and say the sounds for the black letters.
First sound. (Signal.) *p.*
Next sound. (Signal.) *AAA.*
Last sound. (Signal.) *nnn.*

• Say those sounds again. Get ready. (Tap 3 times.) *p   AAA   nnn.*

• What word? (Signal.) *Pane.*
Yes, a window **pane.**

e. Touch word 3. ✔

• Does it have a blue letter? (Signal.) *Yes.*
So what do you say for the letter **A?** (Signal.) *AAA.*

• Touch and say the sounds for the black letters.
First sound. (Signal.) *AAA.*
Next sound. (Signal.) *t.*

• Say the sounds again. Get ready. (Tap 2 times.) *AAA   t.*

• What word? (Signal.) *Ate.*

f. Touch word 4. ✔

• Does it have a blue letter? (Signal.) *No.*
So what do you say for the letter **A?** (Signal.) *aaa.*

• Touch and say the sounds.
First sound. (Signal.) *aaa.*
Next sound. (Signal.) *t.*

• What word? (Signal.) *At.*

**Individual Turns**

• Figure out if you'll say **AAA** or **aaa,** then read the word.

• (Call on different children to read one or two of the words.)

═══════ EXERCISE 5 ═══════

**READING WORDS**
**AAA vs. aaa Discrimination**

a. Find the worm. ✔

• (Teacher reference:)

| 1. map   2. ta<u>i</u>l   3. fat |
| --- |

• All of these words have the letter **A.** Some of these words have a blue letter, so you say a letter name. Other words don't have a blue letter, so you don't say a letter name.

b. Word 1. Do you say a letter name? (Signal.) *No.*

• Touch and say the sounds. Get ready. (Tap 3 times.) *mmm   aaa   p.*

• Again. Get ready. (Tap 3 times.) *mmm   aaa   p.*

• What word? (Signal.) *Map.*

c. Word 2. Do you say a letter name? (Signal.) *Yes.*

• Touch and say the sounds. Get ready. (Tap 3 times.) *t   AAA   lll.*

• Again. Get ready. (Tap 3 times.) *t   AAA   lll.*

• What word? (Signal.) *Tail.*

d. Word 3. Do you say a letter name? (Signal.) *No.*

• Touch and say the sounds. Get ready. (Tap 3 times.) *fff   aaa   t.*

• Again. Get ready. (Tap 3 times.) *fff   aaa   t.*

• What word? (Signal.) *Fat.*

e. (Repeat steps b through d until firm.)

**Individual Turns**

• Figure out if you'll say **AAA** or **aaa,** then read the word.

• (Call on different children to read one or two of the words.)

## ═══ EXERCISE 6 ═══
### STORY READING

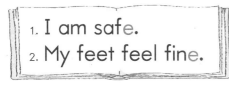

1. I am safe.
2. My feet feel fine.

a. Go to the next page. Find the picture of a book. ✔
• You're going to read the two sentences in the book.
b. Touch sentence 1. ✔
• First word. Everybody, what word? (Signal.) *I.*
• Next word. Touch and say the sounds. Get ready. (Tap 2 times.) *aaa   mmm.* Again. Get ready. (Tap 2 times.) *aaa   mmm.* What word? (Signal.) *Am.*
• Last word. Touch and say the sounds. Get ready. (Tap 3 times.) *sss   AAA   fff.* Again. Get ready. (Tap 3 times.) *sss   AAA   fff.* What word? (Signal.) *Safe.*
• Say all the words in sentence 1. (Signal.) *I am safe.*
c. Those words go with one of the pictures. Touch the first picture. ✔
• Do the bugs look like they are saying, "**I am safe**"? (Signal.) *No.*

• Find the best picture that shows somebody who could say, "**I am safe.**" ✔
• You should be touching the bottom picture. ✔
• The little fish looks like it could say, "**I am safe.**"
d. Touch sentence 2. ✔
• There are a lot of words in that sentence.
• First word. Touch and say the sounds. Get ready. (Tap 2 times.) *mmm   III.* What word? (Signal.) *My.*
• Next word. Touch and say the sounds. Get ready. (Tap 3 times.) *fff   EEE   t.* What word? (Signal.) *Feet.*
• Next word. Touch and say the sounds. Get ready. (Tap 3 times.) *fff   EEE   lll.* What word? (Signal.) *Feel.*
• Next word. Touch and say the sounds. Get ready. (Tap 3 times.) *fff   III   nnn.* What word? (Signal.) *Fine.*
e. Say all the words in sentence 2. (Signal.) *My feet feel fine.*
f. (Repeat step e until firm.)
g. One of the pictures shows somebody who could say, "**My feet feel fine.**" Touch that picture. ✔
h. Which of the people in the picture could say, "**My feet feel fine**"? (Call on a child. Ideas: *The girl; the one in front.*)
• What are the children walking on in that picture? (Call on a child. Idea: *Stones at a beach.*)
• Why do the girl's feet feel fine? (Call on a child. Idea: *Because she is wearing shoes.*)
• How do the boy's feet feel? (Call on a child. Idea: *Sore.*)
• Yes, I don't think it would be much fun to walk barefoot on those stones.

## WORKBOOK

### STORY EXTENSION
### Sentence Writing

a. Close your textbook. Go to lesson 25 in your workbook and write your name. ✔
• Find the picture of the shark and the fish. ✔
This is the same picture that was in your textbook.
b. You're going to write one of the sentences you just read.
• (Write on the board:)

## I am safe.

• Here's one of the sentences you just read. It says, **I am safe.**
• (Touch word **safe**.) The word **safe** is supposed to have a blue **E**, but we'll write it with a black **E.**
• You'll write that sentence two times.
c. Touch line 1 below the picture. ✔
• Find the space for the first word. ✔
• You'll write the word **I** in that space. It will be a capital **I.** Write capital **I** in the space for the first word. Pencils down when you're finished.
(Observe children and give feedback.)
d. Touch the space for the next word. ✔
• Write the word **am** in the space for the second word. Pencils down when you're finished.
(Observe children and give feedback.)
e. Touch the space for the last word. ✔
• Write the word **safe** in the space for that word. The word **safe** is always spelled with that **E** on the end. Pencils down when you've written the word **safe.**
(Observe children and give feedback.)
f. Later, you'll write the same thing on line 2. You'll write: **I am safe.**
• Then you'll color the picture.

### SOUNDING OUT vs. SPELLING

a. Find the dog. ✔
• (Teacher reference:)

| **1. mean   2. an** |
| --- |

• Remember: When you spell, you say the letter names. When you say the sounds, that's not spelling. That's part of reading.
b. Touch word 1. ✔
Tell me if I say the sounds or spell. Follow along.
• My turn: **M-E-A-N.** Did I say the sounds or spell? (Signal.) *Spell.*
• My turn again: **mmm   EEE   nnn.** Did I say the sounds or spell? (Signal.) *Say the sounds.*
• Your turn to **spell** word 1. Remember, say the letter names. Get ready. (Tap 4 times.) *M-E-A-N.*
• Did you say the sounds or spell? (Signal.) *Spell.*
• Now touch and say the sounds. Get ready. (Tap 3 times.) *mmm   EEE   nnn.*
• Did you say the sounds or spell? (Signal.) *Say the sounds.*
• Raise your hand when you know word 1. Everybody, what word? (Signal.) *Mean.*
• Good reading.
c. Word 2. Tell me if I say the sounds or spell: **A-N.** Did I say the sounds or spell? (Signal.) *Spell.*
• My turn again: **aaa   nnn.** Did I say the sounds or spell? (Signal.) *Say the sounds.*
• Your turn to **spell** the word. Get ready. (Tap 2 times.) *A-N.*
• Now touch and say the sounds. Get ready. (Tap 2 times.) *aaa   nnn.*
• What word did you sound out? (Signal.) *An.*

### Individual Turns
• (Call on different children to spell word 2 and then say the sounds for word 2.)

═══════ EXERCISE 9 ═══════

## SPELLING WORDS

### Oral

a. I'll say words. You'll say the sounds and spell them.
b. Listen: **at.** What word? (Signal.) *At.*
- Say the sounds in **at.** Get ready. (Tap 2 times.) *aaa    t.*
- Spell the word **at,** and I'll write it on the board. (Signal.) *A-T.*
- (Write on the board:)

| **at** |
|---|

c. New word. Listen: **fat.** What word? (Signal.) *Fat.*
- Say the sounds in **fat.** Get ready. (Tap 3 times.) *fff    aaa    t.*
- Spell the word **fat,** and I'll write it on the board. (Signal.) *F-A-T.*
- (Write on the board:)

| **fat** |
|---|

d. New word. Listen: **or.** What word? (Signal.) *Or.*
- Say the sounds in **or.** Get ready. (Tap 2 times.) *OOO    rrr.*
- Spell the word **or,** and I'll write it on the board. (Signal.) *O-R.*
- (Write on the board:)

| **or** |
|---|

e. New word. Listen: **an.** What word? (Signal.) *An.*
- Say the sounds in **an.** Get ready. (Tap 2 times.) *aaa    nnn.*
- Spell the word **an,** and I'll write it on the board. (Signal.) *A-N.*
- (Write on the board:)

| **an** |
|---|

f. Everybody, read the words that are on the board.
- First word. What word? (Signal.) *At.*
- Next word. What word? (Signal.) *Fat.*
- Next word. What word? (Signal.) *Or.*
- Last word. What word? (Signal.) *An.*

### Individual Turns

- (Call on different children to spell one of the words on the board.)
- You're spelling words. Good for you.

### Written

g. (Erase the board.)
h. Find the hamburger. ✔
- Your turn to write the words we just spelled.
i. Touch line 1. ✔
- Write the word **fat** on line 1. Pencils down when you're finished. (Observe children and give feedback.)
- (Write on the board:)

| **1. fat** |
|---|

- Here's what you should have. **Fat** is spelled **F-A-T.**
j. Touch line 2. ✔
- Write the word **at** on line 2. Pencils down when you're finished. (Observe children and give feedback.)
- (Write on the board:)

| **2. at** |
|---|

- Here's what you should have. **At** is spelled **A-T.**
k. Touch line 3. ✔
- Write the word **an** on line 3. Pencils down when you're finished. (Observe children and give feedback.)
- (Write on the board:)

| **3. an** |
|---|

- Here's what you should have. **An** is spelled **A-N.**
l. Touch line 4. ✔
- Write the word **or** on line 4. Pencils down when you're finished. (Observe children and give feedback.)
- (Write on the board:)

| **4. or** |
|---|

- Here's what you should have. **Or** is spelled **O-R.**

m. Raise your hand if you got everything right.
- You're spelling and writing some hard words.

==========**EXERCISE 10**==========

**INDEPENDENT WORK**

**Matching: Capitals and Combinations**

a. Find the matching game. ✔
- The lines are already drawn for the combinations. You'll follow the lines to where the other combination should be and write it in that space. You'll draw lines to match the capital letters with the regular letters.

**Cross-Out and Circle Game**

b. Find the cross-out game. ✔
- You're going to cross out a word and circle a different word.
c. Raise your hand when you know the word you'll cross out. ✔
- Everybody, what word will you cross out? (Signal.) *Ear.*
- The little 3 means you'll cross out three words.
d. Raise your hand when you know which word you'll circle. ✔
- Everybody, which word will you circle? (Signal.) *At.*
- The little 3 means you'll circle three words.
e. Remember, cross out the word **ear** and circle the word **at.**

**Cut-Out: Words**

*Note:* Each child will need scissors and paste.

f. Find the pictures at the bottom of the page. ✔
- Touch the first picture. ✔
- What's in that picture? (Signal.) *An ear.*
- In the picture next to the **ear** is a **pan.** Below the **ear** are **feet.**
- What's in the last picture? (Signal.) *Tail.*

g. The words at the bottom of the page tell about the pictures. You'll read those words to yourself, cut them out, and paste them under the right pictures.

==========**EXERCISE 11**==========

**TAKE HOME**

a. Go to the next page in your workbook. ✔
- (Remove perforated story sheet. Direct children to fold sheet so the title, *A Fan,* is the cover page.)
b. This is like a story you read before. The first page is the title of the story. (Call on a child to read the title. *A Fan.*)
c. Turn to the next page. ✔
- Read what it says in the picture. (Call on a child. *A man. A fan.*)
d. On the next page, an ant is saying something. Read what that is. (Call on a child. *I see no man.*)
e. Turn to the last page. ✔
- The farmer is saying something in that picture. Read what he says. (Call on a child. *My fan ran.*)
f. You can color this book and take it home to read to your family. I think they'll like it.
g. (Check out each child on reading the entire story.)

**LINED PAPER**
==========**EXERCISE 12**==========

**LETTER PRINTING**

a. (Write on the board:)

p   oa   ai   ea   y

b. Get ready to write on lined paper. ✔
- The letter combination you'll write on the first line makes the sound **AAA** in some words. What sound? (Signal.) *AAA.*
- That combination is on the board.

- Which letter combination makes that sound? (Signal.) *A-I.*
- I'll show you how to write **A-I.**
- (Trace **ai.**)
- Write the letter combination for **AAA.** Pencils down when you're finished.
(Observe children and give feedback.)

c. Write **A-I** again. Remember to leave a space after the first **A-I.** ✔

d. Touch the next line. ✔

- The letter combination you'll write on the next line makes the sound **OOO** in some words. What sound? (Signal.) *OOO.*
- Which letter combination makes that sound? (Signal.) *O-A.*
- I'll show you how to write **O-A.**
- (Trace **oa.**)
- Write the letter combination for **OOO.** Pencils down when you're finished.
(Observe children and give feedback.)

e. Write **O-A** again. Remember to leave a space after the first **O-A.** ✔

f. Touch the next line. ✔

- The letter you'll write on that line makes the sound **p** in words. What sound? (Signal.) *p.*
- Write the letter for **p.** Pencils down when you're finished.
(Observe children and give feedback.)

g. Later, you'll complete the lines.

**Independent Work Summary**

*Note:* Check out each child on reading *A Fan.*

- Story extension (copy once more: **I am safe.**)
- Color story picture.
- Matching game.
- Cross-out (**ear**=3) and circle (**at**=3) game.
- Cut-out game.
- Color and take home *A Fan.*
- Letter printing (finish lines of **ai, oa, p**).

# 26

**Materials:** Each child will need scissors, paste and lined paper.

## TEXTBOOK

### EXERCISE 1
**READING SOUNDS**

a. Open your textbook to lesson 26. Find the box at the top of the page. ✔
- (Teacher reference:)

| y i th ai p t th |
|---|

- These are letters and combinations. You'll tell me the sounds.
- First letter. Everybody, what sound? (Signal.) *III.*
- Next sound. Get ready. (Signal.) *III.*
b. Next sound. Get ready. (Signal.) *ththth.*
c. (Repeat step b for remaining items.)

**Individual Turns**
- (Call on different children to identify one or two sounds.)
d. This time, I'll say sounds for the green letters. You'll touch the letter or combination and tell me the name.
- (Teacher reference:)

| i th ai p t |
|---|

e. Listen: One of the green sounds is **ththth.** Touch it. ✔
- Everybody, spell what you are touching. Get ready. (Signal.) *T-H.*
f. Listen: One of the green sounds is **III.** Touch it. ✔
- Everybody, spell what you are touching. Get ready. (Signal.) *I.*
g. Listen: One of the green sounds is **AAA.** Touch it. ✔
- Everybody, spell it. Get ready. (Signal.) *A-I.*

h. Listen: One of the green sounds is **t.** Touch it. ✔
- Everybody, spell it. Get ready. (Signal.) *T.*
i. Listen: One of the green sounds is **ththth.** Touch it. ✔
- Everybody, spell it. Get ready. (Signal.) *T-H.*
j. Listen: One of the green sounds is **p.** Touch it. ✔
- Everybody, spell it. Get ready. (Signal.) *P.*
k. (Repeat steps e through j until firm.)

### EXERCISE 2
**READING WORDS**
**Mix**

a. Everybody, find the circle. ✔
- (Teacher reference:)

| 1. fly   2. near   3. feel   4. sat |
|---|

b. Word 1. Touch and say the sounds. Get ready. (Tap 3 times.) *fff   lll   III.*
- What word? (Signal.) *Fly.*
c. Word 2. Touch and say the sounds. Get ready. (Tap 3 times.) *nnn   EEE   rrr.*
- What word? (Signal.) *Near.*
d. Word 3. Touch and say the sounds. Get ready. (Tap 3 times.) *fff   EEE   lll.*
- What word? (Signal.) *Feel.*
e. Word 4. Touch and say the sounds. Get ready. (Tap 3 times.) *sss   aaa   t.*
- Again. Get ready. (Tap 3 times.) *sss   aaa   t.*
- What word? (Signal.) *Sat.*

**Individual Turns**
- (Call on different children to read one of the words.)

### EXERCISE 3
**READING WORDS**
**Blue-Letter Discrimination**

a. Find the triangle. It's next to the circle. ✔
- (Teacher reference:)

| 1. Sam   2. same   3. name   4. more |
|---|

- Some of these words have the letter **A**. Remember, if the word has a blue letter, the letter **A** says its name.
b. Word 1. Does it have a blue letter? (Signal.) *No.*
- Touch and say the sounds. Get ready. (Tap 3 times.) *sss    aaa    mmm.*
- Again. Get ready. (Tap 3 times.) *sss    aaa    mmm.*
- What word? (Signal.) *Sam.*
c. Word 2. Does it have a blue letter? (Signal.) *Yes.*
- Touch and say the sounds. Get ready. (Tap 3 times.) *sss    AAA    mmm.*
- Again. Get ready. (Tap 3 times.) *sss    AAA    mmm.*
- What word? (Signal.) *Same.*
d. Word 3. Does it have a blue letter? (Signal.) *Yes.*
- Touch and say the sounds. Get ready. (Tap 3 times.) *nnn    AAA    mmm.*
- Again. Get ready. (Tap 3 times.) *nnn    AAA    mmm.*
- What word? (Signal.) *Name.*
e. Word 4. Does it have a blue letter? (Signal.) *Yes.*
- Touch and say the sounds. Get ready. (Tap 3 times.) *mmm    OOO    rrr.*
- Again. Get ready. (Tap 3 times.) *mmm    OOO    rrr.*
- What word? (Signal.) *More.*
- Yes, you are reading **more** and **more.**

**Individual Turns**
- Remember what to say if there's a blue letter.
- (Call on different children to read one or two of the words.)

================ EXERCISE 4 ================

**SIMILAR WORDS**
**Blue-Letter Discrimination**

a. Find the square at the bottom of the page. ✔
- (Teacher reference:)

> 1. pal    2. pail    3. pile

- All these words have the letter **P**.
b. Word 1 doesn't have a blue letter. Touch and say the sounds. Get ready. (Tap 3 times.) *p    aaa    lll.*
- What word? (Signal.) *Pal.*
c. Word 2 has a blue letter. Touch and say the sounds. Get ready. (Tap 3 times.) *p    AAA    lll.*
- Again. Get ready. (Tap 3 times.) *p    AAA    lll.*
- What word? (Signal.) *Pail.*
d. Word 3. Touch and say the sounds. Get ready. (Tap 3 times.) *p    III    lll.*
- Again. Get ready. (Tap 3 times.) *p    III    lll.*
- What word? (Signal.) *Pile.*

**Individual Turns**
- (Call on different children to read one of the words.)

================ EXERCISE 5 ================

**STORY READING**

1. A fly sat ne͟a͟r me.
2. My feet feel sore.

a. Find the book. ✔
- These are the same pictures you had in the last lesson. You'll read the sentences

and find the right pictures.

b. Touch sentence 1. ✔

- First word. Everybody, what word? (Signal.) *A.*
- Next word. Touch and say the sounds. Get ready. (Tap 3 times.) *fff lll III.* What word? (Signal.) *Fly.*
- Next word. Touch and say the sounds. Get ready. (Tap 3 times.) *sss aaa t.* What word? (Signal.) *Sat.*
- Next word. Touch and say the sounds. Get ready. (Tap 3 times.) *nnn EEE rrr.* What word? (Signal.) *Near.*
- Next word. Touch and say the sounds. Get ready. (Tap 2 times.) *mmm EEE.* What word? (Signal.) *Me.*

c. Say all the words in sentence 1. (Signal.) *A fly sat near me.*

d. (Repeat step c until firm.)

e. Those words go with one of the pictures. Touch the picture that shows somebody who is saying, **"A fly sat near me."** ✔

- Who is talking? (Call on a child. Idea: *A ladybug.*)

f. Touch sentence 2. ✔

- First word. Touch and say the sounds. Get ready. (Tap 2 times.) *mmm III.* What word? (Signal.) *My.*
- Next word. Touch and say the sounds. Get ready. (Tap 3 times.) *fff EEE t.* What word? (Signal.) *Feet.*
- Next word. Touch and say the sounds. Get ready. (Tap 3 times.) *fff EEE lll.* What word? (Signal.) *Feel.*
- Yes, so far somebody is saying, **"My feet feel . . ."**
- Last word. Touch and say the sounds. Get ready. (Tap 3 times.) *sss OOO rrr.* What word? (Signal.) *Sore.*

g. Say all the words in sentence 2. (Signal.) *My feet feel sore.*

h. (Repeat step g until firm.)

i. One of the pictures shows somebody who is saying, **"My feet feel sore."** Touch that picture. ✔

- That's the same picture we had in the last lesson.
- Which person is saying, **"My feet feel sore"**? (Call on a child. Idea: *The boy.*)

**Second Reading**

- Let's read the sentences again. (Call on different children to read one or two words.)

========EXERCISE 6========

**STORY EXTENSION**
**Sentence Writing**

a. Close your textbook. Go to lesson 26 in your workbook and write your name. ✔

- You're going to write a sentence like one you just read.

b. (Write on the board:)

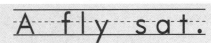

- (Call on a child to read the sentence.)

c. Touch line 1 above the picture. ✔

- Write all three words on line 1. Remember, the first letter is capital **A.** (Observe children and give feedback.)

d. Later, you'll write the same sentence on line 2: **A fly sat.**

========EXERCISE 7========

**STORY EXTENSION**
**Coloring**

a. Find the picture of the fly and the ladybug. ✔

- This is the same picture that was in your textbook.

b. Later, you can color the picture.

- Under the picture is a sentence you can read to your family.

========EXERCISE 8========

**SPELLING WORDS**

**Oral**

a. You're going to spell some words. Then you'll write those words.

b. Listen: **man.** Say the sounds in **man.** Get ready. (Tap 3 times.) *mmm    aaa    nnn.*
• Spell the word **man.** Get ready. (Signal.) *M-A-N.*
c. New word. Listen: **sat.** Say the sounds in **sat.** Get ready. (Tap 3 times.) *sss    aaa    t.*
• Spell the word **sat.** Get ready. (Signal.) *S-A-T.*
d. New word. Listen: **or.** Say the sounds in **or.** Get ready. (Tap 2 times.) *OOO    rrr.*
• Spell the word **or.** Get ready. (Signal.) *O-R.*
e. New word: **mat.** Say the sounds in **mat.** Get ready. (Tap 3 times.) *mmm    aaa    t.*
• Spell the word **mat.** Get ready. (Signal.) *M-A-T.*

## Written
f. Find the horse. ✔
• Your turn to write the words we just spelled.
g. Touch line 1. ✔
• Write the word **sat** on line 1. Pencils down when you're finished. (Observe children and give feedback.)
• (Write on the board:)

> **1. sat**

• Here's what you should have. **Sat** is spelled **S-A-T.**
h. Touch line 2. ✔
• Write the word **mat** on line 2. Pencils down when you're finished. (Observe children and give feedback.)
• (Write on the board:)

> **2. mat**

• Here's what you should have. **Mat** is spelled **M-A-T.**
i. Touch line 3. ✔
• Write the word **man** on line 3. Pencils down when you're finished. (Observe children and give feedback.)
• (Write on the board:)

> **3. man**

• Here's what you should have. **Man** is spelled **M-A-N.**

j. Touch line 4. ✔
• Write the word **or** on line 4. Pencils down when you're finished. (Observe children and give feedback.)
• (Write on the board:)

> **4. or**

• Here's what you should have. **Or** is spelled **O-R.**
k. Raise your hand if you got everything right.

═══════════════ EXERCISE 9 ═══════════════
## INDEPENDENT WORK

### Matching: Letter Combinations
a. Find the matching game. ✔
• I think that's an owl. These are letter combinations. The lines show where you'll write each combination. Remember to write the complete combination in each space.

### Cross-Out and Circle Game
b. Find the cross-out game. ✔
• The little boxes show what you'll circle and what you'll cross out.
c. Everybody, spell the combination you'll **circle.** (Signal.) *T-H.*
• Then you'll cross out a word. Raise your hand when you know that word.
• Everybody, what word? (Signal.) *My.*
d. Remember, circle **T-H.** Cross out the word **my.** The numbers tell you how many words you'll cross out and how many combinations you'll circle.

### Cut-Out: Words

> *Note:* Each child will need scissors and paste.

e. Find the box below the cross-out game. ✔
• There's a sentence in the box. (Call on a child to read the sentence. *My feet feel fine.*)
• The sentence says: **My feet feel fine.**

f. You'll cut out the pictures at the bottom of the page and put the words over the words in the box. Then you'll see the mystery picture.

---

**LINED PAPER**
**═══ EXERCISE 10 ═══**

## LETTER PRINTING

a. (Write on the board:)

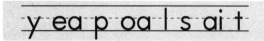

- Get ready to write on lined paper.
b. Touch the top line. ✔
- The letter you'll write on the first line makes the sound **III** in some words. What sound? (Signal.) *III.*
- Which letter on the board makes that sound? (Signal.) *Y.*
- Write **Y.** Pencils down when you're finished.
  (Observe children and give feedback.)
c. Touch the next line. ✔
- The letter combination you'll write on that line makes the sound **EEE** in some words. What sound? (Signal.) *EEE.*

- Spell the letter combination that makes the sound **EEE.** (Signal.) *E-A.*
- I'll show you how to write **E-A.**
- (Trace **ea.**)
- Write the letter combination for **EEE.** Pencils down when you're finished. (Observe children and give feedback.)
d. Write **E-A** again. Remember to leave a space after the first **E-A.** ✔
e. Touch the next line. ✔
- The letter you'll write on that line makes the sound **sss** in words. What sound? (Signal.) *sss.*
- Write the letter for **sss.** Pencils down when you're finished. (Observe children and give feedback.)
f. Later, you'll complete the lines of letters.

**Independent Work Summary**
- Story extension (copy once more: **A fly sat.**).
- Color story picture.
- Matching game.
- Cross-out (**my**=3) and circle (**th**=3) game.
- Cut and paste words in sentence order.
- Letter printing (finish lines of **y**, **ea**, **s**).

**Materials:** Each child will need a brown, a black and a green crayon and lined paper.

=EXERCISE 1=

**SOUNDS**
**Introducing d**

a. (Write on the board:)

**p   d**

- You know the sound for the letter **P.** The sound is the first part of the name. Say the name in two parts. Get ready. (Tap 2 times.) *p   EEE.*
- Say the first part of the name. Get ready. (Signal.) *p.*
b. The letter **D** works the same way. Say the name **D** in two parts. Get ready. (Tap 2 times.) *d   EEE.*
- Say the first part of the name. Get ready. (Signal.) *d.*
- That's the sound **D** makes in words.
c. Tell me the sound for the letter **P.** Get ready. (Signal.) *p.*
- Tell me the sound for the letter **D.** Get ready. (Signal.) *d.*
- Remember the sound for **D.**

**TEXTBOOK**

=EXERCISE 2=

**READING SOUNDS**

a. Open your textbook to lesson 27. Find the mouse. ✔
- (Teacher reference:)

| ai   t   y   p   th   oa   t   ea   th |

- That mouse looks like a detective. I think she's going to follow those footprints. Let's help her.
- These are letters and letter combinations.
- Touch the first combination. Say the sound. Get ready. (Signal.) *AAA.*

b. Next sound. Get ready. (Signal.) *t.*
c. (Repeat step b for remaining items.)

**Individual Turns**
- (Call on different children to identify one or two sounds.)

d. This time, I'll say sounds for the red footprints. You'll touch the letters or combinations and tell me the names.
- (Teacher reference:)

| ai   t   y   p   th   oa |

e. Listen: The sound for one of the red footprints is **t.**
- Touch that footprint. ✔
- Everybody, spell what's in the footprint you are touching. Get ready. (Signal.) *T.*
f. Listen: The sound for one of the red footprints is **ththth.**
- Touch that footprint. ✔
- Everybody, spell what's in that footprint. Get ready. (Signal.) *T-H.*
g. Listen: The sound for one of the red footprints is **p.**
- Touch it. ✔
- Everybody, spell it. Get ready. (Signal.) *P.*
h. Listen: The sound for one of the red footprints is **III.**
- Touch it. ✔
- Everybody, spell it. Get ready. (Signal.) *Y.*
i. Listen: The sound for one of the red footprints is **AAA.**
- Touch it. ✔
- Everybody, spell it. Get ready. (Signal.) *A-I.*
j. (Repeat steps e through i until firm.)

## EXERCISE 3

**READING WORDS**
**Words with T-H**

a. Find the monkey. ✔
• (Teacher reference:)

> 1. that
> 2. the
> 3. ma<u>th</u>

• These words have the new letter combination.
b. Word 1. Touch and say the sounds. Get ready. (Tap 3 times.) *ththth    aaa    t.*
• Again. Get ready. (Tap 3 times.) *ththth    aaa    t.*
• What word? (Signal.) *That.*
c. Word 2. Touch and say the sounds. Get ready. (Tap 2 times.) *ththth    EEE.*
• Again. Get ready. (Tap 2 times.) *ththth    EEE.*
• What word? (Signal.) *The.*
• Yes, we say **thuh.**
• Tell me the word that's spelled **T-H-E.** (Signal.) *The.*
d. Word 3. Touch and say the sounds. Get ready. (Tap 3 times.) *mmm    aaa    ththth.*
• Again. Get ready. (Tap 3 times.) *mmm    aaa    ththth.*
• What word? (Signal.) *Math.*
• Yes, you learn **math** in school.
e. (Repeat steps b through d until firm.)

**Individual Turns**
• (Call on different children to read one or two of the words.)
• You're reading words that have the combination **T-H.** Good for you.

## EXERCISE 4

**READING WORDS**
**Blue-Letter Discrimination**

a. Find the hippopotamus. ✔
• (Teacher reference:)

> 1. pail   2. pal   3. mole   4. late

• Some of these words have the letter **A.** Remember, if the word has a blue letter, the letter **A** says its name.
b. Word 1. Does it have a blue letter? (Signal.) *Yes.*
• Touch and say the sounds for the black letters. Get ready. (Tap 3 times.) *p    AAA    lll.*
• Again. Get ready. (Tap 3 times.) *p    AAA    lll.*
• What word? (Signal.) *Pail.*
c. Word 2. Does it have a blue letter? (Signal.) *No.*
• Touch and say the sounds. Get ready. (Tap 3 times.) *p    aaa    lll.*
• Again. Get ready. (Tap 3 times.) *p    aaa    lll.*
• What word? (Signal.) *Pal.*
d. Word 3. Does it have a blue letter? (Signal.) *Yes.*
• Touch and say the sounds for the black letters. Get ready. (Tap 3 times.) *mmm    OOO    lll.*
• Again. Get ready. (Tap 3 times.) *mmm    OOO    lll.*
• What word? (Signal.) *Mole.*
• Yes, a **mole** is an animal that lives underground.
e. Word 4. Does it have a blue letter? (Signal.) *Yes.*
• Touch and say the sounds for the black letters. Get ready. (Tap 3 times.) *lll    AAA    t.*
• Again. Get ready. (Tap 3 times.) *lll    AAA    t.*
• What word? (Signal.) *Late.*

**Individual Turns**
• (Call on different children to read one or two of the words.)

## EXERCISE 5

### STORY READING

a. Find the book. ✔
• (Teacher reference:)

> **1. I am a fly.**
>
> **2. I fly ne͟a͟r an e͟a͟r.**

• This is a story. A fly is telling this story.
b. Touch the first word on line 1. ✔
• Everybody, what word? (Signal.) *I.*
• Next word. Say the sounds. Get ready. (Tap 2 times.) *aaa    mmm.* What word? (Signal.) *Am.*
• Next word. What word? (Signal.) *A.*
• Last word. Say the sounds. Get ready. (Tap 3 times.) *fff    lll    III.* What word? (Signal.) *Fly.*
• Everybody, say all the words in sentence 1. Get ready. (Signal.) *I am a fly.* ✔
c. Touch the first word of sentence 2. ✔
• Everybody, what word? (Signal.) *I.*
• Next word. Say the sounds. Get ready. (Tap 3 times.) *fff    lll    III.* What word? (Signal.) *Fly.*
• Next word. Say the sounds. Get ready. (Tap 3 times.) *nnn    EEE    rrr.* What word? (Signal.) *Near.*
• Yes, so far the sentence says, **I fly near . . .**
• Next word. Say the sounds. Get ready. (Tap 2 times.) *aaa    nnn.* What word? (Signal.) *An.*
• Last word. Say the sounds. Get ready. (Tap 2 times.) *EEE    rrr.* What word? (Signal.) *Ear.*
• Everybody, say all the words in sentence 2. (Signal.) *I fly near an ear.*

## EXERCISE 6

### COMPREHENSION

a. The pictures show the fly telling the story.
• Touch picture 1. ✔

• That fly is looking right at us. We'll read what the fly is saying.
b. First word. What word? (Signal.) *I.*
• Next word. Say the sounds. Get ready. (Tap 2 times.) *aaa    mmm.* What word? (Signal.) *Am.*
• Next word. What word? (Signal.) *A.*
• Last word. Say the sounds. Get ready. (Tap 3 times.) *fff    lll    III.* What word? (Signal.) *Fly.*
• Say the whole sentence the fly is saying. Get ready. (Signal.) *I am a fly.*
c. Find picture 2. ✔

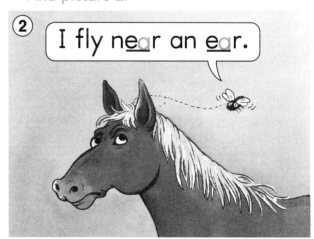

• Where is the fly in that picture? (Call on a child. Idea: *Near a horse's ear.*)
• We'll read what the fly is saying.
d. First word. What word? (Signal.) *I.*
• Next word. Say the sounds. Get ready. (Tap 3 times.) *fff    lll    III.* What word? (Signal.) *Fly.*

- Next word. Say the sounds. Get ready.
  (Tap 3 times.) *nnn   EEE   rrr.*
  What word? (Signal.) *Near.*
- Next word. Say the sounds. Get ready.
  (Tap 2 times.) *aaa   nnn.*
  What word? (Signal.) *An.*
- Last word. Say the sounds. Get ready.
  (Tap 2 times.) *EEE   rrr.*
  What word? (Signal.) *Ear.*
- Say the whole sentence the fly is saying.
  Get ready. (Signal.) *I fly near an ear.*

=========== EXERCISE 7 ===========

## WORD FINDING

a. Look at the words under picture 2.
   They're in a magnifying glass. ✔

- That's because we're going to play a find-the-word game.
- These are words from the story you just read. I'll read those words the fast way.
b. Touch the first word. ✔
- That word is **near.** What word?
  (Signal.) *Near.*
- Next word. That word is **ear.** What word?
  (Signal.) *Ear.*
- Next word. That word is **am.** What word?
  (Signal.) *Am.*
- Last word. That word is **fly.** What word?
  (Signal.) *Fly.*
c. I'll say words. You'll put your finger right over the word I name. Then, when I give you the signal, you'll touch the word. Let's see what good detectives you can be.
d. One of the words is **near.** Put your finger right over the word **near.** Don't touch it yet.

(Observe children and give feedback.)
- Everybody, touch the word **near.**
  (Signal.) ✔
- Good finding the word. Fingers up.
e. One of the words is **fly.** Put your finger right over the word **fly.**
   (Observe children and give feedback.)
- Everybody, touch the word **fly.** (Signal.) ✔
- Fingers up.
f. One of the words is **near.** Put your finger right over the word **near.**
   (Observe children and give feedback.)
- Everybody, touch the word **near.**
  (Signal.) ✔
- Fingers up.
g. One of the words is **am.** Put your finger right over the word **am.**
   (Observe children and give feedback.)
- Everybody, touch the word **am.**
  (Signal.) ✔
h. One of the words is **ear.** Put your finger right over the word **ear.**
   (Observe children and give feedback.)
- Everybody, touch the word **ear.** (Signal.) ✔
i. (Repeat steps e through h until firm.)

=========== EXERCISE 8 ===========

## STORY EXTENSION
### Sentence Writing

a. Close your textbook. Go to lesson 27 in your workbook and write your name. ✔
- Find the hamburger. ✔
- You're going to write part of the story on that line.
- (Write on the board:)

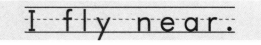

- (Call on a child to read the sentence.)
b. Write all three words on the top line. Remember, the first letter is a capital **I.** Pencils down when you're finished.

**(Observe children and give feedback.)**

c. Later, you can write the same sentence on the line below. You'll write: **I fly near.**

════════ EXERCISE 9 ════════

## STORY EXTENSION
### Coloring

a. Find the story picture. ✔
• Later, you can color the picture.
b. All the words from the story are under the picture. That's so you can read the whole story to your family.

════════ EXERCISE 10 ════════

## FOLLOWING DIRECTIONS
### Spelling

a. Find the tree trunk. ✔
• There's a column of words on the tree trunk.
• I'll tell you rules for the words. But I won't **say** the words. I'll **spell** the words.
b. The first rule is for the word that is spelled **R-A-T.** How is the word spelled? (Signal.) *R-A-T.*
• Here's the rule: The word that is spelled **R-A-T** should have a box around it. Fix up the word. Pencils down when you're finished.
**(Observe children and give feedback.)**
c. The next rule Is for the word that Is spelled **S-A-M.** How is the word spelled? (Signal.) *S-A-M.*
• Here's the rule: That word should be written under the picture. Find the place

under the picture of **S-A-M** and write it. Remember the capital **S.** Pencils down when you're finished.
**(Observe children and give feedback.)**
d. The last rule is for a word that is spelled **F-A-N.** Touch the word that is spelled **F-A-N.** ✔
• Here's the rule: There should be a picture of that thing in the empty box. Draw a picture of the thing that's spelled **F-A-N.** Draw it in the empty box. Pencils down when you're finished.
**(Observe children and give feedback.)**

════════ EXERCISE 11 ════════

## INDEPENDENT WORK
### Hidden Picture

***Note:*** Each child needs a brown, a black and a green crayon.

a. Find the hidden picture at the bottom of your worksheet. ✔
• I'll tell you the coloring rules for the picture.
b. Touch the box for the combination **E-A** at the top of the picture. ✔
• Listen: All the parts with **E-A** are brown. Make a brown mark for **E-A.** ✔
c. Touch the box for the combination spelled **T-H.** ✔
• All the parts with **T-H** are black. Make a black mark for **T-H.** ✔
d. Touch the combination spelled **A-I.** All the parts with **A-I** are green. Make a green mark for **A-I.** ✔
e. Later, you'll color the picture.

## LINED PAPER
### EXERCISE 12

## LETTER PRINTING

a. (Write on the board:)

e oa a i ai ea o

- Get ready to write on lined paper.
b. You're going to write some letter combinations that make the same sound.
c. Touch the top line. ✔
- You'll write the letter combination that makes the sound **EEE**. What sound? (Signal.) *EEE.*
- Which letter combination makes that sound? (Signal.) *E-A.*
- Write the letter combination for **EEE**. Pencils down when you're finished. (Observe children and give feedback.)
d. Touch the next line. ✔
- You'll write the letter that makes the sound **EEE**. Which letter makes that sound? (Signal.) *E.*
- Write the letter for **EEE**. Pencils down when you're finished. (Observe children and give feedback.)

e. Touch the next line. ✔
- You'll write the letter combination that makes the sound **AAA**. What sound? (Signal.) *AAA.*
- Which letter combination makes that sound? (Signal.) *A-I.*
- Write the letter combination for **AAA**. Pencils down when you're finished. (Observe children and give feedback.)
f. Touch the next line. ✔
- You'll write the letter that makes the sound **AAA**. Which letter makes that sound? (Signal.) *A.*
- Write the letter for **AAA**. Pencils down when you're finished. (Observe children and give feedback.)
g. Later, you'll complete the rows.

**Independent Work Summary**
- Story extension (copy once more: **I fly near.**).
- Color story picture.
- Hidden picture (**th**=black, **ai**=green, **ea**=brown).
- Letter printing (finish lines of **ea**, **e**, **ai**, **a**).

**Materials:** Each child will need lined paper.

## TEXTBOOK

═══════ EXERCISE 1 ═══════

### SOUNDS

a. Last time, you learned a sound for the letter **D.** Remember, it's the first part of the letter name. Everybody, what sound does the letter **D** make? (Signal.) *d.*

b. Open your textbook to lesson 28. Find the crocodile. ✔
That crocodile is getting on a log.

• (Teacher reference:)

| d  t  p  i  r  d |
|---|

• Say the sounds for the letters on the crocodile.
• First letter. What sound? (Signal.) *d.*
• Next letter. What sound? (Signal.) *t.*

c. Next letter. What sound? (Signal.) *p.*
d. (Repeat step c for remaining items.)

e. I'll say words that are spelled with the letter **D.**
• **Mad.** What word? (Signal.) *Mad.*
• It has three sounds. Say the sounds in **mad.** Get ready. (Tap 3 times.) *mmm   aaa   d.*
• What word? (Signal.) *Mad.*

f. Next word: **did.** What word? (Signal.) *Did.*
• Say the three sounds in **did.** Get ready. (Tap 3 times.) *d   iii   d.*
• What word? (Signal.) *Did.*

g. New word: **add.** What word? (Signal.) *Add.*
• Say the sounds in **add.** Get ready. (Tap 2 times.) *aaa    d.*
• What word? (Signal.) *Add.*

h. New word: **road.** What word? (Signal.) *Road.*
• Say the sounds in **road.** Get ready. (Tap 3 times.) *rrr   OOO   d.*

• What word? (Signal.) *Road.*

i. Last word: **seed.** What word? (Signal.) *Seed.*
• Say the sounds in **seed.** Get ready. (Tap 3 times.) *sss   EEE   d.*
• What word? (Signal.) *Seed.*

j. In all those words, the sound **d** is spelled with the letter **D.**

═══════ EXERCISE 2 ═══════

### LETTER COMBINATIONS

a. Touch the log. ✔
• (Teacher reference:)

| ai   th   oa   ea |
|---|

• These are letter combinations.
b. Touch the first combination. ✔
There is a blue letter in that combination.
• First combination. What sound? (Signal.) *AAA.*
c. Next combination. What sound? (Signal.) *ththth.*
• Next combination. What sound? (Signal.) *OOO.*
• Last combination. What sound? (Signal.) *EEE.*

**Individual Turns**
• (Call on different children to identify one or two combinations.)

═══════ EXERCISE 3 ═══════

### READING WORDS
### Words with Blue E

a. Find the frog. ✔
I think that's a tree frog and it's sitting in a tree.
• (Teacher reference:)

| 1. mile   2. time   3. fine   4. pile |
|---|

• There are blue letters in these words, so you say the letter name for the letter **I.**
b. Word 1. Touch and say the sounds. Get ready. (Tap 3 times.) *mmm   III   lll.*
• What word? (Signal.) *Mile.*

- Yes, a **mile** is a pretty long distance. If you ran a **mile,** you'd be pretty tired.
c. Word 2. Touch and say the sounds. Get ready. (Tap 3 times.) *t   III   mmm.*
- What word? (Signal.) *Time.*
d. Word 3. Touch and say the sounds. Get ready. (Tap 3 times.) *fff   III   nnn.*
- What word? (Signal.) *Fine.*
e. Word 4. Touch and say the sounds. Get ready. (Tap 3 times.) *p   III   lll.*
- What word? (Signal.) *Pile.*

**Individual Turns**
- (Call on different children to read one or two of the words.)
- In all these words the letter **I** says its name. In some of the words you'll read soon, you'll learn another sound for the letter **I.**

════════════ EXERCISE 4 ════════════
**READING WORDS**

a. Find the tree that the frog's sitting on. ✔
- (Teacher reference:)

| 1. <u>th</u>e | 2. <u>th</u>at | 3. map |
|---|---|---|
| 4. name | 5. rope | 6. m<u>ea</u>l |

- Some of these words have the new letter combination **T-H.**
b. Word 1. Touch and say the sounds. Get ready. (Tap 2 times.) *ththth   EEE.*
- What word? (Signal.) *The.*
c. Word 2. Touch and say the sounds. Get ready. (Tap 3 times.) *ththth   aaa   t.*
- What word? (Signal.) *That.*
d. Word 3 does not have a blue letter. Touch and say the sounds. Get ready. (Tap 3 times.) *mmm   aaa   p.*
- What word? (Signal.) *Map.*
e. Word 4 has a blue letter. Touch and say the sounds. Get ready. (Tap 3 times.) *nnn   AAA   mmm.*
- What word? (Signal.) *Name.*
f. Word 5. Touch and say the sounds. Get ready. (Tap 3 times.) *rrr   OOO   p.*
- What word? (Signal.) *Rope.*

g. Word 6. Touch and say the sounds. Get ready. (Tap 3 times.) *mmm   EEE   lll.*
- What word? (Signal.) *Meal.*

**Individual Turns**
- (Call on different children to read one or two of the words.)

════════════ EXERCISE 5 ════════════
**STORY READING**

a. Find the book. ✔
- (Teacher reference:)

| 1. I rop<u>e</u> a ram. |
|---|
| 2. See my pal fly. |
| 3. I <u>ea</u>t a m<u>ea</u>l. |

- The person telling this story works at a wildlife park.
b. Touch the first word on line 1. ✔
  Everybody, what word? (Signal.) *I.*
- Next word. Say the sounds for the black letters. Get ready. (Tap 3 times.)
  *rrr   OOO   p.*
  What word? (Signal.) *Rope.*
- Next word. What word? (Signal.) *A.*
- Last word. Say the sounds. Get ready. (Tap 3 times.) *rrr   aaa   mmm.*
  What word? (Signal.) *Ram.*
c. Everybody, say all the words in sentence 1. Get ready. (Signal.) *I rope a ram.*
- (Repeat step c until firm.)
d. Touch the first word of sentence 2. ✔
  Everybody, say the sounds. Get ready. (Tap 2 times.) *sss   EEE.*
  What word? (Signal.) *See.*
- Next word. Say the sounds. Get ready. (Tap 2 times.) *mmm   III.*
  What word? (Signal.) *My.*
- Next word. Say the sounds. Get ready. (Tap 3 times.) *p   aaa   lll.*
  What word? (Signal.) *Pal.*
- Next word. Say the sounds. Get ready. (Tap 3 times.) *fff   lll   III.*
  What word? (Signal.) *Fly.*
e. Everybody, say all the words in sentence 2. (Signal.) *See my pal fly.*
- (Repeat step e until firm.)

f. Touch the first word in sentence 3. ✔
Everybody, what word? (Signal.) *I.*

- Next word. Say the sounds. Get ready.
(Tap 2 times.) *EEE    t.*
What word? (Signal.) *Eat.*
- Next word. What word? (Signal.) *A.*
- Last word. Say the sounds. Get ready.
(Tap 3 times.) *mmm    EEE    lll.*
Again. Get ready. (Tap 3 times.)
*mmm    EEE    lll.*
What word? (Signal.) *Meal.*

g. Everybody, say all the words in sentence
3. (Signal.) *I eat a meal.*
- (Repeat step g until firm.)

=========== EXERCISE 6 ===========

## COMPREHENSION

a. Now you're going to look at pictures of
the story.

b. Find picture 1. ✔

- What's happening in that picture? (Call
on a child. Idea: *The ranger is roping
a ram.*)
- Let's read the words the ranger is saying
in the picture.
- First word. What word? (Signal.) *I.*
- Next word. Say the sounds. Get ready.
(Tap 3 times.) *rrr    OOO    p.*
What word? (Signal.) *Rope.*
- Next word. What word? (Signal.) *A.*
- Last word. Say the sounds. Get ready.
(Tap 3 times.) *rrr    aaa    mmm.*

- Say the words the ranger is saying. Get
ready. (Signal.) *I rope a ram.*

c. Find picture 2. ✔

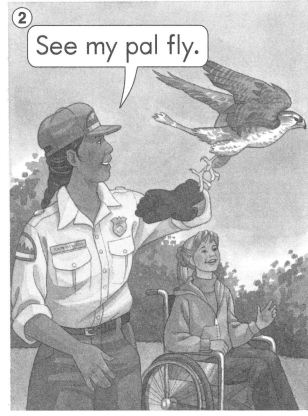

- What's happening in that picture? (Call
on a child. Idea: *The ranger is letting a
hawk fly.*)
- Let's read the words the ranger is saying.
- First word. Say the sounds. Get ready.
(Tap 2 times.) *sss    EEE.*
What word? (Signal.) *See.*
- Next word. Say the sounds. Get ready.
(Tap 2 times.) *mmm    III.*
What word? (Signal.) *My.*
- Next word. Say the sounds. Get ready.
(Tap 3 times.) *p    aaa    lll.*
What word? (Signal.) *Pal.*
- Last word. Say the sounds. Get ready.
(Tap 3 times.) *fff    lll    III.*
What word? (Signal.) *Fly.*
- Say the words the ranger is saying. Get
ready. (Signal.) *See my pal fly.*

d. Find picture 3. ✔

I e**a**t a m**ea**l.

- Let's read the words.
- First word. What word? (Signal.) *I.*
- Next word. Say the sounds. Get ready. (Tap 2 times.) *EEE    t.*
  What word? (Signal.) *Eat.*
- Next word. What word? (Signal.) *A.*
- Last word. Say the sounds. Get ready. (Tap 3 times.) *mmm    EEE    lll.*
  What word? (Signal.) *Meal.*
- Say the words the ranger is saying. Get ready. (Signal.) *I eat a meal.*
- Who is she talking to? (Call on a child. Idea: *Old man.*)

====== EXERCISE 7 ======

**WORD FINDING**

a. Look at the sentence in the magnifying glass. ✔
- (Teacher reference:)

> **I rope a ram.**

- We're going to play the find-the-word game again.
- I'll read the words the fast way.
b. Touch the first word. ✔
- That word is **I.**
- Next word. That word is **rope.** What word? (Signal.) *Rope.*
- Next word. That word is **a.**
- Last word. That word is **ram.** What word? (Signal.) *Ram.*
c. I'll say words. You'll put your finger right over the word I say. Then, when I give you the signal, you'll touch the word.

d. One of the words is **rope.** Put your finger right over the word **rope,** but don't touch it.
  (Observe children and give feedback.)
- Everybody, touch the word **rope.** (Signal.) ✔
- Good finding the word. Fingers up.
e. One of the words is **I.** Put your finger right over the word **I.**
  (Observe children and give feedback.)
- Everybody, touch the word **I.** (Signal.) ✔
- Fingers up.
f. One of the words is **ram.** Put your finger right over the word **ram.**
  (Observe children and give feedback.)
- Everybody, touch the word **ram.** (Signal.) ✔
- Fingers up.
g. One of the words is **a.** Put your finger right over the word **a.**
  (Observe children and give feedback.)
- Everybody, touch the word **a.** (Signal.) ✔
h. (Repeat steps d through g until firm.)

====== EXERCISE 8 ======

**STORY EXTENSION**
**Writing Words in Pictures**

a. Close your textbook. Go to lesson 28 in your workbook and write your name. ✔
b. Touch the picture of the ranger eating. ✔
- One of the sentences above that picture tells what she should say.
- Later, you'll write that sentence in the picture.
- Then you'll write what she is saying in the picture of her roping a ram.
c. After you write the sentences, you can color the pictures.

===== EXERCISE 9 =====

## SENTENCE WRITING

a. Find the ladybug at the top of side 2. ✔
• You're going to write a sentence.
• (Write on the board:)

The man ran.

b. Write all three words on the top line. Remember, the first letter is a capital **T.** Pencils down when you're finished.
(Observe children and give feedback.)
c. Later, you can write the same sentence on the line below. You'll write: **The man ran.**

===== EXERCISE 10 =====

## SPELLING WORDS

### Oral

a. You're going to spell some words. Then you'll write those words.
b. Listen: **an.** Say the sounds in **an.** Get ready. (Tap 2 times.) *aaa    nnn.*
• Listen: Spell the word **an.** Get ready. (Signal.) *A-N.*
c. New word. Listen: **am.** Say the sounds in **am.** Get ready. (Tap 2 times.) *aaa    mmm.*
• Listen: Spell the word **am.** Get ready. (Signal.) *A-M.*
d. New word. Listen: **at.** Say the sounds in **at.** Get ready. (Tap 2 times.) *aaa    t.*
• Listen: Spell the word **at.** Get ready. (Signal.) *A-T.*
e. New word: **ram.** Say the sounds in **ram.** Get ready. (Tap 3 times.) *rrr    aaa    mmm.*
• Listen: Spell the word **ram.** Get ready. (Signal.) *R-A-M.*

### Written

f. Find the pig. ✔
• Your turn to write the words we just spelled.
g. Touch line 1. ✔
• Write the word **at** on line 1. Pencils down when you're finished.

(Observe children and give feedback.)
• (Write on the board:)

**1. at**

• Here's what you should have. **At** is spelled **A-T.**
h. Touch line 2. ✔
• Write the word **am** on line 2. Pencils down when you're finished.
(Observe children and give feedback.)
• (Write on the board:)

**2. am**

• Here's what you should have. **Am** is spelled **A-M.**
i. Touch line 3. ✔
• Write the word **ram** on line 3. Pencils down when you're finished.
(Observe children and give feedback.)
• (Write on the board:)

**3. ram**

• Here's what you should have. **Ram** is spelled **R-A-M.**
j. Touch line 4. ✔
• Write the word **an** on line 4. Pencils down when you're finished.
(Observe children and give feedback.)
• (Write on the board:)

**4. an**

• Here's what you should have. **An** is spelled **A-N.**
k. Raise your hand if you got everything right.

**28**

═══════ **EXERCISE 11** ═══════

**INDEPENDENT WORK**

**Matching: Words**

a. Find the truck. ✔

• This is a matching game. You're going to draw lines to connect words that are the same.

b. Raise your hand when you can tell me the first word.

• Everybody, what's the first word? (Signal.) *Tan.*

• You'll find the word **tan** in the second column and draw a line to connect the words. Then you'll do the other words on your own.

**Cross-Out and Circle Game**

c. Find the cross-out game. ✔

• Raise your hand when you know the word you'll cross out.

• Everybody, what word will you cross out? (Signal.) *At.*

• How many will you cross out? (Signal.) *Four.*

d. Raise your hand when you know which word you'll circle.

• Everybody, which word will you circle? (Signal.) *Ate.*

• How many will you circle? (Signal.) *Four.*

e. You'll cross out the word **at** and circle the word **ate.**

LINED PAPER
═══════ **EXERCISE 12** ═══════

**LETTER PRINTING**

a. (Write on the board:)

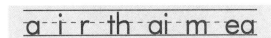

• Get ready to write on lined paper.

b. Touch the top line. ✔

• You'll write the letter combination that makes the sound **thththth.** What sound? (Signal.) *thththth.*

• What two letters make that sound? (Signal.) *T-H.*

• I'll show you how to write the combination **T-H.**

• (Trace **th.**)

• Write the letters for **thththth.** Pencils down when you're finished.
(Observe children and give feedback.)

c. Touch the next line. ✔

• You'll write the letter combination that makes the sound **AAA.** What sound? (Signal.) *AAA.*

• What two letters make that sound? (Signal.) *A-I.*

• I'll show you how to write the combination **A-I.**

• (Trace **ai.**)

• Write the letters for **AAA.** Pencils down when you're finished.
(Observe children and give feedback.)

d. Touch the next line. ✔

• You'll write the letter combination that makes the sound **EEE.** What sound? (Signal.) *EEE.*

• What two letters make that sound? (Signal.) *E-A.*

• I'll show you how to write the combination **E-A.**

• (Trace **ea.**)

• Write the letters for **EEE.** Pencils down when you're finished.
(Observe children and give feedback.)

e. Later, you'll complete the rows.

**Independent Work Summary**

• Story extension (write appropriate sentences in story pictures).

• Color story pictures.

• Sentence writing (copy once more: **The man ran.**).

• Matching game.

• Cross-out (**at**=4) and circle (**ate**=4) game.

• Letter printing (finish lines of **th, ai, ea**).

**Materials:** Each child will need scissors, paste and lined paper.

━━━━━━━ EXERCISE 1 ━━━━━━━

## SOUNDS
### Introducing iii

a. Listen: I'm going to say the word **sit** a sound at a time: **sss iii t.**
- Your turn: Say **sit** a sound at a time. Get ready. (Tap 3 times.) *sss iii t.*

b. New word: **if.** What word? (Signal.) *If.*
- Say **if** a sound at a time. Get ready. (Tap 2 times.) *iii fff.*

c. New word: **fin.** What word? (Signal.) *Fin.*
- Say **fin** a sound at a time. Get ready. (Tap 3 times.) *fff iii nnn.*

d. New word: **this.** What word? (Signal.) *This.*
- Here are the sounds: **ththth iii sss.**
- Say **this** a sound at a time. Get ready. (Tap 3 times.) *ththth iii sss.*

e. In all the words you just said, the sound **iii** is spelled with the letter **I.**
- What letter makes the sound **iii?** (Signal.) *I.*

### TEXTBOOK

f. Open your textbook to lesson 29. Find the tree. ✔
- (Teacher reference:)

| i a |
| --- |

- You know two sounds for each of these letters.

g. Touch the first letter. ✔
- Listen: Tell me the sound that **I** often makes when there is **no blue letter** in the word. Get ready. (Signal.) *iii.*
- Say the sound the letter makes when there **is** a blue letter in the word. Get ready. (Signal.) *III.*

h. Touch the next letter. ✔
- Tell me the sound that letter makes when there is **no blue letter.** Get ready. (Signal.) *aaa.*
- Tell me the sound that letter makes when there **is** a blue letter. Get ready. (Signal.) *AAA.*

i. Let's do those again.
- (Repeat steps g and h until firm.)

### Individual Turns
- (Call on different children to do these tasks for one of the letters:)

a. Say the blue-letter sound.
b. Say the other sound.

━━━━━━━ EXERCISE 2 ━━━━━━━

## READING WORDS
### Words with I as III

a. Find the house. ✔
- (Teacher reference:)

| pile time mile |
| --- |

- There are blue letters in these words, so you say the letter name for the letter **I.**

b. First word. Touch and say the sounds. Get ready. (Tap 3 times.) *p III lll.*
- What word? (Signal.) *Pile.*

c. Next word. Touch and say the sounds. Get ready. (Tap 3 times.) *t III mmm.*
- Again. Get ready. (Tap 3 times.) *t III mmm.*
- What word? (Signal.) *Time.*

d. Last word. Touch and say the sounds. Get ready. (Tap 3 times.) *mmm III lll.*
- Again. Get ready. (Tap 3 times.) *mmm III lll.*
- What word? (Signal.) *Mile.*

### Individual Turns
- (Call on different children to read one or two of the words.)
- In all these words, the letter **I** says its name. In some of the words you'll read soon, you say the other sound for the letter **I.**

## SOUNDS

a. Find the path to the house. ✔
• (Teacher reference:)

| t  p  d  r  d  y |
| --- |

• Say the sounds for these letters. First letter. What sound? (Signal.) *t.*
• Next letter. What sound? (Signal.) *p.*
b. Next letter. What sound? (Signal.) *d.*
c. (Repeat step b for remaining items.)
d. This time, I'll say sounds for the orange letters. You'll touch the letters and tell me the names.
• (Teacher reference:)

| t  p  d  r |
| --- |

e. Listen: The sound for one of the orange letters is **rrr.**
• Touch it. ✔
• Everybody, spell what you are touching. Get ready. (Signal.) *R.*
f. Listen: The sound for one of the orange letters is **p.**
• Touch it. ✔
• Everybody, spell what you are touching. Get ready. (Signal.) *P.*
g. Listen: The sound for one of the orange letters is **t.**
• Touch it. ✔
• Everybody, spell it. Get ready. (Signal.) *T.*
h. Listen: The sound for one of the orange letters is **d.**
• Touch it. ✔
• Everybody, spell it. Get ready. (Signal.) *D.*
i. (Repeat steps e through h until firm.)

## SIMILAR WORDS
### Words with D

a. Find the dog. ✔
• (Teacher reference:)

| 1. re<u>a</u>d    2. ro<u>a</u>d    3. dad |
| --- |

• These are words that have the letter **D.**
b. Word 1. Touch and say the sounds. Get ready. (Tap 3 times.) *rrr   EEE   d.*
• Again. Get ready. (Tap 3 times.) *rrr   EEE   d.*
• What word? (Signal.) *Read.*
• Yes, you read the word **read.**
c. Word 2. Touch and say the sounds. Get ready. (Tap 3 times.) *rrr   OOO   d.*
• Again. Get ready. (Tap 3 times.) *rrr   OOO   d.*
• What word? (Signal.) *Road.*
• Yes, the car went down the **road.**
d. Word 3. Touch and say the sounds. Get ready. (Tap 3 times.) *d   aaa   d.*
• Again. Get ready. (Tap 3 times.) *d   aaa   d.*
• What word? (Signal.) *Dad.*
e. Let's read those words again.
• Word 1. Touch and say the sounds. Get ready. (Tap 3 times.) *rrr   EEE   d.* What word? (Signal.) *Read.*
• Word 2. Touch and say the sounds. Get ready. (Tap 3 times.) *rrr   OOO   d.* What word? (Signal.) *Road.*
• Word 3. Touch and say the sounds. Get ready. (Tap 3 times.) *d   aaa   d.* What word? (Signal.) *Dad.*

**Individual Turns**
• (Call on different children to read one or two of the words.)

## READING WORDS
### Words with T-H

a. Find the ball. ✔
• (Teacher reference:)

| <u>th</u>at |
| --- |
| pa<u>th</u> |

• These words have the letter combination **T-H.**
b. Top word. Touch and say the sounds. Get ready. (Tap 3 times.) *ththth   aaa   t.*
• What word? (Signal.) *That.*

c. Bottom word. Touch and say the sounds. Get ready. (Tap 3 times.) *p    aaa    ththth.*
- Again. Get ready. (Tap 3 times.) *p    aaa    ththth.*
- What word? (Signal.) *Path.*
- Yes, we went down a **path.**
d. Good reading.

**Individual Turns**
- (Call on different children to read one or two of the words.)

━━━━━━━━ EXERCISE 6 ━━━━━━━━

## READING WORDS
### aaa vs. AAA Discrimination

a. Find the cat. ✔
- (Teacher reference:)

> **1. saf**e    **2. rat**    **3. map**    **4. nam**e

- These words have the letter **A.**
b. Word 1. Is there a blue letter? (Signal.) *Yes.*
- Say the sounds for the black letters. Get ready. (Tap 3 times.) *sss    AAA    fff.*
- What word? (Signal.) *Safe.*
c. Word 2. Is there a blue letter? (Signal.) *No.*
- Say the sounds. Get ready. (Tap 3 times.) *rrr    aaa    t.*
- What word? (Signal.) *Rat.*
d. Word 3. Is there a blue letter? (Signal.) *No.*
- Say the sounds. Get ready. (Tap 3 times.) *mmm    aaa    p.*
- What word? (Signal.) *Map.*
e. Word 4. Is there a blue letter? (Signal.) *Yes.*
- Say the sounds. Get ready. (Tap 3 times.) *nnn    AAA    mmm.*
- What word? (Signal.) *Name.*

**Individual Turns**
- (Call on different children to read one of the words.)

━━━━━━━━ EXERCISE 7 ━━━━━━━━

## STORY READING
### Lineation

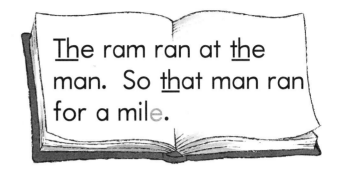

The ram ran at the man. So that man ran for a mile.

a. Find the book. ✔
- This is a story. It has two sentences. You're going to learn how to read sentences.
- Here's the rule: At the end of each sentence is a period. A period is just a little dot.
b. Touch the first word of the story. ✔ Now go all the way along the first line and stop.
- Touch the first word of the next line. That word is **man.** ✔
- Now go along the second line until you find that dot. Keep touching the period after you find it.
  (Observe children and give feedback.)
c. Touch the first word of the story again. ✔ You'll read all the words to the period. Those are the words in the first sentence.
d. First word. Touch and say the sounds. Get ready. (Tap 2 times.) *ththth    EEE.* What word? (Signal.) *The.*
- Next word. Say the sounds. Get ready. (Tap 3 times.) *rrr    aaa    mmm.* What word? (Signal.) *Ram.*
- Next word. Say the sounds. Get ready. (Tap 3 times.) *rrr    aaa    nnn.* What word? (Signal.) *Ran.* Yes, **the ram ran** somewhere.
- Next word. Say the sounds. Get ready. (Tap 2 times.) *aaa    t.* What word? (Signal.) *At.*
- Next word. Say the sounds. Get ready. (Tap 2 times.) *ththth    EEE.* What word? (Signal.) *The.*

- The next word starts with the letter **M.** Touch the word. Get ready.
(Tap 3 times.) *mmm   aaa   nnn.*
What word? (Signal.) *Man.*
- Where did the ram run? (Signal.) *At the man.*

e. I'll read that sentence. You touch the words. I'll read: **The . . . ram . . . ran . . . at . . . the . . . man.**

f. Everybody, say all the words in the first sentence. Get ready. (Signal.) *The ram ran at the man.*

g. (Repeat steps e and f until firm.)

h. Touch the first word of the next sentence. It begins with a capital **S,** right after the period.
(Observe children and give feedback.)

- The sentence starts with that word and goes to the next period.
- Go along the line and then down to the next line until you find the period.
(Observe children and give feedback.)

i. Go back to the word that begins with capital **S**. You'll read all the words in the sentence.

- (Teacher reference:)

---
**So that man ran for a mile.**
---

j. The first word is spelled **S-O.** Touch and say the sounds. Get ready.
(Tap 2 times.) *sss   OOO.*
What word? (Signal.) *So.*
- Next word. Say the sounds. Get ready.
(Tap 3 times.) *ththth   aaa   t.*
What word? (Signal.) *That.*
- Next word. Say the sounds. Get ready.
(Tap 3 times.) *mmm   aaa   nnn.*
What word? (Signal.) *Man.*
- Next word. Say the sounds. Get ready.
(Tap 3 times.) *rrr   aaa   nnn.*
What word? (Signal.) *Ran.*
- Touch the next word. It begins with the letter **F.** ✔
- Say the sounds. Get ready. (Tap 3 times.)
*fff   OOO   rrr.*
What word? (Signal.) *For.*
- Next word. What word? (Signal.) *A.*

- Next word. Say the sounds for the black letters. Get ready.
(Tap 3 times.) *mmm   lll   lll.*
What word? (Signal.) *Mile.*

k. Go back to the word **so.**
- I'll read all the words in that sentence. You touch the words: **So . . . that . . . man . . . ran . . . for . . . a . . . mile.**

l. Everybody, say that sentence.
(Signal.) *So that man ran for a mile.*

m. (Repeat step l until firm.)

n. That man ran pretty far, didn't he?
- I'm going to read the whole story to you. Touch the words as I read them. When I get to the end of a sentence, say "Stop."

o. Touch the first word. Listen and remember to tell me when to stop:
**The . . . ram . . . ran . . . at . . . the . . . man.** (Children say *Stop.*)
- Good saying **stop.** That's the end of the first sentence.
- Everybody, say the first sentence.
(Signal.) *The ram ran at the man.*

p. (Repeat step o until firm.)

q. The first word of the next sentence is **so.** Touch that word. ✔
- Listen and tell me when to stop: **So . . . that . . . man . . . ran . . . for . . . a . . . mile.** (Children say *Stop.*)
- Good saying **stop.** That's the end of the second sentence.
- Everybody, say that sentence.
(Signal.) *So that man ran for a mile.*

r. (Repeat step q until firm.)

=========== EXERCISE 8 ===========

**WORD FINDING**
**In the Story**

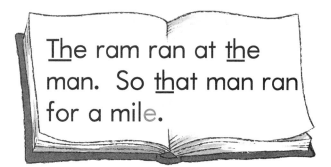

The ram ran at <u>the</u>
man.  So <u>that</u> man ran
for a mile.

a. Touch the first word of the story. ✔
Now you'll find words in the first sentence.

• Touch the period at the end of the first sentence. ✔

• Remember, part of the first sentence is on the second line. Don't get fooled.

b. Listen: One of the words is **ram.** What word? (Signal.) *Ram.*

• Put your finger right over the word **ram.** (Observe children and give feedback.)

• Everybody, touch the word **ram.** (Signal.) ✔

c. New word. Listen: One of the words is **man.** What word? (Signal.) *Man.*

• Put your finger right over the word **man.** (Observe children and give feedback.)

• Everybody, touch the word **man** in the first sentence. (Signal.) ✔ (Observe children and give feedback.)

d. New word. Listen: One of the words is **ran.** What word? (Signal.) *Ran.*

• Put your finger right over the word **ran.** (Observe children and give feedback.)

• Everybody, touch the word **ran.** (Signal.) ✔

e. (Repeat steps b through d until firm.)

• You're getting good at finding words.

===== **EXERCISE 9** =====

**COMPREHENSION**

a. Now you're going to look at pictures of the story.

• Find the first picture. ✔

The ram ran at the man.

• What's happening in that picture? (Call on a child. Idea: *Ram is running at man.*)

• Yes, I don't think he wants that ram to catch up to him.

b. The sentence under the first picture tells about that picture. You'll read the sentence.

c. First word. Say the sounds. Get ready. (Tap 2 times.) *ththth   EEE.* What word? (Signal.) *The.*

• Next word. Say the sounds. Get ready. (Tap 3 times.) *rrr   aaa   mmm.* What word? (Signal.) *Ram.*

• (Repeat for remaining words: **ran, at, the, man.**)

d. Say the sentence that tells about the picture. Get ready. (Signal.) *The ram ran at the man.*

e. Find the next picture. ✔

So that man ran
for a mile.

• What's happening in the picture? (Call on a child. Ideas: *Man and ram are still running hard; Ram is catching up to man.*)

• That man is really sweating, and that ram has its tongue hanging out.

- Why do you think the man and the ram look so tired? (Call on a child. Idea: *They ran for a mile.*)
f. You'll read the sentence under the picture.
g. First word. Say the sounds. Get ready. (Tap 2 times.) *sss   OOO.*
  What word? (Signal.) *So.*
- Next word. Say the sounds. Get ready. (Tap 3 times.) *ththth   aaa   t.*
  What word? (Signal.) *That.*
- (Repeat for remaining words: **man, ran, for, a, mile.**)
h. Say the sentence that tells about the picture. Get ready.
  (Signal.) *So that man ran for a mile.*
- How far did the man run?
  (Signal.) *A mile.*
- I hope the ram stopped chasing him after a mile.

**WORKBOOK**

━━━━━━ EXERCISE 10 ━━━━━━

**STORY EXTENSION**
**Writing Words in Pictures**

a. Close your textbook. Go to lesson 29 in your workbook and write your name. ✔
- Find the picture from the story. ✔
- Below the picture are sentences. The first sentence says: **The ram ran at the** something. What should that sentence say? (Signal.) *The ram ran at the man.*
- Touch the blank for the missing word in the sentence. ✔
- That should be the word **man.** What word? (Signal.) *Man.*
b. Touch the last sentence of the story. ✔ That sentence says: **So that man ran for a** something. What should that sentence say? (Signal.) *So that man ran for a mile.*
- Touch the blank for the missing word in the sentence. ✔
- That should be the word **mile.** What word? (Signal.) *Mile.*

c. You'll find the missing words above the picture. Read those words to yourself, and find the words that go in the sentences. Later, you can write the words where they belong and then read the story to your family.
- Remember to color the picture.

━━━━━━ EXERCISE 11 ━━━━━━

**SENTENCE WRITING**

a. Find the skunk. ✔
- You're going to write a sentence.
- (Write on the board:)

- (Call on a child to read the sentence.)
b. Write all four words on the top line. Remember, the first letter is a capital **I.** Pencils down when you're finished.
  (Observe children and give feedback.)
c. Later, you can write the same sentence on the line below. You'll write: **I rope a ram.**

━━━━━━ EXERCISE 12 ━━━━━━

**SPELLING WORDS**

**Oral**
a. You're going to spell some words. Then you'll write those words.
b. Listen: **so.** Say the sounds in **so.** Get ready. (Tap 2 times.) *sss   OOO.*
- Listen: Spell the word **so.** Get ready. (Signal.) *S-O.*
c. New word. Listen: **or.** Say the sounds in **or.** Get ready. (Tap 2 times.) *OOO   rrr.*
- Spell the word **or.** Get ready. (Signal.) *O-R.*
d. New word. Listen: **pan.** Say the sounds in **pan.** Get ready. (Tap 3 times.) *p   aaa   nnn.*
- Listen: Spell the word **pan.** Get ready. (Signal.) *P-A-N.*
e. New word: **me.** Say the sounds in **me.** Get ready. (Tap 2 times.) *mmm   EEE.*

- Spell the word **me**. Get ready. (Signal.) *M-E.*
f. Find the cat. ✔
- Your turn to write the words we just spelled.

**Written**

g. Touch line 1. ✔
- Write the word **me** on line 1. Pencils down when you're finished.
  (Observe children and give feedback.)
- (Write on the board:)

> **1. me**

- Here's what you should have. **Me** is spelled **M-E.**
h. Touch line 2. ✔
- Write the word **so** on line 2. Pencils down when you're finished.
  (Observe children and give feedback.)
- (Write on the board:)

> **2. so**

- Here's what you should have. **So** is spelled **S-O.**
i. Touch line 3. ✔
- Write the word **pan** on line 3. Pencils down when you're finished.
  (Observe children and give feedback.)
- (Write on the board:)

> **3. pan**

- Here's what you should have. **Pan** is spelled **P-A-N.**
j. Touch line 4. ✔
- Write the word **or** on line 4. Pencils down when you're finished.
  (Observe children and give feedback.)
- (Write on the board:)

> **4. or**

- Here's what you should have. **Or** is spelled **O-R.**
k. Raise your hand if you got everything right.

---

**EXERCISE 13**

**INDEPENDENT WORK**

**Cross-Out and Circle Game**
a. Find the cross-out game. ✔
- Raise your hand when you know the word you'll cross out. ✔
- Everybody, what word will you cross out? (Signal.) *My.*
b. Raise your hand when you know the word you'll circle. ✔
- Everybody, which word will you circle? (Signal.) *Me.*
c. You'll cross out the word **my** and circle the word **me.**

**Cut-Out: Words**

> **Note:** Each child will need scissors and paste.

d. Find the pictures at the bottom of the page. ✔
- Touch the first picture. ✔
  That is a pail.
- What's in the picture next to the pail? (Signal.) *Rope.*
- What's below the pail? (Signal.) *A fly.*
- What's in the last picture? (Signal.) *A rat.*
e. The words at the bottom of the page tell about the pictures. You'll read those words to yourself, cut them out, and paste them on the right pictures.

## LINED PAPER
### EXERCISE 14

**LETTER PRINTING**

a. (Write on the board:)

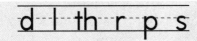

- Get ready to write on lined paper.
b. Touch the top line. ✔
- The letter you'll write on that line makes the sound **d** in some words. What sound? (Signal.) *d.*
- Get ready to tell me which letter on the board makes that sound.
- Everybody, which letter? (Signal.) *D.*
- I'll show you how to write **D.**
- (Trace **d.**)
- Write **D.** Pencils down when you're finished.
(Observe children and give feedback.)
c. Touch the next line. ✔
- The letter combination you'll write on that line makes the sound **ththth** in some words. What sound? (Signal.) *ththth.*
- What two letters make that sound? (Signal.) *T-H.*
- Write the letter combination for **ththth.** Pencils down when you're finished. (Observe children and give feedback.)

d. Touch the next line. ✔
- The letter you'll write on that line makes the sound **p** in words. What sound? (Signal.) *p.*
- What letter makes that sound? (Signal.) *P.*
- Write the letter for **p.** Pencils down when you're finished.
(Observe children and give feedback.)
e. Touch the next line. ✔
- The letter you'll write on that line makes the sound **sss** in words. What sound? (Signal.) *sss.*
- What letter makes that sound? (Signal.) *S.*
- Write the letter for **sss.** Pencils down when you're finished.
(Observe children and give feedback.)
f. Later, you'll complete the lines of letters.

**Independent Work Summary**
- Story extension (write missing words).
- Color story picture.
- Sentence writing (copy once more: **I rope a ram.**).
- Cross-out (**my**=4) and circle (**me**=4) game.
- Cut and paste words under appropriate pictures.
- Letter printing (finish lines of **d, th, p, s**).

Materials: Each child will need scissors and crayons.

**Note:** Administer WORD WRITING to the entire group. Individually administer WORD READING.

### TEST–Group Administered

#### Part 1: WORD WRITING

a. Open your workbook to lesson 30, test 3. ✔
   This is another test.
- Write your name at the top of the page. ✔
b. Find the dog. ✔
- You're going to write some words.
c. Touch line 1. ✔
- The word for that line is **pan.** What word? (Signal.) *Pan.*
- Say the sounds in **pan.** Get ready. (Tap 3 times.) *p aaa nnn.*
- Write the word on line 1. Pencils down when you're finished.
  (Observe children but do not give feedback.)
d. Touch line 2. ✔
- The word for that line is **or.** What word? (Signal.) *Or.*
- Say the sounds in **or.** Get ready. (Tap 2 times.) *OOO rrr.*
- Write the word on line 2. Pencils down when you're finished.
  (Observe children.)
e. Touch line 3. ✔
- The word for that line is **sat.** What word? (Signal.) *Sat.*
- Say the sounds in **sat.** Get ready. (Tap 3 times.) *sss aaa t.*
- Write the word on line 3. Pencils down when you're finished.
  (Observe children.)

### STORYBOOK
### Coloring

**Note:** Each child needs crayons.

a. While I'm listening to each child read, you can color the pictures on side 1 and side 2.
b. You have to write your name on the first page and draw a picture of yourself. Then you can read what the other pages say and color the pictures.

### TEST–Individually Administered

**Note:** Individually administer the rest of the test: WORD READING. Mark all errors. Record the test results on the Test Summary Sheet for test 3.

#### Part 2: WORD READING

a. Go to the top of side 2. ✔
b. Touch number 1. ✔
- Touch and say the sounds. [*rrr aaa t.*]
- What word? [*Rat.*]
c. Touch number 2. ✔
- Touch and say the sound for each black letter. [*lll OOO fff.*]
- What word? [*Loaf.*]
d. Touch number 3. ✔
- Touch and say the sounds. [*mmm aaa p.*]
- What word? [*Map.*]
e. Touch number 4. ✔
- Touch and say the sounds. [*t rrr lll.*]
- What word? [*Try.*]
f. Touch number 5. ✔
- Touch and say the sound for each black letter. [*sss AAA lll.*]
- What word? [*Sail.*]
g. Touch number 6. ✔
- Touch and say the sound for each black letter. [*nnn EEE rrr.*]
- What word? [*Near.*]

h. Touch number 7. ✔
• Touch and say the sounds.
  [*ththth    aaa    t.*]
• What word? [*That.*]
i. Touch number 8. ✔
• Touch and say the sound for each black
  letter. [*nnn    AAA    mmm.*]
• What word? [*Name.*]
j. Touch number 9. ✔
• Touch and say the sounds.
  [*fff    EEE    t.*]
• What word? [*Feet.*]
k. Touch number 10. ✔
• Touch and say the sounds.
  [*fff    OOO    rrr.*]
• What word? [*For.*]

══════════ EXERCISE 4 ══════════

## STORYBOOK
### Take Home

**Note:** Each child needs scissors.

a. (Remove perforated test sheet from
   workbook.)
b. (Direct children to cut along the dotted
   line.)
c. (Collect test part of sheets.)

d. (Direct children to fold their booklet along
   the fold line.)
e. Now you can take the storybook home
   and read it to your family.
f. (After testing all children, check out each
   child on reading the entire story.)

══════════ EXERCISE 5 ══════════

## MARKING THE TEST

• (Record all test results on the lesson 30,
  Test 3 Summary Sheet. Reproducible
  Summary Sheets are at the back of the
  Teacher's Guide.)

══════════ EXERCISE 6 ══════════

## TEST REMEDIES

• (Provide any necessary remedies for Test
  3 before presenting lesson 31. Test
  Remedies are discussed in the Teacher's
  Guide.)

══════════ EXERCISE 7 ══════════

## LITERATURE BOOK

• (See Teacher's Guide.)

**Materials:** Each child will need an orange, a green and a brown crayon and lined paper.

---

================= EXERCISE 1 =================

## SOUNDS
### S Ending Pronounced zzz

a. Some words end with the sound **zzz** that is spelled with the letter **S.**
- Listen: **is.** What word? (Signal.) *Is.*
- Say the sounds in **is.** Get ready. (Tap 2 times.) *iii   zzz.*
- The sound **zzz** is spelled with the letter **S** in that word.

b. New word: **was.** What word? (Signal.) *Was.*
- Say the three sounds in **was.** Get ready. (Tap 3 times.) *www   uuu   zzz.*
- The sound **zzz** is spelled with the letter **S** in that word.

c. New word: **as.** What word? (Signal.) *As.*
- Say **as** a sound at a time. Get ready. (Tap 2 times.) *aaa   zzz.*
- The sound **zzz** is spelled with the letter **S.**

## TEXTBOOK

================= EXERCISE 2 =================

## READING WORDS
### S Ending Pronounced zzz

a. Open your textbook to lesson 31. Find the apple. ✔
- (Teacher reference:)

| as |
|----|
| <u>thos</u>e |

- Both these words have an **S** that makes the sound **zzz.** That's the sound you'll say for the **S.**
- What sound will you say for **S?** (Signal.) *zzz.*

b. Top word. Touch and say the sounds. Get ready. (Tap 2 times.) *aaa   zzz.*
- Again. Get ready. (Tap 2 times.) *aaa   zzz.*
- What word? (Signal.) *As.*
- Yes, she was **as** fast **as** the wind.

c. Bottom word. Touch and say the three sounds. Get ready. (Tap 3 times.) *ththth   OOO   zzz.*
- Again. Get ready. (Tap 3 times.) *ththth   OOO   zzz.*
- What word? (Signal.) *Those.*
- Yes, **those** words are hard.

d. Let's read those words again.

e. (Repeat steps b and c until firm.)

**Individual Turns**
- (Call on different children to read one or both of the words.)

================= EXERCISE 3 =================

## SOUND DISCRIMINATION
### AAA vs. aaa and III vs. iii

a. Find the worm. ✔
- (Teacher reference:)

| a | i |
|---|---|

- You know two sounds for each of these letters.

b. Touch the first letter. ✔
- Tell me the sound that letter usually makes when there is **no** blue letter. Get ready. (Signal.) *aaa.*
- Say the sound that letter usually makes when there **is** a blue letter. Get ready. (Signal.) *AAA.*

c. Touch the next letter. ✔
- Tell me the sound that letter usually makes when there is **no** blue letter. Get ready. (Signal.) *iii.*
- Tell me the sound that letter usually makes when there **is** a blue letter. Get ready. (Signal.) *III.*

d. (Repeat steps b and c until firm.)

**Individual Turns**
- (Call on different children to do these tasks for one of the letters.)

a. Say the blue-letter sound.
b. Say the other sound.

═══════ EXERCISE 4 ═══════

## READING WORDS
### Words with iii

a. Find the leaf. ✔
• (Teacher reference:)

> **in**
> **sit**
> **did**

• These words have the letter **I,** but there are no blue letters. So what sound does the letter **I** make? (Signal.) *iii.*
b. Top word. Touch and say the sounds. Get ready. (Tap 2 times.) *iii nnn.*
• What word? (Signal.) *In.*
• Yes, I put it **in** a cup.
c. Middle word. Touch and say the sounds. Get ready. (Tap 3 times.) *sss iii t.*
• Again. Get ready. (Tap 3 times.) *sss iii t.*
• What word? (Signal.) *Sit.*
d. Bottom word. Touch and say the sounds. Get ready. (Tap 3 times.) *d iii d.*
• Again. Get ready. (Tap 3 times.) *d iii d.*
• What word? (Signal.) *Did.*
• Yes, you **did** it.

### Individual Turns
• (Call on different children to read one or two of the words.)

═══════ EXERCISE 5 ═══════

## READING WORDS
### Words with T-H

a. Find the little nut. ✔
That's an acorn.
• (Teacher reference:)

> **pa<u>th</u>**
> **<u>th</u>at**

• These words have the letter combination **T-H.**
b. Top word. Touch and say the sounds. Get ready. (Tap 3 times.) *p aaa ththth.*
• What word? (Signal.) *Path.*
c. Bottom word. Touch and say the sounds. Get ready. (Tap 3 times.) *ththth aaa t.*
• Again. Get ready. (Tap 3 times.) *ththth aaa t.*
• What word? (Signal.) *That.*

### Individual Turns
• (Call on different children to read one of the words.)

═══════ EXERCISE 6 ═══════

## READING WORDS
### Words with A

a. Find the pumpkin. ✔
• (Teacher reference:)

> **1. made   2. dad   3. and   4. ta<u>i</u>l**

• These words have the letter **A.**
b. Word 1. Is there a blue letter? (Signal.) *Yes.*
• Say the sounds for the black letters. Get ready. (Tap 3 times.) *mmm AAA d.*
• Again. Get ready. (Tap 3 times.) *mmm AAA d.*
• What word? (Signal.) *Made.*
c. Word 2. Is there a blue letter? (Signal.) *No.*
• Say the sounds. Get ready. (Tap 3 times.) *d aaa d.*
• What word? (Signal.) *Dad.*
d. Word 3. Is there a blue letter? (Signal.) *No.*
• Say the sounds. Get ready. (Tap 3 times.) *aaa nnn d.*
• Again. Get ready. (Tap 3 times.) *aaa nnn d.*
• What word? (Signal.) *And.*
• Yes, you **and** me.
e. Word 4. Is there a blue letter? (Signal.) *Yes.*
• Say the sounds for the black letters. Get ready. (Tap 3 times.) *t AAA lll.*

- What word? (Signal.) *Tail.*
f. Let's do those words again.
- Word 1. Get ready. (Tap 3 times.)
  *mmm  AAA  d.*
  What word? (Signal.) *Made.*
- Word 2. Get ready. (Tap 3 times.)
  *d  aaa  d.*
  What word? (Signal.) *Dad.*
- Word 3. Get ready. (Tap 3 times.)
  *aaa  nnn  d.*
  What word? (Signal.) *And.*
- Word 4. Get ready. (Tap 3 times.)
  *t  AAA  lll.*
  What word? (Signal.) *Tail.*

================= EXERCISE 7 =================

**STORY READING**

I see foam and
a tail.  I see no
soap near me.

a. Find the book. ✔
- This is a story. It has two sentences.
  Remember the name of the dot that is at
  the end of each sentence. Everybody,
  what's that dot called? (Signal.) *A period.*
b. Touch the first word of the story. ✔
- Now go all the way along the first line.
  Then go along the second line until you
  find the period. Keep touching it after you
  find it.
  **(Observe children and give feedback.)**
- You should be touching the period that is
  right before the word **I.**
c. Touch the first word of the story again. ✔
- You'll read all the words in the first
  sentence.
d. First word. What word? (Signal.) *I.*
- Next word. Say the sounds. Get ready.
  (Tap 2 times.) *sss  EEE.*
  What word? (Signal.) *See.*
- Next word. Say the sounds. Get ready.

(Tap 3 times.) *fff  OOO  mmm.*
Again. Get ready. (Tap 3 times.)
*fff  OOO  mmm.*
What word? (Signal.) *Foam.*
- Next word. Say the sounds. Get ready.
  (Tap 3 times.) *aaa  nnn  d.*
  What word? (Signal.) *And.*
- Yes, so far the sentence says, **I . . . see
  . . . foam . . . and** something else.
- Go to the beginning of the next line. What
  word? (Signal.) *A.*
- Last word. Say the sounds. Get ready.
  (Tap 3 times.) *t  AAA  lll.*
  What word? (Signal.) *Tail.*
- Go back to the first word of the story. ✔
  I'll read all the words in that sentence.
  You touch the words: **I . . . see . . .
  foam . . . and . . . a . . . tail.**
e. Everybody, say all the words in the first
  sentence. (Signal.) *I see foam and a tail.*
f. (Repeat step e until firm.)
g. Everybody, touch the first word of the
  next sentence. It's the word **I** right after
  the period. ✔
- You'll start with that word and read all the
  words to the next period.
h. First word. What word? (Signal.) *I.*
- Next word. Touch and say the sounds.
  (Tap 2 times.) *sss  EEE.*
  What word? (Signal.) *See.*
- Next word. Say the sounds. Get ready.
  (Tap 2 times.) *nnn  OOO.*
- What word? (Signal.) *No.*
- Go to the beginning of the next line. Say
  the sounds. Get ready. (Tap 3 times.)
  *sss  OOO  p.*
  What word? (Signal.) *Soap.*
- So far the sentence says: **I . . . see . . .
  no . . . soap.**
- Next word. Say the sounds. Get ready.
  (Tap 3 times.) *nnn  EEE  rrr.*
  What word? (Signal.) *Near.*
- Last word. Say the sounds. Get ready.
  (Tap 2 times.) *mmm  EEE.*
  What word? (Signal.) *Me.*
i. Everybody, say all the words in the last
  sentence.
  (Signal.) *I see no soap near me.*
j. (Repeat step i until firm.)

k. Does the person see any soap? (Signal.) *No.*

l. I'm going to read the whole story to you. Touch the words as I read them. When I get to the end of a sentence, say "Stop."

• Touch the first word. ✔

m. Touch the words and tell me when to stop: I . . . see . . . foam . . . and . . . a . . . tail. (Children say: *Stop.*)

• Good saying "Stop." That's the end of the first sentence.

n. Everybody, say that sentence. (Signal.) *I see foam and a tail.*

o. (Repeat step n until firm.)

p. The first word of the next sentence is I. Touch the word. ✔

• Touch the words and tell me when to stop: I . . . see . . . no . . . soap . . . near . . . me. (Children say: *Stop.*)

• Good saying "Stop." That's the end of the second sentence.

q. Everybody, say the second sentence. (Signal.) *I see no soap near me.*

r. (Repeat step q until firm.)

═══════ EXERCISE 8 ═══════

**WORD FINDING**

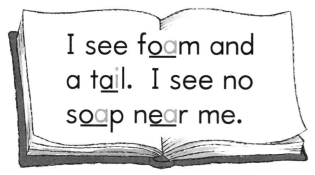

a. This time, you'll find words in the second sentence.

b. Listen: One of the words is **near.** What word? (Signal.) *Near.*

• Put your finger right over the word **near.** (Observe children and give feedback.)

• Everybody, touch the word **near.** (Signal.) ✔

c. Listen: One of the words is **soap.** What word? (Signal.) *Soap.*

• Put your finger right over the word **soap.** (Observe children and give feedback.)

• Everybody, touch the word **soap.** (Signal.) ✔

d. Listen: One of the words is **me.** What word? (Signal.) *Me.*

• Put your finger right over the word **me.** (Observe children and give feedback.)

• Everybody, touch the word **me.** (Signal.) ✔

e. (Repeat steps b through d until firm.)

f. You're getting good at finding words. You're going to see a picture of somebody who can't find soap and who sees a tail and foam.

═══════ EXERCISE 9 ═══════

**COMPREHENSION**

a. Find the first picture of the story. ✔

• This picture shows the girl who is telling the story.

b. Raise your hand when you can read the words that she is saying. (Call on a child to read. *I see foam and a tail.*)

• Touch the foam in the picture. ✔

• Touch the tail. ✔

• That's what things look like to the girl. Can you tell who the tail belongs to in that picture? (Signal.) *No.*

c. Touch the second picture. ✔

I see no soap near me.

- That picture shows the joke. From this side of the room, we can see who the tail belongs to. Who is that? (Signal.) *A dog.*
- We can also see something in the dog's mouth. What is that? (Signal.) *Soap.* Oh, dear.
- Raise your hand when you can read the words that she is saying in that picture. (Call on a child to read. *I see no soap near me.*)
- Does the girl see where the soap is? (Signal.) *No.*
- What is in the way of her seeing the dog? (Signal.) *Foam.*
- d. Sure, if you look at the first picture, you can't see a dog at all, just the tail. Those pictures show a pretty good joke.

**WORKBOOK**

====EXERCISE 10====
**STORY EXTENSION**
**Sentence Completion**

tail ✱ soap ✱ me

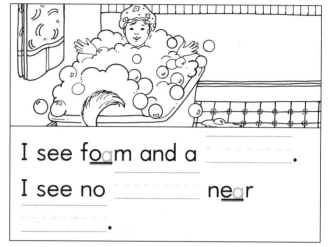

I see foam and a _____.

I see no _____ near

_____.

a. Close your textbook. Go to lesson 31 in your workbook and write your name. ✔
- Find the picture for the story. ✔
- Above the picture are words. Below the picture are sentences.
- b. The first sentence says **I see foam and a** something. What should that sentence say? (Call on a child. *I see foam and a tail.*)
- (Repeat step b until firm.)
- c. Touch the space for the missing word in that sentence. What word goes in the blank? (Signal.) *Tail.*
- d. Touch the last sentence of the story. ✔
- That sentence says, **I see no** something **near** something. What should that sentence say? (Call on a child. *I see no soap near me.*)
- Touch the space for the first missing word in that sentence. ✔
- That should be the word **soap.** What word? (Signal.) *Soap.*
- Touch the space for the other missing word in the last sentence. ✔
That should be the word **me.** What word? (Signal.) *Me.*

e. You'll find the missing words above the picture. Read those words to yourself, and find the words that go in the sentences.

• Later, you'll write the words where they belong. Then you can color the picture.

═══════ EXERCISE 11 ═══════

**INDEPENDENT WORK**

**Matching: Words**

a. Find the lunchbox. ✔

• This is a matching game.

• Later, you'll draw lines to connect words that are the same.

**Words for Pictures**

b. Go to side 2 of your worksheet and touch the first picture. ✔
What's that? (Signal.) *A mole.*

• Touch the picture next to the **mole.** ✔
That shows somebody who is **mad.**

• What's that below the **mole?**
(Signal.) *An ear.*

• What's in the last picture? (Signal.) *Rain.*

c. The words at the top of the page tell about the pictures.

• Later, you'll read the words and write them below the pictures they tell about.

**Hidden Picture**

*Note:* Each child needs an orange, a green and a brown crayon.

d. Find the hidden picture. ✔

• I'll tell you the coloring rules. You'll need an orange crayon, a green crayon and a brown crayon.

e. Touch the box for the combination **E-A** at the top of the picture. ✔

• Here's the rule for combination **E-A:** All parts of the picture that have **E-A** are green. Make a green mark in the box for **E-A.** Raise your hand when you're finished.
(Observe children and give feedback.)

f. Here's the rule for combination **A-I:**
All parts of the picture that have **A-I** are brown. Make a brown mark in the box for **A-I.** Raise your hand when you're finished.
(Observe children and give feedback.)

g. Here's the rule for the combination **T-H:**
All parts of the picture that have **T-H** are orange. Make an orange mark in the box for **T-H.** Raise your hand when you're finished.
(Observe children and give feedback.)

h. Later, you can color the whole picture.

═══════ EXERCISE 12 ═══════

**SPELLING WORDS**
**Words With Y**

a. You're going to spell some words that have the letter **Y.**

• Listen: **my.** Say the sounds in **my.** Get ready. (Tap 2 times.) *mmm    III.*

• The sound III is spelled with **Y.**

• Everybody, spell the word **my.**
(Signal.) *M-Y.*

• New word: **fly.** I'll say the three sounds:
**fff    III    III.**

b. Your turn. Say the sounds in **fly.** Get ready. (Tap 3 times.) *fff    III    III.*

• (Repeat until firm.)

c. **Fly** is spelled **F-L-Y.**

• Your turn. Spell **fly.** (Tap 3 times.) *F-L-Y.*

• Let's do that again. Say the sounds in **fly.** Get ready. (Tap 3 times.)
*fff    III    III.*

• Spell **fly.** (Tap 3 times.) *F-L-Y.*

d. New word: **me.** Say the sounds in **me.** Get ready. (Tap 2 times.) *mmm    EEE.*

• Everybody, spell the word **me.** (Tap 2 times.) *M-E.*

e. New word: **sat.** Say the sounds in **sat.** Get ready. (Tap 3 times.) *sss    aaa    t.*

• Everybody, spell the word **sat.** (Tap 3 times.) *S-A-T.*

## LINED PAPER

f. Now you'll write the words we just spelled. From now on, you'll write your sentences and spelling words on lined paper

• Write your name on your paper. Raise your hand when you're finished.

g. (Write on the board:)

> 1
> 2
> 3
> 4

• You'll number four lines on your paper. Start with the top line and write the number 1. Pencils down when you've done that much.
(Observe children and give feedback.)

• Write 2 on the next line and then number the other lines. Pencils down when you're finished.
(Observe children and give feedback.)

h. Touch number 1. ✔

• Word 1 is **fly.** Leave a little space after the number and write the word **fly.** Remember the letter you write for the **III** sound in that word. Pencils down when you've written the word **fly.**
(Observe children and give feedback.)

• (Write on the board:)

> **1 fly**

• Here's what you should have. **Fly** is spelled **F-L-Y.**

i. Touch number 2. ✔

• Write the word **my** on that line. Remember how the **III** sound is spelled in that word. Pencils down when you've written **my.**
(Observe children and give feedback.)

• (Write on the board:)

> **2 my**

• Here's what you should have. **My** is spelled **M-Y.**

j. Touch number 3. ✔

• Write the word **me** on that line. Pencils down when you're finished.
(Observe children and give feedback.)

• (Write on the board:)

> **3 me**

• Here's what you should have. **Me** is spelled **M-E.**

k. Touch number 4. ✔

• Write the word **sat** on that line. Pencils down when you're finished.
(Observe children and give feedback.)

• (Write on the board:)

> **4 sat**

• Here's what you should have. **Sat** is spelled **S-A-T.**

l. Raise your hand if you got everything right.

• You're spelling and writing some hard words.

═══════ EXERCISE 13 ═══════

## LETTER PRINTING

a. (Write on the board:)

> m r t p n d

• Turn to the back of your paper. ✔

b. On the top line you'll write the letter that makes the sound **d** in words. What sound? (Signal.) *d.*

• Get ready to tell me which letter. Everybody, which letter? (Signal.) *D.*

• Write the letter for **d.** Pencils down when you're finished.
(Observe children and give feedback.)

c. Touch the next line. ✔
• The letter you'll write on that line makes the sound **p** in some words. What sound? (Signal.) *p.*
• What letter makes that sound? (Signal.) *P.*
• Write the letter for **p.** Pencils down when you're finished. (Observe children and give feedback.)
d. Touch the next line. ✔
• The letter you'll write on that line makes the sound **t** in words. What sound? (Signal.) *t.*
• What letter makes that sound? (Signal.) *T.*
• Write the letter for **t.** Pencils down when you're finished. (Observe children and give feedback.)
e. Later, you'll complete the lines of letters.

━━━━━━━ EXERCISE 14 ━━━━━━━
**SENTENCE WRITING**
a. (Write on the board:)

I see no soap.

b. This is a sentence like one in the story. Raise your hand when you can read it. (Call on a child to read the sentence.)
c. Touch the next line on your paper. ✔
• Write all four words on that line. Remember, the first letter is a capital **I.** Make sure you leave a space after each word. Pencils down when you're finished. (Observe children and give feedback.)
d. Later, you can write the same sentence on the line below. You'll write: **I see no soap.**

**Independent Work Summary**
• Story extension (write missing words).
• Color story picture.
• Matching game.
• Write appropriate words for pictures.
• Hidden picture (**th**=orange, **ea**=green, **ai**=brown).
• Letter printing (finish lines of **d, p, t**).
• Sentence writing (copy once more: **I see no soap.**).

**Materials:** Each child will need lined paper.

## TEXTBOOK

### EXERCISE 1

**SOUNDS**
**Introducing A-Y**

a. Open your textbook to lesson 32. Find the mole. ✔
- (Teacher reference:)

| ay | y | d | t | p |
|---|---|---|---|---|

- I think that mole is trying to find his way back to the pile of dirt he made. Let's help him.
- There's a new letter combination. It's spelled **A-Y.** Touch that combination.
- This combination says **AAA.** There's a blue **Y,** so the **A** says its name.

b. What sound does the combination **A-Y** make? (Signal.) *AAA.*
- Touch the next letter. What sound? (Signal.) *III.*
- Next letter. What sound? (Signal.) *d.*
- Next letter. What sound? (Signal.) *t.*
- Last letter. What sound? (Signal.) *p.*

c. Go back to the first combination and say all the sounds.
- First sound. (Signal.) *AAA.*
- Next sound. (Signal.) *III.*
- Next sound. (Signal.) *d.*
- Next sound. (Signal.) *t.*
- Last sound. (Signal.) *p.*

### EXERCISE 2

**READING WORDS**
**Words with I**

a. Find the rabbit. ✔
- (Teacher reference:)

| 1. it | 2. pile | 3. pill |
|---|---|---|
| 4. time | 5. <u>th</u>is | |

These words have the letter **I.**
- Remember, if there's a blue letter in the word, you say the sound **III.**
- If there's not a blue letter, you say the sound **iii.**

b. Word 1. Does it have a blue letter? (Signal.) *No.*
So what do you say for the letter **I?** (Signal.) *iii.*
- Word 2. Does it have a blue letter? (Signal.) *Yes.*
So what sound do you say for the letter **I?** (Signal.) *III.*
- Word 3. Does it have a blue letter? (Signal.) *No.*
So what do you say for the letter **I?** (Signal.) *iii.*
- Word 4. Does it have a blue letter? (Signal.) *Yes.*
So what sound do you say for the letter **I?** (Signal.) *III.*
- Word 5. Does it have a blue letter? (Signal.) *No.*
So what sound do you say for the letter **I?** (Signal.) *iii.*

c. Go back to word 1.
It does not have a blue letter. So what do you say for the letter **I?** (Signal.) *iii.*
- Say the sounds for the letters.
First sound. (Signal.) *iii.*
Next sound. (Signal.) *t.*
- Say those sounds again. Get ready. (Tap 2 times.) *iii   t.*
- What word? (Signal.) *It.*
Yes, **it.** I found **it.**

d. Word 2. Does it have a blue letter? (Signal.) *Yes.*
So what do you say for the letter **I?** (Signal.) *III.*
- Say the sounds. Get ready. (Tap 3 times.) *p   III   lll.*
- Again. Get ready. (Tap 3 times.) *p   III   lll.*
- What word? (Signal.) *Pile.*

e. Word 3. Does it have a blue letter? (Signal.) *No.*

So what do you say for the letter **I?** (Signal.) *iii.*

- Say the sounds. Get ready. (Tap 3 times.) *p   iii   lll.*
- Again. Get ready. (Tap 3 times.) *p   iii   lll.*
- What word? (Signal.) *Pill.* Yes, **pill.**

f. Word 4. Does it have a blue letter? (Signal.) *Yes.*
  So what do you say for the letter **I?** (Signal.) *III.*

- Say the sounds. Get ready. (Tap 3 times.) *t   III   mmm.*
- Again. Get ready. (Tap 3 times.) *t   III   mmm.*
- What word? (Signal.) *Time.*

g. Word 5. Does it have a blue letter? (Signal.) *No.*
  So what do you say for the letter **I?** (Signal.) *iii.*

- Say the sounds. Get ready. (Tap 3 times.) *ththth   iii   sss.*
- Again. Get ready. (Tap 3 times.) *ththth   iii   sss.*
- What word? (Signal.) *This.*

**Individual Turns**

- (Call on different children to read one of the words.)

═══════ EXERCISE 3 ═══════

**SOUNDS**
**S Ending Pronounced zzz**

a. Some words end with the sound **zzz** that is spelled with the letter **S.**

b. Listen: **is.** What word? (Signal.) *Is.*

- Say **is** a sound at a time. Get ready. (Tap 2 times.) *iii   zzz.*
- The sound **zzz** is spelled with the letter **S** in that word.

c. New word: **these.** What word? (Signal.) *These.*

- Say **these** a sound at a time. Get ready. (Tap 3 times.) *ththth   EEE   zzz.*
- The sound **zzz** is spelled with the letter **S** in that word, too.

d. New word: **as.** What word? (Signal.) *As.*

- Say **as** a sound at a time. Get ready. (Tap 2 times.) *aaa   zzz.*
- The sound **zzz** is spelled with the letter **S** in that word.

e. New word: **those.** What word? (Signal.) *Those.*

- Say **those** a sound at a time. Get ready. (Tap 3 times.) *ththth   OOO   zzz.*
- The sound **zzz** is spelled with the letter **S** in that word.

f. Find the head of cabbage. It's next to the bunny. ✔

- (Teacher reference:)

| as |
|---|
| is |
| <u>thos</u>e |

- All these words have an **S** that makes the sound **zzz.** That's the sound you'll say for the **S.**

g. Top word. Touch and say the sounds. Remember to say **zzz.** Get ready. (Tap 2 times.) *aaa   zzz.*

- Yes, she was **as** fast **as** the wind.

h. Middle word. There's no blue letter. So what will you say for the letter **I?** (Signal.) *iii.*

- Touch and say the sounds. Get ready. (Tap 2 times.) *iii   zzz.*
- What word? (Signal.) *Is.*
- Yes, that **is** good reading.

i. Bottom word. Touch and say the sounds. Get ready. (Tap 3 times.) *ththth   OOO   zzz.*

- Again. Get ready. (Tap 3 times.) *ththth   OOO   zzz.*
- What word? (Signal.) *Those.*
- Yes, **those** words are hard.

j. (Repeat steps g through i until firm.)

**Individual Turns**

- (Call on different children to read a word.)

## EXERCISE 4

**READING WORDS**
   **Words with A**

a. Find the mouse. ✔
• (Teacher reference:)

| |
|---|
| **made** |
| **mad** |
| **ra̱i̱n** |

• These words have the letter **A.**
b. Top word. Is there a blue letter?
   (Signal.) *Yes.*
• Say the sounds for the black letters. Get
   ready. (Tap 3 times.) *mmm   AAA   d.*
• Again. Get ready. (Tap 3 times.)
   *mmm   AAA   d.*
• What word? (Signal.) *Made.*
c. Middle word. Is there a blue letter?
   (Signal.) *No.*
• Say the sounds. Get ready. (Tap 3 times.)
   *mmm   aaa   d.*
• Again. Get ready. (Tap 3 times.)
   *mmm   aaa   d.*
• What word? (Signal.) *Mad.*
d. Bottom word. Is there a blue letter?
   (Signal.) *Yes.*
• Say the sounds for the black letters. Get
   ready. (Tap 3 times.) *rrr   AAA   nnn.*
• Again. Get ready. (Tap 3 times.)
   *rrr   AAA   nnn.*
• What word? (Signal.) *Rain.*
e. Let's do those words again.
• Top word. Get ready. (Tap 3 times.)
   *mmm   AAA   d.*
• What word? (Signal.) *Made.*
• Middle word. Get ready. (Tap 3 times.)
   *mmm   aaa   d.*
• What word? (Signal.) *Mad.*
• Bottom word. Get ready. (Tap 3 times.)
   *rrr   AAA   nnn.*
• What word? (Signal.) *Rain.*

**Individual Turns**
• (Call on different children to read a word.)

## EXERCISE 5

**STORY READING**

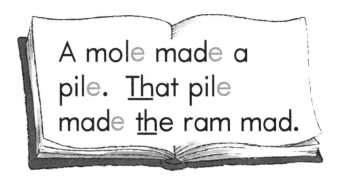

A mole made a
pile. T̲h̲at pile
made t̲h̲e ram mad.

a. Find the book. ✔
• Let's read another story. It has two
   sentences.
• Remember the name of the dot that is at
   the end of each sentence. Everybody,
   what's that dot called? (Signal.) *A period.*
b. Touch the first word of the story. Then go
   along the first line and keep going until
   you find the period. Keep touching it after
   you find it.
   (Observe children and give feedback.)
c. Everybody, touch the first word of the
   story again. You'll read all the words in
   the first sentence.
• First word. What word? (Signal.) *A.*
• Next word. Touch and say the sounds.
   Get ready. (Tap 3 times.)
   *mmm   OOO   lll.*
   What word? (Signal.) *Mole.*
• Next word. Say the sounds. Get ready.
   (Tap 3 times.) *mmm   AAA   d.*
   What word? (Signal.) *made.*
   Yes, a **mole made** something.
• Next word. What word? (Signal.) *A.*
• Go to the beginning of the next line. Say
   the sounds. Get ready. (Tap 3 times.)
   *p   lll   lll.*
   What word? (Signal.) *Pile.*
d. Everybody, say all the words in the first
   sentence. (Signal.) *A mole made a pile.*
e. (Repeat step d until firm.)
f. Touch the first word of the next sentence.
   It starts with the letter **T,** right after the
   period.
   (Observe children and give feedback.)
• You'll start with that word and read all the
   words to the next period.

**g.** First word. Say the sounds. Get ready.
(Tap 3 times.) *ththth   aaa   t.*
What word? (Signal.) *That.*

• Next word. Say the sounds. Get ready.
(Tap 3 times.) *p   III   lll.*
What word? (Signal.) *Pile.*

• Next word. Say the sounds. Get ready.
(Tap 3 times.) *mmm   AAA   d.*
What word? (Signal.) *Made.*

• Next word. Say the sounds. Get ready.
(Tap 2 times.) *ththth   EEE.*
What word? (Signal.) *The.*

• Yes, so far the sentence says: **That pile made the** something.

• Next word. Say the sounds. Get ready.
(Tap 3 times.) *rrr   aaa   mmm.*
What word? (Signal.) *Ram.*

• Last word. Say the sounds Get ready.
(Tap 3 times.) *mmm   aaa   d.*
What word? (Signal.) *Mad.*

• Go back to the first word of that sentence. I'll read all the words in that sentence. You touch the words: **That . . . pile . . . made . . . the . . . ram . . . mad.**

**h.** Everybody, say that sentence.
(Signal.) *That pile made the ram mad.*

**i.** (Repeat step h until firm.)

**j.** I'm going to read the whole story to you. Touch the words as I read them. When I get to the end of a sentence, say "Stop."

• Touch the first word. ✔

• Listen and remember to tell me when to stop: **A . . . mole . . . made . . . a . . . pile.** (Children say: *Stop.*)

• Good saying "Stop." That's the end of the first sentence.

**k.** Everybody, say the first sentence.
(Signal.) *A mole made a pile.*

**l.** (Repeat step k until firm.)

**m.** The first word of the next sentence is **that.** Touch that word. ✔

• Listen and tell me when to stop: **That . . . pile . . . made . . . the . . . ram . . . mad.** (Children say: *Stop.*)

• Good saying "Stop." That's the end of the second sentence.

**n.** Everybody, say that sentence.
(Signal.) *That pile made the ram mad.*

**o.** (Repeat step n until firm.)

=====EXERCISE 6=====
**WORD FINDING**

**a.** This time, you'll find words in the first sentence of the story.

**b.** Listen: One of the words is **pile.** What word? (Signal.) *Pile.*

• Put your finger right over the word **pile.** ✔

• Everybody, touch the word **pile.** (Signal.) ✔

**c.** Listen: One of the words is **made.** What word? (Signal.) *Made.*

• Put your finger right over the word **made.** ✔

• Everybody, touch the word **made.** (Signal.) ✔

**d.** Listen: One of the words is **mole.** What word? (Signal.) *Mole.*

• Put your finger right over the word **mole.** ✔

• Everybody, touch the word **mole.** (Signal.) ✔

**e.** (Repeat steps b through d until firm.)

=====EXERCISE 7=====
**COMPREHENSION**

**a.** Find the first picture of the story. ✔

A mole made a pile.

• That picture shows what the mole made. The words under the picture tell what the mole did.

• Raise your hand when you can read the words that tell what the mole did. (Call on a child to read. *A mole made a pile.*)

- Touch the pile in the picture. ✔
  That's a pretty big pile.
b. Touch the next picture of the story. ✔

That pile made the ram mad.

- That picture shows how the ram feels about the pile. How does the ram feel? (Signal.) *Mad.*
- Raise your hand when you can read the words below the picture. (Call on a child to read. *That pile made the ram mad.*)
- Why do you think it made him mad? (Call on a child. Child's preference.)
- What is the ram going to try to do to that pile? (Call on a child. Idea: *Knock it down.*)
- That may be a pretty big job.

====EXERCISE 8====

**STORY EXTENSION**
**Writing Words in Pictures**

a. Close your textbook. Go to lesson 32 of your workbook and write your name. ✔

- Find the picture for the story. ✔
b. Below the picture are sentences. Touch the first sentence. ✔
- The first sentence says: **A** something **made a** something. What should that sentence say? (Signal.) *A mole made a pile.*
- Touch the space for the first missing word in the sentence. ✔
  That word should be **mole.** What word? (Signal.) *Mole.*
- Touch the space for the other missing word in the sentence. ✔
  What should that word be? (Signal.) *Pile.*
c. Touch the last sentence of the story. ✔
- That sentence says: **That pile made the** something **mad.** What should the sentence say? (Signal.) *That pile made the ram mad.*
- Touch the space for the missing word in the sentence. ✔
  What word goes in the blank? (Signal.) *Ram.*
d. You'll find the missing words above the picture. Read those words to yourself and find the words that go in the sentences.
e. Later, you'll write the words where they belong.

====EXERCISE 9====

**INDEPENDENT WORK**

**Matching: Letter Combinations**
a. Find the matching game. ✔
- The lines are already drawn for each letter combination. You'll follow the lines to where the other letter combination should be and write it in that space.

**Words for Pictures**
b. Find the picture of the feet. ✔
- For each picture on this page, you're going to complete the word independently.

• (Teacher key:)

| 1. feet | 2. na_i_l | 3. rat |
|---|---|---|
| 4. mol_e_ | 5. saf_e_ | 6. ra_i_n |

c. Picture 1 shows some feet, so the word below picture 1 should be: **fff   EEE   t.**

d. Picture 2. Everybody, what does it show? (Signal.) *A nail.*

• That's what the word below should be: **nnn   AAA   lll.**

e. Picture 3 is a: **rrr   aaa   t.**

• Picture 4 is a: **mmm   OOO   lll.**

• Picture 5 is a: **sss   AAA   fff.**

• Picture 6 is: **rrr   AAA   nnn.**

f. You'll complete the word for each picture later.

═══════════ EXERCISE 10 ═══════════
## SPELLING WORDS

a. You're going to spell words.

b. Listen: **my.** Say the sounds in **my.** Get ready. (Tap 2 times.) *mmm   lll.*

• The sound **lll** is spelled with the letter **Y.**

• Everybody, spell the word **my.** (Tap 2 times.) *M-Y.*

c. New word: **me.** Say the sounds in **me.** Get ready. (Tap 2 times.) *mmm   EEE.*

• Everybody, spell the word **me.** (Tap 2 times.) *M-E.*

d. New word: **fly.** Say the sounds in **fly.** Get ready. (Tap 3 times.) *fff   lll   lll.*

• Everybody, spell the word **fly.** (Tap 3 times.) *F-L-Y.*

e. New word: **so.** Say the sounds in **so.** Get ready. (Tap 2 times.) *sss   OOO.*

• Everybody, spell the word **so.** (Tap 2 times.) *S-O.*

f. (Repeat steps b through e until firm.)

### LINED PAPER

g. Now you'll write the words we just spelled. Write your name on your lined paper. Pencils down when you're finished.

• (Write on the board:)

```
          1
          2
          3
          4
```

• Number four lines on your paper. Start with the top line and write the number 1. Write 2 on the next line and then number the other lines. Pencils down when you're finished.
(Observe children and give feedback.)

h. Touch number 1. ✔

• Word 1 is **my.** Leave a little space after the number and write the word **my.** Remember the letter you write for the **lll** sound in that word. Pencils down when you've written the word **my.**
(Observe children and give feedback.)

• (Write on the board:)

> **1 my**

• Here's what you should have. **My** is spelled **M-Y.**

i. Touch number 2. ✔

• Write the word **me** on that line. Pencils down when you're finished.
(Observe children and give feedback.)

• (Write on the board:)

> **2 me**

• Here's what you should have. **Me** is spelled **M-E.**

j. Touch number 3. ✔

• Write the word **so** on that line. Pencils down when you're finished.
(Observe children and give feedback.)

• (Write on the board:)

> **3 so**

• Here's what you should have. **So** is spelled **S-O.**

k. Touch line 4. ✔

• Write the word **fly** on that line. Pencils down when you're finished.
(Observe children and give feedback.)

• (Write on the board:)

**4 fly**

- Here's what you should have. **Fly** is spelled **F-L-Y.**
l. Raise your hand if you got everything right.
- You're spelling and writing some hard words.

━━━━━ EXERCISE 11 ━━━━━

**LETTER PRINTING**

a. (Write on the board:)

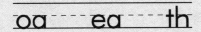

- Turn to the back of your paper. ✔
- You're going to write some letter combinations.
b. On the top line you'll write the letter combination that makes the sound **EEE.** What sound? (Signal.) *EEE.*
- Spell the letter combination for that sound. (Tap 2 times.) *E-A.*
- Write the letter combination for **EEE.** Pencils down when you're finished. (Observe children and give feedback.)
c. Touch the next line. ✔
- The letter combination you'll write on that line makes the sound **ththth** in some words. What sound? (Signal.) *ththth.*
- Spell the letter combination for that sound. (Tap 2 times.) *T-H.*
- Write the letter combination for **ththth.** Pencils down when you're finished. (Observe children and give feedback.)
d. Touch the next line. ✔

- You'll write the letter combination that makes the sound **OOO.** What sound? (Signal.) *OOO.*
- Which letter combination makes that sound? (Signal.) *O-A.*
- Write the letter combination for **OOO.** Pencils down when you're finished. (Observe children and give feedback.)
e. Later, you'll complete the lines of letter combinations.

━━━━━ EXERCISE 12 ━━━━━

**SENTENCE WRITING**

a. (Write on the board:)

A mole made it.

b. This is a sentence like one in the story. The sentence starts with a capital **A.** Raise your hand when you can read this sentence. (Call on a child to read the sentence.)
c. Touch the next line on your paper. Write all four words on that line. Make sure you leave a space after each word. Pencils down when you're finished. (Observe children and give feedback.)
d. Later, you can write the same sentence on the line below.

**Independent Work Summary**
- Story extension (write missing words).
- Color story picture.
- Matching game.
- Word completion (write missing letters).
- Letter printing (finish lines of **ea, th, oa**).
- Sentence writing (copy once more: **A mole made it.**).

**33**

## TEXTBOOK

━━━━━━━ EXERCISE 1 ━━━━━━━

### SOUNDS

a. Open your textbook to lesson 33. Find the train. ✔

- (Teacher reference:)

| ay th d t y p |
|---|

b. The first combination is spelled **A-Y.** Touch that combination.
- Everybody, what sound does that combination make? (Signal.) *AAA.*
- Yes, there's a blue **Y,** so the **A** says its name.
c. Touch the next combination. Say the outloud sound for that combination. (Signal.) *thhth.*
- I'll say the whispered sound **thhth.**
- Your turn. Say the whispered sound for that combination. (Signal.) *thhth.*
d. Next letter. What sound? (Signal.) *d.*
- Next letter. What sound? (Signal.) *t.*
- Next letter. What sound? (Signal.) *III.*
- Last letter. What sound? (Signal.) *p.*
e. Go back to the first combination and say all the sounds.
- First sound. (Signal.) *AAA.*
- Next sound. (Signal.) *thhth.*
- Next sound. (Signal.) *d.*
- Next sound. (Signal.) *t.*
- Next sound. (Signal.) *III.*
- Last sound. (Signal.) *p.*

━━━━━━━ EXERCISE 2 ━━━━━━━

### READING WORDS
### S Ending Pronounced zzz

a. Find the ball. ✔

- (Teacher reference:)

| 1. is | 2. as |
|---|---|
| 3. <u>tho</u>se | 4. <u>the</u>se |

- All these words have an **S** that makes the sound **zzz.** That's the sound you'll say for the **S.**
b. Word 1. There's no blue letter. So what will you say for the **I?** (Signal.) *iii.*
- Touch and say the sounds. Get ready. (Tap 2 times.) *iii   zzz.*
- What word? (Signal.) *Is.*
c. Word 2. There's no blue letter. So what will you say for the **A?** (Signal.) *aaa.*
- Touch and say the sounds. Get ready. (Tap 2 times.) *aaa   zzz.*
- What word? (Signal.) *As.*
d. Word 3. Touch and say the sounds. Get ready. (Tap 3 times.) *thhth   OOO   zzz.*
- What word? (Signal.) *Those.*
e. Word 4. Touch and say the sounds. Get ready. (Tap 3 times.) *thhth   EEE   zzz.*
- What word? (Signal.) *These.*
- Yes, we read **these** words.
f. Let's read those words again.
- Word 1. Say the sounds. Get ready. (Tap 2 times.) *iii   zzz.*
  What word? (Signal.) *Is.*
- Word 2. Say the sounds. Get ready. (Tap 2 times.) *aaa   zzz.*
  What word? (Signal.) *As.*
- Word 3. Say the sounds. Get ready. (Tap 3 times.) *thhth   OOO   zzz.*
  What word? (Signal.) *Those.*
- Word 4. Say the sounds. Get ready. (Tap 3 times.) *thhth   EEE   zzz.*
  What word? (Signal.) *These.*

### Individual Turns
- (Call on different children to read one of the words.)

━━━━━━━ EXERCISE 3 ━━━━━━━

### READING WORDS
### Words with Y or A-Y

a. Find the baseball bat. ✔

• (Teacher reference:)

| 1. try | 2. fly | 3. dry |
| 4. ma_y_ | 5. da_y_ | |

• These words have the letter **Y.** Some of the words have the letter combination **A-Y.** Remember, the **Y** is blue. So the **A** says its name.

b. Word 1. Touch and say the sounds. Get ready. (Tap 3 times.) *t   rrr   III.*
• What word? (Signal.) *Try.*

c. Word 2. Touch and say the sounds. Get ready. (Tap 3 times.) *fff   lll   III.*
• What word? (Signal.) *Fly.*

d. Word 3. Touch and say the sounds. Get ready. (Tap 3 times.) *d   rrr   III.*
• What word? (Signal.) *Dry.*

e. Word 4 has a blue letter. So the **A** says its name. Touch and say the sounds for the black letters. Get ready. (Tap 2 times.) *mmm   AAA.*
• What word? (Signal.) *May.*

f. Word 5 has a blue letter. Touch and say the sounds for the black letters. Get ready. (Tap 2 times.) *d   AAA.*
• What word? (Signal.) *Day.*

g. (Repeat steps b through f until firm.)

**Individual Turns**
• (Call on different children to read one of the words.)

━━━━━ EXERCISE 4 ━━━━━

**READING WORDS**
**Words with I**

a. Find the box of crayons. ✔
• (Teacher reference:)

| 1. time | 2. t_hi_s | 3. did |
| 4. mil_e_ | 5. sit | |

• All these words have the letter **I.** Some of these words have a blue letter.

b. Word 1. Is there a blue letter? (Signal.) *Yes.*
So what sound does the letter **I** make? (Signal.) *III.*

• Word 2. Is there a blue letter? (Signal.) *No.*
So what sound does the letter **I** make? (Signal.) *iii.*

• Word 3. Is there a blue letter? (Signal.) *No.*
So what sound does the letter **I** make? (Signal.) *iii.*

• Word 4. Is there a blue letter? (Signal.) *Yes.*
So what sound does the letter **I** make? (Signal.) *III.*

• Word 5. Is there a blue letter? (Signal.) *No.*
So what sound does the letter **I** make? (Signal.) *iii.*

c. Go back to word 1. ✔
• Is there a blue letter? (Signal.) *Yes.*
• What do you say for the letter **I**? (Signal.) *III.*
• Touch and say the sounds. Get ready. (Tap 3 times.) *t   III   mmm.*
• What word? (Signal.) *Time.*

d. Word 2. Is there a blue letter? (Signal.) *No.*
• What do you say for the letter **I**? (Signal.) *iii.*
• Say the sounds. Get ready. (Tap 3 times.) *ththth   iii   sss.*
• What word? (Signal.) *This.*

e. Word 3. Is there a blue letter? (Signal.) *No.*
• What do you say for the letter **I**? (Signal.) *iii.*
• Say the sounds. Get ready. (Tap 3 times.) *d   iii   d.*
• What word? (Signal.) *Did.*

f. Word 4. Is there a blue letter? (Signal.) *Yes.*
• What do you say for the letter **I**? (Signal.) *III.*
• Touch and say the sounds. Get ready. (Tap 3 times.) *mmm   III   lll.*
• What word? (Signal.) *Mile.*

g. Word 5. Is there a blue letter? (Signal.) *No.*
• What do you say for the letter **I**? (Signal.) *iii.*
• Say the sounds. Get ready. (Tap 3 times.) *sss   iii   t.*

- What word? (Signal.) *Sit.*
h. Let's read those words again.
- Word 1. Touch and say the sounds. Get ready. (Tap 3 times.) *t  III  mmm.* What word? (Signal.) *Time.*
- Word 2. Touch and say the sounds. Get ready. (Tap 3 times.) *ththth  iii  sss.* What word? (Signal.) *This.*
- Word 3. Touch and say the sounds. Get ready. (Tap 3 times.) *d  iii  d.* What word? (Signal.) *Did.*
- Word 4. Touch and say the sounds. Get ready. (Tap 3 times.) *mmm  III  lll.* What word? (Signal.) *Mile.*
- Word 5. Touch and say the sounds. Get ready. (Tap 3 times.) *sss  iii  t.* What word? (Signal.) *Sit.*

**Individual Turns**
- (Call on different children to read one of the words.)

═══════ **EXERCISE 5** ═══════

**STORY READING**

I see ra<u>i</u>n.  So it is tim<u>e</u> for ma<u>th</u>.

a. Find the book. ✔
- This is a story. It has two sentences.
b. Touch the period at the end of the first sentence.
  (Observe children and give feedback.)
- You should be touching the period that is right before the capital letter **S**.
c. Everybody, touch the first word of the story.
  (Observe children and give feedback.)
- You'll read all the words in the first sentence.
- First word. What word? (Signal.) *I.*
- Next word. Touch and say the sounds. Get ready. (Tap 2 times.) *sss  EEE.* What word? (Signal.) *See.*

- Next word. Say the sounds. Get ready. (Tap 3 times.) *rrr  AAA  nnn.* What word? (Signal.) *Rain.*
⌐d. Everybody, say all the words in the first
└  sentence. (Signal.) *I see rain.*
 e. (Repeat step d until firm.)
 f. Touch the first word of the next sentence. It starts with capital **S** right after the period.
  (Observe children and give feedback.)
- Say the sounds. Get ready. (Tap 2 times.) *sss  OOO.* What word? (Signal.) *So.*
- Next word. Say the sounds. Get ready. (Tap 2 times.) *iii  t.* What word? (Signal.) *It.*
- Next word. Say the sounds. Get ready. (Tap 2 times.) *iii  sss.* What word? (Signal.) *Is.*
- Next word. Say the sounds. Get ready. (Tap 3 times.) *t  III  mmm.* What word? (Signal.) *Time.*
- Yes, so far the sentence says: **So it is time.**
  Say that much of the sentence. Get ready. (Signal.) *So it is time.*
- Next word. Say the sounds. Get ready. (Tap 3 times.) *fff  OOO  rrr.* What word? (Signal.) *For.*
- Last word. Say the sounds. Get ready. (Tap 3 times.) *mmm  aaa  ththth.* What word? (Signal.) *Math.*
⌐g. Everybody, say the whole sentence. Get
└  ready. (Signal.) *So it is time for math.*
 h. (Repeat step g until firm.)
 i. I'm going to read the whole story to you. Touch the words as I read them. When I get to the end of the sentence, say "Stop." **I . . . see . . . rain.** (Children say: *Stop.*)
- Good saying "Stop." That's the end of the first sentence.
⌐j. Everybody, say the first sentence.
└  (Signal.) *I see rain.*
 k. (Repeat step j until firm.)
 l. Touch the first word of the next sentence. ✔

- Listen and tell me when to stop:
  **So . . . it . . . is . . . time . . . for . . . math.** (Children say: *Stop.*)
- Good saying "Stop."
m. Everybody, say that sentence. (Signal.) *So it is time for math.*

## Second Reading

- Your turn to read the story one more time. (Call on different children to read two or three words each.)

=========== EXERCISE 6 ===========

## WORD FINDING

a. This time, you'll find words in the **second** sentence.
b. Listen: One of the words is **for.** What word? (Signal.) *For.*
- Put your finger right over the word **for.** ✔
- Everybody, touch the word **for.** ✔
c. Listen: One of the words is **it.** What word? (Signal.) *It.*
- Put your finger right over the word **it.** ✔
- Everybody, touch the word **it.** ✔
d. Listen: One of the words is **is.** What word? (Signal.) *Is.*
- Put your finger right over the word **is.** ✔
- Everybody, touch the word **is.** ✔
e. (Repeat steps b through d until firm.)

=========== EXERCISE 7 ===========

## PICTURE COMPREHENSION

a. Find the picture of the girl. ✔
- Look at the book the girl is holding. Raise your hand when you know what word is on the cover of that book.
- Everybody, what word? (Signal.) *Math.*
- That's her math book.
b. Why do you think she's going to do math rather than play outside? (Call on a child. Idea: *Because it's raining.*)
- If you look carefully in the picture, you may be able to see an animal outside that seems to like the rain. What animal is that? (Signal.) *A dog.*

=========== WORKBOOK ===========

=========== EXERCISE 8 ===========

## STORY EXTENSION
### Sentence Completion

a. Close your textbook. Go to lesson 33 in your workbook and write your name. ✔
b. Find the picture from the story. ✔
- Below the picture are sentences. Later, you'll read the sentences to yourself and figure out the missing words. You'll find the missing words above the picture. You'll read those words to yourself and complete the sentences with the right words.

=========== EXERCISE 9 ===========

## INDEPENDENT WORK

### Matching: Words with Pictures

a. Go to side 2 of your worksheet. ✔
- You're going to draw lines to connect words with pictures of those words.
b. Raise your hand when you can tell me the first word.
- Everybody, what's the first word? (Signal.) *Rat.*
c. Find the right picture in the second column and draw a line to connect the word and the picture.
  (Observe children and give feedback.)
- Later, you'll do the other words on your own.

### Cross-Out and Circle Game

d. Find the cross-out game. ✔
- The little boxes show what you'll circle and what you'll cross out. Raise your hand when you know what you'll circle.
- Everybody, what word? (Signal.) *Is.*
- Then you'll cross out a word. Raise your hand when you know that word. Everybody, what word? (Signal.) *It.*
- Remember, circle **is.** Cross out **it.**

**33**

===== EXERCISE 10 =====

## SPELLING WORDS

a. You're going to spell words that have double **E.**

b. Listen: **see.** Say the sounds in **see.** Get ready. (Tap 2 times.) *sss   EEE.*
• The sound **EEE** is spelled with the letters **E-E.** So **see** is spelled **S-E-E.**
• Everybody, spell the word **see.** (Tap 3 times.) *S-E-E.*

c. New word: **feet.** Say the three sounds in **feet.** Get ready. (Tap 3 times.) *fff   EEE   t.*
• The sound **EEE** is spelled with the letters **E-E.**
• Everybody, spell the word **feet.** (Tap 4 times.) *F-E-E-T.*

d. New word: **seem.** Say the sounds in **seem.** Get ready. (Tap 3 times.) *sss   EEE   mmm.*
• The sound **EEE** is spelled with the letters **E-E.**
• Everybody, spell the word **seem.** (Tap 4 times.) *S-E-E-M.*

e. (Repeat steps b through d until firm.)

f. New word: **fan.** Say the sounds in **fan.** Get ready. (Tap 3 times.) *fff   aaa   nnn.*
• Everybody, spell the word **fan.** (Tap 3 times.) *F-A-N.*

### LINED PAPER

g. Get ready to write the words we just spelled on lined paper. ✔
• (Write on the board:)

|   |
|---|
| 1 |
| 2 |
| 3 |
| 4 |

• Number four lines on your paper. Pencils down when you're finished.
(Observe children and give feedback.)

h. Touch number 1. ✔
• Word 1 is **feet.** Remember the letters you write for the **EEE** sound in that word. Pencils down when you're finished.
(Observe children and give feedback.)

• (Write on the board:)

| **1  feet** |
|---|

• Here's what you should have. **Feet** is spelled **F-E-E-T.**
i. Touch number 2. ✔
• Write the word **fan** on that line. Pencils down when you're finished.
(Observe children and give feedback.)
• (Write on the board:)

| **2  fan** |
|---|

• Here's what you should have. **Fan** is spelled **F-A-N.**
j. Touch number 3. ✔
• Write the word **see** on that line. Pencils down when you're finished.
(Observe children and give feedback.)
• (Write on the board:)

| **3  see** |
|---|

• Here's what you should have. **See** is spelled **S-E-E.**
k. Touch number 4. ✔
• Write the word **seem** on that line. Pencils down when you're finished.
(Observe children and give feedback.)
• (Write on the board:)

| **4  seem** |
|---|

• Here's what you should have. **Seem** is spelled **S-E-E-M.**
l. Raise your hand if you got everything right.
• You're spelling and writing some hard words.

===== EXERCISE 11 =====

## LETTER PRINTING

a. (Write on the board:)

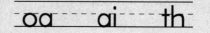

• Turn to the back of your paper. ✔
• You're going to write some letter combinations.

b. On the top line you'll write the letter combination that makes the sound **ththth.** What sound? (Signal.) *ththth.*
- Spell the letter combination that makes that sound. (Signal.) *T-H.*
- Write the letter combination for **ththth.** Pencils down when you're finished. (Observe children and give feedback.)

c. Touch the next line. ✔
- On that line you'll write the letter combination that makes the sound **AAA.** What sound? (Signal.) *AAA.*
- Spell the letter combination from the board that makes that sound. (Signal.) *A-I.*
- Write the letter combination **AAA.** Pencils down when you're finished. (Observe children and give feedback.)

d. Touch the next line. ✔
- On that line you'll write the letter combination that makes the sound **OOO.** What sound? (Signal.) *OOO.*
- Spell the letter combination that makes that sound. (Signal.) *O-A.*
- Write the letter combination for **OOO.** Pencils down when you're finished. (Observe children and give feedback.)

e. Later, you'll complete the lines of letter combinations.

## SENTENCE WRITING

a. (Write on the board:)

I see rain.

b. This is a sentence from the story. Raise your hand when you can read it. (Call on a child to read the sentence.)

c. Touch the next line on your paper. ✔
- Write this sentence on that line. Make sure you leave a space after each word. Pencils down when you're finished. (Observe children and give feedback.)

d. Later, you can write the same sentence **two** more times on the lines below.

### Independent Work Summary
- Story extension (write missing words).
- Color story picture.
- Matching game (connect words with pictures).
- Cross-out (**it**=8) and circle (**is**=7) game.
- Letter printing (finish lines of **th, ai, oa**).
- Sentence writing (copy two more times: **I see rain.**).

---

**Materials:** Each child will need a brown crayon and lined paper.

---

## TEXTBOOK

=====EXERCISE 1=====

**SOUNDS**
### Introducing V, K, J

a. Open your textbook to lesson 34. Find the seashells. ✔
• (Teacher reference:)

| d v k j |
| --- |

• You can figure out the sound for each letter by saying the first part of the letter name. Remember, say the name in two parts. The **first part** is the sound it makes.
b. The first letter is **D.** Say the name a part at a time. Get ready. (Tap 2 times.) *d EEE.*
• What sound does the letter **D** make? (Signal.) *d.*
c. The next letter is **V.** Listen: *vvv EEE.* Say the name a part at a time. Get ready. (Signal.) *vvv EEE.*
• What sound does the letter **V** make? (Signal.) *vvv.*
d. The next letter is **K.** Listen: *k AAA.* Say the name a part at a time. Get ready. (Tap 2 times.) *k AAA.*
• What sound does the letter **K** make? (Signal.) *k.*
e. The next letter is **J.** Listen: *j AAA.* Say the name a part at a time. Get ready. (Tap 2 times.) *j AAA.*
• What sound does the letter **J** make? (Signal.) *j.*
f. Let's do those again.
• Touch **D.** What sound? (Signal.) *d.*
• Touch **V.** What sound? (Signal.) *vvv.*
• Touch **K.** What sound? (Signal.) *k.*
• Touch **J.** What sound? (Signal.) *j.*
g. (Repeat step f until firm.)

**Individual Turns**
• (Repeat step f with different children.)

=====EXERCISE 2=====

**READING WORDS**
### Review

a. Find the beach pail. ✔
• (Teacher reference:)

| 1. and | 2. it | 3. <u>tho</u>se | 4. is |
| --- | --- | --- | --- |
| 5. <u>the</u>se | 6. <u>this</u> | 7. as | 8. <u>the</u> |

• I wonder if someone's going to use that pail to collect the shells.
• These are words you've read before.
b. Word 1. Touch and say the sounds. Get ready. (Tap 3 times.) *aaa nnn d.*
• What word? (Signal.) *And.*
• Yes, you **and** I.
c. Word 2. Touch and say the sounds. Get ready. (Tap 2 times.) *iii t.*
• What word? (Signal.) *It.*
d. Word 3. Touch and say the sounds. Get ready. (Tap 3 times.) *thththth OOO sss.*
• What word? (Signal.) *Those.*
e. Word 4. Touch and say the sounds. Get ready. (Tap 2 times.) *iii sss.*
• What word? (Signal.) *Is.*
f. Word 5. Touch and say the sounds. Get ready. (Tap 3 times.) *thththth EEE sss.*
• What word? (Signal.) *These.*
g. Word 6. Touch and say the sounds. Get ready. (Tap 3 times.) *thththth iii sss.*
• What word? (Signal.) *This.*
h. Word 7. Touch and say the sounds. Get ready. (Tap 2 times.) *aaa sss.*
• What word? (Signal.) *As.*
i. Word 8. Touch and say the sounds. Get ready. (Tap 2 times.) *thththth EEE.*
• What word? (Signal.) *The.*

**Individual Turns**
• (Call on different children to read one or two of the words.)

## EXERCISE 3

### READING WORDS
#### Words with Y or A-Y

a. Find the shovel. ✔
• (Teacher reference:)

| 1. dry | 2. sa<u>y</u> | 3. da<u>y</u> |
|--------|--------|--------|
| 4. ma<u>y</u> | 5. my | |

• These are words that have the letter **Y**. Some words have the combination **A-Y**. What sound does that combination make? (Signal.) *AAA.*
• Yes, the **Y** is blue, so the **A** says its name.
b. Word 1 doesn't have a blue letter. Touch and say the sounds. Get ready. (Tap 3 times.) *d   rrr   III.*
• What word? (Signal.) *Dry.*
c. Word 2 has a blue letter. Touch and say the sounds. Get ready. (Tap 2 times.) *sss   AAA.*
• What word? (Signal.) *Say.*
d. Word 3. Get ready. (Tap 2 times.) *d   AAA.*
• What word? (Signal.) *Day.*
e. Word 4. Get ready. (Tap 2 times.) *mmm   AAA.*
• What word? (Signal.) *May.*
 f. Word 5 doesn't have a blue letter. Don't get fooled. Get ready. (Tap 2 times.) *mmm   III.*
• What word? (Signal.) *My.*
g. Let's read those words again.
• Word 1. Get ready. (Tap 3 times.) *d   rrr   III.*
 What word? (Signal.) *Dry.*
• Word 2. Get ready. (Tap 2 times.) *sss   AAA.*
 What word? (Signal.) *Say.*
• Word 3. Get ready. (Tap 2 times.) *d   AAA.*
 What word? (Signal.) *Day.*
• Word 4. Get ready. (Tap 2 times.) *mmm   AAA.*
 What word? (Signal.) *May.*
• Word 5. Get ready. (Tap 2 times.) *mmm   III.*
 What word? (Signal.) *My.*

### Individual Turns
• (Call on different children to read one or two of the words.)

## EXERCISE 4

### STORY READING

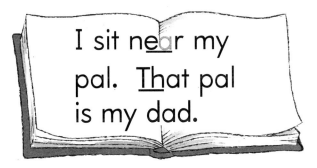

I sit ne<u>a</u>r my pal. <u>Th</u>at pal is my dad.

a. Find the book. ✔
• This is another story with two sentences. The first sentence ends on the second line.
b. Touch the period at the end of the first sentence.
 (Observe children and give feedback.)
• You should be touching the period that is right before the capital letter **T.**
c. Everybody, touch the first word of the story. ✔
• You'll read all the words in the first sentence.
• First word. What word? (Signal.) *I.*
• Next word. Touch and say the sounds. Get ready. (Tap 3 times.) *sss   iii   t.* What word? (Signal.) *Sit.*
• Next word. Get ready. (Signal.) *nnn   EEE   rrr.* What word? (Signal.) *Near.*
• So far the sentence says, **I sit near** something.
• Next word. Get ready. (Tap 2 times.) *mmm   III.* What word? (Signal.) *My.*
• Next word. Get ready. (Tap 3 times.) *p   aaa   lll.* What word? (Signal.) *Pal.*
⌐d. Everybody, say all the words in the first sentence. (Signal.) *I sit near my pal.*
└
e. (Repeat step d until firm.)
 f. Touch the first word of the next sentence. It starts with capital **T.** (Observe children and give feedback.)

- Touch and say the sounds. Get ready. (Tap 3 times.) *thththth   aaa    t.*
  What word? (Signal.) *That.*
- Next word. Get ready. (Tap 3 times.) *p   aaa   lll.*
  What word? (Signal.) *Pal.*
- Next word. Say the sounds. Get ready. (Tap 2 times.) *iii   sss.*
  What word? (Signal.) *Is.*
- Next word. Say the sounds. Get ready. (Tap 2 times.) *mmm    lll.*
  What word? (Signal.) *My.*
- Last word. Get ready. (Tap 3 times.) *d   aaa   d.*
  What word? (Signal.) *Dad.*
g. Say that sentence.
   (Signal.) *That pal is my dad.*
h. (Repeat step g until firm.)
i. The person saying this story has a pal. That pal is the person's. . . (Signal.) *Dad.*
j. I'm going to read the whole story to you. Touch the words as I read them. When I get to the end of a sentence, say "Stop."
   **I . . . sit . . . near . . . my . . . pal.**
   (Children say: *Stop.*)
- Good saying "Stop." That's the end of the first sentence.
k. Everybody, say the first sentence.
   (Signal.) *I sit near my pal.*
l. (Repeat step k until firm.)
m. Touch the first word of the next sentence. ✔
- Listen and tell me when to stop:
  **That . . . pal . . . is . . . my . . . dad.**
  (Children say: *Stop.*)
- Good saying "Stop."
n. Everybody, say that sentence.
   (Signal.) *That pal is my dad.*
o. (Repeat step n until firm.)

**Second Reading**
- Your turn to read the story one more time. (Call on different children to read two or three words each.)

══════════ EXERCISE 5 ══════════
**WORD FINDING**

a. This time, you'll find words in the **second**
sentence. Be careful because some of the words are also in the first sentence.
b. Listen: One of the words in the second sentence is **pal.** What word? (Signal.) *Pal.*
- Put your finger right over the word **pal** in the **second** sentence. ✔
- Everybody, touch the word **pal.** ✔
c. Listen: One of the words in the second sentence is **my.** What word? (Signal.) *My.*
- Put your finger right over the word **my** in the **second** sentence. ✔
- Everybody, touch the word **my.** ✔
d. Listen: One of the words in the second sentence is **is.** What word? (Signal.) *Is.*
- Put your finger right over the word **is** in the second sentence. ✔
- Everybody, touch the word **is.** ✔
e. (Repeat steps b through d until firm.)

══════════ EXERCISE 6 ══════════
**PICTURE COMPREHENSION**

a. Find the picture below the story. ✔
- You see a dad and a youngster. The youngster told the story. What kind of animals are those? (Signal.) *Squirrels.*
- What are they sitting on? (Call on a child. Idea: *A skinny branch.*)
- It looks like they are sitting in a pretty dangerous spot. I don't think I'd like to be sitting there with them.
b. If you look carefully in the picture, you may be able to see another animal. Raise your hand if you can find it.
- Everybody, what kind of animal? (Signal.) *A dog.*

══════════ EXERCISE 7 ══════════
**STORY EXTENSION**
**Sentence Completion**

a. Close your textbook. Go to lesson 34 in your workbook and write your name. ✔
- Find the picture from the story. ✔

b. Below the picture are sentences. Later, you'll read the sentences to yourself and figure out the missing words.

c. The second sentence has two missing words at the end. The sentence says: **That pal is** something something.

• What are the missing words? (Signal.) *My dad.*

• Yes, **That pal is my dad.**

d. You'll find the missing words above the picture. You'll read those words to yourself and complete the sentences with the right words.

══════════ EXERCISE 8 ══════════

## INDEPENDENT WORK

### Matching: Words with Pictures

a. Go to the top of side 2. ✔

• There are two words below each picture. One of the words tells about the picture. The other word doesn't tell about the picture.

b. Find the first picture. ✔

• Touch and say the sounds for the first word under the picture. Get ready. (Tap 3 times.) *sss   aaa   mmm.*

• What word? (Signal.) *Sam.*

• Does the picture show Sam the bunny? (Signal.) *No.*

• Touch and say the sounds for the other word under the picture. Get ready. (Tap 3 times.) *mmm   aaa   nnn.*

• What word? (Signal.) *Man.*

• Does the picture show a man? (Signal.) *Yes.*

• Circle the word **man.** That's the word that tells about the picture.

c. Read the two words that are under the next picture. Find the word that tells about that picture and circle it. Pencils down when you've done that much. (Observe children and give feedback.) (*Key:* **mail.**)

d. Read the two words that are under the last picture. Find the word that tells about the picture and circle it.

(Observe children and give feedback.) (*Key:* **fly.**)

### Hidden Picture

*Note:* Each child needs a brown crayon.

e. Find the hidden picture. ✔

f. Touch the word in the box. ✔

• Raise your hand when you can read that word.
Everybody, what word? (Signal.) *Lay.*

g. Here's the rule for the hidden picture: Color all parts with the word **lay** brown. What color? (Signal.) *Brown.*

• Make a brown mark to remind yourself of the rule. ✔

• Later, you'll color the picture.

══════════ EXERCISE 9 ══════════

## SPELLING WORDS

a. You're going to spell words. Some of them have double **E.**

b. Listen: **my.** Say the sounds in **my.** Get ready. (Tap 2 times.) *mmm   III.*

• Everybody, spell the word **my.** (Tap 2 times.) *M-Y.*

c. New word: **seem.** Say the three sounds in **seem.** Get ready. (Tap 3 times.) *sss   EEE   mmm.*

• The sound **EEE** in **seem** is spelled with the letters **E-E.**

• Everybody, spell the word **seem.** (Tap 4 times.) *S-E-E-M.*

d. New word: **man.** Say the sounds in **man.** Get ready. (Tap 3 times.) *mmm   aaa   nnn.*

• Everybody, spell the word **man.** (Tap 3 times.) *M-A-N.*

e. New word: **feet.** Say the sounds in **feet.** Get ready. (Tap 3 times.) *fff   EEE   t.*

• The sound **EEE** in **feet** is spelled with the letters **E-E.**

• Everybody, spell the word **feet.** (Tap 4 times.) *F-E-E-T.*

f. (Repeat steps b through e until firm.)

**LINED PAPER**

g. Get ready to write the words we just spelled on lined paper.

• (Write on the board:)

> 1
> 2
> 3
> 4

• Number four lines on your paper. Pencils down when you're finished.
  (Observe children and give feedback.)

h. Touch number 1. ✔

• Word 1 is **seem.** Remember the letters you write for the **EEE** sound in that word. Pencils down when you're finished.
  (Observe children and give feedback.)

• (Write on the board:)

> **1 seem**

• Here's what you should have. **Seem** is spelled **S-E-E-M.**

i. Touch number 2. ✔

• Write the word **feet** on that line. Pencils down when you're finished.
  (Observe children and give feedback.)

• (Write on the board:)

> **2 feet**

• Here's what you should have. **Feet** is spelled **F-E-E-T.**

j. Touch number 3. ✔

• Write the word **man** on that line. Pencils down when you're finished.
  (Observe children and give feedback.)

• (Write on the board:)

> **3 man**

• Here's what you should have. **Man** is spelled **M-A-N.**

k. Touch number 4. ✔

• Write the word **my** on that line. Pencils down when you're finished.
  (Observe children and give feedback.)

• (Write on the board:)

> **4 my**

• Here's what you should have. **My** is spelled **M-Y.**

l. Raise your hand if you got everything right.

═══════════ EXERCISE 10 ═══════════

**LETTER PRINTING**

a. (Write on the board:)

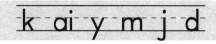

• Turn to the back of your paper. ✔
• You're going to write some letters or combinations.

b. On the top line you'll write the letter or combination that makes the sound **III.** What sound? (Signal.) *III.*
• Which letter or combination makes that sound? (Signal.) *Y.*
• Write the letter for **III.** Pencils down when you're finished.
  (Observe children and give feedback.)

c. Touch the next line. ✔
• On that line you'll write the letter that makes the sound **d.** What sound? (Signal.) *d.*
• What letter makes that sound? (Signal.) *D.*
• Write the letter for **d.** Pencils down when you're finished.
  (Observe children and give feedback.)

d. Touch the next line. ✔
• On that line you'll write the letter that makes the sound **k.** What sound? (Signal.) *k.*
• What letter makes that sound? (Signal.) *K.*
• I'll show you how to write **K.**
• (Trace **k**.)
• Write the letter for **k.** Pencils down when you're finished.
  (Observe children and give feedback.)

e. Later, you'll complete the lines of letters.

## EXERCISE 11

**SENTENCE WRITING**

a. (Write on the board:)

That pal is dad.

b. This is a sentence like one in the story. Raise your hand when you can read it. (Call on a child to read the sentence.)

c. Touch the next line on your paper. ✔

• Write this sentence on that line. Make sure you leave a space after each word. Pencils down when you're finished.

(Observe children and give feedback.)

d. Later, you can write the same sentence two more times on the lines below.

**Independent Work Summary**

• Story extension (write missing words).
• Color story picture.
• Hidden picture (**lay**=brown).
• Letter printing (finish lines of **y**, **d**, **k**).
• Sentence writing (copy two more times: **That pal is dad.**).

| **Materials:** Each child will need lined paper. |
| --- |

### TEXTBOOK

═══════ EXERCISE 1 ═══════

## SOUNDS
### V, D, J, K

a. Open your textbook to lesson 35. Find the raindrops. ✔
• (Teacher reference:)

| v  d  j  k |
| --- |

• These are the new letters. Remember, you can figure out the sound for each letter by saying the first part of the letter name.
b. Touch **V.** Say the name a part at a time. Get ready. (Tap 2 times.) *vvv   EEE.*
• The first part is the sound **V** makes in words. What sound does the letter **V** make? (Signal.) *vvv.*
c. The next letter is **D.** Say the name a part at a time. Get ready. (Tap 2 times.) *d   EEE.*
• What sound does the letter **D** make? (Signal.) *d.*
d. The next letter is **J.** Say the name a part at a time. Get ready. (Tap 2 times.) *j   AAA.*
• What sound does the letter **J** make? (Signal.) *j.*
e. The last letter is **K.** Say the name a part at a time. Get ready. (Tap 2 times.) *k   AAA.*
• What sound does the letter **K** make? (Signal.) *k.*
f. Let's do those again.
• Touch **V.** What sound? (Signal.) *vvv.*
• Touch **D.** What sound? (Signal.) *d.*
• Touch **J.** What sound? (Signal.) *j.*
• Touch **K.** What sound? (Signal.) *k.*
g. (Repeat step f until firm.)

**Individual Turns**
• (Repeat step f with different children.)

═══════ EXERCISE 2 ═══════

## READING WORDS
### Words with A or I

a. Find the boot. ✔
• (Teacher reference:)

| 1. tape |
| --- |
| 2. tap |
| 3. pin |
| 4. pine |

• Some of these words have a blue letter.
b. Word 1. Does it have a blue letter? (Signal.) *Yes.*
So what sound does the letter **A** make? (Signal.) *AAA.*
• Word 2. Does it have a blue letter? (Signal.) *No.*
So what sound does the letter **A** make? (Signal.) *aaa.*
• Word 3. Does it have a blue letter? (Signal.) *No.*
So what sound does the letter **I** make? (Signal.) *iii.*
• Word 4. Does it have a blue letter? (Signal.) *Yes.*
So what sound does the letter **I** make? (Signal.) *III.*
c. Go back to word 1. ✔
• Does it have a blue letter? (Signal.) *Yes.*
So what sound does **A** make? (Signal.) *AAA.*
• Touch and say the sounds. Get ready. (Tap 3 times.) *t   AAA   p.*
• What word? (Signal.) *Tape.*
d. Word 2.
• Does it have a blue letter? (Signal.) *No.*
So what sound does **A** make? (Signal.) *aaa.*
• Touch and say the sounds. Get ready. (Tap 3 times.) *t   aaa   p.*
• What word? (Signal.) *Tap.*
e. Word 3.
• Does it have a blue letter? (Signal.) *No.*
So what sound does **I** make? (Signal.) *iii.*

- Touch and say the sounds. Get ready. (Tap 3 times.) *p iii nnn.*
- What word? (Signal.) *Pin.*

f. Word 4.
- Does it have a blue letter? (Signal.) *Yes.* So what sound does **I** make? (Signal.) *III.*
- Touch and say the sounds. Get ready. (Tap 3 times.) *p III nnn.*
- What word? (Signal.) *Pine.*

g. (Repeat steps c through f until firm.)

**Individual Turns**
- (Call on different children to read one or two of the words.)

========= EXERCISE 3 =========

**PLURALS**
**S Ending Pronounced sss**

a. Here's a rule about some words: The name for more than one thing ends with the sound **sss.**
- Listen: **rope.** That tells about one thing. Here's the name that tells about more than one thing: **ropes.**

b. New word: **note.** That tells about one thing. What's the word that tells about more than one **note**? (Signal.) *Notes.*
- New word: **mat.** That tells about one thing. What's the word that tells about more than one **mat**? (Signal.) *Mats.*
- New word: **top.** That tells about one thing. What's the word that tells about more than one **top**? (Signal.) *Tops.*
- New word: **joke.** That tells about one thing. What's the word that tells about more than one **joke**? (Signal.) *Jokes.*

c. (Repeat step b until firm.)

d. When you write words that tell about more than one thing, you write a letter for the **sss** sound. What letter is that? (Signal.) *S.*

========= EXERCISE 4 =========

**WORDS WITH DIFFICULT BEGINNINGS**

a. Soon you're going to read some words that have very difficult beginning sounds.

b. Listen: **sleep.** It has four sounds. I'll say it a sound at a time: **sss lll EEE p.**
- Your turn. Say **sleep** a sound at a time. Get ready. (Tap 4 times.) *sss lll EEE p.*

c. New word: **tree.** It has three sounds. Listen: **t rrr EEE.**
- Your turn. Say **tree** a sound at a time. Get ready. (Tap 3 times.) *t rrr EEE.*

d. New word: **play.** It has three sounds. Listen: **p lll AAA.**
- Your turn. Say **play** a sound at a time. Get ready. (Tap 3 times.) *p lll AAA.*

e. Let's do those one more time.
- Everybody, say the four sounds in **sleep.** Get ready. (Tap 4 times.) *sss lll EEE p.*
- Say the three sounds in **tree.** Get ready. (Tap 3 times.) *t rrr EEE.*
- Say the three sounds in **play.** Get ready. (Tap 3 times.) *p lll AAA.*

f. (Repeat step e until firm.)

**Individual Turns**
- (Call on different children to say the sounds in one of these words: **sleep, tree, play.**)

========= EXERCISE 5 =========

**READING WORDS**
**Words with Y or A-Y**

a. Find the rain hat. ✔
- (Teacher reference:)

| 1. **try** |
|---|
| 2. **may** |
| 3. **lay** |
| 4. **play** |

- These are words that have the letter **Y.** Some words have the combination **A-Y.** What sound does that combination make? (Signal.) *AAA.*
- Yes, the **Y** is blue, so the **A** says its name.

b. Word 1 does not have a blue letter. Touch and say the sounds. Get ready. (Tap 3 times.) *t rrr III.*
- What word? (Signal.) *Try.*

c. Word 2 has a blue letter. Touch and say the sounds. Get ready. (Tap 2 times.) *mmm   AAA.*
- What word? (Signal.) *May.*

d. Word 3. Touch and say the sounds. Get ready. (Tap 2 times.) *lll   AAA.*
- What word? (Signal.) *Lay.*

e. Word 4 is a tough word. Touch the letters as I say the sounds. Get ready.
*p   lll   AAA.*
- Your turn. Touch and say the sounds. Get ready. (Tap 3 times.) *p   lll   AAA.*
- What word? (Signal.) *Play.*
- You just read a very tough word.

f. Let's read those words again.
- Word 1. Get ready. (Tap 3 times.) *t   rrr   III.*
  What word? (Signal.) *Try.*
- Word 2. Get ready. (Tap 2 times.) *mmm   AAA.*
  What word? (Signal.) *May.*
- Word 3. Get ready. (Tap 2 times.) *lll   AAA.*
  What word? (Signal.) *Lay.*
- Word 4. Get ready. (Tap 3 times.) *p   lll   AAA.*
  What word? (Signal.) *Play.*

**Individual Turns**
- (Call on different children to read one or two of the words.)

====== EXERCISE 6 ======
**SOUND DISCRIMINATION**
  **AAA vs. aaa and III vs. iii**

a. Find the mouse. ✔
- (Teacher reference:)

| a | i |
|---|---|

- You know two sounds for each of these letters.

b. Touch the first letter. ✔
- Listen: Tell me the sound that letter makes when there is no blue letter. Get ready. (Signal.) *aaa.*

- Say the sound that letter makes when there **is** a blue letter. Get ready. (Signal.) *AAA.*

c. Touch the next letter. ✔
- Tell me the sound that letter makes when there is **no** blue letter. (Signal.) *iii.*
- Tell me the sound that letter makes when there **is** a blue letter. (Signal.) *III.*

d. (Repeat steps b and c until firm.)

**Individual Turns**
- (Call on different children for these tasks:)
a. Say the blue-letter sound.
b. Say the other sound.

====== EXERCISE 7 ======
**READING WORDS**
  **Words with iii or aaa**

a. Find the umbrella. ✔
- (Teacher reference:)

| 1. in | 2. an | 3. sit |
|-------|-------|--------|
| 4. sat | 5. did | |

- These words have the letter **I** or the letter **A,** but there are no blue letters. So what sound does the **I** make? (Signal.) *iii.*
- What sound does the **A** make? (Signal.) *aaa.*

b. Word 1. Touch and say the sounds. Get ready. (Tap 2 times.) *iii   nnn.*
- What word? (Signal.) *In.*
- Yes, put it **in** the cup.

c. Word 2. Touch and say the sounds. Get ready. (Tap 2 times.) *aaa   nnn.*
- What word? (Signal.) *An.*

d. Word 3. Touch and say the sounds. Get ready. (Tap 3 times.) *sss   iii   t.*
- Again. Get ready. (Tap 3 times.) *sss   iii   t.*
- What word? (Signal.) *Sit.*

e. Word 4. Touch and say the sounds. Get ready. (Tap 3 times.) *sss   aaa   t.*
- What word? (Signal.) *Sat.*

f. Word 5. Touch and say the sounds. Get ready. (Tap 3 times.) *d   iii   d.*
- Again. Get ready. (Tap 3 times.) *d   iii   d.*

- What word? (Signal.) *Did.*

================ EXERCISE 8 ================

**STORY READING**

It is time for the mail. That mail is for me. My soap is in that mail.

a. Find the book. ✔
- This is a story with **three** sentences.
b. Touch the period at the end of the first sentence.
  (Observe children and give feedback.)
- You should be touching the period that is right before the capital **T.**
- Touch the period at the end of the second sentence. Remember, that sentence **begins** with the capital **T.**
  (Observe children and give feedback.)
- You should be touching the period that is right before the capital **M.**
- Touch the period at the end of the third sentence.
  (Observe children and give feedback.)
c. (Repeat step b until firm.)
d. Everybody, touch the first word of the story. ✔
- You'll read all the words in the first sentence.
- First word. Touch and say the sounds. Get ready. (Tap 2 times.) *iii   t.*
  What word? (Signal.) *It.*
- Next word. Get ready. (Tap 2 times.) *iii   sss.*
  What word? (Signal.) *Is.*
- The next word has a blue letter. Touch and say the sounds. Get ready. (Tap 3 times.) *t   III   mmm.*
  What word? (Signal.) *Time.*

- Next word. Touch and say the sounds. Get ready. (Tap 3 times.) *fff   OOO   rrr.*
  What word? (Signal.) *For.*
- So far the sentence says: **It is time for** something.
- Next word. Touch and say the sounds. Get ready. (Tap 2 times.) *ththth   EEE.*
  What word? (Signal.) *The.*
  Yes, **It is time for the . . .**
- Next word. Touch and say the sounds. Get ready. (Tap 3 times.)
  *mmm   AAA   lll.*
  What word? (Signal.) *Mail.*
e. Everybody, say all the words in the first sentence. (Signal.) *It is time for the mail.*
f. (Repeat step e until firm.)
g. Touch the first word in the next sentence. It starts with a capital **T.**
  (Observe children and give feedback.)
- Everybody, touch and say the sounds. Get ready. (Tap 3 times.)
  *ththth   aaa   t.*
  What word? (Signal.) *That.*
- Next word. Touch and say the sounds. Get ready. (Tap 3 times.)
  *mmm   AAA   lll.*
  What word? (Signal.) *Mail.*
- Next word. Touch and say the sounds. Get ready. (Tap 2 times.) *iii   sss.*
  What word? (Signal.) *Is.*
- Next word. Touch and say the sounds. Get ready. (Tap 3 times.) *fff   OOO   rrr.*
  What word? (Signal.) *For.*
- Next word. Touch and say the sounds. Get ready. (Tap 2 times.) *mmm   EEE.*
  What word? (Signal.) *Me.*
h. Everybody, say that sentence.
  (Signal.) *That mail is for me.*
i. (Repeat step h until firm.)
j. Touch the first word of the last sentence. It starts with a capital **M.**
  (Observe children and give feedback.)
- Touch and say the sounds. Get ready. (Tap 2 times.) *mmm   III.*
  What word? (Signal.) *My.*
- Next word. Say the sounds. Get ready. (Tap 3 times.) *sss   OOO   p.*
  What word? (Signal.) *Soap.*

- Next word. Touch and say the sounds. Get ready. (Tap 2 times.) *iii    sss.* What word? (Signal.) *Is.*
- Next word. Say the sounds. Get ready. (Tap 2 times.) *iii    nnn.* What word? (Signal.) *In.*
- Next word. Say the sounds. Get ready. (Tap 3 times.) *ththth    aaa    t.* What word? (Signal.) *That.*
- Last word. Say the sounds. Get ready. (Tap 3 times.) *mmm    AAA    lll.* What word? (Signal.) *Mail.*

k. Everybody, say that sentence. (Signal.) *My soap is in that mail.*
l. (Repeat step k until firm.)
m. I'm going to read the whole story to you. Touch the words as I read them. When I get to the end of a sentence, say "Stop." **It . . . is . . . time . . . for . . . the . . . mail.** (Children say: *Stop.*)
- Good saying "Stop." That's the end of the first sentence.
n. Everybody, say the first sentence. (Signal.) *It is time for the mail.*
o. (Repeat step n until firm.)
p. Listen and tell me when to stop. **That . . . mail . . . is . . . for . . . me.** (Children say: *Stop.*)
- Good saying "Stop."
q. Everybody, say that sentence. (Signal.) *That mail is for me.*
r. (Repeat step q until firm.)
s. Touch the first word of the last sentence. Listen and tell me when to stop. **My . . . soap . . . is . . . in . . . that . . . mail.** (Children say: *Stop.*)
- Good saying "Stop."
t. Everybody, say that sentence. (Signal.) *My soap is in that mail.*
u. (Repeat step t until firm.)

==== EXERCISE 9 ====

**COMPREHENSION**

a. Find the first picture for the story. ✔

It is time for the mail.

- What's in that picture? (Call on a child. Idea: *Mailbox.*)
- Read the sentence under the first picture. (Call on different children to read one or two words. *It is time for the mail.*)
b. Touch the next picture. ✔

That mail is for me.

- This is a picture of the person telling the story. Who is that? (Signal.) *A boy.*
- What is the boy saying in the picture? (Call on different children to read one or two words. *That mail is for me.*)
- Why do you think he needs the mail? (Call on a child. Idea: *To clean himself up.*)

c. Touch the last picture. ✔

- What is the mail carrier handing the boy? (Signal.) *A box.*
- What is the boy saying in that picture? (Call on different children to read one or two words. *My soap is in that mail.*)
- What do you think the boy will do with that soap? (Call on a child. Idea: *Wash.*)

═══════ EXERCISE 10 ═══════

## STORY EXTENSION
### Writing Words in Picture

*Note:* Children are not to write their names yet.

a. Close your textbook. Open your workbook to lesson 35. ✔
- Find the picture from the story. The boy is saying something in the picture. A word is missing.

b. Later, you'll read what the boy is saying and write the missing word. It's one of the words above the picture.

═══════ EXERCISE 11 ═══════

## SENTENCE COMPLETION
### Child's Name

a. Find the big number 35 on the top of your worksheet and touch it. ✔
- Keep touching it. Right after the number 35 is part of a sentence.
- (Teacher reference:)

b. Touch the first word. Say the sounds. Get ready. (Tap 2 times.) *mmm III.* What word? (Signal.) *My.*
- Next word. Get ready. (Tap 3 times.) *nnn AAA mmm.* What word? (Signal.) *Name.*
- Next word. Get ready. (Tap 2 times.) *iii sss.* What word? (Signal.) *Is.*
- Say the words. Get ready. (Signal.) *My name is.*

c. When you write your name in the blank, you will have a complete sentence. Write your name. Pencils down when you're finished. (Observe children and give feedback.)

d. Get ready to read the sentence at the top of your worksheet. (Call on different children. Praise children who correctly read: *My name is _____.*)
- Good reading and writing.

═══════ EXERCISE 12 ═══════

## INDEPENDENT WORK

### Matching: Words with Pictures
a. Go to the top of side 2. ✔
- You're going to draw lines to connect words with pictures of those words.
b. Touch the column of words. ✔

- Raise your hand when you can tell me the first word.
- Everybody, what's the first word? (Signal.) *Tape.*

c. Find the right picture in the second column and draw a line to connect the word and the picture. Later, you'll do the other words on your own.

**Cross-Out and Circle Game**

d. Find the cross-out game. ✔
- The little boxes show what you'll circle and what you'll cross out.

e. Everybody, what will you **circle?** (Signal.) *And.*
- Then you'll cross out a word. Raise your hand when you know that word. Everybody, what word? (Signal.) *Day.*
- Remember, circle **and.** Cross out **day.**

===== EXERCISE 13 =====

**TAKE HOME**

a. Go to the next page in your workbook. ✔
- (Remove perforated story sheet. Direct children to fold sheet so the title, ***The Fly,*** is the cover page.)

b. This is like a story you read before. The first page is the title of the story. (Call on a child to read the title.)

c. The rest of the story shows different things the fly does and says. (Call on different children to read the other sentences.)

d. You can color this book and take it home to read to your family.

e. (Check out each child on reading the entire story.)

===== EXERCISE 14 =====

**SPELLING WORDS**
**Words with Blue E**

a. You're going to spell words that end with a blue **E.** You won't write the **E** in blue, but you will write it.
- What letter will you write on the end of the words? (Signal.) *E.*

b. Here's a word that ends in **E: name.**

- Everybody, say the sounds in the word **name.** Get ready. (Tap 3 times.) *nnn   AAA   mmm.*
- This time, I'll say each sound. You tell me the letter you'll write.
- Listen: **nnn.** What letter? (Signal.) *N.*
- **AAA.** What letter? (Signal.) *A.*
- **mmm.** What letter? (Signal.) *M.*
- And what goes on the end of the word? (Signal.) *E.*

c. New word: **ate.**
- Everybody, say the sounds in the word **ate.** Get ready. (Tap 2 times.) *AAA   t.*
- This time, I'll say each sound. You tell me the letter you'll write.
- Listen: **AAA.** What letter? (Signal.) *A.*
- **t.** What letter? (Signal.) *T.*
- And what letter do you write on the end of the word? (Signal.) *E.*
- Once more: **AAA.** What letter? (Signal.) *A.*
- **t.** What letter? (Signal.) *T.*
- And what goes on the end of the word? (Signal.) *E.*

**LINED PAPER**

d. Get ready to write on lined paper. Some of the words are the words we just spelled.
- (Write on the board:)

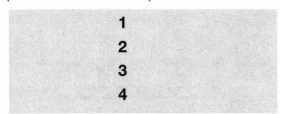

- Number four lines on your paper. Pencils down when you're finished. (Observe children and give feedback.)

e. Touch number 1. ✔
- Word 1 is **ate.** Pencils down when you're finished. (Observe children and give feedback.)
- (Write on the board:)

| 1 ate |
|-------|

- Here's what you should have. **Ate** is spelled **A-T-E.**

f. Touch number 2. ✔
- Write the word **name** on that line. Pencils down when you're finished.
  (Observe children and give feedback.)
- (Write on the board:)

> **2  name**

- Here's what you should have. **Name** is spelled **N-A-M-E.** ✔
g. Touch number 3. ✔
- Word 3 is a word you've spelled before. It does not have an **E** on the end. Word 3 is **fan.** What word? (Signal.) *Fan.*
- Write the word **fan.** Pencils down when you're finished.
  (Observe children and give feedback.)
- (Write on the board:)

> **3  fan**

- Here's what you should have. **Fan** is spelled **F-A-N.**
h. Touch number 4. ✔
- Write the word **feet** on that line. Remember, it does not have an **E** on the end. Pencils down when you're finished.
  (Observe children and give feedback.)
- (Write on the board:)

> **4  feet**

- Here's what you should have. **Feet** is spelled **F-E-E-T.**
i. Raise your hand if you got everything right.

═══════ EXERCISE 15 ═══════

**LETTER PRINTING**

a. (Write on the board:)

> j v y s t k l

- Turn to the back of your paper. ✔
- You're going to write some letters.
b. On the top line you'll write the letter that makes the sound **j.** What sound?
  (Signal.) *j.*
- What letter makes that sound?
  (Signal.) *J.*

- Write the letter for **j.** Pencils down when you're finished.
  (Observe children and give feedback.)
c. Touch the next line. ✔
- On that line you'll write the letter that makes the sound **k.** What sound?
  (Signal.) *k.*
- What letter makes that sound?
  (Signal.) *K.*
- Write the letter for **k.** Pencils down when you're finished.
  (Observe children and give feedback.)
d. Touch the next line. ✔
- On that line you'll write the letter that makes the sound **III.** What sound?
  (Signal.) *III.*
- Which letter on the board makes that sound? (Signal.) *Y.*
- Write the letter for **III.** Pencils down when you're finished.
  (Observe children and give feedback.)
e. Later, you'll complete the lines of letters.

═══════ EXERCISE 16 ═══════

**SENTENCE WRITING**

a. (Write on the board:)

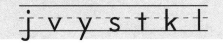

b. This is a sentence like one in the story. Raise your hand when you can read it.
  (Call on a child to read the sentence.)
c. Touch the next line on your paper. ✔
- Write this sentence on that line. Make sure you leave a space after each word. Pencils down when you're finished.
  (Observe children and give feedback.)
d. Later, you can write the same sentence two more times on the lines below.

## Independent Work Summary

*Note:* Check out each child on reading
*The Fly.*

- Story extension (write missing word).
- Color story picture.
- Matching game.
- Cross-out (**day**=2) and circle (**and**=2) game.
- Color and take home *The Fly.*
- Letter printing (finish lines of **j**, **k**, **y**).
- Sentence writing (copy two more times: **I need that mail.**).

**Materials:** Each child will need a blue, a green, and a black crayon and lined paper.

# TEXTBOOK

━━━━━━━━ EXERCISE 1 ━━━━━━━━

## SOUNDS
### D, V, J, K

a. Open your textbook to lesson 36. Find the banana. ✔
• (Teacher reference:)

| d   v   j   k |
|---|

b. Say the sounds for the letters.
• First letter. Everybody, what sound? (Signal.) *d.*
• Next letter. Get ready. (Signal.) *vvv.*
• Next letter. Get ready. (Signal.) *k.*
• Last letter. Get ready. (Signal.) *j.*
c. This time, I'll say the sounds. You'll touch the letters.
d. Listen: You'll touch the letter that makes the sound **vvv.** What sound? (Signal.) *vvv.*
• Get ready. Touch it. ✔
• Everybody, what letter are you touching? (Signal.) *V.*
e. Listen: You'll touch the letter that makes the sound **k.** What sound? (Signal.) *k.*
• Get ready. Touch it. ✔
• Everybody, what letter are you touching? (Signal.) *K.*
f. Listen: You'll touch the letter that makes the sound **j.** What sound? (Signal.) *j.*
• Get ready. Touch it. ✔
• Everybody, what letter are you touching? (Signal.) *J.*
g. Listen: You'll touch the letter that makes the sound **d.** What sound? (Signal.) *d.*
• Get ready. Touch it. ✔
• Everybody, what letter are you touching? (Signal.) *D.*
h. (Repeat steps d through g until firm.)

## Individual Turns
• (Repeat steps d through g with different children.)

━━━━━━━━ EXERCISE 2 ━━━━━━━━

## READING WORDS

a. Find the pear. ✔
• (Teacher reference:)

| 1. dive | 2. save |
|---|---|
| 3. make | 4. keep |

• These words have the new sounds.
b. Word 1 has a blue letter. Touch and say the sounds. Get ready. (Tap 3 times.) *d III vvv.*
• Again. Get ready. (Tap 3 times.) *d III vvv.*
• What word? (Signal.) *Dive.*
• Yes, **dive** into that pool.
c. Word 2 has a blue letter. Touch and say the sounds. Get ready. (Tap 3 times.) *sss AAA vvv.*
• Again. Get ready. (Tap 3 times.) *sss AAA vvv.*
• What word? (Signal.) *Save.*
• Yes, **save** money when you can.
d. Word 3 has a blue letter. Touch and say the sounds. Get ready. (Tap 3 times.) *mmm AAA k.*
• Again. Get ready. (Tap 3 times.) *mmm AAA k.*
• What word? (Signal.) *Make.*
• Yes, **make** a pretty picture.
e. Word 4. Get ready. (Tap 3 times.) *k EEE p.*
• Again. Get ready. (Tap 3 times.) *k EEE p.*
• What word? (Signal.) *Keep.*
• Yes, **keep** off the lawn.
f. Let's do those words again.
• Word 1. Get ready. (Tap 3 times.) *d III vvv.*
  What word? (Signal.) *Dive.*
• Word 2. Get ready. (Tap 3 times.) *sss AAA vvv.*
  What word? (Signal.) *Save.*
• Word 3. Get ready. (Tap 3 times.) *mmm AAA k.*

What word? (Signal.) *Make.*
- Word 4. Get ready. (Tap 3 times.)
k   EEE   p.
What word? (Signal.) *Keep.*
g. (Repeat step f until firm.)

**Individual Turns**
- (Call on different children to read one or two of the words.)

══════════ EXERCISE 3 ══════════
**PLURALS**
**S Ending Pronounced zzz**

a. Some words that tell about more than one thing end with a **zzz** sound.
- Here's a word that tells about one thing: **fan.**
Here's a word that tells about more than one thing: **fans.**
b. New word: **tire.** That word tells about one thing. What's the word that tells about more than one thing?
(Signal.) *Tires.*
- New word: **key.** That word tells about one thing. What's the word that tells about more than one thing?
(Signal.) *Keys.*
- New word: **pole.** That word tells about one thing. What's the word that tells about more than one thing?
(Signal.) *Poles.*
c. Here's the rule about all those words: The letter that you write for the **zzz** sound in all those words is the letter **S.**
- What letter? (Signal.) *S.*
d. Listen: **tires.** What's the last sound in **tires?** (Signal.) *zzz.*
- What letter makes the sound **zzz** in **tires?** (Signal.) *S.*
e. (Repeat step d for: **poles, keys, fans.**)

══════════ EXERCISE 4 ══════════
**READING WORDS**

a. Find the strawberry. ✔
- (Teacher reference:)

| 1. **and** | 2. ta͟il | 3. sa͟y |

- These are words you have read before.
b. Word 1. Touch and say the sounds. Get ready. (Tap 3 times.) *aaa   nnn   d.*
- What word? (Signal.) *And.*
- Yes, you **and** I.
c. Word 2 has a blue letter. Get ready. (Tap 3 times.) *t   AAA   lll.*
- What word? (Signal.) *Tail.*
d. Word 3 has a blue letter. Get ready. (Tap 2 times.) *sss   AAA.*
- What word? (Signal.) *Say.*
e. Let's do those words again.
- Word 1. Get ready. (Tap 3 times.)
*aaa   nnn   d.*
What word? (Signal.) *And.*
- Word 2. Get ready. (Tap 3 times.)
*t   AAA   lll.*
What word? (Signal.) *Tail.*
- Word 3. Get ready. (Tap 2 times.)
*sss   AAA.*
What word? (Signal.) *Say.*

══════════ EXERCISE 5 ══════════
**WORDS WITH DIFFICULT BEGINNINGS**

a. Later, you're going to read some words that have very difficult beginning sounds.
b. Listen: **sleep.** It has four sounds. Say **sleep** a sound at a time. Get ready. (Tap 4 times.) *sss   lll   EEE   p.*
- New word: **slide.** It has four sounds. Say **slide** a sound at a time. Get ready. (Tap 4 times.) *sss   lll   III   d.*
- New word: **tree.** It has three sounds. Say **tree** a sound at a time. Get ready. (Tap 3 times.) *t   rrr   EEE.*
- New word: **play.** It has three sounds. Say **play** a sound at a time. Get ready. (Tap 3 times.) *p   lll   AAA.*
c. Let's do some of those one more time.
- Everybody, say the four sounds in **slide.** Get ready. (Tap 4 times.)
*sss   lll   III   d.*
- Say the three sounds in **tree.** Get ready. (Tap 3 times.) *t   rrr   EEE.*
d. (Repeat step c until firm.)

**Individual Turns**
- (Repeat step c with different children.)

═══════ EXERCISE 6 ═══════

## READING WORDS
### Difficult Beginning Sounds

a. Find the bunch of grapes. ✔
* (Teacher reference:)

| 1. pl<u>a</u>y | 2. tree |
|---|---|
| 3. sleep | 4. slip |

b. Word 1 has a blue letter. Touch and say the sounds. Get ready. (Tap 3 times.)
*p lll AAA.*
* What word? (Signal.) *Play.*
c. Word 2. Get ready. (Tap 3 times.)
*t rrr EEE.*
* Again. Get ready. (Tap 3 times.)
*t rrr EEE.*
* What word? (Signal.) *Tree.*
d. Word 3. Get ready. (Tap 4 times.)
*sss lll EEE p.*
* Again. Get ready. (Tap 4 times.)
*sss lll EEE p.*
* What word? (Signal.) *Sleep.*
e. Word 4 does not have a blue letter. Get ready. (Tap 4 times.) *sss lll iii p.*
* Again. Get ready. (Tap 4 times.)
*sss lll iii p.*
* What word? (Signal.) *Slip.*
* Yes, don't **slip** on that ice.
f. Let's read those tough words one more time.
* Word 1. Get ready. (Tap 3 times.)
*p lll AAA.*
What word? (Signal.) *Play.*
* Word 2. Get ready. (Tap 3 times.)
*t rrr EEE.*
What word? (Signal.) *Tree.*
* Word 3. Get ready. (Tap 4 times.)
*sss lll EEE p.*
What word? (Signal.) *Sleep.*
* Word 4. Get ready. (Tap 4 times.)
*sss lll iii p.*
* What word? (Signal.) *Slip.*

### Individual Turns
* (Call on different children to read one of the words.)

═══════ EXERCISE 7 ═══════

## STORY READING

Sam may e<u>a</u>t a rop<u>e</u>. <u>Th</u>at rop<u>e</u> is no rop<u>e</u>. It is a t<u>ai</u>l.

a. Find the book. ✔
* This is another story with three sentences.
b. Touch the period at the end of the first sentence.
(Observe children and give feedback.)
* You should be touching the period on the second line that is right before the capital **T**.
* Touch the period at the end of the second sentence.
(Observe children and give feedback.)
* You should be touching the period that is right before the capital **I**.
* Touch the period at the end of the third sentence.
(Observe children and give feedback.)
c. Everybody, touch the first word of the story. ✔
* You'll read all the words in the first sentence.
* First word. Touch and say the sounds. Get ready. (Tap 3 times.)
*sss aaa mmm.*
What word? (Signal.) *Sam.*
* The next word has a blue letter. Get ready. (Tap 2 times.) *mmm AAA.*
What word? (Signal.) *May.*
* Next word. Get ready. (Tap 2 times.)
*EEE t.*
What word? (Signal.) *Eat.*
* Next word. What word? (Signal.) *A.*
* Next word. Get ready. (Tap 3 times.)
*rrr OOO p.*
What word? (Signal.) *Rope.*

d. Everybody, say all the words in the first sentence. (Signal.) *Sam may eat a rope.*

e. (Repeat step d until firm.)

f. Touch the first word of the next sentence. ✔

• Touch and say the sounds. Get ready. (Tap 3 times.) *ththth   aaa   t.*
What word? (Signal.) *That.*

• Next word. Get ready. (Tap 3 times.) *rrr   OOO   p.*
What word? (Signal.) *Rope.*

• Next word. Get ready. (Tap 2 times.) *iii   sss.*
What word? (Signal.) *Is.*

• Next word. Get ready. (Tap 2 times.) *nnn   OOO.*
What word? (Signal.) *No.*

• Next word. Get ready. (Tap 3 times.) *rrr   OOO   p.*
What word? (Signal.) *Rope.*

g. Everybody, say that sentence. (Signal.) *That rope is no rope.*

h. (Repeat step g until firm.)

i. Touch the first word of the last sentence. It starts with capital I. ✔

• Touch and say the sounds. Get ready. (Tap 2 times.) *iii   t.*
What word? (Signal.) *It.*

• Next word. Get ready. (Tap 2 times.) *iii   sss.*
What word? (Signal.) *Is.*

• Next word. What word? (Signal.) *A.*

• Next word. Get ready. (Tap 3 times.) *t   AAA   lll.*
What word? (Signal.) *Tail.*

j. Say that sentence. (Signal.) *It is a tail.*

k. (Repeat step j until firm.)

**Second Reading**

l. I'm going to call on different children to read sentences in the story. Everybody else follow along and touch the words as they are read and say "Stop" as soon as the last word of the sentence is read.

m. (Call on a child to read the first sentence: *Sam may eat a rope.*) (Children say: *Stop.* Praise accurate reading.)

• That's the end of the first sentence.

n. Everybody, say the first sentence. (Signal.) *Sam may eat a rope.*

o. (Repeat step n until firm.)

p. Everybody, touch the first word of the next sentence. ✔

• (Call on a child to read the second sentence: *That rope is no rope.*) (Children say: *Stop.*)

q. Everybody, say that sentence. (Signal.) *That rope is no rope.*

r. (Repeat step q until firm.)

s. Touch the first word of the last sentence. ✔

• (Call on a child to read the last sentence: *It is a tail.*) (Children say: *Stop.*)

t. Everybody, say that sentence. (Signal.) *It is a tail.*

u. (Repeat step t until firm.)

═══════ EXERCISE 8 ═══════

**WORD FINDING**

a. Touch the first word of the story. ✔

• This time, you'll find words in the **first** sentence.

b. Listen: One of the words is **eat.** What word? (Signal.) *Eat.*

• Put your finger right over the word **eat** in the first sentence.
(Observe children and give feedback.)

• Everybody, touch the word **eat.** (Signal.) ✔

c. Listen: One of the words is **may.** What word? (Signal.) *May.*

• Put your finger right over the word **may.** (Observe children and give feedback.)

• Everybody, touch the word **may.** (Signal.) ✔

d. Listen: One of the words is **rope.** What word? (Signal.) *Rope.*

• Put your finger right over the word **rope.** (Observe children and give feedback.)

• Everybody, touch the word **rope.** (Signal.) ✔

e. (Repeat steps b through d until firm.)

═══════ EXERCISE 9 ═══════

**COMPREHENSION**

a. Find the first picture of the story. ✔

Sam may e̲a̲t a rope.

- This picture shows what things looked like to Sam.
- What's Sam doing? (Call on a child. Idea: *Eating.*)
- What's he looking at? (Call on a child. Idea: *Rope.*)
- Who can read the sentence below the picture? (Call on a child to read. *Sam may eat a rope.*)
b. Touch the second picture. ✔

T̲h̲at rope is a ta̲i̲l.

- That picture shows the joke. From this side of the rock, we can see that the rope is a tail. Who does the tail belong to? (Signal.) *A bull.*

- Oh, dear. When Sam takes a bite out of that tail, he'd better be able to get out of the field the fast way.
- Who can read the sentence below the picture? (Call on a child to read. *That rope is a tail.*)

**WORKBOOK**

━━━━━━ EXERCISE 10 ━━━━━━

**STORY EXTENSION**
**Sentence Completion**

a. Close your textbook. Open your workbook to lesson 36. ✔
b. Find the picture. This is like the picture from your textbook, but one of the words is missing in the first sentence. Later, you'll figure out which word is missing and write it.

━━━━━━ EXERCISE 11 ━━━━━━

**HIDDEN PICTURE**

*Note:* Each child needs a green, a blue and a black crayon.

a. Find the hidden picture at the bottom of your worksheet. ✔
- I'll tell you the coloring rules for the picture.
b. Touch the box for the combination spelled **E-A.** ✔
- Listen: All the parts with **E-A** are green. Make a green mark for **E-A.** ✔
c. Touch the combination spelled **A-Y.** ✔
- All the parts with **A-Y** are blue. Make a blue mark for **A-Y.** ✔
d. Touch the combination spelled **A-I.** All the parts with **A-I** are black. Make a black mark for **A-I.** ✔
e. Later, you'll color the picture.

## EXERCISE 12

### SENTENCE WRITING
### Child's Name

a. You're going to write sentences in your workbook today.
- Touch the capital **M** at the top of your worksheet. ✔
- Keep touching it. Read the sentence to yourself and write the missing part. Pencils down when you're finished. (Observe children and give feedback.)

b. I'm going to call on different children to read the sentence at the top of their worksheet. (Call on different children. Praise children who correctly read: *My name is _____.)*

c. Touch the capital **M** on side 2 of your worksheet. ✔
- Later, you're going to complete the first sentence and copy that sentence on the lines below.

## EXERCISE 13

### INDEPENDENT WORK

### Words for Pictures
a. Touch the dog. ✔
- Next to the dog is a box with words in it. You'll write them where they belong under the pictures.
b. Touch the first word. ✔
  Read it to yourself. Raise your hand when you know what the first word says.
- Everybody, what's the first word? (Signal.) *Fan.*
- Touch the picture that shows a fan. ✔
c. Later, you'll write the word **fan** under that picture. Then you'll do the same thing with the rest of the words. You'll read them to yourself. Then you'll write them under the correct pictures.

## EXERCISE 14

### SPELLING WORDS
### Words with Blue E

a. You're going to spell words that end with

a blue **E.** You won't write it in blue, but you will write it.
b. Listen: **name.** Everybody, say the sounds in **name.** Get ready. (Tap 3 times.) *nnn    AAA    mmm.*
- Say the letter you'll write for the sound **nnn.** (Signal.) *N.*
- Say the letter you'll write for the sound **AAA.** (Signal.) *A.*
- Say the letter you'll write for the sound **mmm.** (Signal.) *M.*
- Then what letter will you write? (Signal.) *E.*
c. Everybody, spell the word **name.** (Tap 4 times.) *N-A-M-E.*
- (Repeat until firm.)
d. New word: **ate.** Say the sounds in **ate.** Get ready. (Tap 2 times.) *AAA    t.*
- Say the letter you'll write for the sound **AAA.** (Signal.) *A.*
- Say the letter you'll write for the sound **t.** (Signal.) *T.*
- Then what letter will you write? (Signal.) *E.*
e. Everybody, spell **ate.** (Tap 3 times.) *A-T-E.*
- (Repeat until firm.)
f. New word: **same.** Say the sounds in **same.** Get ready. (Tap 3 times.) *sss    AAA    mmm.*
g. Spell the word **same.** (Tap 4 times.) *S-A-M-E.*
- (Repeat until firm.)

### LINED PAPER

h. Get ready to write the words we just spelled on lined paper.
- (Write on the board:)

| |
|---|
| 1 |
| 2 |
| 3 |
| 4 |

- Number four lines on your paper. Pencils down when you're finished. (Observe children and give feedback.)
i. Touch number 1. ✔

- Write the word **same** on that line. Pencils down when you're finished.
  (Observe children and give feedback.)
- (Write on the board:)

**1 same**

- Here's what you should have. **Same** is spelled **S-A-M-E.**
j. Touch number 2. ✔
- Write the word **name** on that line. Pencils down when you're finished.
  (Observe children and give feedback.)
- (Write on the board:)

**2 name**

- Here's what you should have. **Name** is spelled **N-A-M-E.**
k. Touch number 3. ✔
- Write the word **ate** on that line. Pencils down when you're finished.
  (Observe children and give feedback.)
- (Write on the board:)

**3 ate**

- Here's what you should have. **Ate** is spelled **A-T-E.**
l. Touch number 4. ✔
- Write the word **my** on that line. Pencils down when you're finished.
  (Observe children and give feedback.)
- (Write on the board:)

**4 my**

- Here's what you should have. **My** is spelled **M-Y.**
m. Raise your hand if you got everything right.

===== EXERCISE 15 =====
**LETTER PRINTING**

a. (Write on the board:)

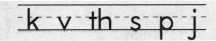

b. Turn to the back of your paper. You're going to write some letters.
c. Touch the top line. ✔
- On that line you'll write the letter that makes the sound **vvv.** What sound? (Signal.) *vvv.*
- What letter makes that sound? (Signal.) *V.*
- I'll show you how to write **V.**
- (Trace **V.**)
- Write the letter for **vvv.** Pencils down when you're finished.
  (Observe children and give feedback.)
d. Touch the next line. ✔
- On that line you'll write the letter that makes the sound **k.** What sound? (Signal.) *k.*
- What letter makes that sound? (Signal.) *K.*
- Write the letter for **k.** Pencils down when you're finished.
  (Observe children and give feedback.)
e. Touch the next line. ✔
- On that line you'll write the letter that makes the sound **j.** What sound? (Signal.) *j.*
- What letter makes that sound? (Signal.) *J.*
- Write the letter for **j.** Pencils down when you're finished.
  (Observe children and give feedback.)
f. Later, you'll complete the lines of letters.

**Independent Work Summary**
- Sentence extension (write missing word).
- Color story picture.
- Hidden picture (**ay**=blue, **ea**=green, **ai**=black).
- Sentence writing (copy two more times: **My name is _____.**).
- Write words under appropriate pictures.
- Letter printing (finish lines of **v, k, j**).

## 37

**Materials:** Each child will need scissors, paste and lined paper.

---

### ═══ EXERCISE 1 ═══
### SOUNDS
#### Introducing C-K and C

a. (Write on the board:)

| k | ck | c |
|---|----|---|

- You know the sound for **K.**
- Everybody, what sound does **K** make? (Signal.) *k.*

b. Everything on the board makes the same sound. The letters **C-K** make the same sound as **K.** The letter **C** by itself usually makes the same sound as **K.**

- That's unusual. You'd think that the letter **C** would make the sound **sss.** And it does in a few words. But most of the time, it makes the sound **k.**
- Raise your hand if you're going to remember the three ways to write the **k** sound.

#### Individual Turns
- (Call on different children.) Tell me one of the ways to write the **k** sound. *[C, C-K or K.]*

---

### TEXTBOOK

---

### ═══ EXERCISE 2 ═══
### SOUNDS

a. Open your textbook to lesson 37. Find the ant. ✔
- I think that ant is going to follow some bread crumbs. Maybe it's going to a picnic.
- (Teacher reference:)

| p | j | k | v | ck | j | c | t |
|---|---|---|---|----|---|---|---|

- Say the sounds for these letters.

b. First letter. Everybody, what sound? (Signal.) *p.*
- Next sound. Get ready. (Signal.) *j.*
- (Repeat for remaining sounds.)

c. (Repeat step b until firm.)

d. Listen: You'll touch the letter that makes the sound **j.** What sound? (Signal.) *j.*
- Get ready. Touch it. ✔
- Everybody, what letter are you touching? (Signal.) *J.*

#### Individual Turns
- This time, I'll call on different children to say all the sounds.
- (Call on different children.)

---

### ═══ EXERCISE 3 ═══
### READING WORDS
#### Words with A

a. Find the little teddy bear. ✔
- (Teacher reference:)

| **than** |
|----------|
| **and** |
| **ant** |

- These words have the letter **A.**

b. Top word. Touch and say the sounds. Get ready. (Tap 3 times.) *ththth    aaa    nnn.*
- What word? (Signal.) *Than.*
- Yes, I am older **than** you.

c. Middle word. Touch and say the sounds. Get ready. (Tap 3 times.) *aaa    nnn    d.*
- Again. Get ready. (Tap 3 times.) *aaa    nnn    d.*
- What word? (Signal.) *And.*

d. Bottom word. Touch and say the sounds. Get ready. (Tap 3 times.) *aaa    nnn    t.*
- Again. Get ready. (Tap 3 times.) *aaa    nnn    t.*
- What word? (Signal.) *Ant.*

e. Let's do those words again.
- Top word. Get ready. (Tap 3 times.) *ththth    aaa    nnn.* What word? (Signal.) *Than.*
- Middle word. Get ready. (Tap 3 times.) *aaa    nnn    d.*

What word? (Signal.) *And.*
- Bottom word. Get ready. (Tap 3 times.)
  *aaa    nnn    t.*
  What word? (Signal.) *Ant.*
f. (Repeat step e until firm.)

**Individual Turns**
- (Call on different children to read one or two of the words.)

═══════ EXERCISE 4 ═══════
## READING WORDS
### Words with the New Sounds

a. Find the big teddy bear. ✔
- (Teacher reference:)

| 1. mak*e* | 2. sav*e* | 3. jok*e* |
|-----------|-----------|-----------|
| 4. ja*i*l | 5. van    |           |

- These words have the new sounds.
b. Word 1 has a blue letter. Touch and say the sounds. Get ready. (Tap 3 times.)
  *mmm    AAA    k.*
- What word? (Signal.) *Make.*
c. Word 2 has a blue letter. Touch and say the sounds. Get ready. (Tap 3 times.)
  *sss    AAA    vvv.*
- What word? (Signal.) *Save.*
d. Word 3. Get ready. (Tap 3 times.)
  *j    OOO    k.*
- Again. Get ready. (Tap 3 times.)
  *j    OOO    k.*
- What word? (Signal.) *Joke.*
- We like a funny joke.
e. Word 4. Get ready. (Tap 3 times.)
  *j    AAA    lll.*
- Again. Get ready. (Tap 3 times.)
  *j    AAA    lll.*
- What word? (Signal.) *Jail.*
- That's a place for people who break the law.
f. Word 5 doesn't have a blue letter. Get ready. (Tap 3 times.) *vvv    aaa    nnn.*
- What word? (Signal.) *Van.*
- Yes, a van holds a lot of people.
g. Let's do those words again.
- Word 1. Get ready. (Tap 3 times.)
  *mmm    AAA    k.*
  What word? (Signal.) *Make.*

- Word 2. Get ready. (Tap 3 times.)
  *sss    AAA    vvv.*
  What word? (Signal.) *Save.*
- Word 3. Get ready. (Tap 3 times.)
  *j    OOO    k.*
  What word? (Signal.) *Joke.*
- Word 4. Get ready. (Tap 3 times.)
  *j    AAA    lll.*
  What word? (Signal.) *Jail.*
- Word 5. Get ready. (Tap 3 times.)
  *vvv    aaa    nnn.*
  What word? (Signal.) *Van.*
h. (Repeat step g until firm.)

**Individual Turns**
- (Call on different children to read one or two of the words.)

═══════ EXERCISE 5 ═══════
## WORDS WITH DIFFICULT BEGINNINGS

a. I'll say words that have difficult beginning sounds. You'll say the sounds for those words.
b. Flat. Flat has four sounds. Listen:
  *fff    lll    aaa    t.*
- Say the sounds in flat. Get ready. (Tap 4 times.) *fff    lll    aaa    t.*
c. Listen: stove has four sounds. Say the sounds in stove. Get ready. (Tap 4 times.)
  *sss    t    OOO    vvv.*
d. Find the picnic basket. ✔
- (Teacher reference:)

| tree |
|------|
| trip |
| sleep |

- I guess the teddy bears are having a picnic.
e. Top word. Touch and say the sounds. Get ready. (Tap 3 times.) *t    rrr    EEE.*
- What word? (Signal.) *Tree.*
f. Middle word. Get ready. (Tap 4 times.)
  *t    rrr    iii    p.*
- Again. Get ready. (Tap 4 times.)
  *t    rrr    iii    p.*
- What word? (Signal.) *Trip.*
g. Bottom word. Get ready. (Tap 4 times.)
  *sss    lll    EEE    p.*

- What word? (Signal.) *Sleep.*
h. Let's read those tough words one more time.
- Top word. Get ready. (Tap 3 times.) *t   rrr   EEE.*
  What word? (Signal.) *Tree.*
- Middle word. Get ready. (Tap 4 times.) *t   rrr   iii   p.*
  What word? (Signal.) *Trip.*
- Bottom word. Get ready. (Tap 4 times.) *sss   lll   EEE   p.*
  What word? (Signal.) *Sleep.*

**Individual Turns**
- (Call on different children to read one of the words.)

===== **EXERCISE 6** =====

**STORY READING**

A se<u>a</u>l and a ram ma<u>y</u>
pl<u>a</u>y.  Or <u>the</u> se<u>a</u>l ma<u>y</u>
sleep.  And <u>the</u> ram
ma<u>y</u> e<u>a</u>t a s<u>ai</u>l.

a. Find the book. ✔
- This is another story with three sentences.
b. Touch the period at the end of the first sentence.
  (Observe children and give feedback.)
- You should be touching the period that is right before the capital **O.**
- Touch the period at the end of the second sentence.
  (Observe children and give feedback.)
- You should be touching the period that is right before the capital **A.**
- Touch the period at the end of the third sentence.
  (Observe children and give feedback.)
c. Everybody, touch the first word of the story. ✔

- You'll read all the words in the first sentence.
- First word. What word? (Signal.) *A.*
- Next word. Say the sounds. Get ready. (Tap 3 times.) *sss   EEE   lll.*
  What word? (Signal.) *Seal.*
- Next word. Get ready. (Tap 3 times.) *aaa   nnn   d.*
  What word? (Signal.) *And.*
- Next word. What word? (Signal.) *A.*
- Next word. Get ready. (Tap 3 times.) *rrr   aaa   mmm.*
  What word? (Signal.) *Ram.*
- Next word. Get ready. (Tap 2 times.) *mmm   AAA.*
  What word? (Signal.) *May.*
- Next word. Get ready. (Tap 3 times.) *p   lll   AAA.*
  What word? (Signal.) *Play.*
- Listen to that whole sentence: **A seal and a ram may play.**
d. Everybody, say all the words in the first sentence. (Signal.) *A seal and a ram may play.*
- (Repeat step d until firm.)
e. Touch the first word of the next sentence. ✔
- Say the sounds. Get ready. (Tap 2 times.) *OOO   rrr.*
  What word? (Signal.) *Or.*
f. Next word. Get ready. (Tap 2 times.) *ththth   EEE.*
  What word? (Signal.) *The.*
- (Repeat step f for: **seal, may, sleep.**)
g. Everybody, say that sentence. (Signal.) *Or the seal may sleep.*
- (Repeat step g until firm.)
h. Touch the first word of the last sentence. ✔
- Get ready. (Tap 3 times.) *aaa   nnn   d.*
  What word? (Signal.) *And.*
i. Next word. Get ready. (Tap 2 times.) *ththth   EEE.*
  What word? (Signal.) *The.*
- (Repeat step i for: **ram, may, eat, a, sail.**)
j. Say that sentence. (Signal.) *And the ram may eat a sail.*
- (Repeat step j until firm.)

**Second Reading**

k. I'm going to call on different children to read sentences in the story. Everybody else follow along and touch the words as they are read and say "Stop" as soon as the last word of the sentence is read.

l. Everybody, touch the first word of the story. ✔

• (Call on a child to read the first sentence: *A seal and a ram may play.*) (Children say: *Stop.* Praise accurate reading.)

• That's the end of the first sentence.

m. Everybody, say the first sentence. (Signal.) *A seal and a ram may play.*

• (Repeat until firm.)

n. That tells one thing that the seal and the ram may do. What may they do? (Signal.) *Play.*

o. Everybody, touch the first word of the next sentence. ✔

• (Call on a child to read the second sentence: *Or the seal may sleep.*) (Children say: *Stop.*)

p. Everybody, say that sentence. (Signal.) *Or the seal may sleep.*

• (Repeat until firm.)

q. Listen: The seal and the ram may play. Or the seal may do something else. What is that? (Signal.) *Sleep.*

r. Touch the first word of the next sentence. ✔

• (Call on a child to read the last sentence: *And the ram may eat a sail.*) (Children say: *Stop.*)

s. Everybody, say the sentence. (Signal.) *And the ram may eat a sail.*

• (Repeat until firm.)

t. Maybe the seal and the ram will play. That's one thing that may happen. The other thing is that the seal will sleep and the ram will do something else. What's that? (Signal.) *Eat a sail.*

━━━━━ EXERCISE 7 ━━━━━

**COMPREHENSION**

a. Find the pictures for the story. ✔

• The pictures show the two things that may happen.

• Touch the first picture. ✔

A seal may sleep.

• What is happening in that picture? (Call on a child. Idea: *A seal is sleeping on the beach.*)

• Raise your hand when you can read the sentence under the picture. (Call on a child to read. *A seal may sleep.*)

b. Find the second picture. ✔

A ram may eat a sail.

• The second picture shows the other thing that may happen while the seal sleeps.

• What's happening in that picture? (Call on a child. Idea: *The ram is eating a sail.*)

• Raise your hand when you can read the sentence under that picture. (Call on a child to read. *A ram may eat a sail.*)

## WORKBOOK

### STORY EXTENSION
#### Cut-Out: Pictures

> **Note:** Each child needs scissors and paste.

a. Close your textbook. Open your workbook to lesson 37. ✔
• Find the cut-out game. There are two sentences and a place for pictures next to them. ✔
b. You'll read the sentences to yourself and figure out which picture goes with each sentence.
c. Later, you'll cut out the pictures and paste them next to the right sentence.

### INDEPENDENT WORK

#### Sentence Completion: Child's Name
a. Touch the number 37 at the top of your worksheet. ✔
b. There's part of a sentence after 37. Read it to yourself and write the missing part to complete the sentence. There is no period at the end of the sentence. Make sure you write a period at the end.
(Observe children and give feedback.)

#### Words for Pictures
c. Find the words at the top of side 2. ✔
• You'll write the words where they belong under the pictures.
d. Touch the first **word.** Read it to yourself. Raise your hand when you know what the first word says.
• Everybody, what's the first word?
(Signal.) *Tape.*
• Touch the picture that shows **tape.** ✔
• Later, you'll write the word **tape** under that picture. Then you'll do the same

thing with the rest of the words. You'll read them to yourself. Then you'll write them under the correct pictures.

### SPELLING WORDS

a. You're going to spell words that end with a blue **E.** Remember, the **E** is last.
b. Listen: **late.** Everybody, say the sounds in **late.** Get ready. (Tap 3 times.)
*lll   AAA   t.*
• Everybody, spell the word **late.** Get ready. (Tap 4 times.) *L-A-T-E.*
• New word: **safe.** Say the sounds in **safe.** Get ready. (Tap 3 times.) *sss   AAA   fff.*
• Spell the word **safe.** Get ready. (Tap 4 times.) *S-A-F-E.*
c. (Repeat step b until firm.)

#### LINED PAPER
d. Get ready to write on lined paper. Some of the words are the words we just spelled.
• Number four lines on your paper. Pencils down when you're finished.
(Observe children and give feedback.)
e. Touch number 1. ✔
• Word 1 is **fly.** Write **fly.** Pencils down when you're finished.
(Observe children and give feedback.)
• (Write on the board:)

> **1  fly**

• Here's what you should have. **Fly** is spelled **F-L-Y.**
f. Touch number 2. ✔
• Write the word **fat** on that line. Pencils down when you're finished.
(Observe children and give feedback.)
• (Write on the board:)

> **2  fat**

• Here's what you should have. **Fat** is spelled **F-A-T.**
g. Touch number 3. ✔

- Write the word **safe** on that line. Remember where the blue **E** goes. Pencils down when you're finished.
(Observe children and give feedback.)
- (Write on the board:)

**3 safe**

- Here's what you should have. **Safe** is spelled **S-A-F-E.**
h. Touch number 4. ✔
- Write the word **late** on that line. Pencils down when you're finished.
(Observe children and give feedback.)
- (Write on the board:)

**4 late**

- Here's what you should have. **Late** is spelled **L-A-T-E.**
i. Raise your hand if you got everything right.

════════ EXERCISE 11 ════════

## SENTENCE WRITING

a. (Write on the board:)

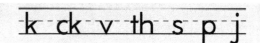

b. This is a sentence like one in the story. Raise your hand when you can read it.
(Call on a child to read the sentence.)
c. Turn to the back of your paper. Write this sentence on the top line. Make sure you leave a space after each word. Pencils down when you're finished.
(Observe children and give feedback.)
d. Later, you can write the same sentence two more times on the lines below.

════════ EXERCISE 12 ════════

## LETTER PRINTING

a. (Write on the board:)

k ck v th s p j

b. You're going to write some letters.
- Skip the next two lines on your paper, and put your pencil at the beginning of the line after that. Keep your pencil in place so I can see it.
(Observe children and give feedback.)
- On that line you'll write the letter that makes the sound **vvv.** What sound? (Signal.) *vvv.*
- What letter makes that sound? (Signal.) *V.*
- Write the letter for **vvv.** Pencils down when you're finished.
(Observe children and give feedback.)
c. Touch the next line. ✔
- On that line you'll write the letter that makes the sound **t.** What sound? (Signal.) *t.*
- What letter makes that sound? (Signal.) *T.*
- Write the letter for **t.** Pencils down when you're finished.
(Observe children and give feedback.)
d. Touch the next line. ✔
- On that line you'll write the **letter,** not the combination, that makes the sound **k.** What sound? (Signal.) *k.*
- The letter you'll write is on the board.
- What **letter** makes that sound? (Signal.) *K.*
- Write the letter for **k.** Pencils down when you're finished.
(Observe children and give feedback.)
e. Later, you'll complete the lines of letters.

**Independent Work Summary**
- Story extension (cut and paste pictures next to appropriate sentences).
- Write words under appropriate pictures.
- Color pictures.
- Sentence writing (copy two more times: **A ram may play.**).
- Letter printing (finish lines of **v, t, k**).

## 38

=== EXERCISE 1 ===

**WORDS WITH DIFFICULT BEGINNINGS**

a. I'll say words that have difficult beginning sounds. You'll say the sounds in those words.

b. The word **flame** has four sounds. Listen: **fff lll AAA mmm.**
Say the sounds in **flame.** Get ready. (Tap 4 times.) *fff lll AAA mmm.*

• The word **drive** has four sounds. Listen: **d rrr lll vvv.**
Say the sounds in **drive.** Get ready. (Tap 4 times.) *d rrr lll vvv.*

• The word **stove** has four sounds. Say the sounds in **stove.** Get ready. (Tap 4 times.) *sss t OOO vvv.*

=== EXERCISE 2 ===

**SOUNDS**
**C-K and C**

a. (Write on the board:)

| ck k c |
| --- |

• The combination and these letters make the same sound in most words. Everybody, what sound is that? (Signal.) *k.*

• Yes, they all make the **k** sound.

**TEXTBOOK**

b. Open your textbook to lesson 38. Find the top clothesline. ✔

• (Teacher reference:)

| v f c k j d ck |
| --- |

• The washcloths on the top clothesline have letters in them. Somebody is hanging them out to dry.

• You'll tell me the sounds for these letters.

c. First letter. Everybody, what sound? Get ready. (Signal.) *vvv.*

• Next sound. Get ready. (Signal.) *fff.*

• (Repeat for remaining items.)

d. (Repeat step c until firm.)

=== EXERCISE 3 ===

**READING WORDS**
**Words with Blue E**

a. Find the shirt. ✔

• (Teacher reference:)

| 1. stove 2. dive 3. like 4. lake |
| --- |

• These words have a blue letter.

b. Word 1 is a tough word. Touch and say the sounds. Get ready. (Tap 4 times.) *sss t OOO vvv.*

• Again. Get ready. (Tap 4 times.) *sss t OOO vvv.*

• What word? (Signal.) *Stove.*

• Yes, we cook on a **stove.**

c. Word 2 has a blue letter. Touch and say the sounds. Get ready. (Tap 3 times.) *d lll vvv.*

• Again. Get ready. (Tap 3 times.) *d lll vvv.*

• What word? (Signal.) *Dive.*

• We will **dive** into the lake.

d. Word 3 has a blue letter. Get ready. (Tap 3 times.) *lll lll k.*

• What word? (Signal.) *Like.*

e. Word 4. Get ready. (Tap 3 times.) *lll AAA k.*

• What word? (Signal.) *Lake.*

f. Let's do those words again.

• Word 1. Get ready. (Tap 4 times.) *sss t OOO vvv.*
What word? (Signal.) *Stove.*

• Word 2. Get ready. (Tap 3 times.) *d lll vvv.*
What word? (Signal.) *Dive.*

• Word 3. Get ready. (Tap 3 times.) *lll lll k.*
What word? (Signal.) *Like.*

• Word 4. Get ready. (Tap 3 times.)
*lll   AAA   k.*
What word? (Signal.) *Lake.*

g. (Repeat step f until firm.)

**Individual Turns**

• (Call on different children to read one or two of the words.)

========= EXERCISE 4 =========

## READING WORDS

a. Find the overalls. ✔
• (Teacher reference:)

| 1. pill | 2. pile | 3. fine |
|---------|---------|---------|
| 4. fin  | 5. sore | 6. ride |

b. Word 1 does not have a blue letter. Touch and say the sounds. Get ready. (Tap 3 times.) *p   iii   lll.*
• What word? (Signal.) *Pill.*

c. Word 2 has a blue letter. Get ready. (Tap 3 times.) *p   III   lll.*
• What word? (Signal.) *Pile.*

d. Word 3 has a blue letter. Get ready. (Tap 3 times.) *fff   III   nnn.*
• What word? (Signal.) *Fine.*

e. Word 4 does not have a blue letter. Get ready. (Tap 3 times.) *fff   iii   nnn.*
• What word? (Signal.) *Fin.*
• Yes, that fish has a big **fin.**

f. Word 5 has a blue letter. Get ready. (Tap 3 times.) *sss   OOO   rrr.*
• What word? (Signal.) *Sore.*

g. Word 6 has a blue letter. Get ready. (Tap 3 times.) *rrr   III   d.*
• What word? (Signal.) *Ride.*

h. Let's read those tough words one more time.
• Word 1. Get ready. (Tap 3 times.)
*p   iii   lll.*
What word? (Signal.) *Pill.*
• Word 2. Get ready. (Tap 3 times.)
*p   III   lll.*
What word? (Signal.) *Pile.*
• Word 3. Get ready. (Tap 3 times.)
*fff   III   nnn.*
What word? (Signal.) *Fine.*

• Word 4. Get ready. (Tap 3 times.)
*fff   iii   nnn.*
What word? (Signal.) *Fin.*
• Word 5. Get ready. (Tap 3 times.)
*sss   OOO   rrr.*
What word? (Signal.) *Sore.*
• Word 6. Get ready. (Tap 3 times.)
*rrr   III   d.*
What word? (Signal.) *Ride.*

**Individual Turns**

• (Call on different children to read one or two of the words.)

========= EXERCISE 5 =========

## READING WORDS
### A Sound at a Time

a. Find the pants. ✔
• (Teacher reference:)

| pin |
|-----|
| need |
| tan |

b. The top word does not have a blue letter. Say the sounds. Get ready. (Tap 3 times.)
*p   iii   nnn.*
• What word? (Signal.) *Pin.*

c. Middle word. Get ready. (Tap 3 times.)
*nnn   EEE   d.*
• What word? (Signal.) *Need.*

d. The bottom word does not have a blue letter. Get ready. (Tap 3 times.)
*t   aaa   nnn.*
• What word? (Signal.) *Tan.*

e. Let's do those words again.
• Top word. Get ready. (Tap 3 times.)
*p   iii   nnn.*
What word? (Signal.) *Pin.*
• Middle word. Get ready. (Tap 3 times.)
*nnn   EEE   d.*
What word? (Signal.) *Need.*
• Bottom word. Get ready. (Tap 3 times.)
*t   aaa   nnn.*
What word? (Signal.) *Tan.*

f. (Repeat step e until firm.)

**Individual Turns**

- (Call on different children to read one or two of the words.)

**Reading Words the Fast Way**

g. This time, you'll read the words the fast way. You won't say the sounds. You'll just tell me the word.

h. Top word. Figure out what the word is. Raise your hand when you know it. Everybody, what's the top word? (Signal.) *Pin.*

- Middle word. Raise your hand when you know it.
  Everybody, what's the middle word? (Signal.) *Need.*

- Bottom word. Raise your hand when you know it.
  Everybody, what's the bottom word? (Signal.) *Tan.*

i. (Repeat step h until firm.)

j. You're reading words the fast way.

**Individual Turns**

a. This time, I'll call on different children to read one of the words the fast way.

b. Everybody, touch the top word.

- (Call on a child.) Read the top word the fast way.

- (Repeat step b for remaining words.)

---

===== EXERCISE 6 =====

**STORY READING**

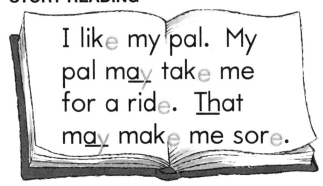

a. Find the book. ✔

b. Everybody, touch the first word of the story. ✔

- You'll read all the words in the first sentence.

- First word. What word? (Signal.) *I.*

- Next word. Say the sounds. Get ready. (Tap 3 times.) *lll lll k.*
  What word? (Signal.) *Like.*

- Next word. Get ready. (Tap 2 times.) *mmm lll.*
  What word? (Signal.) *My.*

- Next word. Get ready. (Tap 3 times.) *p aaa lll.*
  What word? (Signal.) *Pal.*

c. Everybody, say all the words in the first sentence. (Signal.) *I like my pal.*

- (Repeat until firm.)

d. Touch the first word of the next sentence. ✔

- Get ready. (Tap 2 times.) *mmm lll.*
  What word? (Signal.) *My.*

e. Next word. Get ready. (Tap 3 times.) *p aaa lll.*
  What word? (Signal.) *Pal.*

f. (Repeat step e for: **may, take, me, for, a, ride.**)

g. Everybody, say that sentence. (Signal.) *My pal may take me for a ride.*

- (Repeat until firm.)

h. Touch the first word of the next sentence. ✔

- Say the sounds. Get ready. (Tap 3 times.) *ththth aaa t.*
  What word? (Signal.) *That.*

i. Next word. Get ready. (Tap 2 times.) *mmm AAA.*
  What word? (Signal.) *May.*

j. (Repeat step i for: **make, me, sore.**)

k. Everybody, say that sentence. (Signal.) *That may make me sore.*

- (Repeat until firm.)

**Second Reading**

l. I'm going to call on different children to read sentences in the story. Everybody else follow along and touch the words as they are read and say "Stop" as soon as the last word of the sentence is read.

m. Everybody, touch the first word of the story. ✔

- (Call on a child to read the first sentence: *I like my pal.*) (Children say: *Stop.* Praise accurate reading.)

- That's the end of the first sentence.

n. Everybody, say the first sentence.
(Signal.) *I like my pal.*
- (Repeat until firm.)
o. Everybody, touch the first word of the next sentence. ✔
- (Call on a child to read the second sentence: *My pal may take me for a ride.*) (Children say: *Stop.*)
p. Everybody, say that sentence.
(Signal.) *My pal may take me for a ride.*
- (Repeat until firm.)
q. Everybody, touch the first word of the last sentence. ✔
- (Call on a child to read the last sentence: *That may make me sore.*) (Children say: *Stop.*)
r. Everybody, say that sentence.
(Signal.) *That may make me sore.*
- (Repeat until firm.)

========= EXERCISE 7 =========

**WORD FINDING**

a. This time, you'll find the words in the **third** sentence.
b. Listen: One of the words is **may.** What word? (Signal.) *May.*
- Get ready to touch the word **may** in the third sentence. Everybody, touch it. ✔
c. Listen: One of the words is **me.** What word? (Signal.) *Me.*
- Get ready to touch the word **me.** Everybody, touch it. ✔
d. Listen: One of the words is **make.** What word? (Signal.) *Make.*
- Get ready to touch the word **make.** Everybody, touch it. ✔
e. (Repeat steps b through d until firm.)

========= EXERCISE 8 =========

**COMPREHENSION**

a. Find the first picture. ✔

- The girl is the person telling the story. Read what she is saying in that picture. (Call on a child. *I like my pal.*)
- Can you see who her pal is? (Signal.) *No.*
b. Touch the next picture. ✔

- That shows her pal. Who is her pal? (Signal.) *A horse.*
- You can see the girl riding that horse. She does not have a saddle.
- Read what it says under the picture. (Call on a child. *My pal may take me for a ride.*)

c. Find the last picture. ✔

③

That may make me sore.

- The girl's legs are sore in that picture. Why? (Call on a child. Idea: *From riding bareback.*)
- Read what it says under the picture. (Call on a child. *That may make me sore.*)

EXERCISE 9

## STORY EXTENSION
### Writing Words in Picture

a. Close your textbook. Open your workbook to lesson 38. ✔
- Find the picture. The picture shows the girl saying something, but the last word is missing. Later, you'll write that word in.
b. Under the picture are two more sentences, but the last word in each sentence is missing.
- Later, you'll write the missing words. Then you'll have the whole story.

EXERCISE 10

## INDEPENDENT WORK

### Sentence Completion: Child's Name
a. Touch the number 38 at the top of your worksheet. ✔
b. There's part of a sentence after 38. Read it to yourself and write the missing part to complete the sentence. Remember the period.
(Observe children and give feedback.)

### Words for Pictures
c. Find the words at the top of side 2. ✔
- You'll write the words where they belong under the pictures.
d. Find the first word. Read it to yourself. Raise your hand when you know what the word says.
- Everybody, what's the first word? (Signal.) *Tree.*
- Touch the picture that shows a **tree**. ✔
e. Later, you'll write the word **tree** under that picture. Then you'll do the same thing with the rest of the words. You'll read them to yourself. Then you'll write them under the correct picture.

### Matching: Letters
f. Find the matching game. ✔
- You'll draw lines to match the capital letters with the regular letters.

### Cross-Out and Circle Game
g. Find the cross-out game. ✔
- The little boxes show what you'll circle and what you'll cross out.
- Everybody, raise your hand when you know what you will circle. What word? (Signal.) *This.*
- Then you'll cross out a word. Raise your hand when you know that word.
- Everybody, what word? (Signal.) *That.*
- Look at the number below the word that's crossed out. How many words will you cross out? (Signal.) *Three.*
- Look at the number below the word that's circled. How many words will you circle? (Signal.) *Three.*

- Remember, circle **this.** Cross out **that.**

## LINED PAPER
### ═══ EXERCISE 11 ═══
## SPELLING WORDS

a. Get ready to write on lined paper.
- Number four lines on your paper. Pencils down when you're finished.
(Observe children and give feedback.)
b. Word 1 is **ant.** What word? (Signal.) *Ant.*
- **Ant** has three sounds. Say **ant** a sound at a time. Get ready. (Tap 3 times.) *aaa   nnn   t.*
- Again. Say the first sound in **ant.** (Signal.) *aaa.*
- Say the next sound in **ant.** (Signal.) *nnn.*
- Say the last sound in **ant.** (Signal.) *t.*
- The first sound in **ant** is **aaa.** What letter do you write for **aaa?** (Signal.) *A.*
- The next sound is **nnn.** What letter do you write? (Signal.) *N.*
- The last sound is **t.** What letter do you write? (Signal.) *T.*
- Write the word **ant.** Pencils down when you're finished.
(Observe children and give feedback.)
- (Write on the board:)

> **1   ant**

- Here's the word **ant.** It is spelled **A-N-T.**
c. Word 2 is **name.** What word? (Signal.) *Name.*
- Remember, it has an **E** on the end.
- **Name** has three sounds. Say **name** a sound at a time. Get ready. (Tap 3 times.) *nnn   AAA   mmm.*
- Again. Say the first sound in **name.** (Signal.) *nnn.*
- Say the next sound in **name.** (Signal.) *AAA.*
- Say the last sound in **name.** (Signal.) *mmm.*
- Write the word **name.** Pencils down when you're finished.
(Observe children and give feedback.)

- (Write on the board:)

> **2   name**

- Here's the word **name.** It is spelled **N-A-M-E.**
d. Word 3 is **pan.** What word? (Signal.) *Pan.*
- Say **pan** a sound at a time. Get ready. (Tap 3 times.) *p   aaa   nnn.*
- Again. Say the first sound in **pan.** (Signal.) *p.*
- Say the next sound in **pan.** (Signal.) *aaa.*
- Say the last sound in **pan.** (Signal.) *nnn.*
- The middle sound in the word **pan** is **aaa.** What letter do you write for **aaa?** (Signal.) *A.*
- Write the word **pan.** Pencils down when you're finished.
(Observe children and give feedback.)
- (Write on the board:)

> **3   pan**

- Here's the word **pan.** It is spelled **P-A-N.**
e. Word 4 is **sad.** What word? (Signal.) *Sad.*
- Say **sad** a sound at a time. Get ready. (Tap 3 times.) *sss   aaa   d.*
- Again. Say the first sound in **sad.** (Signal.) *sss.*
- Say the next sound in **sad.** (Signal.) *aaa.*
- Say the last sound in **sad.** (Signal.) *d.*
- Write the word **sad.** Pencils down when you're finished.
(Observe children and give feedback.)
- (Write on the board:)

> **4   sad**

- Here's the word **sad.** It is spelled **S-A-D.**
f. Let's spell those words again.
- Word 1: **ant.** Spell **ant.** (Tap 3 times.) *A-N-T.*
- Word 2: **name.** Spell **name.** (Tap 4 times.) *N-A-M-E.*
- Word 3: **pan.** Spell **pan.** (Tap 3 times.) *P-A-N.*
- Word 4: **sad.** Spell **sad.** (Tap 3 times.) *S-A-D.*

════════ EXERCISE 12 ════════

## SENTENCE WRITING

a. (Write on the board: )

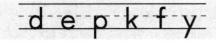

b. This is a sentence like one in the story. (Call on a child to read the sentence.)
c. Turn to the back of your paper. ✔
• Write this sentence on the top line. Make sure you leave a space after each word. Pencils down when you're finished. (Observe children and give feedback.)
d. Later, you can write the same sentence two more times on the lines below.

════════ EXERCISE 13 ════════

## LETTER PRINTING

a. (Write on the board)

d e p k f y

• You're going to write some letters.
b. Skip the next two lines on your paper, and put your pencil at the beginning of the line after that. Keep your pencil in place so I can see it. (Observe children and give feedback.)
• On that line you'll write the letter that makes the sound **k**. What sound? (Signal.) *k.*
• What letter makes that sound? (Signal.) *K.*

• Write the letter for **k**. Pencils down when you're finished. (Observe children and give feedback.)
c. Touch the next line. ✔
• On that line you'll write the letter that makes the sound **EEE**. What sound? (Signal.) *EEE.*
• Look on the board. What letter makes that sound? (Signal.) *E.*
• Write the letter for **EEE**. Pencils down when you're finished. (Observe children and give feedback.)
d. Touch the next line. ✔
• On that line you'll write the letter that makes the sound **d**. What sound? (Signal.) *d.*
• What letter makes that sound? (Signal.) *D.*
• Write the letter for **d**. Pencils down when you're finished. (Observe children and give feedback.)
e. Later, you'll complete the lines of letters.

**Independent Work Summary**
• Story extension (write missing words).
• Color story picture.
• Write appropriate words for pictures.
• Matching game.
• Cross-out (**that**=3) and circle (**this**=3) game.
• Sentence writing (copy two more times: **I ride my pal.**).
• Letter printing (finish lines of **k, e, d**).

**Materials:** Each child will need a pair of scissors, paste, a gray and a blue crayon, and lined paper.

## TEXTBOOK

---
## EXERCISE 1
---

### SOUNDS

a. Open your textbook to lesson 39. Find the cat. ✔
• I think that cat is stuck up in the tree and wants to climb down. Let's help him.
• (Teacher reference:)

| c | v | k | j | ck | j | p | c |

• You'll tell me the sounds for the letters on the tree trunk.
b. First letter. Everybody, what sound? (Signal.) *k.*
• Next sound. Get ready. (Signal.) *vvv.*
• (Repeat for remaining items.)
c. (Repeat step b until firm.)

---
## EXERCISE 2
---

### READING WORDS
### Words with Blue E

a. Find the owl. ✔
• (Teacher reference:)

| 1. tak*e* | 2. lak*e* | 3. jok*e* | 4. stov*e* |

• These words have a blue letter.
b. Word 1. Touch and say the sounds. Get ready. (Tap 3 times.) *t AAA k.*
• Again. Get ready. (Tap 3 times.) *t AAA k.*
• What word? (Signal.) *Take.*
• We will **take** a trip.
c. Word 2. Get ready. (Tap 3 times.) *lll AAA k.*
• What word? (Signal.) *Lake.*
d. Word 3. Get ready. (Tap 3 times.) *j OOO k.*

• What word? (Signal.) *Joke.*
• We like a funny **joke.**
e. Word 4 is a tough word. Get ready. (Tap 4 times.) *sss t OOO vvv.*
• Again. Get ready. (Tap 4 times.) *sss t OOO vvv.*
• What word? (Signal.) *Stove.*
• Yes, we cook on a **stove.**
f. Let's do those words again.
• Word 1. Get ready. (Tap 3 times.) *t AAA k.* What word? (Signal.) *Take.*
• Word 2. Get ready. (Tap 3 times.) *lll AAA k.* What word? (Signal.) *Lake.*
• Word 3. Get ready. (Tap 3 times.) *j OOO k.* What word? (Signal.) *Joke.*
• Word 4. Get ready. (Tap 4 times.) *sss t OOO vvv.* What word? (Signal.) *Stove.*

### Individual Turns

• (Call on different children to read one or two of the words.)

---
## EXERCISE 3
---

### READING WORDS
### Difficult Beginnings

a. I'll say words that have difficult beginning sounds. You'll say the sounds in those words.
b. The word **class** has four sounds. Listen: *c lll aaa sss.* Say the sounds in **class.** Get ready. (Tap 4 times.) *c lll aaa sss.*
• New word: **drive** has four sounds. Listen: *d rrr lll vvv.* Say the sounds in **drive.** Get ready. (Tap 4 times.) *d rrr lll vvv.*
• Listen: **stove** has four sounds. Say the sounds in **stove.** Get ready. (Tap 4 times.) *sss t OOO vvv.*
c. Find the squirrel. ✔
• (Teacher reference:)

| 1. old | 2. told | 3. sleep |
| 4. driv*e* | 5. trip | |

- Some of these words have difficult beginnings.
d. Word 1. Touch and say the sounds. Get ready. (Tap 3 times.) *OOO    lll    d.*
- What word? (Signal.) *Old.*
e. Word 2. Get ready. (Tap 4 times.) *t    OOO    lll    d.*
- What word? (Signal.) *Told.*
f. Word 3. Get ready. (Tap 4 times.) *sss    lll    EEE    p.*
- What word? (Signal.) *Sleep.*
g. Word 4 has a blue letter. Get ready. (Tap 4 times.) *d    rrr    III    vvv.*
- What word? (Signal.) *Drive.*
- Yes, **drive** that car.
h. Word 5 does not have a blue letter. Get ready. (Tap 4 times.) *t    rrr    iii    p.*
- What word? (Signal.) *Trip.*
i. Let's read those tough words one more time.
- Word 1. Get ready. (Tap 3 times.) *OOO    lll    d.*
  What word? (Signal.) *Old.*
- Word 2. Get ready. (Tap 4 times.) *t    OOO    lll    d.*
  What word? (Signal.) *Told.*
- Word 3. Get ready. (Tap 4 times.) *sss    lll    EEE    p.*
  What word? (Signal.) *Sleep.*
- Word 4. Get ready. (Tap 4 times.) *d    rrr    III    vvv.*
  What word? (Signal.) *Drive.*
- Word 5. Get ready. (Tap 4 times.) *t    rrr    iii    p.*
  What word? (Signal.) *Trip.*

**Individual Turns**
- (Call on different children to read one or two of the words.)

===== EXERCISE 4 =====

**READING WORDS**
**A Sound at a Time**

a. Find the dog. ✔
- (Teacher reference:)

---

| pine |
|------|
| ant |
| pa**th** |

- Maybe that's why the cat went up the tree.
b. The top word has a blue letter. Get ready. (Tap 3 times.) *p    III    nnn.*
- What word? (Signal.) *Pine.*
- Yes, a **pine** is a tree.
c. Middle word. Get ready. (Tap 3 times.) *aaa    nnn    t.*
- What word? (Signal.) *Ant.*
d. Bottom word. Get ready. (Tap 3 times.) *p    aaa    ththth.*
- What word? (Signal.) *Path.*
e. Let's do those words again.
- Top word. Get ready. (Tap 3 times.) *p    III    nnn.*
  What word? (Signal.) *Pine.*
- Middle word. Get ready. (Tap 3 times.) *aaa    nnn    t*
- What word? (Signal.) *Ant.*
- Bottom word. Get ready. (Tap 3 times.) *p    aaa    ththth.*
- What word? (Signal.) *Path.*
f. (Repeat step e until firm.)

**Individual Turns**
- (Call on different children to read one or two of the words.)

**Reading Words the Fast Way**
g. This time, you'll read the words the fast way. You won't say the sounds. You'll just tell me the word.
h. Top word. Figure out what the word is. Raise your hand when you know it. Everybody, what's the top word? (Signal.) *Pine.*
- Middle word. Raise your hand when you know it. Everybody, what's the middle word? (Signal.) *Ant.*
- Bottom word. Raise your hand when you know it. Everybody, what's the bottom word? (Signal.) *Path.*
i. (Repeat step h until firm.)

j. You're reading words the fast way.

**Individual Turns**

a. This time, I'll call on different children to read one of the words the fast way.

b. Everybody, touch the top word.
• (Call on a child.) Read the top word the fast way.

• (Repeat step b for remaining words.)

═══════ EXERCISE 5 ═══════

**STORY READING**
**Introducing Question Mark**

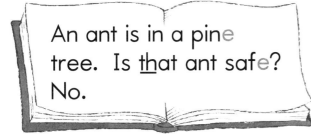

An ant is in a pine
tree. Is that ant safe?
No.

a. Find the book. ✔
• (Write on the board:)

| ? |
|---|

• This is a question mark. Some sentences do not end with a period. They end with a question mark. That means someone is asking a question. One of the sentences in the story you will read ends with a question mark.

b. Touch the period at the end of the first sentence.
(Observe children and give feedback.)

• You should be touching the period that is right before the capital **I.**

• There is no period at the end of the next sentence. There is a question mark. Touch it.
(Observe children and give feedback.)

• You should be touching the question mark that is **at the end of the second line.**

• The next sentence has only one word. Touch the period at the **end** of that sentence.
(Observe children and give feedback.)

c. Everybody, touch the first word of the story. ✔

• You'll read all the words in the first sentence.

• First word. Say the sounds. Get ready. (Tap 2 times.) *aaa    nnn.*
What word? (Signal.) *An.*

d. Next word. Get ready. (Tap 3 times.) *aaa    nnn    t.*
What word? (Signal.) *Ant.*

e. (Repeat step d for remaining words: **is, in, a, pine, tree.**)

f. Listen to that whole sentence: **An ant is in a pine tree.**

g. Everybody, say all the words in the first sentence. (Signal.) *An ant is in a pine tree.*

• (Repeat until firm.)

h. Touch the first word of the next sentence. ✔

• Say the sounds. Get ready. (Tap 2 times.) *iii    sss.*
What word? (Signal.) *Is.*

i. Next word. Get ready. (Tap 3 times.) *ththth    aaa    t.*
What word? (Signal.) *That.*

j. (Repeat step i for remaining words: **ant, safe.**)

k. Everybody, say that sentence. (Signal.) *Is that ant safe?*

• (Repeat until firm.)

l. That sentence is a question.

m. Touch the only word in the last sentence. ✔

• Say the sounds. Get ready. (Tap 2 times.) *nnn    OOO.*
What word? (Signal.) *No.*

n. Say that sentence. (Signal.) *No.*

═══════ EXERCISE 6 ═══════

**COMPREHENSION**

a. Find the first picture. ✔

An ant is in a pine tree.

- What's in that picture? (Call on a child. Idea: *An ant on a pine tree branch.*)
- Read the sentence under the picture. (Call on a child. *An ant is in a pine tree.*)

b. Find the next picture. ✔

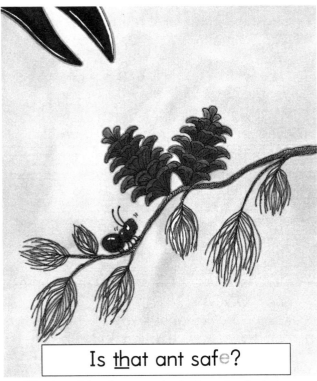

Is that ant safe?

- That ant looks worried. Read what it says under that picture. (Call on a child. *Is that ant safe?*)
- **Is that ant safe?** That's a question.

c. Touch the last picture. ✔

- Everybody, is the ant safe? (Signal.) *No.*
- You can see why the ant is not safe. What could happen? (Call on a child. Idea: *The ant could be eaten by a bird.*)

WORKBOOK

EXERCISE 7

**STORY EXTENSION**
**Cut-Out: Picture**

*Note:* Each child will need a pair of scissors and paste.

a. Close your textbook. Open your workbook to lesson 39. ✔
- Find the picture. This is a picture of the story and the story is below, but the ant is not in the picture. There's a picture of an ant at the top of your worksheet.

b. Later, you'll cut it out and paste it where the ant is safe. If you put it between the pine cones, that bird wouldn't be able to get it.

## EXERCISE 8

**INDEPENDENT WORK**

### Sentence Completion: Child's Name

a. Touch the number 39 at the top of your worksheet. ✔

b. There's part of a sentence after 39. Read it to yourself and write the missing part to complete the sentence. Remember the period.

(Observe children and give feedback.)

### Hidden Picture

> **Note:** Each child needs a gray and a blue crayon.

c. Find the hidden picture at the bottom of your worksheet. ✔
- Touch the word in the first box. ✔
- Raise your hand when you can read that word.
  Everybody, what word? (Signal.) *Seal.*
d. Touch the word in the other box. ✔
- Raise your hand when you can read that word.
  Everybody, what word? (Signal.) *Fine.*
e. I'll tell you the coloring rules for the picture.
- Listen: All the parts with the word **seal** are gray. Make a gray mark for the word **seal.** ✔
- Touch the box for the word **fine.** ✔
- Listen: All the parts with the word **fine** are blue. Make a blue mark for the word **fine.**
f. Later, you'll color the picture.

### Words for Pictures: Plural S

1. \_\_\_\_\_ram\_\_\_\_\_  2. \_\_\_\_ant\_\_\_\_

3. \_\_\_\_rat\_\_\_\_  4. \_\_\_seal\_\_\_

g. Go to side 2 of your worksheet. ✔
- The words under the pictures tell about just one animal. But some of the pictures show more than one animal. You're going to fix up the words under those pictures.
h. Picture 1. How many rams are in that picture? (Signal.) *Two.*
- Touch the word under the picture.
- Say the sounds. Get ready. (Tap 3 times.) *rrr aaa mmm.*
- What word? (Signal.) *Ram.*
- That word tells about one ram. What letter would you write on the end of that word to make it tell about more than one ram? (Signal.) *S.*
i. Fix up the word under picture 1. Pencils down when you're finished.

(Observe children and give feedback.)
- (Write on the board:)

> **1. rams**

- Here's what you should have. You should have the word **rams** under picture 1.
j. Picture 2. How many ants are in the picture? (Signal.) *One.*
- Touch the word under the picture. Say the sounds. Get ready. (Tap 3 times.) *aaa nnn t.*
- What word? (Signal.) *Ant.*
- That word tells about the picture. There is an **ant** in the picture.
- Do you write anything on the end of that word? (Signal.) *No.*

k. Picture 3. How many rats are in the picture? (Signal.) *Three.*
• Touch the word under the picture. Say the sounds. Get ready. (Tap 3 times.) *rrr aaa t.*
• What word? (Signal.) *Rat.*
• Does that word tell how many are in the picture? (Signal.) *No.*
• What letter would you write at the end of the word so it tells about more than one rat? (Signal.) *S.*
• Fix up the word. Pencils down when you're finished.
  (Observe children and give feedback.)
• (Write on the board:)

> **3. rats**

• Here's what you should have for picture 3.
l. Picture 4. How many seals are in the picture? (Signal.) *Four.*
• Touch the word under the picture. Say the sounds. Get ready. (Tap 3 times.) *sss EEE lll.*
• What word? (Signal.) *Seal.*
• Does that word tell how many are in the picture? (Signal.) *No.*
• What letter would you write at the end of the word so it tells about more than one seal? (Signal.) *S.*
• Fix up the word. Pencils down when you're finished.
  (Observe children and give feedback.)
• (Write on the board:)

> **4. seals**

• Here's what you should have for picture 4.
m. Go back to the word under picture 1. Everybody, touch and say the sounds. Get ready. (Tap 4 times.)
  *rrr aaa mmm sss.*
• What word? (Signal.) *Rams.*
• Touch the word under picture 3. Everybody, touch and say the sounds. Get ready. (Tap 4 times.)
  *rrr aaa t sss.*
• What word? (Signal.) *Rats.*
• You are reading some difficult words.

**Matching: Words**
n. Find the matching game. ✔
• Two of the words are missing. You'll write those words in the blanks.
• Some of the lines are missing.
• Later, you'll draw a line to connect the words that are the same. Write the missing words.

LINED PAPER
========EXERCISE 9========
**SPELLING WORDS**

a. Get ready to write on lined paper.
• You're going to write words that do not have a letter that says its name.
• Number four lines on your paper. Pencils down when you're finished.
  (Observe children and give feedback.)
b. Word 1 is **if.** What word? (Signal.) *If.*
• **If** has two sounds. Say **if** a sound at a time. Get ready. (Tap 2 times.) *iii fff.*
• Again. Say the first sound in **if.** (Signal.) *iii.*
• Say the next sound in **if.** (Signal.) *fff.*
• The first sound in **if** is **iii.** What letter do you write for **iii?** (Signal.) *I.*
• Write the word **if.** Pencils down when you're finished.
  (Observe children and give feedback.)
• (Write on the board:)

> **1 if**

• Here's the word **if.** It is spelled **I-F.**
c. Word 2 is **in.** What word? (Signal.) *In.*
• **In** has two sounds. Say **in** a sound at a time. Get ready. (Tap 2 times.)
  *iii nnn.*
• Again. Say the first sound in **in.** (Signal.) *iii.*
• Say the next sound in **in.** (Signal.) *nnn.*
• Write the word **in.** Pencils down when you're finished.
  (Observe children and give feedback.)
• (Write on the board:)

> **2 in**

• Here's the word **in.** It is spelled **I-N.**

d. Word 3 is **fan.** What word? (Signal.) *Fan.*
- Say **fan** a sound at a time. Get ready. (Tap 3 times.) *fff   aaa   nnn.*
- Again. Say the first sound in **fan.** (Signal.) *fff.*
- Say the next sound in **fan.** (Signal.) *aaa.*
- Say the last sound in **fan.** (Signal.) *nnn.*
- The middle sound in the word **fan** is **aaa.** What letter do you write for **aaa?** (Signal.) *A.*
- Write the word **fan.** Pencils down when you're finished.
  (Observe children and give feedback.)
- (Write on the board:)

### 3 fan

- Here's the word **fan.** It is spelled **F-A-N.**

e. Word 4 is **pin.** What word? (Signal.) *Pin.*
- Say **pin** a sound at a time. Get ready. (Tap 3 times.) *p   iii   nnn.*
- Again. Say the first sound in **pin.** (Signal.) *p.*
- Say the next sound in **pin.** (Signal.) *iii.*
- Say the last sound in **pin.** (Signal.) *nnn.*
- The middle sound in the word **pin** is **iii.** What letter do you write for **iii?** (Signal.) *I.*
- Write the word **pin.** Pencils down when you're finished.
  (Observe children and give feedback.)
- (Write on the board:)

### 4 pin

- Here's the word **pin.** It is spelled **P-I-N.**

f. Let's spell those words again.
- Word 1: **if.** Spell **if.** (Tap 2 times.) *I-F.*
- Word 2: **in.** Spell **in.** (Tap 2 times.) *I-N.*
- Word 3: **fan.** Spell **fan.** (Tap 3 times.) *F-A-N.*
- Word 4: **pin.** Spell **pin.** (Tap 3 times.) *P-I-N.*

===== EXERCISE 10 =====
## LETTER PRINTING

a. (Write on the board:)

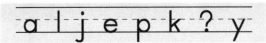

b. Turn to the back of your paper. ✔
- Touch the top line. ✔
  On that line you'll write a question mark. I'll show you how to make it. (Demonstrate.)
- Write a question mark. Pencils down when you're finished.
  (Observe children and give feedback.)
c. Touch the next line. ✔
- On that line you'll write the letter that makes the sound **j.** What sound? (Signal.) *j.*
- What letter makes that sound? (Signal.) *J.*
- Write the letter for **j.** Pencils down when you're finished.
  (Observe children and give feedback.)
d. Touch the next line. ✔
- On that line you'll write the letter that makes the sound **III.** What sound? (Signal.) *III.*
- Look at the board. Which letter on the board makes the sound **III?** (Signal.) *Y.*
- Write the letter for **III.** Pencils down when you're finished.
  (Observe children and give feedback.)
e. Touch the next line. ✔
- On that line you'll write the letter that makes the sound **p.** What sound? (Signal.) *p.*
- What letter makes that sound? (Signal.) *P.*
- Write the letter for **p.** Pencils down when you're finished.
  (Observe children and give feedback.)
f. Later, you'll complete the lines.

===== EXERCISE 11 =====
## SENTENCE WRITING

a. (Write on the board:)

Is that ant safe?

b. This is a sentence like one in the story. (Call on a child to read the sentence.)

c. You'll write this sentence on the next line. You'll make a question mark, not a period, when you write this sentence on your paper. Pencils down when you're finished.
(Observe children and give feedback.)

d. Later, you can write the same sentence two more times on the lines below.

**Independent Work Summary**
- Story extension (cut and paste ant between cones).
- Color story picture.
- Hidden picture (**seal**=gray, **fine**=blue).
- Matching game.
- Letter printing (finish lines of **?**, **j**, **y**, **p**).
- Sentence writing (copy two more times: **Is that ant safe?**).

- The word for that line is **pin**. What word?
  (Signal.) *Pin.*
- Say the sounds in **pin**. Get ready.
  (Tap 3 times.) *p   iii   nnn.*
- Write the word **pin** on line 4. Pencils
  down when you're finished.
  (Observe children.)

=========== EXERCISE 2 ===========

**STORYBOOK**
  **Cut-Out: Pictures**

*Note:* Each child needs scissors, paste
and crayons.

a. Today you'll get to do something special.
   While I'm listening to each child read,
   you're going to make a booklet.
b. There are four sentences.
- First you'll read each sentence in the
  booklet. Then you'll cut out each picture
  and glue it above the sentence that tells
  about the picture.
c. When you're all finished, you can color
   the pictures. Be sure to read the story to
   someone at home.

=========== EXERCISE 3 ===========

**TEST—Individually Administered**

*Note:* Individually administer the rest
of the test: WORD READING. Mark all
errors. Record the test results on the
Test Summary Sheet for test 4.

**Part 2: WORD READING**
a. Go to the top of side 2. ✔
b. Touch number 1. ✔
- Touch and say the sounds.
  *[p   lll   AAA.]*
- What word? *[Play.]*
c. Touch number 2. ✔
- Touch and say the sounds.
  *[s   lll   EEE   p.]*
- What word? *[Sleep.]*
d. Touch number 3. ✔
- Touch and say the sounds.
  *[d   rrr   lll   vvv.]*

---

**Materials:** Each child will need scissors,
paste and crayons.

**Note:** Administer WORD WRITING to the
entire group. Individually administer
WORD READING.

---

**WORKBOOK**

=========== EXERCISE 1 ===========

**TEST—Group Administered**
**Part 1: WORD WRITING**

a. Open your workbook to lesson 40,
   test 4. ✔
   This is another test.
- Complete the sentence at the top of
  the page. ✔
b. Find the fish. ✔
- You're going to write some words.
c. Touch line 1. ✔
- The word for that line is **if**. What word?
  (Signal.) *If.*
- Say the sounds in **if**. Get ready.
  (Tap 2 times.) *iii   fff.*
- Write the word **if** on line 1. Pencils down
  when you're finished.
  (Observe children but do not give
  feedback.)
d. Touch line 2. ✔
- The word for that line is **tap**. What word?
  (Signal.) *Tap.*
- Say the sounds in **tap**. Get ready.
  (Tap 3 times.) *t   aaa   p.*
- Write the word **tap** on line 2. Pencils
  down when you're finished.
  (Observe children.)
e. Touch line 3. ✔
- The word for that line is **fan**. What word?
  (Signal.) *Fan.*
- Say the sounds in **fan**. Get ready.
  (Tap 3 times.) *fff   aaa   nnn.*
- Write the word **fan** on line 3. Pencils
  down when you're finished.
  (Observe children.)
f. Touch line 4. ✔

- What word? *[Drive.]*
e. Touch number 4. ✔
- Touch and say the sounds.
  *[k   EEE   p.]*
- What word? *[Keep.]*
f. Touch number 5. ✔
- Touch and say the sounds.
  *[p   aaa   thtth.]*
- What word? *[Path.]*
g. Touch number 6. ✔
- Touch and say the sounds.
  *[t   AAA   k.]*
- What word? *[Take.]*
h. Touch number 7. ✔
- Touch and say the sounds.
  *[thtth   OOO   sss.]*
- What word? *[Those.]*
i. Touch number 8. ✔
- Touch and say the sounds.
  *[mmm   OOO   rrr.]*
- What word? *[More.]*
j. Touch number 9. ✔
- Touch and say the sounds.
  *[j   AAA   lll.]*
- What word? *[Jail.]*
k. Touch number 10. ✔
- Touch and say the sounds.
  *[t   rrr   EEE.]*
- What word? *[Tree.]*

═══════════ EXERCISE 4 ═══════════

## STORYBOOK
### Take Home

**Note:** Each child needs scissors.

a. (Remove perforated test sheet from workbook.)

b. (Direct children to cut along the top dotted line.)
c. (Collect test part of sheets.)
d. (Direct children to fold their booklet along the fold line.)
e. Now you can take the storybook home and read it to your family.
f. (After testing all children, check out each child on the reading the entire story.)

═══════════ EXERCISE 5 ═══════════

## MARKING THE TEST

- (Record all test results on the lesson 40, Test 4 Summary Sheet. Reproducible Summary Sheets are at the back of the Teacher's Guide.)

═══════════ EXERCISE 6 ═══════════

## TEST REMEDIES

- (Provide any necessary remedies for Test 4 before presenting lesson 41. Test Remedies are discussed in the Teacher's Guide.)

═══════════ EXERCISE 7 ═══════════

## LITERATURE BOOK

- (See Teacher's Guide.)

**Materials:** Each child will need scissors, paste and lined paper.

## TEXTBOOK

======= EXERCISE 1 =======

### SOUNDS

a. Open your textbook to lesson 41. Find the crow. ✔
• That crow is sitting on top of a fence.
• Touch the top letter combination on the crow. ✔
• (Teacher reference:)

> th
> ck
> ay

b. Touch and say the sound for each combination.
• First combination. Get ready. (Signal.) *thththth.*
• Next combination. Get ready. (Signal.) *k.*
• Last combination. Get ready. (Signal.) *AAA.*
c. (Repeat step b until firm.)
d. This time, I'll say sounds for the combinations on the crow. You'll touch the combination and tell me the letter names.
e. Listen: The sound for one of the combinations is **k.**
• Touch that combination. ✔
• Everybody, spell the combination. Get ready. (Signal.) *C-K.*
f. Listen: The sound for one of the combinations is **thththth.**
• Touch that combination. ✔
• Everybody, spell the combination. Get ready. (Signal.) *T-H.*
g. Listen: The sound for one of the combinations is **AAA.**
• Touch that combination. ✔
• Everybody, spell the combination. Get ready. (Signal.) *A-Y.*

h. (Repeat steps e through g until firm.)
i. Touch the letter on the first fence post. ✔
• (Teacher reference:)

> v   c   d   j   k

j. Say the sound. Get ready. (Signal.) *vvv.*
• Next sound. Get ready. (Signal.) *k.*
• Next sound. Get ready. (Signal.) *d.*
• Next sound. Get ready. (Signal.) *j.*
• Last sound. Get ready. (Signal.) *k.*
k. Touch the bush. ✔
• (Teacher reference:)

> i   a

• You know two sounds for each letter.
l. Touch the first letter. When there is a blue letter in a word, what sound does it make? (Signal.) *III.*
What's the other sound? (Signal.) *iii.*
• Touch the next letter. When there is a blue letter in a word, what sound does it make? (Signal.) *AAA.*
What's the other sound? (Signal.) *aaa.*
m. (Repeat step l until firm.)

======= EXERCISE 2 =======

### READING WORDS
#### Words with k Sound

a. Find the scarecrow. ✔
• (Teacher reference:)

> 1. cat    4. rake
> 2. kite    5. cold
> 3. si**ck**

• That scarecrow sure doesn't seem to be scaring away that crow.
• All these words have the sound **k** in them.
b. Word 1. Touch the letter or combination that makes the **k** sound.
What is the name of the letter you are touching? (Signal.) *C.*
• Word 2. Touch the letter or combination that makes the **k** sound.
What letter are you touching? (Signal.) *K.*

Word 3. Touch the letter or combination
that makes the **k** sound.
What letters are you touching?
**(Signal.)** *C-K.*

• Word 4. Touch the letter or combination
that makes the **k** sound.
What letter are you touching? **(Signal.)** *K.*

• Word 5. Touch the letter or combination
that makes the **k** sound.
What letter are you touching? **(Signal.)** *C.*

c. Go back to word 1. What sound do you
say for the letter **C?** **(Signal.)** *k.*

• Word 1 does not have a blue letter.
Touch and say the sounds. Get ready.
**(Tap 3 times.)** *c   aaa   t.*

• Again. Get ready. **(Tap 3 times.)**
*c   aaa   t.*

• What word? **(Signal.)** *Cat.*

• I pet a **cat.**

d. Word 2 has a blue letter. Touch and say
the sounds. Get ready. **(Tap 3 times.)**
*k   III   t.*

• Again. Get ready. **(Tap 3 times.)**
*k   III   t.*

• What word? **(Signal.)** *Kite.*

• Yes, go fly a **kite.**

e. Word 3 does not have a blue letter. Get
ready. **(Tap 3 times.)** *sss   iii   k.*

• Again. Get ready. **(Tap 3 times.)**
*sss   iii   k.*

• What word? **(Signal.)** *Sick.*

• Yes, the girl was **sick.**

f. Word 4 has a blue letter. Get ready. **(Tap
3 times.)** *rrr   AAA   k.*

• Again. Get ready. **(Tap 3 times.)**
*rrr   AAA   k.*

• What word? **(Signal.)** *Rake.*

• Yes, **rake** those leaves.

g. Word 5 is a tough word. It has four
sounds. Get ready. **(Tap 4 times.)**
*c   OOO   lll   d.*

• Again. Get ready. **(Tap 4 times.)**
*c   OOO   lll   d.*

• What word? **(Signal.)** *Cold.*

h. Let's do those words again.

i. Word 1. Get ready. **(Tap 3 times.)**
*c   aaa   t.*
What word? **(Signal.)** *Cat.*

j. Next word. Get ready. **(Tap 3 times.)**
*k   III   t.*

L• What word? **(Signal.)** *Kite.*

k. (Repeat step j for remaining words: **sick,
rake, cold.**)

**Individual Turns**
• (Call on different children to read one or
two of the words.)

═══════════ EXERCISE 3 ═══════════

**READING WORDS**
**Words with S Ending**

a. Find the pumpkin. ✔

• (Teacher reference:)

| pins |
| :---: |
| jok**e**s |
| vans |

• All these words tell about more than one
thing. The last letter in each word is **S.**

b. The top word does not have a blue letter.
Touch and say the sounds. Get ready.
**(Tap 4 times.)** *p   iii   nnn   sss.*

• What word? **(Signal.)** *Pins.*

c. Middle word. Get ready. **(Tap 4 times.)**
*j   OOO   k   sss.*

• What word? **(Signal.)** *Jokes.*

d. Bottom word. Get ready. **(Tap 4 times.)**
*vvv   aaa   nnn   sss.*

• What word? **(Signal.)** *Vans.*

e. Let's do those words again.

• Top word. Get ready. **(Tap 4 times.)**
*p   iii   nnn   sss.*
What word? **(Signal.)** *Pins.*

• Middle word. Get ready. **(Tap 4 times.)**
*j   OOO   k   sss.*
What word? **(Signal.)** *Jokes.*

• Bottom word. Get ready. **(Tap 4 times.)**
*vvv   aaa   nnn   sss.*
What word? **(Signal.)** *Vans.*

f. (Repeat step e until firm.)

g. This time, you'll read the words the fast
way. You won't say the sounds. You'll just
tell me the word.

h. Top word. Figure out what the word is.
Raise your hand when you know it.
Everybody, what's the top word?
**(Signal.)** *Pins.*

- Middle word. Raise your hand when you know it.
  Everybody, what's the middle word? (Signal.) *Jokes.*
- Bottom word. Raise your hand when you know it.
  Everybody, what's the bottom word? (Signal.) *Vans.*
  i. (Repeat step h until firm.)

**Individual Turns**
- (Call on different children to read one or two of the words.)

═══════ EXERCISE 4 ═══════
**READING WORDS**
**Difficult Beginnings**

a. I'll say words that have difficult beginning sounds. You'll say the sounds for those words.
- **Class** has four sounds. Listen:
  c lll aaa sss.
- Say the sounds in **class.** (Tap 4 times.)
  *c lll aaa sss.*
b. New word. **Drove** has four sounds.
  Listen: d rrr OOO vvv.
- Say the sounds in **drove.** (Tap 4 times.)
  *d rrr OOO vvv.*
c. New word. **Store** has four sounds. Listen:
  sss t OOO rrr.
- Say the sounds in **store.** (Tap 4 times.)
  *sss t OOO rrr.*
d. Find the haystack. ✔
- (Teacher reference:)

| | | |
|---|---|---|
| 1. **old** | 4. **flip** |
| 2. **sold** | 5. **driv**ₑ |
| 3. **stor**ₑ | 6. **fiv**ₑ |

- Word 1. Touch and say the sounds. Get ready. (Tap 3 times.) *OOO lll d.*
- What word? (Signal.) *Old.*
e. Word 2. Get ready. (Tap 4 times.)
  *sss OOO lll d.*
- Again. Get ready. (Tap 4 times.)
  *sss OOO lll d.*
  What word? (Signal.) *Sold.*

f. Word 3. Get ready. (Tap 4 times.)
  *sss t OOO rrr.*
- Again. Get ready. (Tap 4 times.)
  *sss t OOO rrr.*
  What word? (Signal.) *Store.*
g. Word 4 does not have a blue letter. Get ready. (Tap 4 times.) *fff lll iii p.*
- What word? (Signal.) *Flip.*
h. Word 5. Get ready. (Tap 4 times.)
  *d rrr lll vvv.*
- What word? (Signal.) *Drive.*
i. Word 6. Get ready. (Tap 3 times.)
  *fff lll vvv.*
- What word? (Signal.) *Five.*
j. Let's read those tough words one more time.
- Word 1. Get ready. (Tap 3 times.)
  *OOO lll d.*
  What word? (Signal.) *Old.*
k. Next word. Get ready. (Tap 4 times.)
  *sss OOO lll d.*
- What word? (Signal.) *Sold.*
l. (Repeat step k for remaining words:
  **store, flip, drive, five.**)
m. You are reading some very difficult words. Good for you.

**Individual Turns**
- (Call on different children to read one of the words.)

═══════ EXERCISE 5 ═══════
**STORY READING**

An ant is in a pan.
That pan is in a van.
Is a man in the van? No.
See a molₑ drivₑ.

a. Find the book. ✔
- One sentence in this story is a question. It ends with a question mark, not a period. Touch the mark at the end of the first sentence. You should be touching the period at the end of the first line. ✔

- Touch the mark at the end of the second line. You should be touching the period just after the small letter **N.** ✔
- Touch the mark at the end of the third sentence. ✔
  Everybody, what kind of mark are you touching? (Signal.) *A question mark.*
- You should be touching the question mark just after the small letter **N.** ✔

b. Go back to the first sentence.
- You'll read all the words in the first sentence.
- First word. Say the sounds. Get ready. (Tap 2 times.) *aaa    nnn.*
  What word? (Signal.) *An.*

c. Next word. Get ready. (Tap 3 times.) *aaa    nnn    t.*
   What word? (Signal.) *Ant.*
- (Repeat step c for: **is, in, a, pan.**)

d. Everybody, say all the words in the first sentence. (Signal.) *An ant is in a pan.*
- (Repeat until firm.)

e. Touch the first word of the next sentence. ✔
- Say the sounds. Get ready. (Tap 3 times.) *ththth    aaa    t.*
  What word? (Signal.) *That.*

f. Next word. Get ready. (Tap 3 times.) *p    aaa    nnn.*
   What word? (Signal.) *Pan.*
- (Repeat step f for: **is, in, a, van.**)

g. Everybody, say all the words in that sentence. (Signal.) *That pan is in a van.*
- (Repeat until firm.)

h. Touch the first word of the next sentence. ✔
- Say the sounds. Get ready. (Tap 2 times.) *iii    sss.*
  What word? (Signal.) *Is.*
- Next word. What word? (Signal.) *A.*

i. Next word. Get ready. (Tap 3 times.) *mmm    aaa    nnn.*
   What word? (Signal.) *Man.*
- (Repeat step i for: **in, the, van.**)

j. That sentence is a question.

k. Everybody, say the question. (Signal.) *Is a man in the van?*
   (Repeat until firm.)

l. The next sentence has only one word. Everybody, what word? (Signal.) *No.*

m. Touch the first word of the next sentence. ✔
- Say the sounds. Get ready. (Tap 2 times.) *sss    EEE.*
  What word? (Signal.) *See.*
- Next word. What word? (Signal.) *A.*

n. Next word. Get ready. (Tap 3 times.) *mmm    OOO    lll.*
   What word? (Signal.) *Mole.*
- Last word. Get ready. (Tap 4 times.) *d    rrr    lll    vvv.*
  What word? (Signal.) *Drive.*

o. Everybody, say all the words in that sentence. (Signal.) *See a mole drive.*
- (Repeat until firm.)

**Second Reading**

p. I'm going to call on different children to read sentences in the story. Everybody else follow along and touch the words as they are read and say "Stop" as soon as the last word of the sentence is read.
- (Call on a child to read the first sentence: *An ant is in a pan.*) (Children say: *Stop.*)
- That's the end of the first sentence.

q. Everybody, say the first sentence. (Signal.) *An ant is in a pan.*
- (Repeat until firm.)

r. Everybody, touch the first word of the next sentence. ✔
- (Call on a child to read the second sentence: *That pan is in a van.*) (Children say: *Stop.*)

s. Everybody, say that sentence. (Signal.) *That pan is in a van.*
- (Repeat until firm.)

t. Everybody, touch the first word of the next sentence. ✔
- (Call on a child to read the third sentence: *Is a man in the van?*) (Children say: *Stop.*)

u. Everybody, say that sentence. (Signal.) *Is a man in the van?*
- (Repeat until firm.)

v. The next sentence is **No.**

w. Everybody, touch the first word of the last sentence. ✔
- (Call on a child to read the last sentence: *See a mole drive.*) (Children say: *Stop.*)

x. Everybody, say that sentence.
(Signal.) *See a mole drive.*
- (Repeat until firm.)

━━━━━━━ EXERCISE 6 ━━━━━━━
## WORD FINDING

a. This time you'll find words in the **second** or **third** sentence.
b. Listen: One of the words is **man.** What word? (Signal.) *Man.*
- Touch the word **man.** Get ready. (Signal.) (Observe children and give feedback.)
c. Listen: One of the words is **that.** What word? (Signal.) *That.*
- Touch the word **that.** Get ready. (Signal.) (Observe children and give feedback.)
d. Listen: One of the words is **the.** What word? (Signal.) *The.*
- Touch the word **the.** Get ready. (Signal.) (Observe children and give feedback.)
e. Listen: One of the words is **pan.** What word? (Signal.) *Pan.*
- Touch the word **pan.** Get ready. (Signal.) (Observe children and give feedback.)
f. (Repeat steps b through e until firm.)

━━━━━━━ EXERCISE 7 ━━━━━━━
## COMPREHENSION

a. Find the pictures for the story. ✔
- Touch the first picture. ✔
- What's in that pan? (Signal.) *An ant.*
- Touch the sentence under the picture. It says: **An ant is in a pan.**
b. Touch the next picture. ✔
- You can see the pan inside a vehicle. What kind of vehicle is that? (Signal.) *Van.*
- Touch the sentence under the picture. It says: **That pan is in a van.**
c. Touch the last picture. ✔
- You can see who is driving that van. Who's driving? (Signal.) *Mole.*
- I don't think a mole can see where to go. That could be a dangerous ride.
- There are three sentences under the picture. They say: **Is a man in the van? No. See a mole drive.**

- Oh dear. I hope the mole is just pretending to drive and not really driving.

━━━━━━━ EXERCISE 8 ━━━━━━━
## STORY EXTENSION
### Cut-Out: Pictures

*Note:* Each child will need a pair of scissors and paste.

a. Close your textbook. Open your workbook to lesson 41, and complete the sentence at the top of your worksheet. Pencils down when you're finished. ✔ (Observe children and give feedback.)
b. Find the picture from the story. ✔
- This is a picture of the van with the mole driving it. The story is next to the picture. There is no pan. And there is no ant in the van.
- There's a picture of a pan at the bottom of the page. Touch it. ✔
- You'll draw an ant in that pan. Then you'll cut out the pan and paste it in the van.
- What are you going to draw in the pan? (Signal.) *An ant.*
- Where are you going to paste the pan? (Signal.) *In the van.*

━━━━━━━ EXERCISE 9 ━━━━━━━
## INDEPENDENT WORK

### Matching: Words
a. Find the matching game. None of the words in the right column have blue letters. Some of the words are missing. You'll write the missing words and draw lines to connect the other words.

### Cross-Out and Circle Game
b. Find the cross-out game. Raise your hand when you know the word you'll cross out. Everybody, what word? (Signal.) *Rat.*

- Raise your hand when you know the word you'll circle. Everybody, what word? (Signal.) *Fat.*

## Words for Pictures—Plural S

fan    fans        tree    trees

c. Find the four pictures. ✔
- There are two words under each picture. One of the words is right and one is wrong. You'll cross out the word that is wrong.
d. Touch the first picture. ✔
- What is in that picture? (Signal.) *Fans.*
- Yes, there are **fans** in the picture.
- Read the words under the picture to yourself. Touch the word that is **wrong**. ✔
- Everybody, tell me the word you're touching. (Signal.) *Fan.*
- The word **fans** is right. The word **fan** is wrong.
- Cross out the word **fan.** ✔
e. Touch the picture of a tree. ✔
- Read the words under the **tree** to yourself. Cross out the word that is wrong. Pencils down when you've done that much.
  **(Observe children and give feedback.)**
- You should have crossed out the word **trees.** The picture shows **tree**, not **trees.**
f. Later, you can fix up the rest of the words. Remember, cross out the wrong word under the picture.

═══════ EXERCISE 10 ═══════

## SPELLING WORDS

a. Now you're going to spell words that end with a blue **E.** The words will have either the letter **A** or the letter **I.**
b. Listen: **fine.** What word? (Signal.) *Fine.*
- Everybody, say the sounds in **fine.** Get ready. (Tap 3 times.) *fff    III    nnn.*

- What's the letter name you hear in **fine?** (Signal.) *I.*
- Everybody, spell the word **fine.** Get ready. (Tap 4 times.) *F-I-N-E.*
c. New word: **mile.** What word? (Signal.) *Mile.*
- Say the sounds in **mile.** Get ready. (Tap 3 times.) *mmm    III    lll.*
- What's the letter name you hear in **mile?** (Signal.) *I.*
- Everybody, spell the word **mile.** Get ready. (Tap 4 times.) *M-I-L-E.*
d. New word: **time.** What word? (Signal.) *Time.*
- Say the sounds in **time.** Get ready. (Tap 3 times.) *t    III    mmm.*
- What's the letter name you hear in **time?** (Signal.) *I.*
- Everybody, spell the word **time.** Get ready. (Tap 4 times.) *T-I-M-E.*
e. New word: **tape.** What word? (Signal.) *Tape.*
- Say the sounds in **tape.** Get ready. (Tap 3 times.) *t    AAA    p.*
- What's the letter name you hear in **tape?** (Signal.) *A.*
- Everybody, spell the word **tape.** Get ready. (Tap 4 times.) *T-A-P-E.*

### LINED PAPER
f. Get ready to write the words we just spelled.
- Number four lines on your paper. Pencils down when you're finished.
  **(Observe children and give feedback.)**
g. Touch number 1. ✔
- Write the word **mile.** Pencils down when you're finished.
  **(Observe children and give feedback.)**
- (Write on the board:)

> **1 mile**

- Here's what you should have. **(Touch letters as you spell them.)** Mile is spelled M-I-L-E.
h. Touch number 2. ✔
- Write the word **fine.** Pencils down when you're finished.

(Observe children and give feedback.)
- (Write on the board:)

### 2 fine

- Here's what you should have. (Touch letters as you spell them.) **Fine** is spelled **F-I-N-E.**
i. Touch number 3. ✔
- Write the word **tape.** Pencils down when you're finished.
  (Observe children and give feedback.)
- (Write on the board:)

### 3 tape

- Here's what you should have. (Touch letters as you spell them.) **Tape** is spelled **T-A-P-E.**
j. Touch number 4. ✔
- Write the word **time.** Pencils down when you're finished.
  (Observe children and give feedback.)
- (Write on the board:)

### 4 time

- Here's what you should have. (Touch letters as you spell them.) **Time** is spelled **T-I-M-E.**
k. Raise your hand if you got everything right. You're spelling and writing some hard words.

====== EXERCISE 11 ======

## SENTENCE WRITING

a. (Write on the board:)

-See an ant sit.-

b. You're going to write this sentence. (Call on a child to read the sentence.)
c. Turn to the back of your paper. ✔

- Write this sentence on the top line. Pencils down when you're finished.
  (Observe children and give feedback.)
d. Later, you can write the same sentence two more times on the lines below.

====== EXERCISE 12 ======

## LETTER PRINTING

a. (Write on the board:)

th c a s v ay t

- Get ready to write some letters.
b. Skip the next two lines on your paper, and put your pencil at the beginning of the line after that. Keep your pencil in place so I can see it.
  (Observe children and give feedback.)
- On that line you'll write the letter that makes the sound **vvv.** What sound? (Signal.) *vv.*
- What letter makes that sound? (Signal.) *V.*
- Write the letter for **vvv.** Pencils down when you're finished. ✔
c. Touch the next line. ✔
- On that line you'll write the letter that makes the sound **k.** What sound? (Signal.) *k.*
- Look at the board. What letter makes that sound? (Signal.) *C.*
- I'll show you how to write **C.**
- (Trace **C.**)
- Write the letter for **k.** Pencils down when you're finished. ✔
d. Touch the next line. ✔
- On that line you'll write the letter that makes the sound **t.** What sound? (Signal.) *t.*
- What letter makes that sound? (Signal.) *T.*
- Write the letter for **t.** Pencils down when you're finished. ✔
e. Later, you'll complete the lines of letters.

**Independent Work Summary**
- Story extension (fix the picture).
- Matching game.
- Cross out wrong words under pictures.
- Cross-out (**rat**=3) and circle (**fat**=4) game.
- Sentence writing (copy two more times:
  **See an ant sit.**).
- Letter printing (finish lines of **v**, **c**, **t**).

**TEXTBOOK**

===== EXERCISE 1 =====

## SOUNDS

a. Open your textbook to lesson 42. Find the turkey. ✔
- (Teacher reference:)

| j | ck | ay | k | c | v |

- There are some sounds on the tail feathers of the turkey.
- Touch and say the sound for each letter or combination.

b. First sound. Get ready. (Signal.) *j.*
- Next sound. Get ready. (Signal.) *k.*
- (Repeat for remaining items.)
c. (Repeat step b until firm.)
d. This time, I'll say the sounds for one of the orange feathers.
- (Teacher reference:)

| j | ck | ay | v |

- You'll touch the letter or combination and then tell me the letter name.

e. Listen: The sound of an orange feather is **k.**
- Touch the letter or combination that makes the sound **k.** ✔
- Everybody, spell the letter or combination you are touching. Get ready. (Tap 2 times.) *C-K.*
f. Listen: The sound of an orange feather is **AAA.**
- Touch the letter or combination that makes the sound **AAA.** ✔
- Everybody, spell the letter or combination you are touching. Get ready. (Tap 2 times.) *A-Y.*
g. Listen: The sound of an orange feather is **j.**

- Touch the letter or combination that makes the sound **j.** ✔
- Everybody, spell the letter or combination you are touching. Get ready. (Signal.) *J.*
h. Listen: The sound of an orange feather is **vvv.**
- Touch the letter or combination that makes the sound **vvv.** ✔
- Everybody, spell the letter or combination you are touching. Get ready. (Signal.) *V.*
i. (Repeat steps e through h until firm.)

===== EXERCISE 2 =====

## READING WORDS
### Words with S Ending

a. Find the words on the turkey. ✔
- (Teacher reference:)

| 1. lak**e**s | 2. stor**e**s |
| 3. ja**i**ls | 4. trees |

- All these words tell about more than one thing.
b. Word 1. Touch and say the sounds. Get ready. (Tap 4 times.) *lll AAA k sss.*
- Again. Get ready. (Tap 4 times.) *lll AAA k sss.*
- What word? (Signal.) *Lakes.*
c. Word 2. Touch and say the sounds. Get ready. (Tap 5 times.) *sss t OOO rrr sss.*
- Again. Get ready. (Tap 5 times.) *sss t OOO rrr sss.*
- What word? (Signal.) *Stores.*
d. Word 3. Touch and say the sounds. Get ready. (Tap 4 times.) *j AAA lll sss.*
- What word? (Signal.) *Jails.*
e. Word 4. Touch and say the sounds. Get ready. (Tap 4 times.) *t rrr EEE sss.*
- What word? (Signal.) *Trees.*
f. This time, you'll read the words the fast way. You won't say the sounds. You'll just tell me the word.
g. Word 1. Raise your hand when you know it. Everybody, what's word 1? (Signal.) *Lakes.*

h. Next word. (Pause.) Everybody, what word? (Signal.) *Stores.*
- (Repeat for: **jails, trees.**)

**Individual Turns**
- (Call on different children to read one of the words.)

═══════ EXERCISE 3 ═══════

**READING WORDS**
**Words with Blue Y**

a. Find the pig. ✔
- (Teacher reference:)

| |
|---|
| da<u>y</u> |
| sta<u>y</u> |
| can |

b. Top word. Touch and say the sounds. Get ready. (Tap 2 times.) *d AAA.*
- What word? (Signal.) *Day.*
c. The middle word has a difficult beginning. Touch and say the sounds. Get ready.
   (Tap 3 times.) *sss t AAA.*
- What word? (Signal.) *Stay.*
d. Bottom word. Get ready. (Tap 3 times.) *c aaa nnn.*
- What word? (Signal.) *Can.*
e. Let's read those words again, the fast way.
- Top word. Raise your hand when you know it. Everybody, what's the top word? (Signal.) *Day.*
- Middle word. Raise your hand when you know it. Everybody, what's the middle word? (Signal.) *Stay.*
- Bottom word. Raise your hand when you know it. Everybody, what's the bottom word? (Signal.) *Can.*
f. (Repeat step e until firm.)

**Individual Turns**
- (Call on different children to read one of the words.)

═══════ EXERCISE 4 ═══════

**RHYMING WORDS**

a. The pig is eating from a trough. Find the trough. ✔
- (Teacher reference:)

| | |
|---|---|
| 1. old | 2. cold |
| 3. told | 4. fold |

- You've read most of these words before.
b. Word 1. Touch and say the sounds. Get ready. (Tap 3 times.) *OOO lll d.*
- What word? (Signal.) *Old.*
c. Word 2. Get ready. (Tap 4 times.) *c OOO lll d.*
- What word? (Signal.) *Cold.*
d. Word 3. Get ready. (Tap 4 times.) *t OOO lll d.*
- What word? (Signal.) *Told.*
e. Word 4. Get ready. (Tap 4 times.) *fff OOO lll d.*
- What word? (Signal.) *Fold.*
f. Let's read those words again, the fast way.
- Word 1. Raise your hand when you know it. Everybody, what's word 1? (Signal.) *Old.*
- Next word. (Pause.) Everybody, what word? (Signal.) *Cold.*
- (Repeat for: **told, fold.**)
g. (Repeat step f until firm.)

═══════ EXERCISE 5 ═══════

**READING WORDS**
**Words with Blue W**

a. Find the barn. ✔
- (Teacher reference:)

| | |
|---|---|
| 1. lo<u>w</u> | 2. flo<u>w</u> |
| 3. slo<u>w</u> | 4. y<u>o</u>u |

- The first three words have a blue **W**. One of the other letters in the word says its name.
b. Word 1 is spelled **L-O-W**. Touch the letter that says its name. Everybody, what letter? (Signal.) *O.*

- Word 2 is spelled **F-L-O-W.** Touch the letter that says its name. Everybody, what letter? (Signal.) *O.*
c. Go back to word 1. The word has two sounds. Touch and say them. Get ready. (Tap 2 times.) *lll OOO.*
- What word? (Signal.) *Low.*
- Yes, the temperature was very **low.**
d. Word 2. Touch and say the sounds. Get ready. (Tap 3 times.) *fff lll OOO.*
- Again. Get ready. (Tap 3 times.) *fff lll OOO.*
- What word? (Signal.) *Flow.*
e. Word 3. Get ready. (Tap 3 times.) *sss lll OOO.*
- Again. Get ready. (Tap 3 times.) *sss lll OOO.*
- What word? (Signal.) *Slow.*
f. Word 4 is a very strange word. It is spelled **Y-O-U.** The **Y** and the **O** are blue. So the **U** says its name. This is the word **you.** What word? (Signal.) *You.*
g. Let's read those words again, the fast way.
- Word 1. Raise your hand when you know it. Everybody, what's word 1? (Signal.) *Low.*
- Next word. (Pause.) Everybody, what word? (Signal.) *Flow.*
- (Repeat for: **slow, you.**)
h. (Repeat step g until firm.)

**Individual Turns**
- (Call on different children to read one of the words.)

===== EXERCISE 6 =====
**STORY READING**

a. Find the book. ✔
- This story has a lot of sentences that are questions.
- Touch the mark at the end of the first sentence. ✔ You should be touching the question mark just after the small letter **P.**
- Now find the next question mark. ✔ You should be touching the question mark just after the small letter **E.**
- Now find the last question mark. ✔ You should be touching the question mark just after the combination **T-H.**
b. Go back to the first word of the story. ✔
- Say the sounds. Get ready. (Tap 3 times.) *d iii d.* What word? (Signal.) *Did.*
c. Next word. Get ready. (Tap 2 times.) *thththe EEE.* What word? (Signal.) *The.*
- (Repeat step c for: **tan, ram, sleep.**)
d. Everybody, say all the words in the first sentence. (Signal.) *Did the tan ram sleep?*
- (Repeat until firm.)
e. Touch the only word in the next sentence. ✔
- What word? (Signal.) *No.*
f. Touch the first word of the next sentence. ✔
- Say the sounds. Get ready. (Tap 3 times.) *d iii d.* What word? (Signal.) *Did.*
g. Next word. Get ready. (Tap 3 times.) *thththe aaa t.* What word? (Signal.) *That.*
- (Repeat step g for: **ram, dive, in, a, lake.**)
h. Everybody, say that sentence. (Signal.) *Did that ram dive in a lake?*
- (Repeat until firm.)
i. Touch the only word in the next sentence. ✔
- What word? (Signal.) *No.*
j. Touch the first word of the next sentence. ✔
- Say the sounds. Get ready. (Tap 3 times.) *d iii d.* What word? (Signal.) *Did.*
k. Next word. Get ready. (Tap 3 times.) *thththe aaa t.* What word? (Signal.) *That.*

- (Repeat step k for: **ram, sit, in, the, path.**)
l. Everybody, say that sentence. (Signal.) *Did that ram sit in the path?*
- (Repeat until firm.)
m. Last sentence. Everybody, what word? (Signal.) *No.*

========= EXERCISE 7 =========

**COMPREHENSION**

a. Touch the first picture of the story. ✔

Did <u>the</u> tan ram sleep?

- What are the rams doing in that picture? (Signal.) *Sleeping.*
- I see black rams, gray rams, and white rams. But I don't see the tan ram. Is the tan ram sleeping? (Signal.) *No.*
- The first sentence of the story is below the picture. You'll read all the words in that sentence the fast way.
- First word. Raise your hand when you know it.
  Everybody, what word? (Signal.) *Did.*
b. Next word. (Pause.) Everybody, what word? (Signal.) *The.*
- (Repeat for: **tan, ram, sleep.**)
c. Let's read that sentence one more time.

- First word. Read it the fast way. Get ready. (Signal.) *Did.*
d. Next word. Read it the fast way. Get ready. (Signal.) *The.*
- (Repeat for: **tan, ram, sleep.**)
e. Touch the next picture. ✔

Did <u>that</u> ram dive in a lak<u>e</u>?

- What are the rams doing in that picture? (Call on a child. Idea: *Diving.*)
- Do you see the tan ram? (Signal.) *No.*
- Read the sentence under the picture. (Call on a child to read. *Did that ram dive in a lake?*)
- Everybody, did the tan ram dive in a lake? (Signal.) *No.*
f. Touch the next picture. ✔

Did <u>that</u> ram sit in <u>the</u> pa<u>th</u>?

- What are the rams doing in that picture? (Call on a child. Idea: *Sitting in a path.*)
- Do you see the tan ram in that picture? (Signal.) *No.*
- Read the sentence under the picture. (Call on a child to read. *Did that ram sit in the path?*)

- Everybody, did that tan ram sit in the path? (Signal.) *No.*
- We don't know what the tan ram did. I wish there was a picture that showed us.

g. (Prompt children to look for picture.) ✔

- What's the tan ram doing in that picture? (Call on a child. Idea: *Eating flowers.*)

## WORKBOOK

=== EXERCISE 8 ===

### STORY EXTENSION
### Matching: Words with Pictures

*Note:* Each child will need a tan crayon.

a. Close your textbook. Open your workbook to lesson 42, and complete the sentence at the top of your worksheet. ✔
b. Find the three sentences. ✔

- These are sentences from the story, but things are different.
- Touch the first sentence. ✔
- It says: **Did the tan ram sleep?**
- The next sentence says: **Yes.**
- Touch the word **yes.** It's spelled **Y-E-S.** ✔

c. Find the picture of the rams sleeping.
- Draw a line to connect the first sentence with that picture. ✔
- The tan ram is not in that picture, but it should be.

d. Later, you'll make one of those white rams tan. Then the picture will show the tan ram sleeping with the others.

e. You'll do the same thing with the other sentences. You'll draw a line to the right picture. Then you'll fix up the picture so it shows the tan ram in the picture.

=== EXERCISE 9 ===

### INDEPENDENT WORK

### Matching: Words

a. Find the matching game at the top of side 2. ✔
- None of the words in the right column have blue letters or underlines. One word is missing.
- Later, you'll write the missing word, and draw lines to connect the other words.

### Words for Pictures—Plural S

nail    nails

rat    rats

rope    ropes

tree    trees

b. Find the pictures with words below them. ✔
• There are two words under each picture. One of the words is right and one is wrong. You'll cross out the word that is wrong.
c. Touch the first picture. ✔
• What is in that picture? (Signal.) *Nails.*
• Yes, there are **nails** in the picture.
• Read the words under the picture to yourself. Touch the word that is wrong. ✔
• Everybody, tell me the word you're touching. (Signal.) *Nail.*
• The word **nails** is right. The word **nail** is wrong. Cross out the word **nail.** ✔
d. Touch the picture of the rat. ✔
• Cross out the wrong word under the picture. Pencils down when you've done that much.
• You should have crossed out the word **rats.** The picture shows **rat,** not **rats.**
e. Later, you can fix up the rest of the words. Remember, cross out the word that is wrong.

===== EXERCISE 10 =====

## SPELLING WORDS

a. You're going to spell words that end with a blue **E.**
b. Listen: **mile.** What word? (Signal.) *Mile.*
• Everybody, say the sounds in **mile.** Get ready. (Tap 3 times.) *mmm III lll.*
• What's the letter name you hear in **mile?** (Signal.) *I.*
• Everybody, spell the word **mile.** Get ready. (Tap 4 times.) *M-I-L-E.*
c. Next word: **pine.** What word? (Signal.) *Pine.*
• Say the sounds in **pine.** Get ready. (Tap 3 times.) *p III nnn.*
• What's the letter name you hear in **pine?** (Signal.) *I.*
• Spell the word **pine.** Get ready. (Tap 4 times.) *P-I-N-E.*
d. Next word: **fine.** What word? (Signal.) *Fine.*
• Say the sounds in **fine.** Get ready. (Tap 3 times.) *fff III nnn.*

• What's the letter name you hear in **fine?** (Signal.) *I.*
• Spell the word **fine.** Get ready. (Tap 4 times.) *F-I-N-E.*
e. Next word: **made.** What word? (Signal.) *Made.*
• Say the sounds in **made.** Get ready. (Tap 3 times.) *mmm AAA d.*
• What's the letter name you hear in **made?** (Signal.) *A.*
• Everybody, spell the word **made.** Get ready. (Tap 4 times.) *M-A-D-E.*

### LINED PAPER

f. Get ready to write the words we just spelled.
• Number four lines on your paper. Pencils down when you're finished. (Observe children and give feedback.)
g. Touch number 1. ✔
• Write the word **pine.** Pencils down when you're finished. (Observe children and give feedback.)
• (Write on the board:)

| **1 pine** |
|---|

• Here's what you should have. (Touch the letters as you spell them.) **Pine** is spelled **P-I-N-E.**
h. Touch number 2. ✔
• Write the word **fine.** Pencils down when you're finished. (Observe children and give feedback.)
• (Write on the board:)

| **2 fine** |
|---|

• Here's what you should have. (Touch the letters as you spell them.) **Fine** is spelled **F-I-N-E.**
i. Touch number 3. ✔
• Write the word **made.** Pencils down when you're finished. (Observe children and give feedback.)

- (Write on the board:)

> **3 made**

- Here's what you should have. (Touch the letters as you spell them.) **Made** is spelled **M-A-D-E.**
- j. Touch number 4. ✔
- Write the word **mile.** Pencils down when you're finished.
  (Observe children and give feedback.)
- (Write on the board:)

> **4 mile**

- Here's what you should have. (Touch the letters as you spell them.) **Mile** is spelled **M-I-L-E.**
- k. Raise your hand if you got everything right.

========== EXERCISE 11 ==========
## SENTENCE WRITING

a. (Write on the board:)

> Did the ram dive?

b. You're going to write this sentence.
   (Call on a child to read the sentence.)
c. Turn to the back of your paper. ✔
   Write this sentence on the top line.
   Remember the question mark at the end.
   Pencils down when you're finished.
   (Observe children and give feedback.)
d. Later, you can write the same sentence two more times on the lines below.

========== EXERCISE 12 ==========
## LETTER PRINTING

a. (Write on the board:)

> th n s c v d oa

- Get ready to write some letters.

b. Skip the next two lines on your paper, and put your pencil at the beginning of the line after that. Keep your pencil in place so I can see it.
   (Observe children and give feedback.)
- On that line you'll write the letter combination that makes the sound **k.** What sound? (Signal.) *k.*
- What letter combination makes that sound? (Signal.) *C-K.*
- I'll show you how to write **C-K.**
- (Trace **ck.**)
- Write the letter combination for **k.** Pencils down when you're finished.
   (Observe children and give feedback.)
c. Touch the next line. ✔
- On that line you'll write the letter that makes the sound **sss.** What sound? (Signal.) *sss.*
- What letter makes that sound? (Signal.) *S.*
- Write the letter for **sss.** Pencils down when you're finished.
   (Observe children and give feedback.)
d. Touch the next line. ✔
- On that line you'll write the letter that makes the sound **vvv.** What sound? (Signal.) *vvv.*
- What letter makes that sound? (Signal.) *V.*
- Write the letter for **vvv.** Pencils down when you're finished.
   (Observe children and give feedback.)
e. Later, you'll complete the lines of letters.

**Independent Work Summary**
- Story extension (connect the color pictures to match sentences).
- Matching game.
- Cross out wrong words under pictures.
- Sentence writing (copy two more times: **Did the ram dive?**).
- Letter printing (finish lines of **ck, s, v**).

**43**

**Materials:** Each child will need lined paper.

---

**EXERCISE 1**

**SOUNDS**
**Introducing W**

**Note:** Pronounce **www** as **oo**—the last sound in de**w**, z**oo**.

a. (Write on the board:)

> **W**

- Everybody, what's this letter? (Signal.) *W.*
- The sound that **W** makes is the very last sound of the name.
- Listen: **double yewww.** The very last sound is **www.**
b. I'll say some words with the **www** sound.
- Listen: **we.** What word? (Signal.) *We.*
- What's the first sound in in we. (Signal.) *www.*
- That's the sound that **W** makes.
c. Listen: **win.** What word? (Signal.) *Win.*
- What's the first sound in **win?** (Signal.) *www.*
- What letter makes that sound? (Signal.) *W.*
d. Listen: **war.** What word? (Signal.) *War.*
- What's the first sound in **war?** (Signal.) *www.*
- What letter makes that sound? (Signal.) *W.*
e. Listen: **wood.** What word? (Signal.) *Wood.*
- What's the first sound in **wood?** (Signal.) *www.*
- What letter makes that sound? (Signal.) *W.*

---

**TEXTBOOK**

**EXERCISE 2**

**READING WORDS**
**Words with S Ending**

a. Open your textbook to lesson 43. Find the big owl. ✔
- (Teacher reference:)

> **1. cats   2. sits   3. ants   4. rakes**
> **5. rains   6. pals   7. naps**

- These words end with the letter **S.** Some of these words tell about more than one. Some tell about things that somebody is doing.
b. Word 1. Touch and say the sounds. Get ready. (Tap 4 times.)
  *c   aaa   t   sss.*
- Again. Get ready. (Tap 4 times.)
  *c   aaa   t   sss.*
- What word? (Signal.) *Cats.*
c. Word 2. Get ready. (Tap 4 times.)
  *sss   iii   t   sss.*
- What word? (Signal.) *Sits.*
- Yes, somebody **sits.**
d. Word 3. Get ready. (Tap 4 times.)
  *aaa   nnn   t   sss.*
- What word? (Signal.) *Ants.*
e. Word 4. Get ready. (Tap 4 times.)
  *rrr   AAA   k   sss.*
- Again. Get ready. (Tap 4 times.)
  *rrr   AAA   k   sss.*
- What word? (Signal.) *Rakes.*
- Yes, you collect leaves with **rakes.**
f. Word 5. Get ready. (Tap 4 times.)
  *rrr   AAA   nnn   sss.*
- Again. Get ready. (Tap 4 times.)
  *rrr   AAA   nnn   sss.*
- What word? (Signal.) *Rains.*
- Yes, we get wet when it **rains.**
g. Word 6. Get ready. (Tap 4 times.)
  *p   aaa   lll   sss.*
- What word? (Signal.) *Pals.*
h. Word 7. Get ready. (Tap 4 times.)
  *nnn   aaa   p   sss.*
- Again. Get ready. (Tap 4 times.)
  *nnn   aaa   p   sss.*

- What word? (Signal.) *Naps.*
i. This time, we're going to read those words the fast way.
j. Word 1. (Pause.) What word? (Signal.) *Cats.*
- Next word. (Pause.) What word? (Signal.) *Sits.*
- (Repeat for: **ants, rakes, rains, pals, naps.**)

**Individual Turns**
- (Call on different children to read one or two of the words.)

═══════ EXERCISE 3 ═══════

**READING WORDS**
**Words with Blue W**

a. Find the moon. It's a full moon. ✔
- (Teacher reference:)

| 1. know | 2. no | 3. slow |
|---|---|---|
| 4. snow | 5. fine | 6. you |

- Some of these words have a blue **W**.
b. Word 1 is spelled **K-N-O-W**. It has a blue **K** and a blue **W**. Touch the letter that says its name.
- Everybody, what letter? (Signal.) *O.*
- Touch and say the sounds for the black letters. Get ready. (Tap 2 times.) *nnn OOO.*
- What word? (Signal.) *Know.*
- Yes, you **know** a lot of things.
c. Word 2 is spelled **N-O**. Everybody, say the sounds. Get ready. (Tap 2 times.) *nnn OOO.*
- What word? (Signal.) *No.*
- Yes, this is the word that means: **no, no, no.** So you've learned two different words that say: **no.**
d. Word 3 is spelled **S-L-O-W**. Touch the letter that says its name.
- Everybody, what letter? (Signal.) *O.*
- Touch and say the sounds. Get ready. (Tap 3 times.) *sss lll OOO.*
- What word? (Signal.) *Slow.*
e. Word 4. Touch and say the sounds. Get ready. (Tap 3 times.) *sss nnn OOO.*
- What word? (Signal.) *Snow.*

f. Word 5 has a blue letter. Touch and say the sounds for the black letters. Get ready. (Tap 3 times.) *fff lll nnn.*
- What word? (Signal.) *Fine.*
g. Word 6 is spelled **Y-O-U**. Touch the letter that says its name. What letter are you touching? (Signal.) *U.*
- What's word 6? (Signal.) *You.*
- Yes, the word **you** is spelled **Y-O-U**.
h. Let's read those words again, the fast way.
i. Word 1. Raise your hand when you know it. Everybody, what's word 1? (Signal.) *Know.*
- Next word. (Pause.) What word? (Signal.) *No.*
- (Repeat for: **slow, snow, fine, you.**)
j. (Repeat step i until firm.)

**Individual Turns**
- (Call on different children to read one of the words.)

═══════ EXERCISE 4 ═══════

**READING WORDS**
**Words with A or I**

a. Find the baby owl. ✔
- (Teacher reference:)

| 1. pass | 2. dime | 3. plane | 4. lid |
|---|---|---|---|

- These are new words.
b. Word 1 has no blue letter. It has two **S**s at the end. You'll say the **S** sound just one time.
- Touch and say the sounds for word 1. Get ready. (Tap 3 times.) *p aaa sss.*
- What word? (Signal.) *Pass.*
- Yes, throw me a **pass.**
c. Word 2 has a blue letter. Get ready. (Tap 3 times.) *d lll mmm.*
- What word? (Signal.) *Dime.*
d. Word 3 has a blue letter. Get ready. (Tap 4 times.) *p lll AAA nnn.*
- What word? (Signal.) *Plane.*
- Yes, they flew in a **plane.**
e. Word 4. Get ready. (Tap 3 times.) *lll iii d.*
- What word? (Signal.) *Lid.*

- Put the **lid** on the jar.
f. Let's read those words again, the fast way.
- Word 1. (Pause.) What word? (Signal.) *Pass.*
- Next word. (Pause.) What word? (Signal.) *Dime.*
- (Repeat for: **plane, lid.**)

═══════ EXERCISE 5 ═══════

**STORY READING**

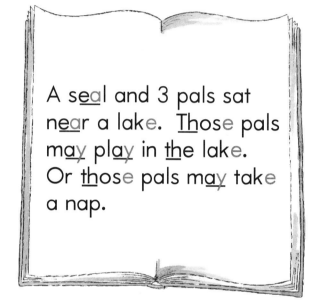

A se͞al and 3 pals sat ne͞ar a lake. Those pals ma͞y pla͞y in the lake. Or those pals ma͞y take a nap.

a. Find the book. ✔
- You'll read all the words in the first sentence.
- First word. What word? (Signal.) *A.*
- Next word. Get ready. (Tap 3 times.)
  *sss  EEE  lll.*
  What word? (Signal.) *Seal.*
- Next word. Get ready. (Tap 3 times.)
  *aaa  nnn  d.*
  What word? (Signal.) *And.*
- The next word is a numeral. What numeral? (Signal.) *3.*
b. Next word. Get ready. (Tap 4 times.)
  *p  aaa  lll  sss.*
  What word? (Signal.) *Pals.*
- (Repeat step b for remaining words: **sat, near, a, lake.**)

c. Everybody, say all the words in the first sentence. (Signal.) *A seal and 3 pals sat near a lake.*
- (Repeat until firm.)
d. Touch the first word of the next sentence. ✔
- Get ready. (Tap 3 times.)
  *ththth  OOO  sss.*
  What word? (Signal.) *Those.*
e. Next word. Get ready. (Tap 4 times.)
  *p  aaa  lll  sss.*
  What word? (Signal.) *Pals.*
- (Repeat step e for remaining words: **may, play, in, the, lake.**)
f. Everybody, say that sentence. (Signal.) *Those pals may play in the lake.*
- (Repeat until firm.)
g. Touch the first word of the next sentence. ✔
- Get ready. (Tap 2 times.)
  *OOO  rrr.*
  What word? (Signal.) *Or.*
h. Next word. Get ready. (Tap 3 times.)
  *ththth  OOO  sss.*
  What word? (Signal.) *Those.*
- (Repeat step h for remaining words: **pals, may, take, a, nap.**)
i. Everybody, say that sentence. (Signal.) *Or those pals may take a nap.*
- (Repeat until firm.)

## EXERCISE 6

**COMPREHENSION**

a. Find the first picture for the story. ✔

A se<u>a</u>l and 3 pals sat
ne<u>a</u>r a lak<u>e</u>.

- Who is in that picture? (Call on a child.
  Idea: *A seal and three skunks.*)
- Who are the seal's three pals?
  (Signal.) *Skunks.*
- The first sentence of the story is below
  the picture. You'll read all the words in
  that sentence the fast way.
- First word. What word? (Signal.) *A.*
- Next word. What word? (Signal.) *Seal.*
- Next word. What word? (Signal.) *And.*
- The next word is a numeral. What
  numeral? (Signal.) *3.*
b. Next word. What word? (Signal.) *Pals.*
- (Repeat for remaining words: **sat, near,
  a, lake.**)
c. Let's read that sentence one more time,
  the fast way.
- First word. Read it the fast way. Get
  ready. (Signal.) *A.*
d. Next word. Get ready. (Signal.) *Seal.*
- (Repeat for remaining words: **and, 3,
  pals, sat, near, a, lake.**)

e. Touch the next picture. ✔

<u>Th</u>ose pals m<u>ay</u> pl<u>ay</u> in
<u>th</u>e lak<u>e</u>.

- What are the pals doing in that picture?
  (Call on a child. Idea: *Playing in a lake.*)
- They are in a cloud. That means the
  picture shows what may happen, not
  what will happen.
- Read the sentence under the picture.
  (Call on a child to read. *Those pals may
  play in the lake.*)
f. Touch the next picture. ✔

Or <u>th</u>ose pals m<u>ay</u> take
a nap.

- What's happening in this picture? (Call
  on a child. Idea: *The seal and the skunks
  are taking a nap.*)
- The cloud shows that it is another thing
  that may happen.
- Read the sentence under the picture.
  (Call on a child. *Or those pals may take
  a nap.*)
g. Those pictures show what the pals may
  do. I wonder what they really did. I wish
  there was a picture that showed it.

- (Prompt children to look for picture.) ✔

What are the pals doing in that picture?
(Call on a child. Idea: *Playing in the lake with other animals.*)

## STORY EXTENSION
### Matching: Words with Pictures

a. Close your textbook. Open your workbook to lesson 43, and complete the sentence at the top of the page. ✔
b. Find the pictures for the story. ✔
- There are sentences from the story and pictures. Later, you'll read each sentence to yourself and draw a line from the sentence to the right picture.

## INDEPENDENT WORK

### Words for Pictures—Plural S
a. Go to side 2 of your worksheet. ✔
- Some of the pictures show more than one.
b. Touch the first picture. That shows kites. ✔
- The word **kites** is not in the box above the pictures. But the word **kite** is in the box. You'll copy the word **kite** below the picture, then fix up the word so it says **kites,** not **kite.** Do it. Pencils down when you're finished.
  (Observe children and give feedback.)
- (Write on the board:)

| kites |
| --- |

- Here's what you should have for the first picture.
c. Later, you'll write words for the other pictures.
- Remember, if the picture shows more than one, find the word that tells about one, copy that word, then fix it so it tells about more than one.

## SPELLING WORDS

a. You're going to spell words. Some of them have a blue **E** as the last letter. The other words don't have any blue letters.
b. Listen: **pin.** What word? (Signal.) *Pin.*
- Say the sounds in **pin.** Get ready. (Tap 3 times.) *p  iii  nnn.*
- Do you say a letter name when you say the sounds? (Signal.) *No.*
- So **pin** does not have a blue **E.**
c. Listen: **pine.** What word? (Signal.) *Pine.*
- Say the sounds in **pine.** Get ready. (Tap 3 times.) *p  III  nnn.*
- Do you say a letter name when you say the sounds? (Signal.) *Yes.*
- What letter name? (Signal.) *I.*
- You say a letter name. So the word **pine** has a blue **E.**

d. Listen: **tape.** What word? (Signal.) *Tape.*
- Say the sounds in **tape.** Get ready.
  (Tap 3 times.) *t   AAA   p.*
- Do you say a letter name when you say
  the sounds? (Signal.) *Yes.*
- What letter name? (Signal.) *A.*
- You say a letter name. So does the word
  **tape** have a blue **E**? (Signal.) *Yes.*
e. Listen: **tap.** What word? (Signal.) *Tap.*
- Say the sounds in **tap.** Get ready.
  (Tap 3 times.) *t   aaa   p.*
- Do you say a letter name when you say
  the sounds? (Signal.) *No.*
- So does the word **tap** have a blue **E**?
  (Signal.) *No.*
- Remember, you write a blue **E** if you hear
  a letter name in the word.

### LINED PAPER
f. Get ready to write the words we just
  spelled.
- Number four lines on your paper. Pencils
  down when you're finished.
  (Observe children and give feedback.)
g. Touch number 1. ✔
- Write the word **tap.** Pencils down when
  you're finished.
  (Observe children and give feedback.)
- (Write on the board:)

> **1 tap**

- Here's what you should have. **Tap** is
  spelled **T-A-P.**
h. Touch number 2. ✔
- Write the word **tape.** Pencils down when
  you're finished.
  (Observe children and give feedback.)
- (Write on the board:)

> **2 tape**

- Here's what you should have. **Tape** is
  spelled **T-A-P-E.**
i. Touch number 3. ✔

- Write the word **pine.** Pencils down when
  you're finished.
  (Observe children and give feedback.)
- (Write on the board:)

> **3 pine**

- Here's what you should have. **Pine** is
  spelled **P-I-N-E.**
j. Touch number 4. ✔
- Write the word **pin.** Pencils down when
  you're finished.
  (Observe children and give feedback.)
- (Write on the board:)

> **4 pin**

- Here's what you should have. **Pin** is
  spelled **P-I-N.**
k. Raise your hand if you got everything
  right.

## EXERCISE 10
### SENTENCE WRITING
a. (Write on the board:)

> Those pals may play.

b. You're going to write this sentence.
  (Call on a child to read the sentence.)
c. Turn to the back of your paper. ✔
- Write the sentence on the top line.
  Pencils down when you're finished.
  (Observe children and give feedback.)
d. Later, you can write the same sentence
  two more times on the lines below.

**Independent Work Summary**
- Story extension (connect sentences to
  pictures).
- Write appropriate words under pictures.
- Sentence writing (copy two more times:
  **Those pals may play.**).

Materials: Each child will need lined paper.

## TEXTBOOK

EXERCISE 1

### SOUNDS

a. Open your textbook to lesson 44. Find the first building. ✔
• (Teacher reference:)

| | |
|---|---|
| ai | ay |
| c | k |
| v | j |
| i | a |

• This is an apartment house. It has four floors. You're going to say the sounds.
b. Touch the top floor. ✔
• First combination. Get ready. (Signal.) *AAA.*
• Next combination. Get ready. (Signal.) *AAA.*
• (Repeat step b until firm.)
c. Touch the next floor. ✔
• First sound. Get ready. (Signal.) *k.*
• Next sound. Get ready. (Signal.) *k.*
d. Touch the next floor. ✔
• First sound. Get ready. (Signal.) *vvv.*
• Next sound. Get ready. (Signal.) *j.*
e. Touch the bottom floor. ✔
• You know two sounds for each letter.
f. Touch the first letter. What's the sound it makes with a blue letter? (Signal.) *III.*
  What's the other sound? (Signal.) *iii.*
• Touch the next letter. What's the sound it makes with a blue letter? (Signal.) *AAA.*
  What's the other sound? (Signal.) *aaa.*
• (Repeat step f until firm.)

EXERCISE 2

### READING WORDS
### Words with W

a. (Write on the board:)

| W |
|---|

• Everybody, what's this letter? (Signal.) *W.*
b. Listen: **now.** What word? (Signal.) *Now.*
  The last sound is **www.**
  What letter makes that sound? (Signal.) *W.*
• Listen: **will.** What word? (Signal.) *Will.*
  What's the **first** sound in **will?** (Signal.) *www.*
  What letter makes that sound? (Signal.) *W.*
• Listen: **wood.** What word? (Signal.) *Wood.*
  What's the **first** sound in **wood?** (Signal.) *www.*
  What letter makes that sound? (Signal.) *W.*
c. Find the yellow building. ✔
• (Teacher reference:)

| | |
|---|---|
| 1. will | 2. wi<u>th</u> |
| 3. wid<u>e</u> | 4. we |

• All these words have the letter **W.**
d. Word 1 does not have a blue letter. Touch and say the sounds. Get ready. (Tap 3 times.) *www   iii   lll.*
• Again. Get ready. (Tap 3 times.) *www   iii   lll.*
• What word? (Signal.) *Will.*
• Yes, we **will** go.
e. Word 2 does not have a blue letter. Touch and say the sounds. Get ready. (Tap 3 times.) *www   iii   ththth.*
• Again. Get ready. (Tap 3 times.) *www   iii   ththth.*
• What word? (Signal.) *With.*
f. Word 3 has a blue letter. Get ready. (Tap 3 times.) *www   III   d.*
• Again. Get ready. (Tap 3 times.) *www   III   d.*
• What word? (Signal.) *Wide.*

g. Word 4. Get ready. (Tap 2 times.) *www   EEE.*
- What word? (Signal.) *We.*
h. Let's read those words again, the fast way.
- Word 1. (Pause.) What word? (Signal.) *Will.*
- Word 2. (Pause.) What word? (Signal.) *With.*
- Word 3. (Pause.) What word? (Signal.) *Wide.*
- Word 4. (Pause.) What word? (Signal.) *We.*

===== EXERCISE 3 =====

**RHYMING WORDS**
**Reading Words the Fast Way**

a. Find the taxicab. ✔
- (Teacher reference:)

> **old**
>
> **cold**
>
> **told**

- These are words you've read before. See if you can read them the fast way without first saying the sounds.
b. Top word. (Pause.) Everybody, what word? (Signal.) *Old.*
- Middle word. (Pause.) Everybody, what word? (Signal.) *Cold.*
- Bottom word. (Pause.) Everybody, what word? (Signal.) *Told.*

===== EXERCISE 4 =====

**READING WORDS**
**Words with S Ending**

a. Find the mailbox. ✔
- (Teacher reference:)

> 1. ki<u>ck</u>s     2. kit<u>e</u>s
>
> 3. cats     4. j<u>ai</u>ls

- These words end with the letter **S.** You'll say the sounds, then tell me each word.
b. Word 1. Touch and say the sounds. Get ready. (Tap 4 times.) *k   iii   k   sss.*
- What word? (Signal.) *Kicks.*
- Yes, that horse **kicks.**
c. Word 2. Get ready. (Tap 4 times.) *k   III   t   sss.*
- What word? (Signal.) *Kites.*
- Yes, we fly **kites.**
d. Word 3. Get ready. (Tap 4 times.) *c   aaa   t   sss.*
- What word? (Signal.) *Cats.*
e. Word 4. Get ready. (Tap 4 times.) *j   AAA   lll   sss.*
- What word? (Signal.) *Jails.*
f. Let's read those words again, the fast way.
- Word 1. (Pause.) Everybody, what word? (Signal.) *Kicks.*
- Word 2. (Pause.) What word? (Signal.) *Kites.*
- Word 3. (Pause.) What word? (Signal.) *Cats.*
- Word 4. (Pause.) What word? (Signal.) *Jails.*

**Individual Turns**

- I'm going to call on different children to read several words on this **page** the fast way.
- Everybody, find the yellow building. (Call on a child to read words.) *Will, with, wide, we.*
- Everybody, find the taxicab. (Call on a child to read words.) *Old, cold, told.*
- Everybody, find the mailbox. (Call on a child to read words.) *Kicks, kites, cats, jails.*

═══════ EXERCISE 5 ═══════

**STORY READING**

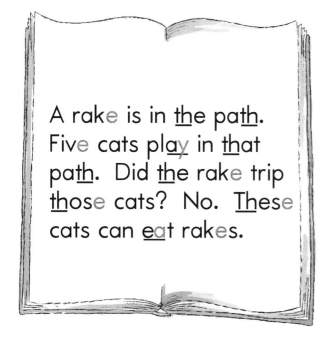

A rake is in <u>the</u> pa<u>th</u>.
Fiv<u>e</u> cats pl<u>ay</u> in <u>th</u>at
pa<u>th</u>. Did <u>the</u> rak<u>e</u> trip
<u>th</u>os<u>e</u> cats? No. <u>These</u>
cats can <u>ea</u>t rak<u>e</u>s.

a. Find the book. ✔
• You'll read all the words in the first sentence.
b. First word. What word? (Signal.) *A.*
• Next word. Touch and say the sounds. Get ready. (Tap 3 times.) *rrr    AAA    k.*
• Again. Get ready. (Tap 3 times.) *rrr    AAA    k.*
What word? (Signal.) *Rake.*
c. Next word. Get ready. (Tap 2 times.) *iii    sss.*
What word? (Signal.) *Is.*
• (Repeat step c for remaining words: **in, the, path.**)
d. Everybody, say all the words in the first sentence. (Signal.) *A rake is in the path.*
• (Repeat until firm.)
e. Touch the first word of the next sentence. ✔
Get ready. (Tap 3 times.) *fff    III    vvv.*
• Again. Get ready. (Tap 3 times.) *fff    III    vvv.*
Everybody, what word? (Signal.) *Five.*
f. Next word. Get ready. (Tap 4 times.) *c    aaa    t    sss.*
What word? (Signal.) *Cats.*
• (Repeat step f for remaining words: **play, in, that, path.**)

g. Everybody, say that sentence. (Signal.) *Five cats play in that path.*
• (Repeat until firm.)
h. Touch the first word of the next sentence. ✔
Get ready. (Tap 3 times.) *d    iii    d.*
Everybody, what word? (Signal.) *Did.*
i. Next word. Get ready. (Tap 2 times.) *ththth    EEE.*
What word? (Signal.) *The.*
• (Repeat step i for remaining words: **rake, trip, those, cats.**)
j. Everybody, say that sentence. (Signal.) *Did the rake trip those cats?*
• (Repeat until firm.)
k. Next sentence. What word? (Signal.) *No.*
• Did the rake trip the cats? (Signal.) *No.*
l. Touch the first word of the last sentence. ✔
Get ready. (Tap 3 times.) *ththth    EEE    sss.*
Everybody, what word? (Signal.) *These.*
m. Next word. Get ready. (Tap 4 times.) *c    aaa    t    sss.*
What word? (Signal.) *Cats.*
• (Repeat step m for remaining words: **can, eat, rakes.**)
n. Everybody, say that sentence. (Signal.) *These cats can eat rakes.*
• (Repeat until firm.)
o. That doesn't sound right. How could cats eat rakes? Maybe the pictures will show us how that could happen.

**EXERCISE 6**

**COMPREHENSION**

a. Touch the first picture of the story. ✔

| A rake is in the path. |

- What's in that picture? (Signal.) *A rake.*
- Where is the rake? (Signal.) *In the path.*
- The first sentence of the story is below the picture. You'll read all the words in that sentence the fast way.
- First word. What word? (Signal.) *A.*
- b. Next word. What word? (Signal.) *Rake.*
- (Repeat for remaining words: **is, in, the, path.**)

c. Touch the next picture. ✔

| Five cats play in that path. |

- That picture shows the cats. Are they the kind of cats you thought they would be? (Signal.) *No.*
- What kind of cats are they? (Signal.) *Lions.*
- How many lions are there? (Signal.) *Five.*
- (Call on a child.) Read the sentence under the picture. *Five cats play in that path.*

d. Touch the next picture. ✔

Did <u>the</u> rake trip <u>those</u> cats? No. <u>These</u> cats can e<u>a</u>t rakes.

- What are the lions doing in that picture? (Call on a child. Idea: *Eating the rake.*)
- I guess they can eat rakes.
- (Call on different children to read one of the sentences below the picture. *Did the rake trip those cats? No. These cats can eat rakes.*)

═══════ **EXERCISE 7** ═══════

## STORY EXTENSION
### Sentence Completion

a. Close your textbook. Open your workbook to lesson 44, and complete the sentence at the top of the page. ✔
b. Find the picture for the story. ✔
- The picture is like one from your textbook. Part of the story is below the picture, but some of the words are missing.

- Later, you'll find the missing words above the picture and complete the story.

═══════ **EXERCISE 8** ═══════

## INDEPENDENT WORK

### Cross-Out and Circle Game
a. Find the cross-out game.
- Raise your hand when you know the word you'll cross out.
  Everybody, what word? (Signal.) *Ant.*
- Raise your hand when you know the word you'll circle.
  Everybody, what word? (Signal.) *And.*
- You'll circle **and** and cross out **ant.**

### Words for Pictures
b. You're going to complete words that tell about pictures. For some pictures, you'll complete a word by writing the letters **A-T.** For other pictures, you'll complete a word by writing the letters **A-I-L.**
c. Everybody, find the star at the top of side 2. ✔
- The first word ending is spelled **A-T.** Touch and say the sounds. Get ready. (Tap 2 times.) *aaa    t.*
- What does this part say? (Signal.) *at.*
- The next word ending is spelled **A-I-L.** Touch and say the sounds. Get ready. (Tap 2 times.) *AAA    lll.*
- What does this part say? (Signal.) *ail.*
d. Find picture 1. ✔
- What is in that picture? (Signal.) *Rat.*
- Fix up the word that is under the picture. The first letter is **R.** Complete the word by writing the correct ending. Don't get fooled. Pencils down when you're finished.
  (Observe children and give feedback.)
- (Write on the board:)

> **rat**

- Everybody, spell the word you wrote under picture 1. Get ready. (Tap 3 times.) *R-A-T.*

- If you wrote the other ending, you wrote the word **rail**. Boo. The word **rail** doesn't tell about the picture.
e. Touch picture 2. ✔
- What does that picture show? (Signal.) *Sail.*
- Complete the word under the picture so it says **sail**. Use one of the endings in the box. Pencils down when you're finished. **(Observe children and give feedback.)**
- (Write on the board:)

> **sail**

- Everybody, spell the word you wrote under picture 2. Get ready. **(Tap 4 times.)** *S-A-I-L.*
- If you wrote the other ending, you wrote the word **sat**. Boo.
f. You'll do the rest of the words later. Remember, look at the picture and figure out the word. Then copy the correct ending.

**Matching: Words**

g. Find the matching game. None of the words in the right column have blue letters or underlines. Some of the words are missing. You'll write the missing words and draw lines to connect the other words.

===== EXERCISE 9 =====

**SPELLING WORDS**

a. You're going to spell words. Some of them have a blue **E** as the last letter.
b. Listen: **tap**. What word? (Signal.) *Tap.*
- Say the sounds in **tap**. Get ready. (Tap 3 times.) *t    aaa    p.*
- Do you say a letter name when you say the sounds? (Signal.) *No.*
- So **tap** does not have a blue **E**.
c. Listen: **tape**. What word? (Signal.) *Tape.*
- Say the sounds in **tape**. Get ready. (Tap 3 times.) *t    AAA    p.*
- Do you say a letter name when you say the sounds? (Signal.) *Yes.*
- What letter name? (Signal.) *A.*

- You say a letter name. Does the word **tape** have a blue **E**? (Signal.) *Yes.*
d. Listen: **pine**. What word? (Signal.) *Pine.*
- Say the sounds in **pine**. Get ready. (Tap 3 times.) *p    III    nnn.*
- Do you say a letter name when you say the sounds? (Signal.) *Yes.*
- What letter name? (Signal.) *I.*
- You say a letter name. Does the word **pine** have a blue **E**? (Signal.) *Yes.*
e. Listen: **pin**. What word? (Signal.) *Pin.*
- Say the sounds in **pin**. Get ready. (Tap 3 times.) *p    iii    nnn.*
- Do you say a letter name when you say the sounds? (Signal.) *No.*
- So does the word **pin** have a blue **E**? (Signal.) *No.*
- Remember, you write a blue **E** if you hear a letter name in these words.

**LINED PAPER**

f. Get ready to write the words we just spelled.
- Number four lines on your paper. Pencils down when you're finished. **(Observe children and give feedback.)**
g. Touch number 1. ✔
- Write the word **pine**. Pencils down when you're finished. **(Observe children and give feedback.)**
- Spell **pine**. Get ready. (Tap 4 times.) *P-I-N-E.*
- (Write on the board:)

> **1 pine**

- Here's what you should have. **Pine** is spelled **P-I-N-E**.
h. Touch number 2. ✔
- Write the word **tape**. Pencils down when you're finished. **(Observe children and give feedback.)**
- Spell **tape**. Get ready. (Tap 4 times.) *T-A-P-E.*
- (Write on the board:)

> **2 tape**

- Here's what you should have. **Tape** is spelled **T-A-P-E**.

i. Touch number 3. ✔
- Write the word **pin.** Pencils down when you're finished.
  (Observe children and give feedback.)
- Spell **pin.** Get ready. (Tap 3 times.)
  *P-I-N.*
- (Write on the board:)

| 3 pin |
|-------|

- Here's what you should have. **Pin** is spelled **P-I-N.**
j. Touch number 4. ✔
- Write the word **tap.** Pencils down when you're finished.
  (Observe children and give feedback.)
- Spell **tap.** Get ready. (Tap 3 times.)
  *T-A-P.*
- (Write on the board:)

| 4 tap |
|-------|

- Here's what you should have. **Tap** is spelled **T-A-P.**
k. Raise your hand if you got everything right. You're spelling and writing some hard words.

═══════ **EXERCISE 10** ═══════

**SENTENCE WRITING**

a. (Write on the board:)

**These cats eat rakes.**

b. You're going to write this sentence. (Call on a child to read the sentence.)
c. Turn to the back of your paper. ✔
- Write this sentence on the top line. Make sure you leave a space after each word. Pencils down when you're finished.
  (Observe children and give feedback.)
d. Later, you can write the same sentence two more times on the lines below.

**Independent Work Summary**
- Story extension (write missing words).
- Cross-out (**ant**=3) and circle (**and**=4) game.
- Write word endings to match pictures.
- Matching game.
- Sentence writing (copy two more times: **These cats eat rakes.**).

**Materials:** Each child will need lined paper.

═══════ EXERCISE 1 ═══════

## SOUNDS
### Introducing g Sound

a. Everybody, say the sound that the letter **C** sometimes makes. Get ready. (Signal.) *k.*
* The letter **G** makes the same sound except that it is not whispered. Listen: **g.**
b. I'll say words that are spelled with the letter **G. Go.** What word? (Signal.) *Go.*
* The first sound is **g.** The next sound is **OOO.**
* Say the sounds in **go.** Get ready. (Tap 2 times.) *g   OOO.*
* The first sound is spelled with the letter **G.**
c. New word: **game.** What word? (Signal.) *Game.*
* Say the sounds in **game.** Get ready. (Tap 3 times.) *g   AAA   mmm.*
d. New word: **rag.** What word? (Signal.) *Rag.*
* Say the sounds in **rag.** Get ready. (Tap 3 times.) *rrr   aaa   g.*
* The last sound in **rag** is spelled with the letter **G.**
e. Last word: **tag.** What word? (Signal.) *Tag.*
* Say the sounds in **tag.** Get ready. (Tap 3 times.) *t   aaa   g.*
* Remember the sound for the letter **G.**

┌─────────────┐
│  **TEXTBOOK**  │
└─────────────┘

f. Open your textbook to lesson 45. Find the circus train. ✔
* (Teacher reference:)

| | | | | | |
|---|---|---|---|---|---|
| r | w | g | p | c | g |

g. Touch and say the sounds.
* First sound. Get ready. (Signal.) *rrr.*
* Next sound. Get ready. (Signal.) *www.*
* (Repeat for remaining items.)
h. (Repeat step g until firm.)

═══════ EXERCISE 2 ═══════

## READING WORDS

a. After you read all the **words** on this page without any mistakes, I'll call on individual children to read some of the words.
* Find the clown. ✔
* (Teacher reference:)

| | | | | | |
|---|---|---|---|---|---|
| **1. deep** | | **4. know** | | **7. trip** | |
| **2. if** | | **5. store** | | **8. train** | |
| **3. you** | | **6. storm** | | **9. trail** | |

* First you'll say these words a sound at a time. Then you'll read them the fast way.
b. Word 1. Get ready. (Tap 3 times.) *d   EEE   p.*
  What word? (Signal.) *Deep.*
* Word 2. Get ready. (Tap 2 times.) *iii   fff.*
  What word? (Signal.) *If.*
* Word 3 has two blue letters. Everybody, what's word 3? (Signal.) *You.*
* Spell **you.** Get ready. (Tap 3 times.) *Y-O-U.*
* Word 4. Touch and say the sounds for the black letters. Get ready. (Tap 2 times.) *nnn   OOO.*
  What word? (Signal.) *Know.*
* I **know** the answer.
c. The rest of the words have difficult beginning sounds.
* Word 5. Get ready. (Tap 4 times.) *sss   t   OOO   rrr.*
  Again. Get ready. (Tap 4 times.) *sss   t   OOO   rrr.*
  What word? (Signal.) *Store.*
* Word 6. Get ready. (Tap 5 times.) *sss   t   OOO   rrr   mmm.*
  What word? (Signal.) *Storm.*
* Word 7. Get ready. (Tap 4 times.) *t   rrr   iii   p.*
  What word? (Signal.) *Trip.*

45

- Word 8. Get ready. (Tap 4 times.)
  *t  rrr  AAA  nnn.*
  What word? (Signal.) *Train.*
- Word 9. Get ready. (Tap 4 times.)
  *t  rrr  AAA  lll.*
  What word? (Signal.) *Trail.*
- d. Let's read those words again, the
  fast way.
- Word 1. What word? (Signal.) *Deep.*
- Next word. What word? (Signal.) *If.*
- (Repeat for: **you, know, store, storm,
  trip, train, trail.**)

========= EXERCISE 3 =========

**READING WORDS**
**Introducing SAID and E-R**

a. Find the big, funny car. ✔
- (Teacher reference:)

| 1. s<u>ai</u>d | 2. ov<u>er</u> | 3. win |
|---|---|---|
| 4. will | 5. wid**e** | |

b. Touch the letter combination in word 1. ✔
- The combination has the funny underline
  because it does not say the sound **AAA.**
  This word is not **sayed.** The word is **said.**
  What word? (Signal.) *Said.*
- Yes, we **said** the sentences.
c. Everybody, spell the word **said.** Get
  ready. (Tap 4 times.) *S-A-I-D.*
- What word did you spell? (Signal.) *Said.*
- (Repeat step c until firm.)
d. Remember, the word **said** has a funny
  underline under the combination **A-I**
  because the combination **doesn't**
  say **AAA.**
e. Word 2 is **over.** What word?
  (Signal.) *Over.*
- The letters **E-R** are underlined because
  they make the sound **ur,** not **ear.** What
  sound do the letters **E-R** make?
  (Signal.) *ur.*
- Word 2 is spelled **O-V-E-R.** Everybody,
  what word? (Signal.) *Over.*
f. The rest of the words start with the
  letter **W.**
- Say the sounds for word 3. Get ready.
  (Tap 3 times.) *www  iii  nnn.*
  What word? (Signal.) *Win.*

- Word 4. Get ready. (Tap 3 times.)
  *www  iii  lll.*
  What word? (Signal.) *Will.*
- Word 5 has a blue letter. Get ready.
  (Tap 3 times.) *www  lll  d.*
  What word? (Signal.) *Wide.*
g. Let's read those words again, the
  fast way.
- Word 1. Remember, the funny underline
  tells you that part of this word is funny.
  Everybody, what's word 1? (Signal.) *Said.*
- Next word. What word? (Signal.) *Over.*
- (Repeat for: **win, will, wide.**)
h. (Repeat step g until firm.)

========= EXERCISE 4 =========

**READING WORDS**
**T-H, No Underline**

a. Find the three balls at the bottom of the
  page. ✔
- The words in those balls have the
  combination **T-H,** but it is not underlined.
b. I'll spell each word. You tell me the word.
- First word: **W-I-T-H.** What word?
  (Signal.) *With.*
- Next word: **T-H-O-S-E.** What word?
  (Signal.) *Those.*
- Last word: **T-H-A-T.** What word?
  (Signal.) *That.*
c. Let's read those words again, the
  fast way.
- First word. What word? (Signal.) *With.*
- Next word. What word? (Signal.) *Those.*
- Last word. What word? (Signal.) *That.*
d. From now on, this is the way those words
  will look in your stories. The **T-H** won't be
  underlined.

## Individual Turns

- (Call on different children to read one or two of the words on the page.)

---

==== EXERCISE 5 ====

## STORY READING

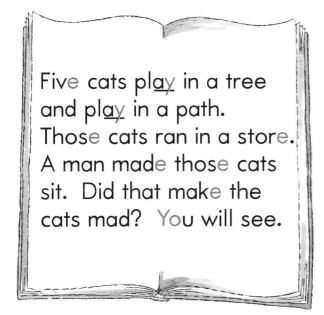

Five cats play in a tree and play in a path. Those cats ran in a store. A man made those cats sit. Did that make the cats mad? You will see.

a. Find the book. ✔
- It's time to read a story.
- You'll read all the words in the first sentence.
- First word. Touch and say the sounds. Get ready. (Tap 3 times.) *fff III vvv.* What word? (Signal.) *Five.*
b. Next word. Get ready. (Tap 4 times.) *c aaa t sss.* What word? (Signal.) *Cats.*

- (Repeat step b for remaining words: **play, in, a, tree, and, play, in, a, path.**)
c. That's a long sentence. Listen: **Five cats play in a tree and play in a path.**
d. Everybody, say all the words in the first sentence. Get ready. (Signal.) *Five cats play in a tree and play in a path.*
- (Repeat until firm.)
e. Touch the first word of the next sentence. Get ready. (Tap 3 times.) *ththth OOO sss.* What word? (Signal.) *Those.*
f. Next word. Get ready. (Tap 4 times.) *c aaa t sss.* What word? (Signal.) *Cats.*
- (Repeat step f for remaining words: **ran, in, a, store.**)
g. Everybody, say that sentence. Get ready. (Signal.) *Those cats ran in a store.*
- (Repeat until firm.)
h. Touch the first word of the next sentence. What word? (Signal.) *A.*
i. Next word. Get ready. (Tap 3 times.) *mmm aaa nnn.* What word? (Signal.) *Man.*
- (Repeat step i for remaining words: **made, those, cats, sit.**)
j. Everybody, say that sentence. Get ready. (Signal.) *A man made those cats sit.*
- (Repeat until firm.)
k. Next sentence. First word. Get ready. (Tap 3 times.) *d iii d.* What word? (Signal.) *Did.*
l. Next word. Get ready. (Tap 3 times.) *ththth aaa t.* What word? (Signal.) *That.*
- (Repeat step l for remaining words: **make, the, cats, mad.**)
m. Everybody, say that sentence. (Signal.) *Did that make the cats mad?*
- (Repeat until firm.)
n. Last sentence. First word. What word? (Signal.) *You.*
- Next word. Get ready. (Tap 3 times.) *www iii lll.* What word? (Signal.) *Will.*
- Next word. Get ready. (Tap 2 times.) *sss EEE.* What word? (Signal.) *See.*

o. Everybody, say that sentence.
(Signal.) *You will see.*
• (Repeat until firm.)

=========== EXERCISE 6 ===========

**COMPREHENSION**

a. You're going to see pictures of the story. Do you think you'll see the same five cats you saw in the last cat story? (Children respond.)

b. Touch the first picture. ✔

Five cats pl<u>ay</u> in a tree
and pl<u>ay</u> in a path.

• Are those the same cats? (Signal.) *No.*
• Those are regular house cats. But they're not in a house. Where are three of those cats? (Call on a child. Idea: *In a tree.*)
• Where are the other two cats? (Call on a child. Idea: *In a path.*)
• The first sentence of the story is below the picture. You'll read all the words in that sentence the fast way.
• First word. What word? (Signal.) *Five.*

c. Next word. What word? (Signal.) *Cats.*
• (Repeat for remaining words: **play, in, a, tree, and, play, in, a, path.**)

d. Say the whole sentence. Get ready. (Signal.) *Five cats play in a tree and play in a path.*

e. Touch the next picture. ✔

Thos<u>e</u> cats ran in a stor<u>e</u>.

• What are the cats doing in that picture? (Call on a child. Idea: *Running into and around a store.*)
• I don't think the man in the store likes those cats running into his store.
• (Call on a child.) Read the sentence under the picture. *Those cats ran in a store.*

f. Touch the next picture. ✔

A man mad<u>e</u> thos<u>e</u> cats
sit. Did that mak<u>e</u> the
cats mad?

• All the cats are doing the same thing in that picture. What are they doing? (Signal.) *Sitting.*

- There are two sentences under the picture. (Call on different children to read the sentences. *A man made those cats sit. Did that make the cats mad?*)
- Do the cats look mad? (Signal.) *No.*
- Who looks mad in the picture? (Call on a child. Idea: *The man.*)
- Why do you think he's mad? (Call on a child. Idea: *He doesn't like the cats all over the store or on his head.*)

## WORKBOOK

=== EXERCISE 7 ===

### STORY EXTENSION
### Sentence Completion

a. Close your textbook. Open your workbook to lesson 45, and complete the sentence at the top of the page. ✔
b. Find the picture for the story. ✔
- The picture is like one from your textbook. Part of the story is below the picture, but some of the words are missing from these sentences.
c. Later, you'll find the missing words above the picture and complete the story.

=== EXERCISE 8 ===

### INDEPENDENT WORK

### Cross-Out Game
a. Find the cross-out game. ✔
- Raise your hand when you know the word you'll cross out.
  Everybody, what word? (Signal.) *Wide.*
- Raise your hand when you know the word you'll circle.
  Everybody, what word? (Signal.) *Low.*
- You'll circle **low** and cross out **wide.**

## Words for Pictures

b. (Write on the board:)

**at   ail**

- You're going to complete words that tell about pictures. For some pictures, you'll complete a word by writing the letters **A-T.** For other pictures, you'll complete a word by writing the letters **A-I-L.**
c. Everybody, find the star. ✔
- The first ending is spelled **A-T.** Say the sounds. Get ready. (Tap 2 times.) *aaa   t.*
- What does this part say? (Signal.) *at.*
- The next ending is spelled **A-I-L.** Say the sounds. Get ready. (Tap 2 times.) *AAA   lll.*
- What does this part say? (Signal.) *ail.*
d. Everybody, touch picture 1. ✔
- That's a **rail.** What is in the picture? (Signal.) *A rail.*
- Fix up the word under the picture. The first letter is shown. Complete the word by writing the correct ending. Pencils down when you're finished.
  (Observe children and give feedback.)
- (Write on the board:)

**rail**

- Everybody, spell the word you wrote under picture 1. Get ready. (Tap 4 times.) *R-A-I-L.*

e. Touch picture 2. ✔
• That person is in **jail.**
• Complete the word under the picture so it says **jail.** Pencils down when you're finished.
   (Observe children and give feedback.)
• (Write on the board:)

**jail**

• Everybody, spell the word you wrote under picture 2. Get ready. **(Tap 4 times.)** *J-A-I-L.*
f. Later, you'll complete the other pictures.
• Touch picture 3. ✔
   That picture shows a **mat.** You'll complete the word under the picture so it says **mat.**
• Touch picture 4. ✔
   That picture shows a **tail.** You'll complete word 4 so it says **tail.**

### Matching: Words

g. Find the matching game. None of the words in the right column have blue letters or underlines. Some of the words are missing. You'll write the missing words, and draw lines to connect the other words.

═══════════ EXERCISE 9 ═══════════
### TAKE HOME

a. Go to the next page in your workbook. ✔
• (Remove perforated story sheet. Direct children to fold sheet so the title, **Me and My Pal**, is the cover page.)
b. This is like a story you read before. The first page is the title of the story. (Call on a child to read the title. *Me and My Pal.*)
c. Turn to the next page. ✔
• Read what the girl is saying. (Call on a child. *I like my pal.*)
• Read what it says at the bottom of the next page. (Call on a child. *My pal may take me for a ride.*)
d. Turn to the last page. ✔
• Read what it says on that page. (Call on a child. *That may make me sore.*)

e. You can color this book and take it home to read to your family. I think they'll like it.
f. (Check out each child on reading the entire story.)

═══════════ EXERCISE 10 ═══════════
### SPELLING WORDS

a. You're going to spell words. Some of them have a blue **E** as the last letter.
b. Listen: **ate.** What word? (Signal.) *Ate.*
• Say the sounds in **ate.** Get ready. (Tap 2 times.) *AAA    t.*
• Do you say a letter name when you say the sounds? (Signal.) *Yes.*
• What letter name? (Signal.) *A.*
• So **ate** has a blue **E.**
c. Listen: **at.** What word? (Signal.) *At.*
• Say the sounds in **at.** Get ready. (Tap 2 times.) *aaa    t.*
• Do you say a letter name when you say the sounds? (Signal.) *No.*
• So **at** does not have a blue **E.**
d. Listen: **made.** What word? (Signal.) *Made.*
• Say the sounds in **made.** Get ready. (Tap 3 times.) *mmm    AAA    d.*
• Do you say a letter name when you say the sounds? (Signal.) *Yes.*
• What letter name? (Signal.) *A.*
• So does the word **made** have a blue **E?** (Signal.) *Yes.*
e. Listen: **mad.** What word? (Signal.) *Mad.*
• Say the sounds in **mad.** Get ready. (Tap 3 times.) *mmm    aaa    d.*
• Do you say a letter name when you say the sounds? (Signal.) *No.*
• Does **mad** have a blue **E?** (Signal.) *No.*
• Remember, you write a blue **E** if you hear a letter name in the word.

## LINED PAPER

f. Get ready to write the words we just spelled.

• Number four lines on your paper. Pencils down when you're finished.
(Observe children and give feedback.)

g. Touch number 1. ✔

• Write the word **mad.** Pencils down when you're finished.
(Observe children and give feedback.)

• (Write on the board:)

> **1 mad**

• Here's what you should have. **Mad** is spelled **M-A-D.**

h. Touch number 2. ✔

• Write the word **made.** Pencils down when you're finished.
(Observe children and give feedback.)

• (Write on the board:)

> **2 made**

• Here's what you should have. **Made** is spelled **M-A-D-E.**

i. Touch number 3. ✔

• Write the word **ate.** Pencils down when you're finished.
(Observe children and give feedback.)

• (Write on the board:)

> **3 ate**

• Here's what you should have. **Ate** is spelled **A-T-E.**

j. Touch number 4. ✔

• Write the word **at.** Pencils down when you're finished.
(Observe children and give feedback.)

• (Write on the board:)

> **4 at**

• Here's what you should have. **At** is spelled **A-T.**

k. Raise your hand if you got everything right.

═══ EXERCISE 11 ═══

## SENTENCE WRITING

a. (Write on the board:)

> Make those cats sit.

b. You're going to write this sentence.
(Call on a child to read the sentence.)

c. Turn to the back of your paper. ✔

• Write this sentence on the top line. Pencils down when you're finished.
(Observe children and give feedback.)

• Later, you'll write the same sentence two more times on the lines below.

═══ EXERCISE 12 ═══

## LETTER PRINTING

a. (Write on the board:)

> ck m y j w r

• You're going to write some letters.

b. Skip the next two lines on your paper and put your pencil at the beginning of the line after that. Keep your pencil in place so I can see it. ✔

• The letter you'll write on that line makes the sound **www.** What sound?
(Signal.) *www.*

• What letter makes that sound?
(Signal.) *W.*

• I'll show you how to write **w.**

• (Trace **W.**)

• Write the letter for **www.** Pencils down when you're finished. ✔

c. Touch the next line. ✔

• The letter you'll write on that line makes the sound **mmm.** What sound?
(Signal.) *mmm.*

• What letter makes that sound?
(Signal.) *M.*

• Write the letter for **mmm.** Pencils down when you're finished. ✔

d. Later, you'll complete the lines of letters.

**45**

## Independent Work Summary

*Note:* Check out each child on reading *Me and My Pal.*

- Story extension (write missing words).
- Cross-out (**wide**=4) and circle (**low**=3) game.
- Write word endings to match pictures.
- Matching game.
- Color and take home *Me and My Pal.*
- Sentence writing (copy two more times: **Make those cats sit.**).
- Letter printing (finish lines of **w**, **m**).

**Materials:** Each child will need lined paper.

━━━━━━━ EXERCISE 1 ━━━━━━━

**SOUNDS**
**g Sound**

a. The letter **G** makes the same sound that **C** makes except that it is not whispered.
• Listen: **g.** Say the sound for **G.** Get ready. (Signal.) *g.*
b. Listen: **gold.** What word? (Signal.) *Gold.*
• There are four sounds in **gold.** I'll say them: **g   OOO   lll   d.**
• Your turn. Say the sounds in **gold.** Get ready. (Tap 4 times.) *g   OOO   lll   d.*
• What letter do you use to spell the first sound in **gold?** (Signal.) *G.*
c. New word: **game.** What word? (Signal.) *Game.*
• Say the sounds in **game.** Get ready. (Tap 3 times.) *g   AAA   mmm.*

**TEXTBOOK**

d. Open your textbook to lesson 46. Find the squirrel. ✔
• I think that squirrel is going to collect those acorns.
• (Teacher reference:)

| k | g | w | c | g |
|---|---|---|---|---|

e. Touch and say the sounds.
• First sound. Get ready. (Signal.) *k.*
• Next sound. Get ready. (Signal.) *g.*
• (Repeat for remaining items.)
f. (Repeat step e until firm.)
g. This time, I'll say the sounds for one of the brown acorns. You'll touch the letter and then tell me the letter name.
• (Teacher reference:)

| g | w | c |
|---|---|---|

h. Listen: The sound of a brown acorn is **g.**
• Touch the brown acorn that makes the sound **g.** ✔
• Everybody, spell the letter you're touching. (Signal.) *G.*
i. Listen: The sound of a brown acorn is **k.**
• Touch the acorn that makes the sound **k.** ✔
• Everybody, spell the letter you're touching. (Signal.) *C.*
j. Listen: The sound of a brown acorn is **www.**
• Touch the acorn that makes the sound **www.** ✔
• Everybody, spell the letter you're touching. (Signal.) *W.*
k. (Repeat steps h through j until firm.)

━━━━━━━ EXERCISE 2 ━━━━━━━

**READING IRREGULAR WORDS**
**Introducing TO and DO**

a. After you read all the words on this page, I'll call on individual children to read some of the words.
b. Find the mouse. ✔
• (Teacher reference:)

| t͜o |
|---|
| d͜o |

• Look at the funny underline in these two words. ✔
• The funny underline means that part of the word does funny things. It does not make the sound you think it should make.
c. Touch the top word. ✔
• Say the sound for the first letter. Get ready. (Signal.) *t.*
• You'd think the sound for the next letter would be **OOO,** but that word is not **toe.** It's **to.**
• What word? (Signal.) *To.*
Yes, I went **to** school.
d. Touch the bottom word. ✔
• What's the first sound? (Signal.) *d.*
• That word is not **dough.** It's **do.**
• What word? (Signal.) *Do.*
We like what we **do.**

e. Those are very strange words, but that's the way they are spelled.
How do you spell the word **to?**
(Signal.) *T-O.*
How do you spell the word **do?**
(Signal.) *D-O.*
• Who will remember how to spell those words?
(Children respond.)
• Who will remember that the funny underline means that part of the word is strange?
(Children respond.)

━━━━━━━━━ EXERCISE 3 ━━━━━━━━━
## READING WORDS

a. Find the raccoon. ✔
• (Teacher reference:)

| 1. s<u>ai</u>d | 2. over | 3. ask |
|---|---|---|
| 4. sno<u>w</u> | 5. if | 6. deep |

b. Word 1 is a word you learned in the last lesson. That word is **said.** It has a funny underline because the letter combination does not say **AAA.** Spell word 1. Get ready. (Tap 4 times.) *S-A-I-D.*
What word? (Signal.) *Said.*
• Word 2 has an ending that makes the sound **ur.** Say the sounds for word 2.
Get ready. (Tap 3 times.) *OOO   vvv   ur.*
What word? (Signal.) *Over.*
• Word 3. Get ready. (Tap 3 times.)
*aaa   sss   k.*
Again. Get ready. (Tap 3 times.)
*aaa   sss   k.*
What word? (Signal.) *Ask.*
We **ask** questions.
c. Next word. Get ready. (Tap 3 times.)
*sss   nnn   OOO.*
What word? (Signal.) *Snow.*
• (Repeat for: **if, deep.**)
d. Let's read those words again, the fast way.
• Word 1. That's a funny word. What word? (Signal.) *Said.*

• Next word. What word? (Signal.) *Over.*
• (Repeat for: **ask, snow, if, deep.**)

━━━━━━━━━ EXERCISE 4 ━━━━━━━━━
## READING WORDS
### S Ending Pronounced zzz

a. Find the bush. ✔
• (Teacher reference:)

| 1. needs | 2. weeds |
|---|---|
| 3. tr<u>ai</u>ls | 4. tr<u>ai</u>ns |

• These are words that end with the letter **S. S** in these words makes the sound **zzz.** First you'll say the sounds. Then you'll read these words the fast way.
b. Word 1. Get ready. (Tap 4 times.)
*nnn   EEE   d   zzz.*
• What word? (Signal.) *Needs.*
• Yes, the cat **needs** to play.
c. Word 2. Get ready. (Tap 4 times.)
*www   EEE   d   zzz.*
• What word? (Signal.) *Weeds.*
• Yes, the garden is full of **weeds.**
d. Word 3 has five sounds. Get ready.
(Tap 5 times.) *t   rrr   AAA   lll   zzz.*
• What word? (Signal.) *Trails.*
• Yes, the **trails** went along the river.
e. Word 4 has five sounds. Get ready.
(Tap 5 times.) *t   rrr   AAA   nnn   zzz.*
• What word? (Signal.) *Trains.*
• Good reading.
f. Let's read those words again, the fast way.
• Word 1. What word? (Signal.) *Needs.*
• Word 2. What word? (Signal.) *Weeds.*
• Word 3. What word? (Signal.) *Trails.*
• Word 4. What word? (Signal.) *Trains.*

## Individual Turns

- (Call on different children to read one or two of the words on the page.)

━━━━━━━━ **EXERCISE 5** ━━━━━━━━

## STORY READING

It is a cold day. Snow is in the stove. A cat and a rat feel cold. Is an ant as cold as the stove? No. That ant is in five coats.

a. Find the story. ✔
b. You'll read all the words in the first sentence.
- First word. Say the sounds. Get ready. (Tap 2 times.) *iii   t.*
  What word? (Signal.) *It.*
c. Next word. Say the sounds. Get ready. (Tap 2 times.) *iii   sss.*
  What word? (Signal.) *Is.*
- (Repeat step c for remaining words: **a, cold, day.**)
d. Everybody, say all the words in the first sentence. (Signal.) *It is a cold day.*
- (Repeat until firm.)
e. Touch the first word of the next sentence. ✔

- Get ready. (Tap 3 times.) *sss   nnn   OOO.*
  What word? (Signal.) *Snow.*
f. Next word. Say the sounds. Get ready. (Tap 2 times.) *iii   sss.*
  What word? (Signal.) *Is.*
- (Repeat step f for remaining words: **in, the, stove.**)
g. Everybody, say that sentence. (Signal.) *Snow is in the stove.*
- (Repeat until firm.)
h. Next sentence. First word. What word? (Signal.) *A.*
i. Next word. Get ready. (Tap 3 times.) *c   aaa   t.*
  What word? (Signal.) *Cat.*
- (Repeat step i for remaining words: **and, a, rat, feel, cold.**)
j. Everybody, say that sentence. (Signal.) *A cat and a rat feel cold.*
- (Repeat until firm.)
k. Next sentence. First word. Get ready. (Tap 2 times.) *iii   sss.*
  What word? (Signal.) *Is.*
l. Next word. Get ready. (Tap 2 times.) *aaa   nnn.*
  What word? (Signal.) *An.*
- (Repeat step l for remaining words: **ant, as, cold, as, the, stove.**)
m. Everybody, say that sentence. (Signal.) *Is an ant as cold as the stove?*
- (Repeat until firm.)
n. The next sentence has one word. Everybody, what word? (Signal.) *No.*
o. Last sentence. First word. Get ready. (Tap 3 times.) *ththth   aaa   t.*
  What word? (Signal.) *That.*
p. Next word. Get ready. (Tap 3 times.) *aaa   nnn   t.*
  What word? (Signal.) *Ant.*
- (Repeat step p for remaining words: **is, in, five, coats.**)
q. Everybody, say that sentence. (Signal.) *That ant is in five coats.*
- (Repeat until firm.)

## 46

====== **EXERCISE 6** ======

### COMPREHENSION

a. You're going to look at pictures of the story.
* Touch the first picture. ✔

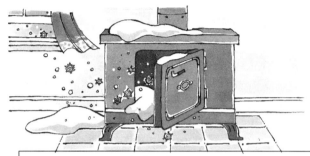

> It is a cold day.  Snow is in the stove.

* It looks pretty cold in that place. Is the stove cold? (Signal.) *Yes.*
* How do you know? (Call on a child. Idea: *It has snow in it and on it.*)
* The first two sentences of the story are below the picture. You'll read all the words in the first sentence the fast way.
* First word. What word? (Signal.) *It.*
b. Next word. What word? (Signal.) *Is.*
* (Repeat for remaining words: **a, cold, day.**)
c. Say the whole sentence. (Signal.) *It is a cold day.*
d. (Call on a child.) Read the next sentence under the picture. *Snow is in the stove.* (Praise accurate and fast reading.)

e. Touch the next picture. ✔

> A cat and a rat feel cold.  Is an ant as cold as the stove?

* Who is in that picture? (Call on a child. Idea: *Cat, rat, and part of an ant.*)
* You can see the head of the ant.
* (Call on a child.) Read the first sentence under the picture. *A cat and a rat feel cold.*
* (Call on a child.) Read the next sentence under the picture. *Is an ant as cold as the stove?*

f. Touch the next picture. ✔

That ant is in five coats.

- You can see what the ant is wearing. Does the ant look cold? (Signal.) *No.*
- (Call on a child to read the sentence. *That ant is in five coats.*)

========= EXERCISE 7 =========
**STORY EXTENSION**
**Sentence Completion**

a. Close your textbook. Go to lesson 46 in your workbook and write your name. ✔
b. Find the picture for the story. ✔
- There are sentences from the story, but words are missing. You'll fill in the missing words and color the picture. Remember, the words are in the box above the picture.

========= EXERCISE 8 =========
**INDEPENDENT WORK**

**Matching: Words and Capitals**
a. Find the matching games. ✔
- There are two matching games.
- For the first matching game, one of the words is missing. Later, you'll write the missing word and draw lines to connect the other words.
- For the other matching game, you'll draw lines to match the capital letters with the regular letters.

**Words for Pictures—Plural S**
b. Find the words at the top of side 2. ✔
- You'll read each word and find the picture it tells about. Then you'll write the word below the picture. If the picture shows more than one, copy the word that tells about one and fix it so it tells about more than one.
- Remember, when you copy words you have to write all of the letters, even the blue ones.

========= EXERCISE 9 =========
**SPELLING WORDS**

a. (Write on the board:)

| ai |
|---|

- You're going to spell words. Some of them have the letter combination **A-I.** They don't have an **E** on the end of the word; they have the combination **A-I.** Remember, when you say the sounds for those words, you say a letter name.
b. Listen: **tail.** What word? (Signal.) *Tail.*
- The dog had a long **tail.**
- Say the sounds in **tail.** Get ready. (Tap 3 times.) *t   AAA   lll.*
- Do you say a letter name when you say the sounds? (Signal.) *Yes.*
- Yes, you say a letter name. What letter name? (Signal.) *A.*
- In the word **tail,** the **AAA** sound is spelled with **A-I.** So **tail** is spelled **T-A-I-L.**

- Everybody, spell the word **tail.** Get ready. (Tap 4 times.) *T-A-I-L.*
- c. Listen: **aim.** What word? (Signal.) *Aim.*
- Say the sounds in **aim.** Get ready. (Tap 2 times.) *AAA   mmm.*
- Do you say a letter name when you say the sounds? (Signal.) *Yes.*
- Yes, you say a letter name. What letter name? (Signal.) *A.*
- In the word **aim,** the **AAA** sound is spelled **A-I-M.**
- Everybody, spell the word **aim.** Get ready. (Tap 3 times.) *A-I-M.*
- d. Listen: **rain.** What word? (Signal.) *Rain.*
- Say the sounds in **rain.** Get ready. (Tap 3 times.) *rrr   AAA   nnn.*
- Do you say a letter name when you say the sounds? (Signal.) *Yes.*
- What letter name? (Signal.) *A.*
- You say a letter name. How do you spell the sound **AAA** in the word **rain?** (Signal.) *A-I.*
- Everybody, spell the word **rain.** Get ready. (Tap 4 times.) *R-A-I-N.*
- e. Listen: **mail.** What word? (Signal.) *Mail.*
- Say the sounds in **mail.** Get ready. (Tap 3 times.) *mmm   AAA   lll.*
- Do you say a letter name when you say the sounds? (Signal.) *Yes.*
- What letter name? (Signal.) *A.*
- You say a letter name. How do you spell the sound **AAA** in the word mail? (Signal.) *A-I.*
- Everybody, spell the word mail. Get ready. (Tap 4 times.) *M-A-I-L.*
- f. Remember, for these words you write **A-I** if you hear a letter name in the word. You don't write any **E**s on the end of these words.

**LINED PAPER**

- g. Your turn to write some of the words we just spelled. All those words have the letter combination **A-I.**
- Number four lines on your paper. Pencils down when you're finished. ✔
- h. Touch number 1. ✔
- Write the word **rain** on that line. Pencils down when you're finished. (Observe children and give feedback.)
- (Write on the board:)

> **1 rain**

- Here's what you should have. **Rain** is spelled **R-A-I-N.**
- i. Touch number 2. ✔
- Write the word **aim** on that line. Pencils down when you're finished. (Observe children and give feedback.)
- (Write on the board:)

> **2 aim**

- Here's what you should have. **Aim** is spelled **A-I-M.**
- j. Touch number 3. ✔
- Write the word **mail** on that line. Pencils down when you're finished. (Observe children and give feedback.)
- (Write on the board:)

> **3 mail**

- Here's what you should have. **Mail** is spelled **M-A-I-L.**
- k. Touch number 4. ✔
- Write the word **sail** on that line. Pencils down when you're finished. (Observe children and give feedback.)
- (Write on the board:)

> **4 sail**

- Here's what you should have. **Sail** is spelled **S-A-I-L.**
- l. Raise your hand if you got everything right.

================= EXERCISE 10 =================

## SENTENCE WRITING

a. (Write on the board:)

The stove is cold.

b. You're going to write this sentence. (Call on a child to read the sentence.)
c. Turn to the back of your paper. ✔
• Write the sentence on the top line. Pencils down when you're finished. (Observe children and give feedback.)
d. Later, you can write the same sentence two more times on the lines below.

================= EXERCISE 11 =================

## LETTER PRINTING

a. (Write on the board:)

ay ai ck th c w m

• You're going to write some letters.
b. Skip the next two lines on your paper, and put your pencil at the beginning of the line after that. Keep your pencil in place so I can see it. ✔
• On that line you'll write the letter combination that makes the sound **k.** What sound? (Signal.) k.

• Look at the board. Spell the letter combination that makes that sound. Get ready. (Tap 2 times.) C-K.
• Write the letter combination for **k.** Pencils down when you're finished. ✔
c. Touch the next line. ✔
• On that line you'll write the letter that makes the sound **www.** What sound? (Signal.) www.
• What letter makes that sound? (Signal.) W.
• Write the letter for **www.** Pencils down when you're finished. ✔
d. Touch the next line. ✔
• On that line you'll write the letter that makes the sound **k.** What sound? (Signal.) k.
• Which letter on the board makes that sound? (Signal.) C.
• Write the letter for **k.** Pencils down when you're finished. ✔
e. Later, you'll complete the lines of letters.

**Independent Work Summary**
• Story extension (write missing words).
• Matching words.
• Matching letters.
• Write appropriate words for pictures.
• Sentence writing (copy two more times: **The stove is cold.**).
• Letter printing (finish lines of **ck, w, c**).

**Materials:** Each child will need a gray and a brown crayon and lined paper.

## TEXTBOOK

=========== EXERCISE 1 ===========

### SOUNDS

a. Open your textbook to lesson 47. Find the fish tank. ✔

• This looks like a pet store. Touch the fish tank. ✔

• (Teacher reference:)

| v   c   j   g   k   w |
|---|

b. Touch and say the sounds on the fish.
• First sound. Get ready. (Signal.) *vvv.*
• Next sound. Get ready. (Signal.) *k.*
• (Repeat for remaining items.)

### Individual Turns
• (Repeat step b with different children.)

=========== EXERCISE 2 ===========

### READING WORDS

a. After you read all the words on this page without any mistakes, I'll call on different children to read some of the words.

b. Find the parrot. ✔
• (Teacher reference:)

| 1. to | 2. do | 3. said | 4. over |
|---|---|---|---|
| 5. ask | 6. more | 7. mail | 8. make |

• The first words have parts with funny underlines. I'll spell each word. Then you'll tell me the word.

c. Word 1 is spelled **T-O.** It is not pronounced **toe.** What's word 1? (Signal.) *To.*
• Word 2 is spelled **D-O.** It is not pronounced **dough.** What's word 2? (Signal.) *Do.*

• Word 3 is spelled **S-A-I-D.** It is not pronounced **sayed.** What's word 3? (Signal.) *Said.*
• (Repeat step c until firm.)

d. Word 4 has an underlined part. Remember, that part says **ur.** What does it say? (Signal.) *ur.*
• Touch and say the sounds. Get ready. (Tap 3 times.) *OOO   vvv   ur.* Again. Get ready. (Tap 3 times.) *OOO   vvv   ur.* What word? (Signal.) *Over.*
• Word 5. Get ready. (Tap 3 times.) *aaa   sss   k.* What word? (Signal.) *Ask.*

e. The rest of the words have problems. They are supposed to have blue letters, but somebody forgot to put them in. Let's try to read these words anyhow.

• Word 6 is supposed to have a blue E. Everybody, say the sounds. Get ready. (Tap 3 times.) *mmm   OOO   rrr.* Again. Get ready. (Tap 3 times.) *mmm   OOO   rrr.* What word? (Signal.) *More.*

• Word 7 is supposed to have a blue letter. Everybody, say the sounds. Get ready. (Tap 3 times.) *mmm   AAA   lll.* Again. Get ready. (Tap 3 times.) *mmm   AAA   lll.* What word? (Signal.) *Mail.*

• Word 8 is supposed to have a blue letter. Everybody, say the sounds. Get ready. (Tap 3 times.) *mmm   AAA   k.* Again. Get ready. (Tap 3 times.) *mmm   AAA   k.* What word? (Signal.) *Make.*

• Good reading words without the blue letters.

f. Let's read those words again the fast way.
• Word 1. What word? (Signal.) *To.*
• Next word. What word? (Signal.) *Do.*
• (Repeat for: **said, over, ask, more, mail, make.**)

## EXERCISE 3

### READING WORDS
#### Words with g

a. Find the rabbit. ✔
• (Teacher reference:)

| | | | |
|---|---|---|---|
| **1.** | **go** | **2.** | **pig** |
| **3.** | **gav**e | **4.** | **gam**es |

• These words have the letter **G**.
b. First word. Touch and say the sounds. Get ready. (Tap 2 times.) *g    OOO.*
Again. Get ready. (Tap 2 times.) *g    OOO.*
What word? (Signal.) *Go.*
• Next word. Get ready. (Tap 3 times.) *p    iii    g.*
Again. Get ready. (Tap 3 times.) *p    iii    g.*
What word? (Signal.) *Pig.*
Yes, we may have some stories that tell about a **pig.**
• The next word has a blue letter. Get ready. (Tap 3 times.) *g    AAA    vvv.*
Again. Get ready. (Tap 3 times.) *g    AAA    vvv.*
What word? (Signal.) *Gave.*
• The last word has four sounds. Get ready. (Tap 4 times.)
*g    AAA    mmm    sss.*
Again. Get ready. (Tap 4 times.)
*g    AAA    mmm    sss.*
What word? (Signal.) *Games.*
c. Let's read those words again the fast way.
• Word 1. What word? (Signal.) *Go.*
• Word 2. What word? (Signal.) *Pig.*
• Word 3. What word? (Signal.) *Gave.*
• Word 4. What word? (Signal.) *Games.*

## EXERCISE 4

### READING WORDS
#### Words with S Ending

a. Find the puppy. ✔
• (Teacher reference:)

| |
|---|
| **weeds** |
| **jok**es |
| **lik**es |

• All these words end with the letter **S**.
b. Top word. Touch and say the sounds. Get ready. (Tap 4 times.)
*www    EEE    d    sss.*
What word? (Signal.) *Weeds.*
• Middle word. Get ready. (Tap 4 times.)
*j    OOO    k    sss.*
What word? (Signal.) *Jokes.*
• Bottom word. Get ready. (Tap 4 times.)
*lll    III    k    sss.*
What word? (Signal.) *Likes.*
c. Let's read those words again the fast way.
• Top word. What word? (Signal.) *Weeds.*
• Middle word. What word? (Signal.) *Jokes.*
• Bottom word. What word? (Signal.) *Likes.*

**Individual Turns**

• (Call on different children to read one or two of the words on the page.)

---

## EXERCISE 5

**E-D ENDING**
   **Oral**
a. (Write on the board:)

> **ed**

- Some words that tell what happened end with the letters **E-D.** What letters? (Signal.) *E-D.*
b. Listen: **fill.** What word? (Signal.) *Fill.*
- That tells what happens now. Here's the word that tells what happened earlier: **filled.**
- What word? (Signal.) *Filled.*
c. Listen: **jump.** What word? (Signal.) *Jump.*
- That tells what happens now. Here's the word that tells what happened earlier: **jumped.**
- What word? (Signal.) *Jumped.*
- The last letters in the word are **E-D.**
- What are the last letters in the word **jumped?** (Signal.) *E-D.*
- Listen: **jump.** What word? (Signal.) *Jump.*
- That tells what happens now. Say the word that tells what happened earlier. (Signal.) *Jumped.*
d. Listen: **walk.** What word? (Signal.) *Walk.*
- That tells what happens now. The word that tells what happened earlier is **walked.** Say the word that tells what happened earlier. (Signal.) *Walked.*
- What are the last letters in the word **walked?** (Signal.) *E-D.*
e. Listen: **clean.** What word? (Signal.) *Clean.*
- That tells what happens now. Say the word that tells what happened earlier. (Signal.) *Cleaned.*
- What are the last letters in the word **cleaned?** (Signal.) *E-D.*
f. Listen: **stop.** What word? (Signal.) *Stop.*
- Say the word that tells what happened earlier. (Signal.) *Stopped.*
- What are the last letters in the word **stopped?** (Signal.) *E-D.*
g. (Repeat steps b through f until firm.)

---

## EXERCISE 6

**STORY READING**

> A mole and a rat like to play. The rat likes to play in the weeds. The mole likes to play jokes.

a. Find the book. ✔
b. You'll read all the words in the first sentence.
- First word. What word? (Signal.) *A.*
c. Next word. Say the sounds. Get ready. (Tap 3 times.) *mmm   OOO   lll.* What word? (Signal.) *Mole.*
- (Repeat step c for: **and, a, rat, like.**)
d. So far you have: **A mole and a rat like . . .**
- The next word is spelled **T-O.** What word? (Signal.) *To.*
- Last word. Say the sounds. Get ready. (Tap 3 times.) *p   lll   AAA.* What word? (Signal.) *Play.*
e. Everybody, say the first sentence. (Signal.) *A mole and a rat like to play.*
- (Repeat until firm.)
f. Touch the first word of the next sentence. ✔
- Get ready. (Tap 2 times.) *ththth   EEE.* What word? (Signal.) *The.*
- Next word. Get ready. (Tap 3 times.) *rrr   aaa   t.* What word? (Signal.) *Rat.*
- Next word. Get ready. (Tap 4 times.) *lll   III   k   sss.* What word? (Signal.) *Likes.*
- The next word is spelled **T-O.** What word? (Signal.) *To.*
g. Next word. Get ready. (Tap 3 times.) *p   lll   AAA.* What word? (Signal.) *Play.*
- (Repeat step g for **in, the, weeds.**)

h. Everybody, say that sentence. (Signal.)
   *The rat likes to play in the weeds.*
• (Repeat until firm.)
i. Touch the first word of the next
   sentence. ✔
• Get ready. (Tap 2 times.) *ththth    EEE.*
   What word? (Signal.) *The.*
• Next word. Get ready. (Tap 3 times.)
   *mmm    OOO    lll.*
   What word? (Signal.) *Mole.*
• Next word. Get ready. (Tap 4 times.)
   *lll    III    k    sss.*
   What word? (Signal.) *Likes.*
• The next word is spelled T-O.
   What word? (Signal.) *To.*
j. Next word. Get ready. (Tap 3 times.)
   *p    lll    AAA.*
   What word? (Signal.) *Play.*
• (Repeat step j for **jokes.**)
k. Everybody, say that sentence.
   (Signal.) *The mole likes to play jokes.*
• (Repeat until firm.)

──────── EXERCISE 7 ────────

**COMPREHENSION**

a. You're going to see pictures of the story.
• Touch the first picture. ✔

A mol e and a rat lik e to
pla y.

• You can see the mole and the rat in that
  picture. What are they doing? (Call on a
  child. Idea: *Playing.*)
• The first sentence of the story is below
  the picture. You'll read all the words in
  the first sentence the fast way.
• First word. What word? (Signal.) *A.*

b. Next word. What word? (Signal.) *Mole.*
• (Repeat for remaining words: **and, a, rat,
  like, to, play.**)
c. Say the whole sentence. Get ready.
   (Signal.) *A mole and a rat like to play.*
• (Repeat until firm.)
d. Touch the next picture. ✔

# The rat likes to play in the weeds.

• Who is in that picture? (Call on a child.
  Idea: *A rat and a mole.*)
• Where is the rat playing? (Call on a child.
  Idea: *In the weeds.*)
• (Call on a child.) Read the sentence
  under the picture. *The rat likes to play in
  the weeds.*

e. Touch the last picture. ✔

## The mole likes to play jokes.

- What happened to the rat? (Call on a child. Idea: *Fell in a hole.*)
- (Call on a child.) Read the sentence under the picture. *The mole likes to play jokes.*

══════ EXERCISE 8 ══════

**READING**
**Introducing Quotes**

a. Go to the next page in your textbook. Find the sentences at the top. ✔
- (Teacher reference:)

> 1. A ram said, "I am a ram."
> 2. A ram said, "You will see trees."
> 3. A ram said, "I am late."

- Each sentence starts with the words: **A ram said.** After **A ram said** are different things that the ram said. The red marks are quote marks. They show everything he said.

b. Sentence 1. Touch the red quote mark after **A ram said.** ✔
Keep touching it and the red quote mark at the end of the sentence. Touch them both.
(Observe children and give feedback.)
- I'm going to read all the words the ram said. Those are the words between the quote marks. The first word he said is **I.** Touch the word **I.** ✔
- I'll read the rest of the words. (Tap 3 times.) **am . . . a . . . ram.**
- Your turn. Touch the words he said and read them the fast way. Get ready. (Tap 4 times.) *I am a ram.*
- What did he say in sentence 1? (Signal.) *I am a ram.*

c. Sentence 2. Touch the quote marks around the words he said in the sentence.
(Observe children and give feedback.)
- I'll read the words he said. (Tap 4 times.) **You . . . will . . . see . . . trees.**
- Read the words he said the fast way. Get ready. (Tap 4 times.) *You . . . will . . . see . . . trees.*
- What did he say in sentence 2? (Signal.) *You will see trees.*

d. Sentence 3. Touch the quote marks around the words he said in the sentence.
(Observe children and give feedback.)
- I'll read the words he said the fast way. (Tap 3 times.) **I . . . am . . . late.**
- Your turn. Get ready. (Tap 3 times.) *I . . . am . . . late.*
- What did he say? (Signal.) *I am late.*

e. Let's go back and read the **whole** sentences.
- Sentence 1. Read all the words, starting with **A.** Get ready. (Tap for each word.) *A . . . ram . . . said . . . I . . . am . . . a . . . ram.*
What did he say? (Signal.) *I am a ram.*
- Sentence 2. Read all the words. Get ready. (Tap for each word.) *A . . . ram . . . said . . . You . . . will . . . see . . . trees.*
What did he say?
(Signal.) *You will see trees.*

- Sentence 3. Read all the words. Get ready. (Tap for each word.) *A . . . ram . . . said . . . I . . . am . . . late.*
  What did he say? (Signal.) *I am late.*
f. You are reading sentences that have quote marks. Remember, those marks show the words that somebody said.
g. Touch the picture of the ram. ✔

- The ram is saying something in that picture. There are no quote marks because when characters talk in pictures, no quote marks are shown.
- (Call on a child to read what the ram said.)
- Everybody, what did the ram say? (Signal.) *I am late.*
  That's what the ram said in one of the sentences you read.
- Where do you think that ram is going? (Call on a child. Idea: *To a party.*)
- Who thinks the party has already started? (Children respond.)
h. Remember, when characters talk in pictures, no quote marks are shown.

**WORKBOOK**

========= **EXERCISE 9** =========

**STORY EXTENSION**
**Writing Words in Pictures**

a. Close your textbook. Go to lesson 47 in your workbook and write your name. ✔
b. Find the picture of the ram. ✔
- I'll read the sentence under the picture. Follow along: **A ram said, "I am a ram."**
- The quote marks aren't red. What color are they? (Signal.) *Black.*
- Later, you'll write the words the ram said in the picture. Everybody, what did the ram say? (Signal.) *I am a ram.*
- Those are the words that go in the picture: **I am a ram.**
- Don't get fooled and write the words the ram didn't say.

========= **EXERCISE 10** =========

**INDEPENDENT WORK**
**Hidden Picture**

*Note:* Each child needs a gray and a brown crayon.

a. Find the hidden picture at the bottom of your worksheet. ✔
- I'll tell you the coloring rules for the picture.
b. Touch the word **day.** ✔
- Listen: All the parts with **day** are gray. Make a gray mark for **day.** ✔
c. Touch the word **and.** ✔
- All the parts with **and** are brown. Make a brown mark for **and.** ✔
d. Later, you'll color the picture.

**Words for Pictures—Plural S**

e. Find the words at the top of side 2. ✔
- You'll read each word and find the picture it tells about. Then you'll write the word below the picture.
- Some of the pictures show more than one. For those pictures, write the word that tells about more than one.

## EXERCISE 11

### SPELLING WORDS

a. (Write on the board:)

> **ai**

- You're going to spell words. Some of them have the letter combination **A-I.** They don't have an **E** on the end of the word. They have **A-I.** Remember, when you say the sounds for those words, you say a letter name.

b. Listen: **tail.** What word? (Signal.) *Tail.*
- Yes, the dog had a short **tail.**
- Say the sounds in **tail.** Get ready. (Tap 3 times.) *t   AAA   lll.*
- Do you say a letter name when you say the sounds? (Signal.) *Yes.*
- Yes, you say a letter name. What letter name? (Signal.) *A.*
- In the word **tail,** the **AAA** sound is spelled with **A-I.** The word **tail** has four letters.
- Everybody, spell the word **tail.** Get ready. (Tap 4 times.) *T-A-I-L.*

c. Listen: **pain.** What word? (Signal.) *Pain.*
- Yes, the tooth gave me some **pain.**
- Say the sounds in **pain.** Get ready. (Tap 3 times.) *p   AAA   nnn.*
- You say a letter name. How do you spell the sound **AAA** in the word **pain?** (Signal.) *A-I.*
- Everybody, spell the word **pain.** Get ready. (Tap 4 times.) *P-A-I-N.*

d. Listen: **rain.** What word? (Signal.) *Rain.*
- Say the sounds in **rain.** Get ready. (Tap 3 times.) *rrr   AAA   nnn.*
- Do you say a letter name when you say the sounds? (Signal.) *Yes.*
- Everybody, spell the word **rain.** Get ready. (Tap 4 times.) *R-A-I-N.*
- Remember, you write **A-I** if you hear the letter name **A** in these words.

**LINED PAPER**

e. Your turn to write the words we just spelled.
- Number four lines on your paper. Pencils down when you're finished. ✔

f. Here's the rule for these words: If you say **AAA** it's spelled **A-I.** Say the rule for these words. (Signal.) *If you say AAA it's spelled A-I.*

g. Touch number 1. ✔
- Write the word **tail** on that line. Pencils down when you're finished. (Observe children and give feedback.)
- (Write on the board:)

> **1 tail**

- Here's what you should have. Tail is spelled **T-A-I-L.**

h. Touch number 2. ✔
- Write the word **rain** on that line. Pencils down when you're finished. (Observe children and give feedback.)
- (Write on the board:)

> **2 rain**

- Here's what you should have. Rain is spelled **R-A-I-N.**

i. Touch number 3. ✔
- Write the word **jail** on that line. Pencils down when you're finished. (Observe children and give feedback.)
- (Write on the board:)

> **3 jail**

- Here's what you should have. Jail is spelled **J-A-I-L.**

j. Touch number 4. ✔
- Write the word **pain** on that line. Pencils down when you're finished. (Observe children and give feedback.)
- (Write on the board:)

> **4 pain**

- Here's what you should have. Pain is spelled **P-A-I-N.**

k. Raise your hand if you got everything right.

## EXERCISE 12

### SENTENCE WRITING

a. (Write on the board:)

That rat likes to play.

b. You're going to write this sentence.
(Call on a child to read the sentence.)
c. Turn to the back of your paper. ✔
• Write the sentence on the top line.
Pencils down when you're finished.
(Observe children and give feedback.)
d. Later, you can write the same sentence
two more times on the lines below.

## EXERCISE 13

### LETTER PRINTING

a. (Write on the board:)

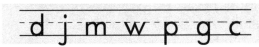

• You're going to write some letters.
b. Skip the next two lines on your paper
and put your pencil at the beginning of
the line after that. ✔
• On that line you'll write the letter that
makes the sound **j**. What sound?
(Signal.) *j*.

• What letter makes that sound?
(Signal.) *J*.
• Write the letter for **j**. Pencils down when
you're finished. ✔
c. Touch the next line. ✔
• On that line you'll write the letter that
makes the sound **k**. What sound?
(Signal.) *k*.
• What letter makes that sound?
(Signal.) *C*.
• Write the letter for **k**. Pencils down when
you're finished. ✔
d. Touch the next line. ✔
• On that line you'll write the letter that
makes the sound **g**. What sound?
(Signal.) *g*.
• What letter makes that sound?
(Signal.) *G*.
• Write the letter for **g**. Pencils down when
you're finished. ✔
e. Later, you'll complete the lines of letters.

**Independent Work Summary**
• Sentence writing (write direct quote
inside word bubble).
• Hidden picture (**and**=brown, **day**=gray).
• Write appropriate words for pictures.
• Sentence writing (copy two more times:
**That rat likes to play.**).
• Letter printing (finish lines of **j**, **c**, **g**).

**Materials:** Each child will need lined paper.

═══════ EXERCISE 1 ═══════

## SOUNDS
### Introducing h

a. (Write on the board:)

| h |
|---|

- You're going to learn the sound for the letter **H.** Here's a word that has that sound: **he.**
- What word? (Signal.) *He.*
- The first sound in **he** is a whispered sound. Listen: **h EEE.**
- Your turn. Say the two sounds in **he.** Get ready. (Tap 2 times.) *h   EEE.*
- What letter do you use to spell the first sound? (Signal.) *H.*

b. New word: **hole.** What word? (Signal.) *Hole.*

- The first sound is the whispered sound for **H.** Say the three sounds in **hole.** Get ready. (Tap 3 times.) *h   OOO   lll.*
- What letter do you use to spell the first sound? (Signal.) *H.*

c. New word: **heat.** What word? (Signal.) *Heat.*

- Say the three sounds in **heat.** Get ready. (Tap 3 times.) *h   EEE   t.*

d. Last word: **hat.** What word? (Signal.) *Hat.*

- Say the three sounds in **hat.** Get ready. (Tap 3 times.) *h   aaa   t.*

**TEXTBOOK**

e. Open your textbook to lesson 48. Find the toolbox. ✔
- (Teacher reference:)

| h | c | g | t | d | h | j |
|---|---|---|---|---|---|---|

f. Touch and say the sounds.
- First sound. Get ready. (Signal.) *h.*
- Next sound. Get ready. (Signal.) *k.*
- (Repeat for remaining items.)

g. (Repeat step f until firm.)

h. This time, I'll say sounds for one of the green letters. You'll touch the letter and then tell me the letter name.
- (Teacher reference:)

| c | g | h | j |
|---|---|---|---|

i. Listen: The sound of a green letter is **h.**
- Touch the letter that makes the sound **h.** ✔
- Everybody, what letter are you touching? (Signal.) *H.*

j. Listen: The sound of a green letter is **g.**
- Touch the letter that makes the sound **g.** ✔
- Everybody, what letter are you touching? (Signal.) *G.*

k. Listen: The sound of a green letter is **j.**
- Touch the letter that makes the sound **j.** ✔
- Everybody, what letter are you touching? (Signal.) *J.*

l. Listen: The sound of a green letter is **k.**
- Touch the letter that makes the sound **k.** ✔
- Everybody, what letter are you touching? (Signal.) *C.*

m. (Repeat steps i through l until firm.)

═══════ EXERCISE 2 ═══════

## READING WORDS

a. After you read all the words on this page without any mistakes, I'll call on different children to read some of the words.
- Find the hammer. ✔
- (Teacher reference:)

| 1. was | 2. do | 3. nine | 4. rats |
|---|---|---|---|
| 5. trails | 6. go | 7. gave | 8. seeds |

b. The first word is a strange word. Everybody, spell word 1. Get ready. (Tap 3 times.) *W-A-S.*

- The **A** has a funny underline because it does not make the sound it is supposed to make. Word 1 is **was.** What word? (Signal.) *Was.*
- c. Word 2 has a funny underline. Spell word 2. Get ready. (Tap 2 times.) *D-O.*
- Everybody, what word? (Signal.) *Do.*
- d. Word 3 has a blue **E.** Say the sounds. Get ready. (Tap 3 times.) *nnn III nnn.*
- What word? (Signal.) *Nine.*
- e. Word 4. Get ready. (Tap 4 times.) *rrr aaa t sss.*
- What word? (Signal.) *Rats.*
- f. Word 5 has five sounds. Get ready. (Tap 5 times.) *t rrr AAA lll sss.*
- Again. Get ready. (Tap 5 times.) *t rrr AAA lll sss.*
- What word? (Signal.) *Trails.*
- g. Word 6. Get ready. (Tap 2 times.) *g OOO.*
- What word? (Signal.) *Go.*
- h. Word 7 has a blue letter. Get ready. (Tap 3 times.) *g AAA vvv.*
- What word? (Signal.) *Gave.*
- i. Word 8. Get ready. (Tap 4 times.) *sss EEE d sss.*
- What word? (Signal.) *Seeds.*
- j. Let's read those words again, the fast way.
- Word 1. Remember that word is **was.** What word? (Signal.) *Was.*
- Next word. What word? (Signal.) *Do.*
- (Repeat for: **nine, rats, trails, go, gave, seeds.**)

═══════ EXERCISE 3 ═══════

**READING WORDS**
**C-K, No Underline**

a. Find the saw. ✔
- (Teacher reference:)

| 1. cave | 2. came | 3. corn |
| 4. kick | 5. kiss | 6. sick |

- All these words have letters that make the sound **k.** In some words the **k** sound is made by the letters **C-K,** but they are not underlined.

- b. Word 1 has a blue letter. Get ready. (Tap 3 times.) *c AAA vvv.* What word? (Signal.) *Cave.*
- Word 2 has a blue letter. Get ready. (Tap 3 times.) *c AAA mmm.* What word? (Signal.) *Came.*
- Word 3. Get ready. (Tap 4 times.) *c OOO rrr nnn.* What word? (Signal.) *Corn.* Yes, we love to eat **corn.**
- Word 4. Get ready. (Tap 3 times.) *k iii k.* What word? (Signal.) *Kick.*
- Word 5. Get ready. (Tap 3 times.) *k iii sss.* What word? (Signal.) *Kiss.* Yes, a **kiss** is better than a **kick.**
- Word 6. Get ready. (Tap 3 times.) *sss iii k.* What word? (Signal.) *Sick.*
- c. Let's read those words again, the fast way.
- Word 1. What word? (Signal.) *Cave.*
- Next word. What word? (Signal.) *Came.*
- (Repeat for: **corn, kick, kiss, sick.**)

═══════ EXERCISE 4 ═══════

**E-D ENDING**
**Oral**

a. (Write on the board:)

**ed**

- Some words that tell what happened end with the letters **E-D.**
- b. Listen: **smell.** What word? (Signal.) *Smell.*
- That tells what happens now. Say the word that tells what happened earlier. (Signal.) *Smelled.*
- What are the last letters in the word **smelled?** (Signal.) *E-D.*
- c. Listen: **hope.** What word? (Signal.) *Hope.*
- That tells what happens now. Say the word that tells what happened earlier. (Signal.) *Hoped.*
- What are the last letters in the word **hoped?** (Signal.) *E-D.*
- d. Listen: **talk.** What word? (Signal.) *Talk.*

- Say the word that tells what happened earlier. (Signal.) *Talked.*
- What are the last letters in the word **talked?** (Signal.) *E-D.*
e. Listen: **smile.** What word? (Signal.) *Smile.*
- That tells what happens now. Say the word that tells what happened earlier. (Signal.) *Smiled.*
- What are the last letters in the word **smiled?** (Signal.) *E-D.*

=== EXERCISE 5 ===

## READING WORDS

a. Find the drill. ✔
- (Teacher reference:)

> **said**
>
> **we**
>
> **slow**

- These are words you've read before. You're going to spell each word, then tell me the word.
b. Spell the top word. Get ready. (Tap 4 times.) *S-A-I-D.*
  What word? (Signal.) *Said.*
- Spell the middle word. Get ready. (Tap 2 times.) *W-E.*
  What word? (Signal.) *We.*
- Spell the bottom word. Get ready. (Tap 4 times.) *S-L-O-W.*
  What word? (Signal.) *Slow.*
c. (Repeat step b until firm.)
d. Let's read those words again, the fast way.
- Top word. What word? (Signal.) *Said.*
- Middle word. What word? (Signal.) *We.*
- Bottom word. What word? (Signal.) *Slow.*

**Individual Turns**

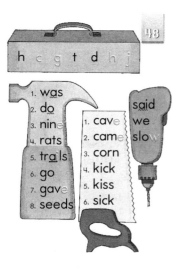

- (Call on different children to read one or two of the words on the page.)

=== EXERCISE 6 ===

## READING
### Sentences with Quotes

a. Find the sentence at the top of the next page. ✔
- (Teacher reference:)

> **A man said, "I like corn."**

- This is a sentence that tells what somebody said. Touch the words as I read them: **A . . . man . . . said . . .** The quote marks are around the words the man said.
- Touch the first quote mark and the quote mark at the end of the sentence. Touch them both.
  (Observe children and give feedback.)
b. I'll read the words the man said. Remember, those are the words inside the quote marks. Listen: **I . . . like . . . corn.**
c. Your turn. I'll tap. You'll read the words in the whole sentence the fast way. Get ready. (Tap for each word.) *A . . . man . . . said . . . I . . . like . . . corn.*
- What did the man say? (Signal.) *I like corn.*
d. (Repeat step c until firm.)

## EXERCISE 7
### STORY READING

> An ant likes to sit.  So that ant sat in a path.  Nine rats like to sit.  So those rats sat with the ant.

a. Find the book. ✔
- This is a story about an ant and some rats.
b. You'll read all the words in the first sentence.
- First word. Get ready. (Tap 2 times.) *aaa nnn.*
  What word? (Signal.) *An.*
- Next word. Get ready. (Tap 3 times.) *aaa nnn t.*
  What word? (Signal.) *Ant.*
- Next word. Get ready. (Tap 4 times.) *lll III k sss.*
  What word? (Signal.) *Likes.*
- The next word is spelled **T-O.** What word? (Signal.) *To.*
- Next word. Get ready. (Tap 3 times.) *sss lll t.*
  What word? (Signal.) *Sit.*
c. Everybody, say the first sentence. (Signal.) *An ant likes to sit.*
- (Repeat until firm.)
d. Touch the first word of the next sentence. ✔
- Get ready. (Tap 2 times.) *sss OOO.*
  What word? (Signal.) *So.*
e. Next word. Get ready. (Tap 3 times.) *ththth aaa t.*
  What word? (Signal.) *That.*
- (Repeat step e for remaining words: **ant, sat, in, a, path.**)
f. Everybody, say that sentence. (Signal.) *So that ant sat in a path.*
- (Repeat until firm.)

g. Touch the first word of the next sentence. ✔
- Get ready. (Tap 3 times.) *nnn III nnn.*
  What word? (Signal.) *Nine.*
h. Next word. Get ready. (Tap 4 times.) *rrr aaa t sss.*
  What word? (Signal.) *Rats.*
- (Repeat step h for remaining words: **like, to, sit.**)
i. Everybody, say that sentence. (Signal.) *Nine rats like to sit.*
- (Repeat until firm.)
j. Touch the first word of the last sentence. ✔
- First word. Get ready. (Tap 2 times.) *sss OOO.*
  What word? (Signal.) *So.*
k. Next word. Get ready. (Tap 3 times.) *ththth OOO sss.*
  What word? (Signal.) *Those.*
- (Repeat step k for remaining words: **rats, sat, with, the, ant.**)
l. Everybody, say that sentence. (Signal.) *So those rats sat with the ant.*
- (Repeat until firm.)

## EXERCISE 8
### COMPREHENSION

a. You're going to see pictures of the story.
- Touch the first picture. ✔

> An ant likes to sit.  So that ant sat in a path.

- Who is in that picture? (Signal.) *An ant.*
- Where is the ant? (Call on a child. Idea: *In a path.*)
- You're going to read both sentences under the picture the fast way.

**48**

- Everybody, first word. What word? (Signal.) *An.*
b. Next word. What word? (Signal.) *Ant.*
- (Repeat for remaining words: **likes, to, sit.**)
c. Say the whole sentence. Get ready. (Signal.) *An ant likes to sit.*
d. Touch the first word of the next sentence. ✔
- Everybody, what word? (Signal.) *So.*
e. Next word. What word? (Signal.) *That.*
- (Repeat for remaining words: **ant, sat, in, a, path.**)
f. Everybody, say the whole sentence. Get ready. (Signal.) *So that ant sat in a path.*
g. Touch the next picture. ✔

## Nine rats like to sit.

- Who is in that picture? (Signal.) *Rats.*
- Count the rats. Everybody, how many rats are in that picture? (Signal.) *Nine.*
- What are those rats doing? (Signal.) *Sitting.*
- (Call on a child.) Read the sentence under the picture. *Nine rats like to sit.*

h. Touch the last picture. ✔

## So those rats sat with the ant.

- Who is in that picture? (Call on a child. Idea: *Nine rats and one ant.*)
- (Call on a child.) Read the sentence under the picture. *So those rats sat with the ant.*

WORKBOOK

════════ EXERCISE 9 ════════

**STORY EXTENSION**
**Sentence Completion**

a. Close your textbook. Go to lesson 48 in your workbook and write your name. ✔
b. Find the picture for the story. ✔
- The picture is supposed to show nine rats and one ant, but I think one of the rats is missing, and I don't see an ant at all. After you complete the sentences under the picture, you can draw in the missing rat and draw in an ant.

## EXERCISE 10

**INDEPENDENT WORK**

**Matching: Words**

a. Find the matching game. ✔
- One of the words is missing. You'll write the missing word, and draw lines to connect the other words.

**Words for Pictures—Plural S**

b. Find the box with words in it. ✔
- Later, you'll read each word, find the picture it tells about, and write the word below. If the picture shows more than one, write the word that tells about more than one.

## EXERCISE 11

**SPELLING WORDS**

a. (Write on the board:)

| ai |
|---|

- You're going to spell words. Some of them have the letter combination **A-I.** They don't have an **E** on the end of the word. They have **A-I.** Other words don't make the sound **AAA.**
b. Listen: **sit.** What word? (Signal.) *Sit.*
- Say the sounds in **sit.** Get ready. (Tap 3 times.) *sss    iii    t.*
- Do you say a letter name when you say the sounds? (Signal.) *No.*
- Everybody, spell the word **sit.** Get ready. (Tap 3 times.) *S-I-T.*
c. Listen: **sat.** What word? (Signal.) *Sat.*
- Say the sounds in **sat.** Get ready. (Tap 3 times.) *sss    aaa    t.*
- Do you say a letter name when you say the sounds? (Signal.) *No.*
- Everybody, spell the word **sat.** Get ready. (Tap 3 times.) *S-A-T.*
d. Listen: **sail.** What word? (Signal.) *Sail.*
- Say the sounds in **sail.** Get ready. (Tap 3 tlmes.) *sss    AAA    lll.*
- Do you say a letter name when you say the sounds? (Signal.) *Yes.*
- What letter name? (Signal.) *A.*

- You say a letter name. How do you spell the sound **AAA** in the word **sail?** (Signal.) *A-I.*
- Everybody, spell the word **sail.** Get ready. (Tap 4 times.) *S-A-I-L.*
e. Listen: **we.** What word? (Signal.) *We.*
- Say the sounds in **we.** Get ready. (Tap 2 times.) *www    EEE.*
- Do you say the letter name **A** when you say the sounds? (Signal.) *No.*
- Remember, you'll write **A-I** if you hear the letter name **A** in the word.

**LINED PAPER**

f. Your turn to write the words we just spelled.
- Number four lines on your paper. Pencils down when you're finished. ✔
g. Touch number 1. ✔
- Write the word **sail** on that line. Pencils down when you're finished. (Observe children and give feedback.)
- (Write on the board:)

| 1 sail |
|---|

- Here's what you should have. **Sail** is spelled **S-A-I-L.**
h. Touch number 2. ✔
- Write the word **sit** on that line. Pencils down when you're finished. (Observe children and give feedback.)
- (Write on the board:)

| 2 sit |
|---|

- Here's what you should have. **Sit** is spelled **S-I-T.**
i. Touch number 3. ✔
- Write the word **we** on that line. Pencils down when you're finished. (Observe children and give feedback.)
- (Write on the board:)

| 3 we |
|---|

- Here's what you should have. **We** is spelled **W-E.**
- j. Touch number 4. ✔
- Write the word **sat** on that line. Pencils down when you're finished.
  (Observe children and give feedback.)
- (Write on the board:)

> **4 sat**

- Here's what you should have. **Sat** is spelled **S-A-T.**
- k. Raise your hand if you got everything right.

---

================ **EXERCISE 12** ================

### SENTENCE WRITING

a. (Write on the board:)

> You will see a rat.

b. You're going to write this sentence.
   (Call on a child to read the sentence.)

c. Turn to the back of your paper. ✔

- Write the sentence on the top line. Pencils down when you're finished.
  (Observe children and give feedback.)

d. Later, you can write the same sentence two more times on the lines below.

### Independent Work Summary
- Story extension (write missing words and draw missing animals).
- Matching game.
- Write appropriate words for pictures.
- Sentence writing (copy two times: **You will see a rat.**).

**Materials:** Each child will need lined paper.

═══════ EXERCISE 1 ═══════

## SOUNDS

a. Listen: **he.** What word? (Signal.) *He.*
- Say the sounds in **he.** Get ready. (Tap 2 times.) *h   EEE.*
- What letter do you use to spell the first sound? (Signal.) *H.*

b. New word: **hill.** What word? (Signal.) *Hill.*
- Say the sounds in **hill.** Get ready. (Tap 3 times.) *h   iii   lll.*
- What letter do you use to spell the first sound? (Signal.) *H.*

## TEXTBOOK

c. Open your textbook to lesson 49. Find the shirts that are hanging on the clothesline. ✔
- (Teacher reference:)

| th | h | j | c | g | k | h |
|----|----|----|----|----|----|----|

d. Touch and say the sounds.
- First sound. Get ready. (Signal.) *ththth.*
- Next sound. Get ready. (Signal.) *h.*
- (Repeat for remaining items.)

═══════ EXERCISE 2 ═══════

## READING WORDS
### Words with H

a. After you read all the words on this page without any mistakes, I'll call on different children to read some of the words.

b. Find the pair of shorts. ✔
- (Teacher reference:)

| 1. he | 2. hole |
|-------|---------|
| 3. hill | 4. hide |

- These words start with the letter **H.**

c. Word 1 has two sounds. Get ready. (Tap 2 times.) *h   EEE.*
- What word? (Signal.) *He.*

d. Word 2. Get ready. (Tap 3 times.) *h   OOO   lll.*
- What word? (Signal.) *Hole.*

e. Word 3 does not have a blue letter. Get ready. (Tap 3 times.) *h   iii   lll.*
- What word? (Signal.) *Hill.*

f. Word 4 has a blue letter. Get ready. (Tap 3 times.) *h   lll   d.*
- What word? (Signal.) *Hide.*

g. Let's read those words again, the fast way.
- Word 1. What word? (Signal.) *He.*
- Word 2. What word? (Signal.) *Hole.*
- Word 3. What word? (Signal.) *Hill.*
- Word 4. What word? (Signal.) *Hide.*
- You're reading some pretty hard words.

═══════ EXERCISE 3 ═══════

## READING IRREGULAR WORDS

a. Find the skirt. ✔
- (Teacher reference:)

| 1. was | 2. do |
|--------|-------|
| 3. to | 4. said |

- All these words have funny underlines. They don't make the sound they're supposed to.

b. Everybody, spell word 1. Get ready. (Tap 3 times.) *W-A-S.*
- The **A** has a funny underline because it does not make the sound it is supposed to make. Everybody, what's word 1? (Signal.) *Was.*

c. Spell word 2. Get ready. (Tap 2 times.) *D-O.*
  Everybody, what word? (Signal.) *Do.*

d. Spell word 3. Get ready. (Tap 2 times.) *T-O.*
  What word? (Signal.) *To.*

e. Spell word 4. Get ready. (Tap 4 times.) *S-A-I-D.*
  What word? (Signal.) *Said.*

f. Let's read those words again the fast way.
- Word 1. What word? (Signal.) *Was.*
- Word 2. What word? (Signal.) *Do.*

- Word 3. What word? (Signal.) *To.*
- Word 4. What word? (Signal.) *Said.*

═══════════ EXERCISE 4 ═══════════

## READING WORDS

a. Find the dress. ✔
- (Teacher reference:)

| 1. pig | 2. to<u>a</u>d | 3. go<u>a</u>t |
|---|---|---|
| 4. cam<u>e</u> | 5. m<u>ea</u>n | |

- These words do not have funny underlines. You'll touch and say the sounds.
b. Word 1. Get ready. (Tap 3 times.)
  *p    iii    g.*
- What word? (Signal.) *Pig.*
c. Word 2. Get ready. (Tap 3 times.)
  *t    OOO    d.*
- What word? (Signal.) *Toad.*
- Yes, a **toad** is an animal that looks like a bumpy frog.
d. Word 3. Get ready. (Tap 3 times.)
  *g    OOO    t.*
- What word? (Signal.) *Goat.*
e. Word 4. Get ready. (Tap 3 times.)
  *c    AAA    mmm.*
- What word? (Signal.) *Came.*
f. Word 5. Get ready. (Tap 3 times.)
  *mmm    EEE    nnn.*
- What word? (Signal.) *mean.*
g. Let's read those words again, the fast way.
- Word 1. What word? (Signal.) *Pig.*
- Next word. What word? (Signal.) *Toad.*
- (Repeat for: **goat, came, mean.**)

═══════════ EXERCISE 5 ═══════════

## READING WORDS
### E-D Ending

a. You've learned that some words that tell what happened earlier end with the letters **E-D.**
b. Find the shirt at the bottom of the page. ✔

- (Teacher reference:)

| 1. play | <u>ed</u> | |
|---|---|---|
| 2. sav | <u>ed</u> | |
| 3. mail | <u>ed</u> | |
| 4. lik | <u>ed</u> | |

- All these words tell what happened earlier. They all have the ending **E-D.** All the **E-D** endings are in that green stripe. The letter **E** is blue in some words because one of the letters in the word says its name.
c. Word 1. Touch and say the sounds for the black letters. Get ready. (Tap 4 times.)
  *p    lll    AAA    d.*
- Again. Get ready. (Tap 4 times.)
  *p    lll    AAA    d.*
- What word? (Signal.) *Played.*
d. Word 2. Get ready. (Tap 4 times.)
  *sss    AAA    vvv    d.*
- Again. Get ready. (Tap 4 times.)
  *sss    AAA    vvv    d.*
- What word? (Signal.) *Saved.*
e. Word 3. Get ready. (Tap 4 times.)
  *mmm    AAA    lll    d.*
- Again. Get ready. (Tap 4 times.)
  *mmm    AAA    lll    d.*
- What word? (Signal.) *Mailed.*
f. Word 4. Get ready. (Tap 4 times.)
  *lll    III    k    d.*
- Again. Get ready. (Tap 4 times.)
  *lll    III    k    d.*
- What word? (Signal.) *Liked.*
- Yes, we **liked** the game.
g. Let's read those words again, the fast way.
- Word 1. What word? (Signal.) *Played.*
- Word 2. What word? (Signal.) *Saved.*
- Word 3. What word? (Signal.) *Mailed.*
- Word 4. What word? (Signal.) *Liked.*

**Individual Turns**

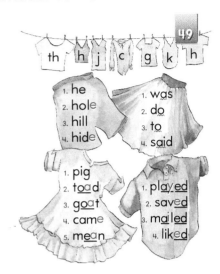

- (Call on different children to read one or two of the words on the page.)

===== EXERCISE 6 =====

**STORY READING**

A mean ant was near a toad. The toad said, "Do you like to play?"

The ant said, "No."

The toad said, "Do you like to sleep?"

The ant said, "No."

The toad said, "Do you like to eat?"

The ant said, "No."

The toad said, "I do." And he did.

a. Find the book. ✔
- This is a long story. It has quote marks because the characters are talking.
b. I'll tap. You'll read all the words in the first sentence the fast way. Get ready. (Tap for each word.) *A . . . mean . . . ant . . . was . . . near . . . a . . . toad.*

c. Everybody, say the first sentence. (Signal.) *A mean ant was near a toad.*
d. Touch the first word of the next sentence. ✔
- What word? (Signal.) *The.*
- Next word. What word? (Signal.) *Toad.*
- The next word is spelled **S-A-I-D.** Everybody, what word? (Signal.) *Said.*
- The quote marks show what the toad said. Touch the first word inside the quote marks. It's spelled **D-O.** ✔ What word? (Signal.) *Do.*
- Next word. Everybody, what word? (Signal.) *You.*
- The next word has a blue letter. What word? (Signal.) *Like.*
- The next word is spelled **T-O.** Everybody, what word? (Signal.) *To.*
- The last word has a blue letter. What word? (Signal.) *Play.*
- Listen to the whole sentence: **The toad said, "Do you like to play?"**
- Say the whole sentence. Get ready. (Signal.) *The toad said, "Do you like to play?"*
- Say the words the toad said. (Signal.) *Do you like to play?*
e. Touch the first word of the next sentence. ✔
- What word? (Signal.) *The.*
- Next word. What word? (Signal.) *Ant.*
- The next word is spelled **S-A-I-D.** Everybody, what word? (Signal.) *Said.*
- The quote marks show that the ant said one word. Everybody, what word? (Signal.) *No.*
- Listen to the whole sentence: **The ant said, "No."**
- Say the whole sentence. (Signal.) *The ant said, "No."*
- Now just say the word the ant said. Get ready. (Signal.) *No.*
f. Next sentence. First word. What word? (Signal.) *The.*
- Next word. What word? (Signal.) *Toad.*
- Next word. Spell that word. Get ready. (Tap 4 times.) *S-A-I-D.* What word? (Signal.) *Said.*

- The quote marks show what the toad said. Spell the first word inside the quote marks. Get ready. (Tap 2 times.) *D-O.* What word? (Signal.) *Do.*
- Next word. What word? (Signal.) *You.*
- The next word has a blue letter. What word? (Signal.) *Like.*
- Spell the next word. Get ready. (Tap 2 times.) *T-O.* What word? (Signal.) *To.*
- Last word. What word? (Signal.) *Sleep.*
- Here's the whole sentence: **The toad said, "Do you like to sleep?"**
- Say the whole sentence. Get ready. (Signal.) *The toad said, "Do you like to sleep?"*
- Now just say the words the toad said. Get ready. (Signal.) *Do you like to sleep?*

g. Next sentence. Let's do it the fast way.
- First word. What word? (Signal.) *The.*
- Next word. What word? (Signal.) *Ant.*
- Next word. What word? (Signal.) *Said.*
- The quote marks show what the ant said. What word? (Signal.) *No.*

h. Next sentence. Let's do it the fast way.
- First word. What word? (Signal.) *The.*
- Next word. What word? (Signal.) *Toad.*
- Next word. What word? (Signal.) *Said.*
- You can see the words he said. First word inside the quote marks. What word? (Signal.) *Do.*
- Next word. What word? (Signal.) *You.*
- Next word. What word? (Signal.) *Like.*
- Next word. What word? (Signal.) *To.*
- Last word. What word? (Signal.) *Eat.*
- What did the toad say? (Signal.) *Do you like to eat?*

i. I'll call on different children to read the rest of the story the fast way.
- (Call on a child.) Read the next sentence. *The ant said, "No."*
- (Call on a child.) Read the next sentence. *The toad said, "I do."*
- The last sentence has a new word in it. (Call on a child.) Read the last sentence. Don't get fooled by the new word. *And he did.*

**Second Reading**
- Let's read the story one more time the fast way.
- (Call on different children to read one of the sentences.)

========= **EXERCISE 7** =========

**COMPREHENSION**

a. You're going to see pictures of the story.
- Touch the first picture. ✔

- The toad is talking and the mean ant is talking. (Call on a child to read what the toad said and then what the ant said.)

b. Touch the next picture. ✔

- (Call on a child to read what the toad said and then what the ant said.)

c. Touch the next picture. ✔

Do you like to eat?

No.

- (Call on a child to read what the toad said and then what the ant said.)

d. Touch the last picture. ✔

I like to eat.

- (Call on a child to read what the toad said.)
- So the toad said he likes to eat.
- The toad is licking his chops. I don't see the ant in that picture. Where do you think that ant is? (Call on a child. Idea: *The toad ate it.*)
- Oh, dear. No more mean ant.

WORKBOOK

─────── EXERCISE 8 ───────

## STORY EXTENSION
### Writing Words in Picture

a. Close your textbook. Go to lesson 49 in your workbook and write your name. ✔
b. Find the picture for the story. ✔

- The toad and the ant are talking. You'll write the word ant under the picture of the ant.
- Touch where you'll write the word ant. ✔
- And what word will you write under the picture of the toad? (Signal.) *Toad.*
- Touch where you'll write the word toad. ✔

c. Then you'll fix up the picture so the toad is asking a question. The toad is saying: Do you like to something. You can complete the sentence with anything you want. You can pick from the words next to the picture.

- Then write what the ant said. You know what that ant will say to anything.

─────── EXERCISE 9 ───────

## INDEPENDENT WORK

### Matching: Words

a. Find the matching game. You'll draw lines to connect the words.

### Missing Words or Pictures

b. Turn to side 2. ✔
- Some of the pictures show things, but there are no words under those pictures. Some pictures are blank, but there are words under those pictures.
c. The first picture is blank. Everybody, read the word that is under that picture. (Signal.) *Kite.*
- You'll have to draw a picture of a kite in that box.
d. Touch the next blank picture. ✔
- It has the word feet under it. You'll draw feet in that picture.
e. Touch the picture of the rope. ✔
- The word is missing under that picture. What word will you write? (Signal.) *Rope.*
- You'll find that word in the box above the pictures.
f. Touch the last picture. ✔
- What's in the picture? (Signal.) *Lake.*
- You'll find the word lake in the box above the pictures.
g. Remember, fix up each picture box so it has a picture in it and a word under it.

========== EXERCISE 10 ==========

## SPELLING WORDS

a. (Write on the board:)

| oa | ea |
|----|----|

- You're going to spell words. Some of them have the letter combination **O-A.** What sound does that combination make? (Signal.) *OOO.*
- Some of the words have the letter combination **E-A.** What sound does that combination make? (Signal.) *EEE.*

b. Listen: **read.** What word? (Signal.) *Read.*
- Say the sounds in **read.** Get ready. (Tap 3 times.) *rrr   EEE   d.*
- Remember, when you spell **read** the **EEE** sound is spelled **E-A.**
- Everybody, spell the word **read.** Get ready. (Tap 4 times.) *R-E-A-D.*
- Again. Spell **read.** Get ready. (Tap 4 times.) *R-E-A-D.*

c. New word: **leaf.** What word? (Signal.) *Leaf.*
- Say the sounds in **leaf.** Get ready. (Tap 3 times.) *lll   EEE   fff.*
- How do you spell the **EEE** sound in the word **leaf?** (Signal.) *E-A.*
- Everybody, spell the word **leaf.** Get ready. (Tap 4 times.) *L-E-A-F.*
- Again. Spell **leaf.** Get ready. (Tap 4 times.) *L-E-A-F.*

d. New word: **loaf.** What word? (Signal.) *Loaf.*
- Say the sounds in **loaf.** Get ready. (Tap 3 times.) *lll   OOO   fff.*
- You spell the **OOO** sound with the combination **O-A.**
- Everybody, spell the word **loaf.** Get ready. (Tap 4 times.) *L-O-A-F.*
- Again. Spell **loaf.** Get ready. (Tap 4 times.) *L-O-A-F.*

e. Last word: **road.** What word? (Signal.) *Road.*
- Say the sounds in **road.** Get ready. (Tap 3 times.) *rrr   OOO   d.*
- How do you spell the **OOO** sound in the word **road?** (Signal.) *O-A.*
- Everybody, spell the word **road.** Get ready. (Tap 4 times.) *R-O-A-D.*

## LINED PAPER

f. Get ready to write the words we just spelled.
- Number four lines on your paper. Pencils down when you're finished. ✔

g. Touch number 1. ✔
- Write the word **road** on that line. Pencils down when you're finished.
  (Observe children and give feedback.)
- (Write on the board:)

| 1 road |
|--------|

- Here's what you should have. **Road** is spelled **R-O-A-D.**

h. Touch number 2. ✔
- Write the word **read** on that line. Pencils down when you're finished.
  (Observe children and give feedback.)
- (Write on the board:)

| 2 read |
|--------|

- Here's what you should have. **Read** is spelled **R-E-A-D.**

i. Touch number 3. ✔
- Write the word **leaf** on that line. Pencils down when you're finished.
  (Observe children and give feedback.)
- (Write on the board:)

| 3 leaf |
|--------|

- Here's what you should have. **Leaf** is spelled **L-E-A-F.**

j. Touch number 4. ✔
- Write the word **loaf** on that line. Pencils down when you're finished.
  (Observe children and give feedback.)
- (Write on the board:)

| 4 loaf |
|--------|

- Here's what you should have. **Loaf** is spelled **L-O-A-F.**

k. Raise your hand if you got everything right.

## EXERCISE 11

**SENTENCE WRITING**

a. (Write on the board:)

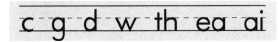

Do you like to eat?

b. You're going to write this sentence. (Call on a child to read the sentence.)
c. Turn to the back of your paper. ✔
• Write the sentence on the top line. Remember the question mark at the end. Pencils down when you're finished. (Observe children and give feedback.)
d. Later, you can write the same sentence two more times on the lines below.

## EXERCISE 12

**LETTER PRINTING**

a. (Write on the board:)

c g d w th ea ai

• You're going to write some letters.
b. Skip the next two lines on your paper and put your pencil at the beginning of the line after that. ✔
• On that line you'll write the letter that makes the sound **g.** What sound? (Signal.) *g.*

• What letter makes that sound? (Signal.) *G.*
• Write the letter for **g.** Pencils down when you're finished. ✔
c. Touch the next line. ✔
• On that line you'll write the letter or letter combination that makes the sound **ththth.** What sound? (Signal.) *ththth.*
• What letter or letter combination makes that sound? (Signal.) *T-H.*
• Write the letter combination for **ththth.** Pencils down when you're finished. ✔
d. Touch the next line. ✔
• On that line you'll write the letter combination that makes the sound **EEE.** What sound? (Signal.) *EEE.*
• What letter combination makes that sound? (Signal.) *E-A.*
• Write the letter combination for **EEE.** Pencils down when you're finished. ✔
e. Later, you'll complete the lines of letters.

**Independent Work Summary**
• Story extension (write missing words).
• Matching game.
• Draw missing pictures; write missing words.
• Sentence writing (copy two times: **Do you like to eat?**).
• Letter printing (finish lines of **g, th, ea**).

 **TEST 5**

**Materials:** Each child will need crayons and scissors.

**Note:** Administer WORD WRITING to the entire group. Individually administer SENTENCE READING, WORD READING, and WORD READING THE FAST WAY.

**WORKBOOK**

**═══ EXERCISE 1 ═══**

**TEST—Group Administered**
**Part 1: WORD WRITING**
a. Open your workbook to lesson 50, test 5. ✔
   This is another test.
• Write your name at the top of the page. ✔
b. Find the fish. ✔
• You're going to write some words. Some of the words end with a blue **E**. Remember how those words work.
c. Touch line 1. ✔
• The word for that line is made. What word? (Signal.) *Made.*
• Say the sounds in made. Get ready. (Tap 3 times.) *mmm   AAA   d.*
• Write the word made on line 1. Pencils down when you're finished.
   (Observe children but do not give feedback.)
d. Touch line 2. ✔
• The word for that line is mad. What word? (Signal.) *Mad.*
• Say the sounds in mad. Get ready. (Tap 3 times.) *mmm   aaa   d.*
• Write the word mad on line 2. Pencils down when you're finished.
   (Observe children.)
e. Touch line 3. ✔
• The word for that line is at. What word? (Signal.) *At.*
• Say the sounds in at. Get ready. (Tap 2 times.) *aaa   t.*

• Write the word at on line 3. Pencils down when you're finished.
   (Observe children.)
f. Touch line 4. ✔
• The word for that line is ate. What word? (Signal.) *Ate.*
• Say the sounds in ate. Get ready. (Tap 2 times.) *AAA   t.*
• Write the word ate on line 4. Pencils down when you're finished.
   (Observe children.)

**═══ EXERCISE 2 ═══**

**STORYBOOK**

**Note:** Each child needs crayons.

a. Today you'll get to make another booklet while I'm listening to each child read.
b. There are four sentences.
• First you'll read each sentence in the booklet. Then you can color the pictures.
• You can write the answer to the last sentence you read.

**═══ EXERCISE 3 ═══**

**TEST—Individually Administered**

**Note:** Individually administer the rest of the test: SENTENCE READING, WORD READING and WORD READING THE FAST WAY. Mark all errors. Record the test results on the Test Summary Sheet for test 5.

**Part 2: SENTENCE READING**
a. Find the star. ✔
b. Read this sentence the fast way. *[A mole and a rat like to play.]*
• (For each word read correctly the fast way, award four points.)
• (For each word read correctly, but not the fast way, award two points.)
• (For each word misidentified, award no points.)

**Part 3: WORD READING**

c. Go to the top of side 2. ✔
d. You'll read the words in the first column.
- Read word 1. (Child reads **ask.**)
- (Repeat for words 2–5.)

e. You'll read all the words in the second column.
- Read word 1. (Child reads **if.**)
- (Repeat for words 2–5.)

**Part 4: WORD READING THE FAST WAY**

f. You'll read all the words in the third column the fast way.
- Read word 1. *[Was.]*
- (Repeat for words 2–5.)

─────── EXERCISE 4 ───────

**STORYBOOK**
    **Take Home**

*Note:* Each child needs scissors.

a. (Remove perforated test sheet from workbook.)
b. (Direct children to cut along the dotted line.)
c. (Collect test part of sheets.)

d. (Direct children to fold their booklet along the fold line.)
e. Now you can take the storybook home and read it to your family.
f. (After testing all children, check out each child on reading the entire storybook.)

─────── EXERCISE 5 ───────

**MARKING THE TEST**

- (Record all test results on the lesson 50, Test 5 Summary Sheet. Reproducible Summary Sheets are at the back of the Teacher's Guide.)

─────── EXERCISE 6 ───────

**TEST REMEDIES**

- (Provide any necessary remedies for Test 5 before presenting lesson 51. Test Remedies are discussed in the Teacher's Guide.)

─────── EXERCISE 7 ───────

**LITERATURE BOOK**

- (See Teacher's Guide.)